Microservices for the Enterprise

Designing, Developing, and Deploying

Kasun Indrasiri

Prabath Siriwardena

Apress®

Microservices for the Enterprise

Kasun Indrasiri
San Jose, CA, USA

Prabath Siriwardena
San Jose, CA, USA

ISBN-13 (pbk): 978-1-4842-3857-8
https://doi.org/10.1007/978-1-4842-3858-5

ISBN-13 (electronic): 978-1-4842-3858-5

Library of Congress Control Number: 2018962968

Managing Director, Apress Media LLC: Welmoed Spahr
Acquisitions Editor: Jonathan Gennick
Development Editor: Laura Berendson
Coordinating Editor: Jill Balzano

Cover image designed by Freepik (www.freepik.com)

Distributed to the book trade worldwide by Springer Science+Business Media New York, 233 Spring Street, 6th Floor, New York, NY 10013. Phone 1-800-SPRINGER, fax (201) 348-4505, e-mail orders-ny@springer-sbm.com, or visit www.springeronline.com. Apress Media, LLC is a California LLC and the sole member (owner) is Springer Science + Business Media Finance Inc (SSBM Finance Inc). SSBM Finance Inc is a **Delaware** corporation.

For information on translations, please e-mail rights@apress.com, or visit http://www.apress.com/rights-permissions.

Apress titles may be purchased in bulk for academic, corporate, or promotional use. eBook versions and licenses are also available for most titles. For more information, reference our Print and eBook Bulk Sales web page at http://www.apress.com/bulk-sales.

Any source code or other supplementary material referenced by the author in this book is available to readers on GitHub via the book's product page, located at www.apress.com/9781484238578. For more detailed information, please visit http://www.apress.com/source-code.

Printed on acid-free paper

Table of Contents

About the Authors

Kasun Indrasiri is an architect, author, microservice and integration evangelist, and director of integration architecture at WSO2. He also founded the Microservices, APIs, and Integration meetup group, which is a vendor-neutral microservices meetup in the San Francisco Bay Area. He is the author of the book *Beginning WSO2 ESB* (Apress) and has worked as a software architect and a product lead with over seven years of experience in enterprise integration. He is an Apache committer and PMC member. Kasun has spoken at several conferences held in San Francisco, London, and Barcelona on topics relating to enterprise integration and microservices. He also conducts talks at Bay Area microservices, container, and cloud-native meetups, and he publishes blogs and articles on microservices. He works with many Fortune 100 companies to provide solutions in the enterprise integration and microservices domain.

Prabath Siriwardena is an identity evangelist, author, blogger, and the VP of Identity Management and Security at WSO2, with more than 11 years of industry experience in designing and building critical Identity and Access Management (IAM) infrastructure for global enterprises, including many Fortune 100/500 companies. As a technology evangelist, Prabath has published five books. He blogs on various topics from blockchain, PSD2, GDPR, and IAM, to microservices security. He also runs a YouTube channel. Prabath has spoken at many conferences, including the RSA Conference, Identiverse, European Identity Conference, Consumer Identity World USA, API World, API Strategy & Practice Con, QCon, OSCON, and WSO2Con. He has also travelled the world conducting workshops/meetups to evangelize IAM communities. He is the founder of the Silicon Valley IAM User Group, which is the largest IAM meetup in the San Francisco Bay Area.

About the Technical Reviewer

 **Alp Tunc** is a software engineer. He graduated from Ege University, Izmir/Turkey. He completed his MSc degree while working as a research assistant. He is a software developer by heart, with 20 years of experience in the industry as a developer/architect/project manager of projects of various sizes. He has a lot of hands-on experience in a broad range of technologies. Besides technology, he loves freezing moments in spectacular photographs, trekking into the unknown, running, and reading and he is a jazz aficionado. He also loves cats and dogs.

Acknowledgments

We would first like to thank Jonathan Gennick, assistant editorial director at Apress, for evaluating and accepting our proposal for this book. Then, Jill Balzano, coordinating editor at Apress, was extremely patient and tolerant of us throughout the publishing process. Thank you very much, Jill, for your support. Laura Berendson, the development editor at Apress, also helped us toward the end. Thanks Laura! Alp Tunc served as the technical reviewer. Thanks, Alp, for your quality reviews.

Dr. Sanjiva Weerawarana, the Founder and Chief Architect at WSO2, is our constant mentor. We are truly grateful to Dr. Sanjiva for his guidance, mentorship, and support. We also express our gratitude to Tyler Jewel, the CEO at WSO2, and Paul Fremantle, the CTO at WSO2, for their direction, which helped us explore the microservices domain. Finally, we'd like to thank our families and parents; without them nothing is possible!

Introduction

The microservices architecture has become one of the most popular architectural styles in the enterprise software architecture landscape. Owing to the benefits that it brings, most enterprises are transforming their existing monolithic applications to microservices architecture-based applications. Hence, for any software architect or software engineer, it's really important to understand the key architectural concepts of the microservices architecture and how you can use those architectural principles in practice to solve real-world business use cases.

In this book, we provide the readers a comprehensive understanding of microservices architectural principles and discuss how to use those concepts in real-world scenarios. Also, without locking into a particular technology or framework, we cover a wide range of technologies and frameworks, which are most suitable for given aspects of the microservices architecture.

One other key difference of this book is that it addresses some of the fundamental challenges in building microservices in the enterprise architecture landscape, such as inter-service communication, service integration with no centralized Enterprise Service Bus (ESB), exposing microservices as APIs avoiding a centralized API gateway, determining the scope and size of a microservice, and leveraging microservices security patterns. All the concepts explained in this book are supported with real-world use cases and incorporated with samples that the reader can try out. Most of these use cases are inspired by existing microservices implementations such as Netflix and Google, as well as the authors' exposure to various meetups and conferences in the San Francisco Bay area.

This book covers some of the widely used and bleeding edge technologies and patterns in realizing microservices architecture, such as technologies for container-native deployment (Docker, Kubernetes, Helm), messaging standards and protocols (gRPC, HTTP2, Kafka, AMQP, OpenAPI, GraphQL, etc.), reactive and active microservices integration, service mesh (Istio and Linkerd), miroservice resiliency patterns (circuit breaker, timeouts, bulk-heads, etc.), security standards (OAuth 2, JWT, and certificates), using APIs, events, and streams with microservices, and building observable microservices using logging, metrics, and tracing.

## CHAPTER 1

The Case for Microservices

Enterprise software architecture always evolves with new architectural styles owing to the paradigm shifts in the technology landscape and the desire to find better ways to build applications in a fast but reliable way.

The microservices architecture has been widely adopted as an architectural style that allows you to build software applications with speed and safety. The microservices architecture fosters building a software system as a collection of independent autonomous services (developed, deployed, and scaled independently) that are loosely coupled. These services form a single software application by integrating all such services and other systems.

In this chapter, we explore what microservices are, the characteristics of microservices with real-world examples, and the pros and cons of microservices in the context of enterprise software architecture.

To better understand what microservices are, we need to look at some of the architectural styles used prior to microservices, and how the enterprise architecture has evolved to embrace the microservices architecture.

From a Monolith to a Microservices Architecture

Exploring the evolution of enterprise architecture from monolithic applications to microservices is a great way to understand the key motivations and characteristics of microservices. Let's begin our discussion with monolithic applications.

© Kasun Indrasiri and Prabath Siriwardena 2018
K. Indrasiri and P. Siriwardena, *Microservices for the Enterprise*, https://doi.org/10.1007/978-1-4842-3858-5_1

Monolithic Applications

Enterprise software applications are designed to facilitate numerous business requirements. In the monolithic architecture style, all the business functionalities are piled into a single monolithic application and built as a single unit.

Consider a real-world example to understand monolithic applications further. Figure 1-1 shows an online retail application, which is built using the monolithic architecture style.

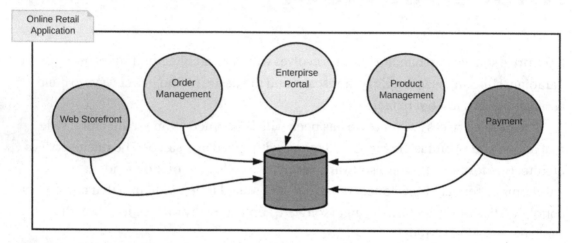

Figure 1-1. *Online retail application developed with a monolithic architecture*

The entire retail application is a collection of several components, such as order management, payments, product management, and so on. Each of these components offers a wide range of business functionalities. Adding or modifying a functionality to a component was extremely expensive owing to its monolithic nature. Also, to facilitate the overall business requirements, these components had to communicate with each other. The communications between these components were often built on top of proprietary protocols and standards, and they were based on the point-to-point communication style. Hence, modifying or replacing a given component was also quite complicated. For example, if the retail enterprise wanted to switch to a new order management system while keeping the rest, doing so would require quite a lot of changes to the other existing components too.

We can generalize the common characteristics of monolithic application as follows:

- Designed, developed, and deployed as a single unit.

- Overwhelmingly complex for most of the real-world business use cases, which leads to nightmares in maintaining, upgrading, and adding new features.

- It's hard to practice Agile development and delivery methodologies. Since the application has to be built as a single unit, most of the business capabilities that it offers cannot have their own lifecycles.

- You must redeploy the entire application in order to update any part of it.

- As the monolithic app grows, it may take longer and longer to start up, which adds to the overall cost.

- It has to be scaled as a single application and is difficult to scale with conflicting resource requirements. (For example, since a monolithic application offers multiple business capabilities, one capability may require more CPU while another requires more memory. It's hard to cater to the individual needs of these capabilities.)

- One unstable service can bring the whole application down.

- It's very difficult to adopt new technologies and frameworks, as all the functionalities have to build on homogeneous technologies/ frameworks. (For example, if you are using Java, all new projects have to be based on Java, even if that are better alternative technologies out there.)

As a solution to some of the limitations of the monolithic application architecture, Service Oriented Architecture (SOA) and Enterprise Service Bus (ESB) emerged.

SOA and ESB

SOA tries to combat the challenges of large monolithic applications by segregating the functionalities of monolithic applications into reusable, loosely coupled entities called *services*. These services are accessible via calls over the network.

- A service is a self-contained implementation of a well-defined business functionality that is accessible over the network. Applications in SOA are built based on services.

- Services are software components with well-defined interfaces that are implementation-independent. An important aspect of SOA is the separation of the service interface (the what) from its implementation (the how).

- The consumers are only concerned about the service interface and do not care about its implementation.

- Services are self-contained (perform predetermined tasks) and loosely coupled (for independence).

- Services can be dynamically discovered. The consumers often don't need to know the exact location and other details of a service. They can discover the service's metadata via a service metadata repository or a service registry. When there's a change to the service metadata, the service can update its metadata in the service registry.

- Composite services can be built from aggregates of other services.

With the SOA paradigm, each business functionality is built as a (coarse-grained) service (often implemented as Web Services) with several sub-functionalities. These services are deployed inside an application server. When it comes to the consumption of business functionalities, we often need to integrate/plumb multiple such services (and create composite services) and other systems. Enterprise Service Bus (ESB) is used to integrate those services, data, and systems. Consumers use the composite services exposed from the ESB layer. Hence, ESB is used as the centralized bus (see Figure 1-2) that connects all these services and systems.

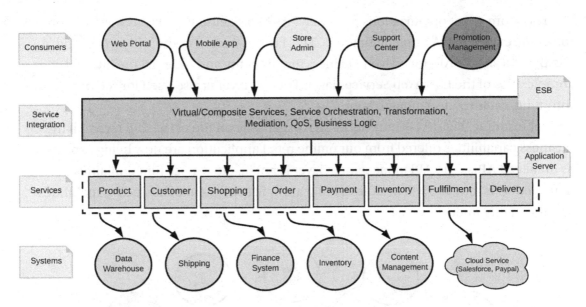

Figure 1-2. *SOA/ESB style based online retail system*

For example, let's go back to our online retail application use case. Figure 1-2 illustrates the implementation of the online retail application using SOA/web services. Here we have defined multiple web services that cater to various business capabilities such as products, customers, shopping, orders, payments, etc. At the ESB layer, we may integrate such business capabilities and create composite business capabilities, which are exposed to the consumers. Or the ESB layer may just be used to expose the functionalities as it is, with additional cross-cutting features such as security. So, obviously the ESB layer also contains a significant portion of the business logic of the entire application. Other cross-cutting concerns such as security, monitoring, and analytics may also be applied at the ESB layer. The ESB layer is a monolithic entity where all developers share the same runtime to develop/deploy their service integrations.

APIs

Exposing business functionalities as managed services or APIs has become a key requirement of the modern enterprise architecture. However, web services/SOA is not really the ideal solution to cater to such requirements, due to the complexity of the Web Service-related technologies such as SOAP (used as the message format for inter-service communication), WS-Security (to secure messaging between services), WSDLs (to define the service contract), etc., and the lack of features to build an ecosystem around APIs (self-servicing, etc.)

Therefore, most organizations put a new API Management/API Gateway layer on top of the existing SOA implementations. This layer is known as the *API façade*, and it exposes a simple API for a given business functionality and hides all the internal complexities of the ESB/Web Services layer. The API layer is also used for security, throttling, caching, and monetization.

For example, Figure 1-3 introduces an API gateway on top of the ESB layer. All the business capabilities offered from our online retail application are now being exposed as managed APIs. The API management layer is not just to expose functionalities as managed APIs, but you will be able to build a whole ecosystem of business capabilities and their consumers.

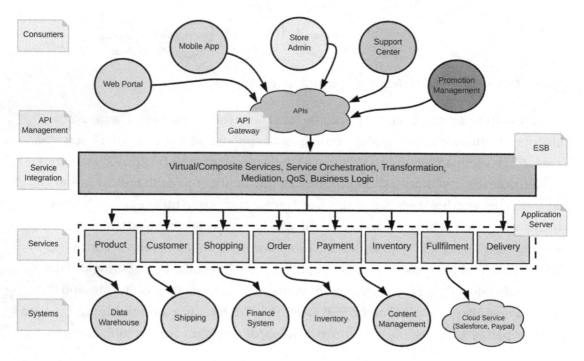

Figure 1-3. *Exposing business functionalities as managed APIs through an API Gateway layer*

With the increasing demand for complex business capabilities, the monolithic architecture can no longer cater to the modern enterprise software application development. The centralized nature of monolithic applications results in the lack of being able to scale applications independently, inter-application dependencies that hinder independent application development and deployment, reliability issues due to the centralized nature and the constraints on using diverse technologies for application development. To overcome most of these limitations and to cater to the modern, complex, and decentralized application needs, a new architecture paradigm must be conceived.

The microservices architecture has emerged as a better architecture paradigm to overcome the drawbacks of the ESB/SOA architecture as well as the conventional monolithic application architecture.

What Is a Microservice?

The foundation of the microservices architecture is about developing a single application as a suite of small and independent services that are running in their own processes, developed and deployed independently.

As illustrated in Figure 1-4, the online retail software application can be transformed into a microservices architecture by breaking the monolithic application layer into independent and business functionality oriented services. Also, we got rid of the central ESB by breaking its functionalities into each service, so that the services take care of the inter-service communication and composition logic.

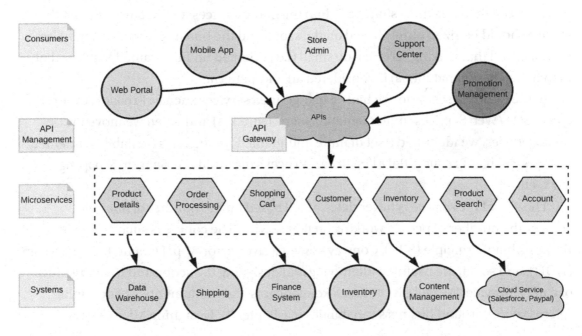

Figure 1-4. *An online retail application built using a microservices architecture*

Therefore, each microservice at the microservices layer offers a well-defined business capability (preferably with a small scope), which are designed, developed, deployed, and administrated independently.

The API management layer pretty much stays the same, despite the changes to the ESB and services layers that it communicates with. The API gateway and management layer exposes the business functionalities as managed APIs; we have the option of segregating the gateway into independent per-API based runtimes.

Since now you have a basic understanding of the microservices architecture, we can dive deep into the main characteristics of microservices.

Business Capability Oriented

One of the key concepts of the microservices architecture is that your service has to be designed based on the business capabilities, so that a given service will serve a specific business purpose and has a well-defined set of responsibilities. A given service should focus on doing only one thing and doing it well.

It's important to understand that a coarse-grained service (such as a web service developed in the SOA context) or a fine-grained service (which doesn't map to a business capability) is not a suitable fit into the microservices architecture. Rather, the service should be sized purely based on the scope and the business functionality. Also, keep in mind that making services too small (i.e., oriented on fine grained features that map to business capabilities) is considered an anti-pattern.

In the example scenario, we had coarse-grained services such as `Product`, `Order`, etc. in SOA/Web Services implementation (see Figure 1-3) and when we move into microservices, we identified a set of more fine-grained, yet business capability-oriented services, such as `Product Details`, `Order Processing`, `Product Search`, `Shopping Cart`, etc.

The size of the service is never determined based on the number of lines of code or the number of people working on that service. The concepts such as Single Responsibility Principle (SRP), Conway's law, Twelve Factor App, Domain Driven Design (DDD), and so on, are useful in identifying and designing the scope and functionalities of a microservice. We will discuss such key concepts and fundamentals of designing microservices around business capabilities in Chapter 2, "Designing Microservices".

Autonomous: Develop, Deploy, and Scale Independently

Having autonomous services could well be the most important driving force behind the realization of the microservices architecture. Microservices are developed, deployed, and scaled as independent entities. Unlike web services or a monolithic application architecture, services don't share the same execution runtime. Rather they are deployed as isolated runtimes by leveraging technologies such as containers. The successful and increasing adaptation of containers and container management technologies such as Docker, Kubernetes, and Mesos are vital for the realization of service autonomy and contribute to the success of the microservices architecture as a whole. We dig deep into the deployment aspect of microservices in Chapter 8, "Deploying and Running Microservices".

The autonomous services ensure the resiliency of the entire system as we have isolated the failures along with service isolation. These services are loosely coupled through messaging via inter-service communication over the network. The inter-service communication can be built on top of various interaction styles and message formats (we cover these things in detail in Chapter 3, "Inter-Service Communication"). They expose their APIs via technology-agnostic service contracts and consumers can use those contracts to collaborate with that service. Such services may also be exposed as managed APIs via an API gateway.

The independent deployment of services provides the innate ability to scale services independently. As the consumption of business functionalities varies, we can scale the microservices that get more traffic without scaling other services.

We can observe these microservices' characteristics in our e-commerce application use case, which is illustrated in Figure 1-3. The coarse-grained services, such as `Product`, `Order`, etc., share the same application server runtime as in the SOA/Web Services approach. So, a failure (such as out of memory or CPU spinning) in one of those services could blow off the entire application server runtime. Also, in many cases the functionalities such as product search may be very frequently used compared to other functionalities. With the monolithic approach, you can't scale the product searching functionalities because it shares the same application server runtime with other services (you have to share the entire application server runtime instead). As illustrated in Figure 1-4, the segregation of these coarse-grained services into microservices makes them independently deployable, isolates failures into each service level, and allows you to independently scale a given microservice depending how it is consumed.

No Central ESB: Smart Endpoints and Dumb Pipes

The microservices architecture fosters the elimination of the Enterprise Service Bus (ESB). The ESB used to be the where most of the smarts lived in the SOA/Web Services based architecture. The microservices architecture introduces a new style of service integration called *smart endpoints and dumb pipes* instead of using an ESB. As discussed earlier in this chapter, most of the business functionalities are implemented at the ESB level through the integration or plumbing of the underlying services and systems. With *smart endpoints and dumb pipes*, all the business logic (which includes the inter-service communication logic) resides at each microservice level (they are the *smart-endpoints*) and all such services are connected to a primitive messaging system (a *dumb pipe*), which doesn't have any business logic.

Most naive microservices adopters think that by just transforming the system into a microservices architecture, they can simply get rid of all the complexities of the centralized ESB architecture. However, the reality is that with microservices architecture, the centralized capabilities of the ESB are dispersed into all the microservices. The capabilities that the ESB has offered now have to be implemented at the microservices level.

So, the key point here is that the complexity of the ESB won't go away. Rather it gets distributed among all the microservices that you develop. The microservices compositions (using synchronous or asynchronous styles), inter-services communication via different communication protocols, application of resiliency patterns such as circuit breakers, integrating with other applications, SaaS (e.g., Salesforce), APIs, data and proprietary systems, and observability of integrated services need to be implemented as part of the microservices that you develop. In fact, the complexity of creating compositions and inter-services communication can be more challenging due to the number of services that you have to deal with in a microservices architecture (services are more prone to errors due to the inter-service communications over the network).

Most of the early microservices adopters such as Netflix just implemented most of these capabilities from scratch. However, if we are to fully replace ESB with a microservices architecture, we have to select specific technologies to build those ESB's capabilities at our microservices level rather re-implementing them from scratch.

We will take a detailed look at all these requirements and discuss some of the available technologies to realize them in Chapter 3, "Inter-service Communication" and Chapter 7, "Integrating Microservices".

Failure Tolerance

As discussed in the previous section, microservices are more prone to failures due to the proliferation of the services and their inter-service network communications. A given microservice application is a collection of fine-grained services and therefore a failure of one or more of those services should not bring down the entire application. Therefore, we should gracefully handle a given failure of a microservice so that it has minimum impact on the business functionalities of the application. Designing microservices in failure-tolerable fashion requires the adaptation of the required technologies from the design, development, and deployment phases.

For example, in the retail example, let's say the `Product Details` microservices is critical to the functionality of the e-commerce application. Hence we need to apply all the resiliency-related capabilities, such as circuit breakers, disaster recovery, load-balancing, fail-over, and dynamic scaling based on traffic patterns, which we discuss in detail in Chapter 7, "Integrating Microservices".

It is really important to mimic all such possible failures as part of the service development and testing, using tools such as Netflix's Chaos Monkey. A given service implementation should also be responsible for all the resiliency related activities; such behaviors are automatically verified as part of the CICD (continuous integration, continuous delivery) process.

The other aspect of failure tolerance is the ability to observe the behavior of the microservices that you run in production. Detecting or predicting failures in a service and restoring such services is quite important. For example, suppose that you have monitoring, tracing, logging, etc. enabled for all your microservices in the online retail application example. Then you observe a significant latency and low TPS (Transactions Per Second) in the `Product Search` service. This is an indication of a possible future outage of that service. If the microservices are observable, you should be able to analyze the reasons for the current symptoms. Therefore, even if you have employed chaos testing during the development phase, it's important to have a solid observability infrastructure in place for all your microservices to achieve failure tolerance. We will discuss the observability techniques in detail in Chapter 13, "Observability".

We cover failure tolerance techniques and best practices in Chapter 7, "Integrating Microservices" and Chapter 8, "Deploying and Running Microservices" in detail.

Decentralized Data Management

In a monolithic architecture, the application stores data in single and centralized logical databases to implement various functionalities/capabilities of the application. In a microservices architecture, the functionalities are dispersed across multiple microservices. If we use the same centralized database, the microservices will be no longer independent from each other (for instance, if the database schema is changed by one microservice, that will break several other services). Therefore, each microservice must have its own database and database schema.

Each microservice can have a private database to persist the data that requires implementing the business functionality offered by it. A given microservice can only access the dedicated private database and not the databases of other microservices.

In some business scenarios, you might have to update several databases for a single transaction. In such scenarios, the databases of other microservices should be updated through the corresponding service API only (they are not allowed to access the database directly).

The decentralized data management gives you the fully decoupled microservices and the liberty of choosing disparate data-management techniques (SQL or NoSQL etc., different database management systems for each service). We look at the data management techniques of the microservices architecture in detail in Chapter 5, "Data Management".

Service Governance

SOA governance was one of a key driving forces behind the operational success of SOA; it provides the cooperation and coordination between the different entities in an organization (development teams, service consumers, etc.). Although it defines a comprehensive set of theoretical concepts as part of SOA governance, only a handful of concepts are being actively used in practice. When we shift into a microservices architecture, most of the useful governance concepts are discarded and the governance in microservices is interpreted as a decentralized process, which allows each team/entity to govern its own domain, as it prefers. Decentralized governance is applicable to the service development, deployment, and execution process, but there's a lot more to it than that. Hence we deliberately didn't use the term *decentralized governance*.

We can identify two key aspects of governance: design-time governance of services (selecting technologies, protocols, etc.) and runtime governance (service definitions, service registry and discovery, service versioning, service runtime dependencies, service ownerships and consumers, enforcing QoS, and service observerability).

Design-time governance in microservices is mostly a decentralized process where each service owner is given the freedom to design, develop, and run their services. Then they can use the right tool for the job, rather than standardize on a single technology platform. However, we should define some common standards that are applicable across the organization (for example, irrespective of the development language, all code should go through a review process and automatically be merged into the mainline).

The runtime governance aspect of microservices is implemented at various levels and often we don't call it *runtime governance* in a microservices context (service registry and discovery is one such popular concept that is extremely useful in a microservices architecture). So, rather than learn about these concepts as a set of discrete concepts, it's easier to understand them if we look at the runtime-governance perspective.

Runtime governance is absolutely critical in the microservices architecture (it is even more important than SOA runtime governance), simply because of the number of microservices that we have to deal with. The implementation of runtime governance is often done as a centralized component. For example, suppose that we need to discover service endpoints and metadata in our online retail application scenario. Then all the services have to call a centralized registry service (which can have its own scaling capabilities, yet a logically centralized component). Similarly, if we want to apply QoS (quality of service) enforcements such as security, by throttling centrally, we need a central place such as an API Manager/gateway to do that. In fact, some of the runtime governance aspects are implemented at the API gateway layer too.

We'll look at microservices governance aspects in detail in Chapter 6, "Microservices Governance" and API Management in Chapter 10, "APIs, Events and Streams".

Observability

Service observability can be considered a combination of monitoring, distributed logging, distributed tracing, and visualization of a service's runtime behavior and dependencies. Hence observability can be also considered part of runtime governance. With the proliferation of fine-grained services, the ability to observe the runtime behavior of a service is absolutely critical. Observability components are often a centralized component in the microservices implementation and each service pushes data into those components (rather, observability runtimes pull data from services). Observability is useful for identifying and debugging potential issues, while services are in production and can be also used for business functionality purposes (such as monetization). We'll discuss the wide range of tools and techniques for building observable services in Chapter 13, "Observability".

Microservices: Benefits and Liabilities

As with any architecture or technology, there are benefits and liabilities with the microservices architecture. Since you have a good understanding of the key microservices characteristics, this is a good time to talk about them. Let's start with the benefits of microservices.

Benefits

One of the main reasons for the popularity of the microservices architecture are the benefits that it provides over the conventional software architecture patterns. Let's have a closer look at the key benefits of the microservices architecture.

Agile and Rapid Development of Business Functionalities

The microservices architecture favors autonomous service development, which helps us with Agile and rapid development of business functionalities. In a conventional architecture, converting a business functionality to a production-ready software application functionality takes many cycles, primarily due to the size of the system, codebase, and dependencies. With autonomous service development, you just need to focus on the interface and the functionality of the service (not the functionality of the entire system, which is far more complex), as all the other services only communicate through the network calls via service interfaces.

Replaceability

Due to its autonomous nature, microservices are also *replaceable*. Since we are building services as an independent entity, which is communicating via network calls and defined APIs, we can easily replace that functionality with another better implementation. Being focused on a specific functionality, having a limited scope and size, and deploying it in an independent runtime, all make it much easier to build a replaceable service.

Failure Isolation and Predictability

Replaceability also helps us to achieve failure isolation and prediction. As discussed, a microservices-based application cannot blow up like a conventional monolithic application due to the failure of any given component or service. Having proper observability features also helps us to identify or predict potential failures.

Agile Deployment and Scalability

Ease of deployment and scaling could well be the most important value proposition of microservices. With the modern cloud-based container native infrastructures, the ability to easily deploy a service and scale it dynamically is becoming trivial. Since we are building capabilities as autonomous services, we can easily leverage all such container and cloud-native technologies to facilitate Agile deployment and scalability.

Align with Organizational Structure

Since microservices are business capability oriented, they can well be aligned with the organizational/team structure. Often a given organization is structured in a way that it delivers the business capabilities. Therefore, the ownership of each service can easily be given to the teams who own the business functionality. Therefore, given that a microservice focuses on specific business functionality, you can pick a relatively small team to own that microservice. This has a positive impact on the development team, because the scope of a given service is simple and well defined. That way, the team can fully own service's entire lifecycle.

Liabilities

Most of the liabilities of the microservices architecture are primarily due to the proliferation of services that you need to cope with.

Inter-Service Communication

Inter-service communication complexity could possibly be more challenging than the implementation of the actual services. As discussed earlier, the smart endpoints and dumb pipes concept forces us to have inter-service communication logic as part of our microservices. The service developers have to spend a substantial amount of time on plumbing microservices together to create a composite business functionality.

Service Governance

Having a number of services communicated over the network also *complicates the governance and observability aspect of services.* If you don't have the proper governance and observability tools in place, it will be a nightmare to identify service dependencies and detect failures. For example, service lifecycle management, testing, discovery, monitoring, quality of service, and various other service governance capabilities will become more complex with a microservices architecture.

Heavily Depends on Deployment Methodologies

The success of deploying and scaling microservices is heavily dependent on the adoption of containers and container orchestration systems. If you don't have such an infrastructure in place, you will need to invest time and energy on it (and don't even think about having a successful microservices architecture without containers). Ultimately, a successful microservices architecture is also up to the teams and people. The ownership of services, thinking about making service lightweight and container-native, not having a central point to integrate services, etc., requires organization-level engineering culture changes.

Complexity of Distributed Data and Transaction Management

Since a microservices architecture promotes localizing the data to a given service, distributed data management will be quite daunting. The same applies to distributed transactions. Implementing transaction boundaries that span across multiple microservices will be quite challenging.

How and When to Use Microservices

We discussed how the microservices architecture has evolved from the conventional centralized enterprise architecture, covered the key characteristics of it, and discussed the pros and cons of using it. However, we need to have a solid set of guidelines on when to use the microservices architecture and when to avoid it.

- The microservices architecture is ideal when your current enterprise architecture requires modularity.

- If the business problem that you are trying to solve with your software application is quite simple, you may not need microservices at all (having a simple monolithic web application and a database is usually sufficient).

- Your software application has to embrace container-based deployment.

- If your system is far too complex to be segregated into microservices, you should identify the areas into which you can introduce microservices with minimal impact. Then, start implementing a small use case on microservices and build the required ecosystem components around that.

- Understanding business capabilities is quite critical for designing microservices. Understanding microservices design techniques, as explained in Chapter 2, "Designing Microservices," are essential prior to service implementation

- For each specific microservice domain (such as data management, inter-service communication, security, etc.), we discuss in detail the best practices and anti-patterns in the upcoming chapters.

Summary

The key objective of this chapter is to give you an overview on the current state of the enterprise architecture and how microservices fit into it. In this chapter, we discussed how enterprise architecture has been evolving from monolithic applications to microservices. And we discussed how the role of ESB and API gateway changes when we move into microservices. We also discussed the key characteristics of the microservices architecture and its pros and cons, which will be the foundation to understand the rest of this book.

CHAPTER 2

Designing Microservices

Steve Jobs believed that design is not just what something looks like and feels like, but how it works. How a microservice works within itself and interacts with other microservices highly depends on its design. Most of the architectural concepts and design principles discussed in terms of microservices don't just relate to microservices. They've been here for some time, even during the early days when SOA (Service Oriented Architecture) was popular. Some even call microservices SOA done right! The fundamental issue with SOA was that people didn't get the design right. They got caught up in the hype and left behind the key design principles. Over time, SOA became just another buzzword, while the original need for it was left unaddressed. Microservices as a concept has emerged to fill this vacuum. Unless you pay close attention to microservices architectural concepts and design principles, you are not doing microservices!

Sir Charles Antony Richard Hoare is the British scientist who developed the quicksort-sorting algorithm. During his speech accepting the Turing award in 1980, he mentioned that there are two ways to design software: one way is to make the software so simple that there are obviously no deficiencies, and the other way is to make it so complicated that there are no obvious deficiencies—the first method is far more difficult. In a microservices design, you need to worry about its inner and outer architecture. The inner architecture defines how you design a microservice itself, and the outer architecture talks about how it communicates with other microservices. Unless you make both the designs simple and easy to evolve, you make the system error prone and move away from key microservices design goals. At its core in any microservices design, time to production, scalability, complexity localization, and resiliency are key elements. Unless you make the design simple, it's hard to reach these expectations.

19

© Kasun Indrasiri and Prabath Siriwardena 2018
K. Indrasiri and P. Siriwardena, *Microservices for the Enterprise*, https://doi.org/10.1007/978-1-4842-3858-5_2

Domain-Driven Design

Domain-driven design (DDD) is not a new concept introduced with microservices and has been around for quite some time. Eric Evans, in his book, *Domain-Driven Design: Tackling Complexity in the Heart of Software,* coined the term Domain-Driven Design. As microservices became a mainstream architectural pattern, people started to realize the applicability of domain-driven design concepts in designing microservices. This design plays a key role in scoping out microservices.

Note   An in-depth explanation of domain-driven design is out of the scope of this book. This chapter focuses on the application of domain-driven design for building microservices. Readers who are keen on learning more about domain-driven design are encouraged to go through the book by Eric Evans. In addition to Eric's book, we also recommend reading the book *Patterns, Principles, and Practices of Domain-Driven Design*, by Scott Millett and Nick Tune.

What is domain-driven design? It is mainly about modeling complex business logic, or building an abstraction over complex business logic. The *domain* is at the heart of a domain-driven design. All software we develop is related to some user activity or interest. Eric Evans says that the subject area to which the user applies the program is the domain of the software. Some domains involve the physical world. In the retail business, you find buyers, sellers, suppliers, partners, and many other entities. Some domains are intangible. For example, in the crypto-currency domain, a Bitcoin wallet application deals with intangible assets. Whatever it is, the domain is related to the business, not the software. Of course, software can be a domain itself when you build software to work in the software domain, for example a configuration management program.

Throughout this book we'll be using many examples to elaborate on these concepts. Let's say we have an enterprise retailer that is building an e-commerce application. The retailer has four main departments: inventory and order management, customer management, delivery, and billing and finance. Each department may have multiple sections. The order processing section of the inventory and order management department accepts an order, locks the items in the inventory, and then passes the control to billing and finance to work on the payment. Once the payment is successfully processed, the delivery department makes the order ready for delivery. The customer management department takes the ownership of managing all customer personal data and all the interactions with the customer. See Figure 2-1.

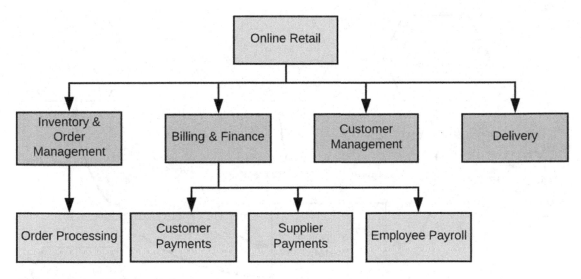

Figure 2-1. *Divide and conquer*

One key principle behind domain-driven design is *divide and conquer*. The retail domain is the core business domain in our example. Each department can be treated as a sub-domain. Identifying the core business domain and the related sub-domains is critically important. This helps us build an e-commerce application for our retailer following microservices architectural principles. One of the key challenges many architects face in building a microservices architecture is to come up with the right level of granularity for each service. Domain-driven design helps here. As the name implies, under domain-driven design, *domain* is the king!

Let's take a step back and look at *Conway's law*. It says any organization that designs a system will produce a design whose structure is a copy of the organization's communication structure. This justifies identifying sub-domains in an enterprise in terms of departments. A given department is formed for a purpose. A department has it own internal communication structure, as well as a communication structure between departments. Even a given department can have multiple sections, where we can identify each such section as a sub-domain. See Figure 2-1 for the details.

Let's see how we can map this domain structure into the microservices architecture. Possibly we can start building our e-commerce application with four microservices (see Figure 2-2): `Order Processing`, `Customer`, `Delivery`, and `Billing`.

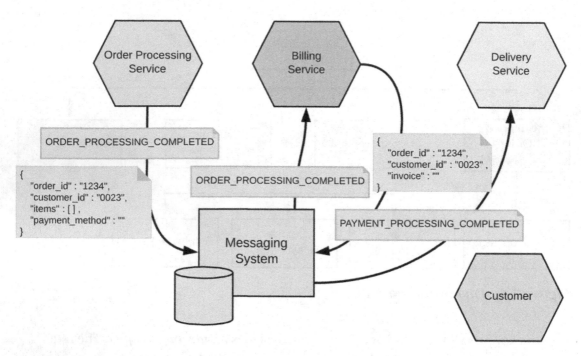

Figure 2-2. *Communication between microservices*

Suppose that these microservices communicate with each other via messages, which are sent as events. The request first hits the Order Processing microservice, and once it locks the items in the inventory, fires the ORDER_PROCESSING_COMPLETED event. Events are a way of communicating between microservices. There can be multiple other services listening to the ORDER_PROCESSING_COMPLETED event and once they are notified, start acting upon it accordingly. As per Figure 2-2, the Billing microservice receives the ORDER_PROCESSING_COMPLETED event and starts processing the payment. Amazon, for example, does not process payments at the time an order is placed, but only when it is ready to ship. Just like Amazon, the Order Processing microservice will fire the ORDER_ PROCESSING_COMPLETED event only when the order is ready to ship. This event itself contains the data required to process the payment by the Billing microservice. In this particular example, it carries the customer ID and the payment method. The Billing microservice stores customer payment options in its own repository, including the credit card information, so it can now independently process the payment.

Note   Using events to communicate between microservices is one of the commonly used patterns in inter-microservice communication. It removes point-to-point connections between microservices and the communication happens via a messaging system. Each microservice, once it's done with its own processing, publishes an event to a topic, while the other microservices, which register themselves as listeners to the interested topics, will act accordingly once they receive a notification. Messaging technologies used in microservices, microservice integration patterns, and event-driven messaging patterns are covered in Chapter 3, "Inter-Service Communication," Chapter 7, "Integrating Microservices," and Chapter 10, "APIs, Events, and Streams," respectively.

Once the `Billing` microservice completes processing the payment, it will fire the `PAYMENT_PROCESSING_COMPLETED` event and the `Delivery` microservice will capture it. This event carries the customer ID, order ID, and invoice. Now the `Delivery` microservice loads the customer delivery address from its own repository and prepares the order for delivery. Even though the `Customer` microservice is shown in Figure 2-2, it is not being used during the order processing flow. When new customers are on-boarded into the system or existing customers want to update their personal data, the `Customer` microservice will be used.

A project faces serious problems when its language is fractured.

—Eric Evans

Each microservice in Figure 2-2 belongs to a business domain. The inventory and order management is the domain of the `Order Processing` microservice; customer management is the domain of the `Customer` microservice; delivery is the domain of the `Delivery` microservice; and billing & finance is the domain of the `Billing` microservice. Each of these domains or departments can have its own communication structure internally along with its own terminology to represent business activities.

Each domain can be modeled independently. As much as one can be independent from the others, it gains more flexibility to evolve on its own. Domain-driven design defines best practices and guidelines on how you can model a given domain. It highlights the need to have a *ubiquitous language* to define the domain model. The ubiquitous language is a shared team language, which is shared by domain experts and the developers. In fact, ubiquitous means that the same language must be used everywhere within a given context (or to be precise, within a bounded context, which we discuss in the section to follow), from conversations to code. This bridges the gap in communication between domain experts and developers. Domain experts are thorough with their own jargons, but have limited or no understanding of the technical terms used in software development, while the developers know how to describe a system in technical terms, but have no or limited domain expertise. The ubiquitous language fills this gap and brings everyone to the same page.

The terminology defined by the ubiquitous language must be bounded by the corresponding context. The context is related to a domain. For example, the ubiquitous language can be used to define an entity called *customer*. The definition of the customer entity in the inventory and order management domain does not necessarily need to be the same as in the customer management domain. For example, the customer entity in the inventory and order management domain may have properties such as order history, open orders, and scheduled orders, while the customer entity in the customer management domain has properties such as first name, last name, home address, email address, mobile number, etc. The customer entity in the billing & finance domain may have properties like credit card number, billing address, billing history, and scheduled payments. Any term defined by ubiquitous language must only be interpreted under the corresponding context.

Note   A typical software project involves domain experts only during the requirement-gathering phase. A business analyst (BA) translates the business use cases into a technical requirements specification. The business analyst completely owns the requirements and there is no feedback cycle. The model is developed, as heard by the business analyst. One key aspect in domain-driven design is to encourage more, lengthy communication between domain experts and developers. This goes well beyond the initial requirement-gathering phase and finally ends up with building a domain model well understood by both the domain experts and developers.

Let's delve deep in to this example. In our architecture, a given microservice belongs to a single business domain and the communication between microservices happens via message passing. The message passing can be based on an event-driven architecture or just over HTTP. Each message from one microservice to another carries domain objects.

For example, the ORDER_PROCESSING_COMPLETED event carries the *order* domain object, while the PAYMENT_PROCESSING_COMPLETED event carries the *invoice* domain object (see Figure 2-2). The definition of these domain objects must be carefully derived via domain-driven design with the collaboration between domain experts and developers.

Note   Domain-driven design has its own inherent challenges. One challenge is to get domain experts involved in the project throughout its execution. It also takes a considerable amount of time to build the ubiquitous language, which requires good collaboration between domain experts and developers. Unlike developing a monolithic application, which expands across all the domains, building a solution for a given domain and encapsulating domain-specific business logic requires a change in developer mindset, which is also challenging.

Bounded Context

As we discussed, one of the most challenging parts of a microservices design is to scope out a microservice. This is where the SOA and its implementations had poorly defined the scope. In SOA, while doing a design, we take into consideration the entire enterprise. It will not worry about individual business domains, but rather the enterprise as a whole. It will not worry about inventory and order management, billing and finance, delivery and customer management as separate independent domains—but rather will treat the complete system as an enterprise e-commerce application.

Figure 2-3 illustrates the layered architecture of an e-commerce application done by an SOA architect. For anyone from some SOA background, this should look quite familiar. What we have here is a monolithic application. Even though the service layer exposes some functionality as services, none is decoupled from each other. The scoping of services was not done based on the business domain they belong to. For example, the Order Processing service may also deal with billing and delivery. In Chapter 1, "The Case for Microservices," we discussed the deficiencies of such a monolithic architecture.

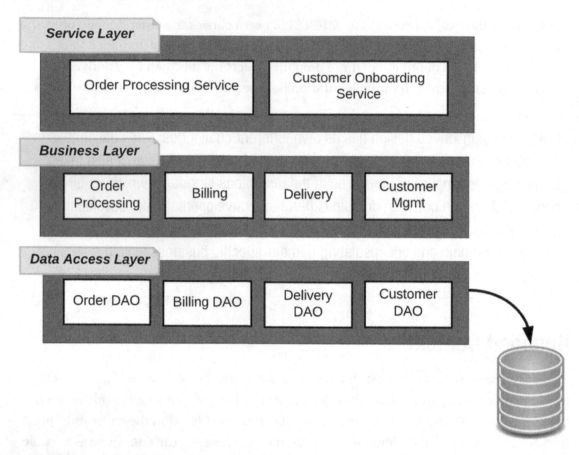

Figure 2-3. *A layered architecture of an e-commerce application*

As we discussed in the previous section, domain-driven design helps scope out microservices. The scoping of a microservice is done around a *bounded context*. The bounded context is at the heart of a microservices design. Eric Evans first introduced bounded context as a design pattern in his book *Domain-Driven Design: Tackling Complexity in the Heart of Software*. The idea is that any given domain consists of multiple bounded contexts, and each bounded context encapsulates related functionalities into domain models and defines integration points to other bounded contexts. In other words, each bounded context has an explicit interface, where it defines what models to share with other contexts. By explicitly defining what models should be shared, and not sharing the internal representation, we can avoid the potential pitfalls that can result in tight coupling. These modular boundaries are great candidates for microservices. In general, microservices should cleanly align to bounded contexts. If the service boundaries are aligned to the bounded contexts of the corresponding domain, and the microservices represent those bounded contexts, that's a great indication that the microservices are loosely coupled and strongly cohesive.

Note   A bounded context is an explicit boundary within which a domain model exists. Inside the boundary all terms and phrases of the ubiquitous language have a specific meaning, and the model reflects the language with exactness.[1]

Let's extend our previous example with bounded contexts. There we identified four domains: inventory and order management, billing and finance, delivery, and customer management. Each microservice we designed attached to one of those domains. Even though we have one-to-one relationship between a microservice to a domain, we know by now that one domain can have more than one bounded context, hence more than one microservices. For example, if you take the inventory & order management domain, we have the Order Processing microservice, but we also can have multiple other microservices as well, based on different bounded contexts (e.g., the Inventory microservice). To do that, we need to take a closer look at the key functions provided under the inventory and order management domain and identify the corresponding bounded contexts.

Note   It is recommended that bounded contexts maintain their separation by each having its own team, codebase, and the database schema.

The inventory and order management department of an enterprise takes care of managing stocks and makes sure customer demand can be met with the existing stocks. It should also know when to order more stocks from suppliers to optimize the sales as well as the storage facilities. Whenever it receives a new order, it has to update the inventory and lock the corresponding items for delivery. Once the payment is done and confirmed by the billing department, the delivery department has to locate the item in its warehouse and make it available for pick up and delivery. At the same time, whenever the available quantity of an item in the store reaches some threshold value, the inventory and order management department should contact the suppliers to get more, and once received, should update the inventory.

---

[1]Implementing Domain-Driven Design, Vaughn Vernon

One of the key highlights of the domain-driven design is the collaboration between domain experts and the developers. Unless you have proper understanding of how an inventory management department works within an enterprise, you will never identify the corresponding bounded contexts. With our limited understanding of inventory management, based on what was discussed before, we can identify the following three bounded contexts.

- *Order processing*: This bounded context encapsulates the functionality related to processing an order, which includes locking the items in the order in the inventory, recording orders against the customer, etc.

- *Inventory*: Inventory itself can be treated as a bounded context. This takes care of updating the stocks upon receiving items from suppliers and releasing for delivery.

- *Supplier management*: This bounded context encapsulates the functionality related to managing suppliers. Upon releasing an item for delivery, supplier management checks whether it has enough stocks in the inventory, and if not, it notifies the corresponding suppliers.

Figure 2-4 illustrates multiple microservices under the inventory and order management domain, representing each of the bounded contexts. Here the service boundaries are aligned to the bounded contexts of the corresponding domain. The communication between bounded contexts happens only via message passing against well-defined interfaces. As per Figure 2-4, the Order Processing microservice first updates the Inventory microservice to lock the items in the order and then triggers the ORDER_PROCESSING_COMPLETED event. The Billing microservice listening to the ORDER_PROCESSING_COMPLETED event executes payment processing and then triggers the PAYMENT_PROCESSING_COMPLETED event. The Supplier Management microservice listening to the PAYMENT_PROCESSING_COMPLETED event checks whether the number of items in the stocks is above the minimal threshold and if not notifies the suppliers. The Delivery microservice listening to the same event executes its operations to look up the items (probably sending instructions to warehouse bots) and then groups the items together to build the order and make it ready for delivery. Once that's done, the Delivery microservice will trigger the ORDER_DISPATCHED event, which notifies the Order Processing microservice, and will update the order status.

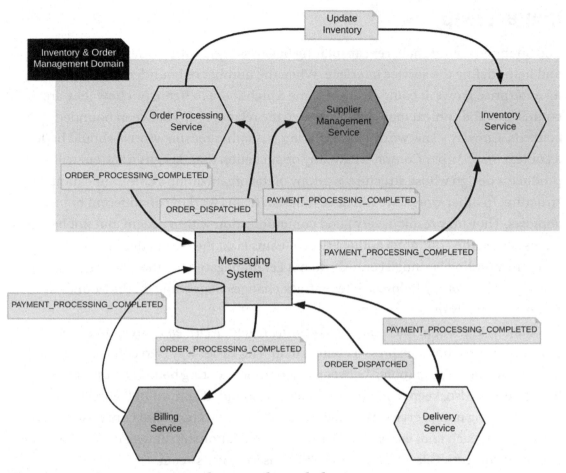

Figure 2-4. *Communication between bounded contexts*

A good design will scope out one microservice to a single bounded context. Any microservice expanding across multiple bounded contexts deviates from the original goals. When we have one microservice, encapsulating the business logic behind a well defined interface and representing one bounded context, bringing in new changes will have no or minimal impact on the complete system.

As we discussed, communication between microservices can happen via events. Under domain-driven design, these events are known as *domain events*. Domain events are triggered as a result of state changes in bounded contexts. Then the other bounded contexts can respond to these events in a loosely coupled manner. The bounded contexts firing events need not to worry about the behaviors that should take place as a result of those events and at the same time bounded contexts, which handle such events, need not to worry about where the events came from. Domain events can be used between bounded contexts within a domain or between domains.

Context Map

The bounded context helps encapsulating business logic within a service boundary and helps define the service interface. When the number of bounded contexts in an enterprise grows, it could easily become a nightmare to figure out how they are connected. The context maps help visualize the relationships between bounded contexts. Conway's Law we discussed earlier is another reason why we should build a context map. As per Conway's Law, any organization that designs a system will produce a design whose structure is a copy of the organization's communication structure. In other words, we will have different teams working on different bounded contexts. They may result in very good communication within a team, but not between teams. When the communication between teams lack, the design decisions made on corresponding bounded contexts do not get propagated to other parties properly. Having a context map helps each team track changes happening on the bounded contexts they rely on.

Vaughn Vernon, in his book *Implementing Domain-Driven Design,* presents multiple approaches to express a context map. The easier way is to come up with a diagram to show the mapping between two or more existing bounded contexts, as in Figure 2-5. Also, keep in mind here that each bounded context in Figure 2-5 has a corresponding microservice. We used a line between two bounded contexts with two identifiers at each end, either U or D, to show the relationship between corresponding bounded contexts. U is for upstream, while D is for downstream.

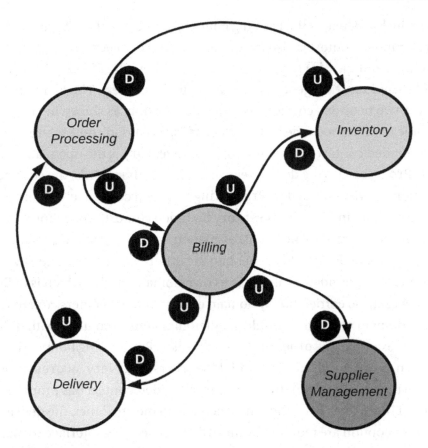

Figure 2-5. *Context map*

In the relationship between the Order Processing bounded context and the
Billing bounded context, the Order Processing bounded context is the upstream
context, while Billing is the downstream context. The upstream context has more
control over the downstream context. In other words, the upstream context defines the
domain model passed between the two contexts. The downstream context should be
well aware of any changes happening to the upstream context. Figure 2-4 shows what
exact messages being passed between these two bounded contexts. There is no direct
coupling. The communication between the Order Processing bounded context and
the Billing bounded context happens via eventing. The upstream bounded context
or the Order Processing bounded context defines the structure of the event, and any
downstream bounded context interested in that event must be compliant.

The relationship between the `Billing` bounded context and the `Supplier Management` bounded context is also the same as what is between the `Order Processing` bounded context and the `Billing` bounded context. There the `Billing` is the upstream context while `Supplier Management` is the downstream context. The communication between these two bounded contexts happens via eventing, as shown in Figure 2-4. The communication between the `Order Processing` bounded context and the `Inventory` bounded context is synchronous. The `Inventory` is the upstream context while `Order Processing` is the downstream context. In other words, the contract for the communication between the `Order Processing` bounded context and the `Inventory` bounded context is defined by the `Inventory` bounded context. Not all the relationships, which are shown in Figure 2-5, need an explanation, as they are self-explanatory.

Let's step back and delve little deeper into the `Order Processing` and `Inventory` bounded contexts. A bounded context has its own domain model, which is defined as a result of a long exercise carried out by domain experts and developers. You may recall that the same domain object may reside in different bounded contexts with different definitions. For example, the `order` entity in the `Order Processing` bounded context has properties such as `order id`, `customer id`, `line items`, `delivery address`, and `payment option`, while the `order` entity in the `Inventory` bounded context has properties such as `order id` and `line items`. Even though a reference to the customer, the deliver address, and the payment option are required by the `Order Processing` interface to maintain the history of all the orders against the customer, none of them are needed by the `Inventory`. Each bounded context should know how to manage such situations, to avoid any conflicts in their domain models. In the following section we discuss some patterns to follow in order to maintain relationships between multiple bounded contexts.

Relational Patterns

Domain-driven design has lead to multiple patterns that facilitate communication between multiple bounded contexts. The same patterns are applicable while designing microservices, which are well aligned with bounded contexts. These relational patterns for bounded contexts were first introduced by Eric Evans in his book *Domain-Driven Design: Tackling Complexity in the Heart of Software.*

Anti-Corruption Layer

Let's revisit the scenario we discussed in the previous section, where the order entity has two different definitions under the Order Processing and Inventory bounded contexts. For the communication between these two bounded contexts, the contract is defined by the Inventory bounded context (see Figure 2-5). When Order Processing updates the Inventory, it has to translate its own order entity to the order entity, which is understood by the Inventory bounded context. We use the anti-corruption layer (ACL) pattern to address this concern. The anti-corruption layer pattern provides a translation layer (see Figure 2-6).

Figure 2-6. *Anti-corruption layer pattern*

Let's see how this pattern is applicable in an enterprise grade microservices deployment. Imagine a scenario where your microservice has to invoke a service exposed by a monolithic application. The design of the monolithic application does not worry about domain-driven design. The best way to facilitate the communication between our microservice and the monolithic application is via an anti-corruption layer. This helps to keep the microservice design much cleaner (or less corrupted).

There are multiple ways to implement the anti-corruption layer. One approach is to build the translation into the microservice itself. You will be using whatever the language you used to implement the microservice to implement the anti-corruption layer as well. This approach has multiple drawbacks. The microservice development team has to own the implementation of the anti-corruption layer; hence they need to worry about any changes happening at the monolithic application side. If we implement this translation layer as another microservice, then we can delegate its implementation and the ownership to a different team. That team only needs to understand the translation and nothing else. This approach is commonly known as the *sidecar* pattern.

As shown in Figure 2-7, the sidecar pattern is derived from the vehicle where a sidecar is attached to a motorcycle. If you'd like, you can attach different sidecars (of different colors or designs) to the same motorcycle, provided that the interface between those two is unchanged. The same applies in the microservices world, where our microservice resembles the motorcycle, while the translation layer resembles the sidecar. If any change happens to the monolithic application, we only need to change the sidecar implementation to be compliant with it—and no changes to the microservice.

Figure 2-7. *Sidecar*

The communication between the microservice and the sidecar happens over the network (not a local, in-process call), but both the microservice and sidecar are co-located in the same host—so it will not be routed over the network. We discuss multiple microservices deployment patterns later in the book, in Chapter 8, "Deploying and Running Microservices". Also, keep in mind the sidecar itself is another microservice. Figure 2-8 shows how to use a sidecar as an anti-corruption layer.

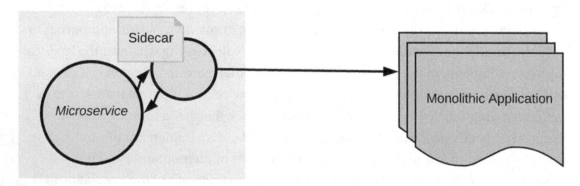

Figure 2-8. *Sidecar acting as the anti-corruption layer*

An anti-corruption layer is one possible way to use a sidecar pattern. It is also used in several other use cases such as a Service Mesh. We discuss what a Service Mesh is and how the sidecar pattern is used in Service Meshes in detail in Chapter 9, "Service Mesh".

Shared Kernel

Even though we discussed how it's important to have clear boundaries between bounded contexts, there are cases in which we need to share domain models. This can happen in a case where we have two or more bounded contexts with certain things in common, and it adds lot of overhead to maintain separate object models under different bounded contexts. For example, each bounded context (or the microservice) has to authorize the user who invokes its operations. Different domains could be using their own authorization policies, but in many cases they share the same domain model as the authorization service (the authorization service itself is a microservice or a separate bounded context). In such cases, the domain model of the authorization service acts as the shared kernel. Since there is a shared code dependency (probably wrapped into a library), to make the shared kernel pattern work in practice, all the teams who use the shared kernel have to collaborate well with each other (see Figure 2-9).

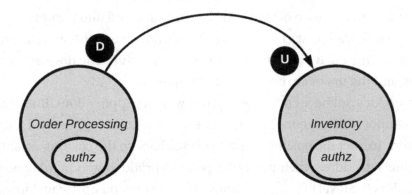

Figure 2-9. *Shared kernel*

Conformist

We already discussed in this chapter the responsibilities of an upstream bounded context and a downstream bounded context. Let's quickly recall. The upstream context has more control over the downstream context. The upstream context defines the domain model passed between the two contexts. The downstream context should be well aware of any changes happening to the upstream context. The conformist pattern states that the downstream context (the conformist) has to conform to the contract defined by the upstream context.

The conformist pattern looks similar to the shared kernel, where both patterns have a shared domain model. The difference is in the decision-making and the development process. The shared kernel is a result of the collaboration between two teams that coordinate tightly, while the conformist pattern deals with integration with a team that is not interested in collaboration—possibly a third-party service, where you have no control. For example, you may use the PayPal API to process payments. PayPal is never going to change its API to fit you, rather your bounded context has to comply with it. In case this integration makes your domain model look ugly, you can possibly introduce an anti-corruption layer to isolate the integration in just one place.

Customer/Supplier

The conformist pattern has its own drawbacks where the downstream context or the service has no say as to how the interface between itself and the upstream context should be. There is no collaboration between the teams who work upstream/downstream bounded contexts. The customer/supplier pattern is one step forward to build better communication between these two teams and find a way to build the interface with collaboration. It's not a total collaboration like in the shared kernel pattern, but something like a customer/supplier relationship. The downstream context is the customer, and the upstream context is the supplier.

A customer does not have complete say over what a supplier does. But, then again, the supplier cannot totally ignore customer feedback. A good supplier will always listen to its customers, extract the positives, give feedback back to the customers, and produce the best products to address their needs. No point in producing something useless to its customers. This is the level of collaboration expected between upstream/downstream contexts adhering to the customer/supplier pattern. This helps the downstream contexts to provide suggestions, and request changes to the interface between the two contexts. Following this pattern, there is more responsibility on the upstream context. A given upstream context not only deals with one downstream context. You need to be extra careful that a suggestion from one downstream context does not break the contract between the upstream context and another downstream context.

Partnership

When we have two or more teams building microservices under different bounded contexts, but overall moving toward the same goal, and there are notable inter-dependencies between them, partnership pattern is an ideal way to build collaboration. Teams can collaborate in making decisions over the technical interfaces, release schedules, and anything of common interest. The partnership pattern is also applicable to any teams using the shared kernel pattern. The collaboration required to build the shared kernel can be established via a partnership. Also keep in mind that the output of the partnership pattern is not necessarily a shared kernel. It can be any interdependent services with nothing concrete to share.

Published Language

Microservices or bounded contexts, which follow the published language pattern, should agree on a published language to communicate. Here the *published* means that the language is readily available to the community that might be interested in using it. This can be XML, JSON, or any other language corresponding to the domain where the microservices are. Here the domain means the core domain. For example, there are domain specific languages used in the financial, e-business, and many other domains.

 This pattern highlights the importance of using a well-documented shared language to express necessary domain information as a common medium of communication. Figure 2-10 shows how the translation works in and out of the published language to the context-specific languages. There we have a Java to JSON parser at the Order Processing microservice end, which knows how to create a JSON document from a Java object model. We use the JSON to C# parser at the Inventory microservice end to build a C# object model from a JSON document.

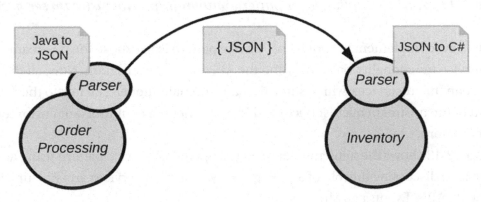

Figure 2-10. *Published language pattern*

Open Host Service

In the anti-corruption layer pattern we have a translation layer between upstream and downstream microservices (or bounded contexts). When we have multiple downstream services, each downstream service has to handle the translation, as shown in Figure 2-11. Both the `Delivery` and `Supplier Management` microservices have to translate the object model they get from the `Billing` upstream microservice to their own respective domain models (see Figure 2-11). If each of these downstream microservice has its own domain model, it doesn't matter. We cannot avoid the translation happening at each end. But, if we have many downstream microservices doing the same translation, then it's a duplication of the effort. The open host service pattern suggests an approach to overcome this.

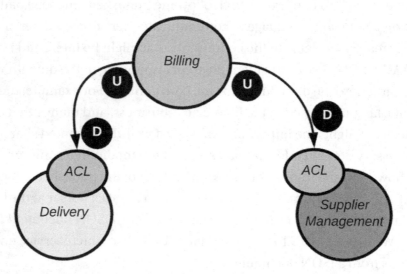

Figure 2-11. *Anti-corruption layer pattern with multiple downstream services*

One way to implement the open host service pattern is to expose the upstream microservice functionality via an API, and the API does the translation. Now, all the downstream microservices, which share the same domain model, can talk to the API (instead of the upstream microservice) and follow either the conformist or customer/supplier pattern.

Figure 2-12 shows the implementation of the open host service pattern using an API. We'll be discussing the role of an API gateway, in a microservices architecture, in Chapter 10: APIs, Events and Streams.

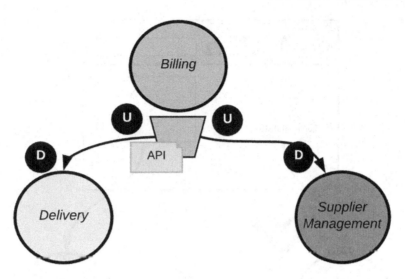

Figure 2-12. *Open host service pattern*

Separate Ways

Let's revisit the microservices design we did for our e-commerce application. There we have a `Customer` microservice and an `Order Processing` microservice (see Figure 2-2). Think of a customer portal, which talks to the `Customer` microservice and displays user profile. It may be useful to the end user to see his/her order history, along with the profile data. But the `Customer` microservice does not have direct access to the order history of a given customer; it's under the control of `Order Processing` microservice. One way to facilitate this is to integrate the `Order Processing` microservice with the `Customer` microservice, and change the domain model of the `Customer` microservice to return the order history along with the profile data, which is a costly integration.

Integration is always expensive and sometimes the benefit is small. The separate ways pattern suggests avoiding such costly integrations, and finds other ways to cater such requests. For example, in this particular scenario, we can avoid the integration between the `Order Processing` microservice and the `Customer` microservice and provide a link to the customer portal, along with the profile data to retrieve order history, and that will directly talk to the `Order Processing` microservice (see Figure 2-13).

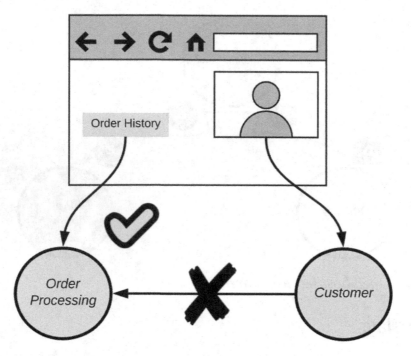

Figure 2-13. *Separate ways pattern*

Big Ball of Mud

Most of the time you don't get a chance to work on a green-field project. Always you find some kind of a legacy system with lots of resistance to integrate with other systems in a standard manner. These systems do not have clear boundaries and clean domain models. The big ball of mud pattern highlights the need to identify such systems and treat them in a special context. We should not try to apply sophisticated modeling to these contexts, but rather find a way to integrate via an API or some kind of a service interface and use an anti-corruption layer pattern at the downstream service end.

Design Principles

Domain-driven design helps us scope out microservices along with bounded contexts. At its core in any microservices design, time to production, scalability, complexity localization, and resiliency are key elements. Adhering to the following design principles helps a microservice reach those design goals.

High Cohesion And Loose Coupling

Cohesion is a measure of how well a given system is self-contained. Gary McLean Hall, in his book *Adaptive Code*, presents cohesion as a measure of the contextual relationship between variables in a method, methods in a class, classes in a module, modules in a solution, solutions in a subsystem, and subsystems in a system. This fractal relationship is important because a lack of cohesion at any scope is problematic. Cohesion can be low or high based on the strength of the contextual relationships. In a microservices architecture, if we have one microservice to address two or more unrelated problems, or in other words two or more problems with weak contextual relationships, this results in a low cohesive system. Low cohesive systems are brittle in nature. When we build one microservice to address many other not-so related requirements, chances are high that we have to change the implementation more frequently.

How do we know, given two requirements, if we have a strong contextual relationship? This is the whole point of the exercise we carried out in the previous section under domain-driven design. If your requirements fall under the same bounded context, then those do have a strong contextual relationship. If the service boundaries of a microservice are aligned to the bounded context of the corresponding domain, then it will produce a highly cohesive microservice.

Note   A highly cohesive and loosely coupled system will naturally follow the *single responsibility principle*. The single responsibility principle states that a component or a system that adheres to it should only have one reason to change.

Cohesion and coupling are two related properties of a system design. A highly cohesive system is naturally loosely coupled. Coupling is a measure of the interdependence between different systems or, in our case, microservices. When we have a high interdependency between microservices, this will result in a tightly coupled system, while a low interdependency will produce a loosely coupled system. Tightly coupled systems build a brittle system architecture. A change done in one system will affect all the related systems. If one system goes down, all the related systems will be dysfunctional. When we have a high cohesive system, we group all the related or interdependent functionalities together, into one system (or group into one bounded context). So, it does not need to heavily rely on other systems.

A microservices architecture must be highly cohesive and loosely coupled, by definition.

Resilience

Resilience is a measure of the capacity of a system or individual components in a system to recover quickly from a failure. In other words it is an attribute of a system that enables it to deal with failure in a way that doesn't cause the entire system to fail. A microservices architecture is naturally a distributed system. A distributed system is a collection of computes (or nodes) connected over the network, with no shared memory, that appears to its users as a single coherent system. In a distributed system, failures are not strange. Now and forever the network will always be unreliable. An underwater fiber optics cable may get damaged by a submarine, a router can be blown up due to the heat, a load balancer can start to malfunction, computers may run out of memory, a power failure can take a database server down, an earthquake may take an entire data center down—and for a thousand and one other reasons the communication in a distributed system may fail.

Note   In 1994, Peter Deutsch, a Sun fellow at the time, drafted seven assumptions architects and designers of distributed systems are likely to make, which prove wrong in the long run and result in all sorts of troubles and pain for the solution and architects who made the assumptions. In 1997, James Gosling added another such fallacy. The assumptions are now collectively known as *the eight fallacies of distributed computing*: 1. The network is reliable. 2. Latency is zero. 3. Bandwidth is infinite. 4. The network is secure. 5. Topology doesn't change. 6. There is one administrator. 7. Transport cost is zero. 8. The network is homogeneous.[2]

Failures are unavoidable. Ariel Tseitlin, in his ACM paper, "Anti-Fragile Organization,"[3] talks about embracing failures to improve resilience and maximize availability, taking Netflix as an example. One way Ariel highlights in his paper to increase the resilience of a system is to reduce uncertainty by regularly inducing failures. Netflix accepts the idea of inducing failures regularly and takes an aggressive approach by writing programs that cause failures and running them in production in daily basis (The Netflix Simian Army). Google too goes beyond simple tests to mimic server failures, and as part of its annual Disaster Recovery Test (DiRT) exercises, it has simulated large-scale disasters such as earthquakes.

---

[2]http://www.rgoarchitects.com/Files/fallacies.pdf
[3]https://queue.acm.org/detail.cfm?id=2499552

Note   Netflix has taken three important steps to build a more anti-fragile system and organization. The first step is to treat every engineer as an operator of the corresponding service. The second step is to treat each failure as an opportunity to learn and the third is to foster a blameless culture.

The most common way to counter attack failures in a distributed system is via redundancy. Each component in the distributed system will have a redundant counterpart. If one component fails, the corresponding counterpart will take over. Not all the time, every component in a system will be able to recover from a failure with zero downtime. Apart from redundancy, having a developer mindset focusing on recovery-oriented development helps in building more resilient software. The following lists a set of patterns that were initially introduced by Michael T. Nygard in his book, *Release It,* to build resilient software. Today, these patterns are part and parcel of microservices development. Many microservices frameworks have first class support for implementing these patterns. What follows is a detailed explanation of resilient communication patterns and we revisit them when we discuss microservice integration in Chapter 7. There we discuss how they are used in practice with most of the common microservice development frameworks.

Timeouts

Almost all the applications we build today do remote calls over the network. It can be an HTTP request to a web service endpoint, a database call over JDBC, or an authentication request to an LDAP server. Anything over the network is fallible; hence we should not wait infinitely expecting a response from the remote endpoint. For example, in a database connection, if we decide to wait infinitely until we see a response, that takes one connection out of the database connection pool for the period of the wait time. And if we have few more like that, the overall performance of the application will start to degrade.

Timeouts decide how much time we want to tolerate waiting for a response. For every remote call we do from our microservice, we must have a timeout. Neither the very long timeouts nor the very short ones are going to help. It will be a learning exercise to figure out the best fit. Make sure every time a connection times out to have a log entry. That helps in the future to adjust the timeout value.

Let's see how this could happen in practice. From our customer portal, to load suggestions for the logged in user, based on his/her previous order patterns, we have to call the `Customer Suggestions` microservice. This service has to talk to a database internally to load the suggestions. If the connection to the database times out, what should we return? If we build the microservice with a recovery-oriented development mindset, we should not just return an error, rather we should return a default set of suggestions, which will not break anything in the customer portal. From a business point of view, this may not be effective, but from the end user's user experience point of view it's a good pattern to follow.

Circuit Breaker

The circuit breaker protects electrical appliances by controlling the flow of electricity (see Figure 2-14). If the flow of electricity is higher than a certain threshold value, the circuit breaker will break the flow and protect the appliances behind it from damages. The circuit breaker pattern brings this same concept to the software world. If our microservice keeps timing out against one endpoint all the time, there is no point keep trying, at least for some time. The circuit breaker pattern suggests wrapping such operations with a component that can circumvent calls when the system is not healthy. This component will maintain some threshold value for failures and, if it is met, then will break the circuit; no more calls will hit the wrapped operation. It may also wait for some configured time interval and close the circuit to see if the operation returns errors, and if does not, it will keep the circuit closed for all the subsequent operations.

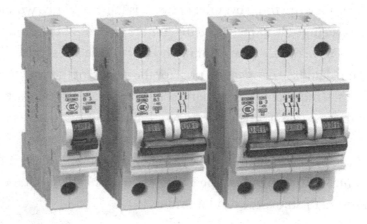

Figure 2-14. *MCBs (miniature circuit breakers), mostly used in homes*

Bulkheads

Bulkheads are mostly used in ships and boats to build watertight compartments, so that if one compartment is caught in the water, the people can move to another compartment for safety. The damage in one compartment will not take the ship completely down, as the compartments are isolated from each other.

The bulkheads pattern borrows this same concept . This pattern highlights how we can allocate resources, such as thread pools, which are connection pools for outbound connections. If we have one single thread pool for all outbound endpoints, then, if one endpoint happens to be slow in responding, releasing the corresponding thread to the pool will take more time. If this repeats consistently then will have an impact on requests directed to other endpoints as well, since more threads are now waiting on the slow endpoint. Following the bulkheads pattern, we can have one thread pool per endpoint— or in a way you can logically group those together. This prevents an issue in one bad endpoint being propagated into other good endpoints. The bulkheads pattern partitions capacity to preserve partial functionality when bad things happen.

Steady State

The steady state pattern highlights the need of adhering to a design that lets your system run in a steady state for a long time without frequent interventions. Every time your DevOps team has to touch the system, they increase the possibility of introducing new errors, no matter how experienced they are. In March 2017, there was a massive AWS (Amazon Web Services) outage. This four-hour outage at AWS S3 system caused disruptions, slowdowns, and failure-to-load errors across the United States. Amazon later published[4] the cause of the issue, which was a trivial human error. An authorized S3 team member using an established playbook executed a command, which was intended to remove a small number of servers for one of the S3 subsystems that is used by the S3 billing process. Unfortunately, one of the inputs to the command was entered incorrectly and a larger set of servers was removed than intended.

The design of a system must be done in a way to keep humans away from it whenever possible. Everything, from development to deployment, must be automated. This includes cleaning up resources that accumulate in the production servers. The best example are the logs. Accumulating log files can easily fill up the filesystem. Later in this chapter we discuss an approach to managing logs in an effective manner in a microservices deployment.

---

[4]https://aws.amazon.com/message/41926/

We also used to store temporary states and time-bound tokens in the database, which causes the database to grow heavily over the time. Even though these tokens and temporary states are no longer valid, they still sit in the database, eating space and slowing down the system. The design of the system should have a way to clean such data periodically via an automated process.

In-memory caching is another area to look into. Memory is a limited, precious resource in a running system. Letting an in-memory cache grow infinitely will cause system performance to degrade and, ultimately, the system will run out of memory. It is always recommend to have an upper limit (in terms of the number of elements in the cache) to the cache and have an LRU (least recently used) strategy to clean up. With the least recently used strategy, when the cache hits its upper limit, the least recently used element will be evicted to find room for the new one. Periodic flush is another strategy to clean up the cache.

The steady state pattern says that, for every mechanism that accumulates a resource, some other mechanism must recycle that resource.

Fail Fast

Fail fast pattern highlights the need for making decisions early in the flow of execution, if the request is going to fail or be rejected. For example, if the load balancer already knows that a given node is down, there is no point in sending requests there again and again to find out its up or not. Rather, that node can be marked as a faulty node until you hear a valid heartbeat from it. The circuit breaker pattern can also be used to implement a fail fast strategy. With the circuit breaker pattern, we can isolate faulty endpoints, and any requests going out for such endpoints can be rejected without retrying, until circuit breaker decides that it's time to recheck.

Let It Crash

There are many cases where doctors decide to cut off the leg of a person after a serious accident to save that person's life. This helps to prevent propagating serious damage from the leg to the other parts of the body. In the Erlang[5] world, this is called the "let it crash" philosophy. It may be useful at sometimes to abandon a subsystem to preserve the stability of the overall system. The let it crash approach suggests getting back to

---

[5]https://www.erlang.org/

a clean startup as rapidly as possible, in case the recovery is difficult and unreliable due to a failure. This is a very common strategy in microservice deployments. A given microservice addresses a limited scope of the overall system, and taking it down and booting up again will have a minimal impact on the system. This is being well supported by the one microservice per host strategy with containers. Having a rapid server startup time, probably a few milliseconds, is also a key aspect in making this strategy successful.

Handshaking

Handshaking is mostly used to share requirements between two parties to establish a communication channel. This happens prior to establishing a TCP (transmission control protocol) connection, which is commonly known as the TCP three-way handshake. Also, we see a handshake before establishing a TLS (transport layer security) connection. These are the two most popular handshaking protocols in computer science. The handshaking pattern suggests the use of a handshake by the server to protect it by throttling its own workload. When a microservice is behind a load balancer, it can use this handshaking technique to inform the load balancer whether it is ready to accept more requests or not. Each server hosting the microservice can provide a lightweight health check endpoint. The load balancer can periodically ping this endpoint and see whether the corresponding microservice is ready to accept requests.

Test Harness

All the failures in a distributed system are hard to catch, either in development testing or in QA (quality assurance) testing. Integration testing possibly looks like a better option, but it has its own limitations. Most of the time we build integration tests as per a specification provided by the corresponding service endpoint. Mostly it covers success scenarios, and even in failure cases it defines what exactly to expect, for example the error codes. Not all the systems all the time work as per the specifications. The test harness pattern suggests an approach for integration testing that would allow us to test most of the failure modes, even outside the service specifications.

The test harness is another remote endpoint that represents each of the remote endpoints you need to connect from your microservice. The difference between the test harness and the service endpoint is that the test harness is just for testing failures and it does not worry about the application logic. Test harness has to be written so that it is capable of generating all sorts of errors covering all seven layers of the OSI (open systems interconnection) model. For example, the test harness may send connection refused responses, invalid TCP packets, slow responses, responses with incorrect content types (XML instead of JSON), and many other errors, that we would never expect from the service endpoint under normal circumstances.

Shed Load

If we look at the way TCP (transmission control protocol) works, it provides a listen queue per port. When the connections are flooded against a given port, then all of them will be queued. Each pool has a maximum limit and when the limit is reached, no more connections will be accepted. When the queue is full, any new attempt to establish a connection will be rejected with an ICMP RST (reset) packet. This is how TCP sheds load at the TCP layer. The applications running on top of the TCP layer will pull requests from the TCP connection pool. In practice, most of the applications are exhausted with connections before the TCP connection pool reaches its maximum. The shed load pattern suggests that the applications or the services also should be modeled after TCP.

The application should shed load when it finds out that it is running behind a given SLA (service level agreement). Usually when the applications are exhausted and the running threads are blocked on certain resources, the response time starts to degrade. Such indicators help show whether a given service is running behind an SLA. If so, this pattern advocates shedding load or notifying the load balancer that the service is not ready to accept more requests. This can be combined with the handshaking pattern to build a better solution.

Observability

Collecting data is cheap, but not having it when you need it can be expensive. In March 2016, Amazon was down for 20 minutes and the estimated revenue loss was $3.75 million. In January 2017, there was a system outage at Delta Airlines that caused cancellation of more than 170 flights and resulted in an estimated loss of $8.5 million. In both these cases, if they had the right level of data collected, they could have predicted such behavior or recovered from it as soon as it happened by identifying the root cause. The more information we have, the better decisions we can make.

Observability is a measure of how well internal states of a system can be inferred from knowledge of their external outputs[6]. A company I know used to monitor its employees effective time at work, by calculating the time difference between ins and outs when they swipe the ID card at the front door. This strategy is effective only if all the employees support it or make themselves observable. At the end of each week the Human Resource (HR) department used to send the effective work time by date to each employee. In most of the cases, figures were completely incorrect. The reason is that most people would go out in groups for lunch and tea, and when they would go out and come in, only one person would swipe the card to open the door. Even though we have monitoring in place, it didn't produce the expected results, as the employees were not cooperating or observable.

There is another company I know that used to track its employees' in and out times, the places they worked from within the company, by the time they connected to the company's wireless network, and the location of the wireless endpoint. Even with this approach, we are not tracking employees, but their laptops. We can keep our laptops on our desks and spend the day at the ping-pong table—or go shopping and come back to take the laptop home. Both of these examples highlight one important fact—monitoring is only effective if we have an observable system in place.

Observability is one of the most important aspects that needs to be baked into any microservices design. We may need to track throughput of each microservice, the number of success/failed requests, utilization of CPU, memory and other network resources, and some business related metrics. Chapter 13, "Observability", includes a detailed discussion on the observability of microservices.

Automation

One of the key rationales behind a microservice architecture is less time to production and shorter feedback cycles. We cannot meet such goals with no automation. A good microservices architecture will only look good on paper (or a whiteboard), if not for the timely advancements in DevOps and tooling around automation. No idea is a good idea if it doesn't appear at the right time. Microservices came as a good idea, as it had all the tooling support at the time it started to become mainstream, in the form of Docker, Ansible, Puppet, Chef, and many more.

---

[6]https://en.wikipedia.org/wiki/Observability

Tooling around automation can be divided into two broad categories—continuous integration tools and continuous deployment tools. Continuous integration enables software development teams to work collaboratively, without stepping on each other's toes. They can automate builds and source code integration to maintain source code integrity. They also integrate with DevOps tools to create an automated code delivery pipeline. Forrester, one of the top analyst firms, in its latest report[7] on continuous integration tools, identifies the top ten tools in the domain: Atlassian Bamboo, AWS CodeBuild, CircleCI, CloudBees Jenkins, Codeship, GitLab CI, IBM UrbanCode Build, JetBrains TeamCity, Microsoft VSTS, and Travis CI.

The continuous delivery tools bundle applications, infrastructure, middleware, and the supporting installation processes and dependencies into release packages that transition across the lifecycle. The latest Forrester report[8] on continuous delivery and release automation highlights 15 most significant vendors in the domain: Atlassian, CA Technologies, Chef Software, Clarive, CloudBees, Electric Cloud, Flexagon, Hewlett Packard Enterprise (HPE), IBM, Micro Focus, Microsoft, Puppet, Red Hat, VMware, and XebiaLabs.

12-Factor App

A microservices architecture is not just built around design principles. Some call it a *culture*. It's a result of many other collaborative efforts. Yes, the design is a key element, but we also need to worry about collaboration between developers and domain experts, the communication between teams and team members, continuous integration and delivery, and many other issues. The 12 Factor App is a manifesto[9] published by Heroku in 2012. This manifesto is a collection of best practices and guidelines to build and maintain scalable, maintainable, and portable applications. Even though these best practices are initially derived from the applications deployed on the Heroku cloud platform, today it has become a mantra for any successful microservices deployment. These 12 factors discussed next are quite common and natural, so chances are very high that you are adhering to them, knowingly or unknowingly.

---

[7]http://bit.ly/2IBWhEz
[8]http://bit.ly/2G2kq8P
[9]https://12factor.net/

Codebase

The codebase factor highlights the importance of maintaining all your source code in a version control system, and having one code repository per application. Here the application could be our microservice. Having one repository per microservice helps release it independently from other microservices. The microservice must be deployed to multiple environments (test, staging, and production) from the same repository. Having per service repositories also helps the governance aspects of the development process.

Dependencies

The *dependencies* factor says, in your application you should explicitly declare and isolate your dependencies and should never rely on implicit system-wide dependencies. In practice, if you are building a Java based microservice, you must declare all your dependencies either with Maven in a `pom.xml` file or with Gradle in a `build.gradle` file. Maven and Gradle are two very popular build automation tools, but with recent developments, Gradle seems to have the edge over Maven and is used by Google, Netflix, LinkedIn and many other top companies. Netflix, in their microservices development process, uses Gradle with their own build automation tool called Nebula[10]. In fact, Nebula is a set of Gradle plugins developed by Netflix.

Managing dependencies for microservices has gone beyond just having them declared under build automation tools. Most of the microservices deployments today rely on containers, for example Docker. If you are new to Docker and containers, do not worry about it now; we discuss those in Chapter 8, when we talk about microservices deployment patterns in detail. With Docker, you can declare not just the core dependencies your microservice needs to run, but also other external dependencies with specific versions, such as the MySQL version, Java version, and so on.

Configuration

The configuration factor emphasizes the need to decouple environment specific settings from the code to configuration. For example, the connection URL of the LDAP or the database server involves environment specific parameters and certificates. These

---

[10]http://nebula-plugins.github.io/

settings should not be baked into the code. Also, even with the configuration files, never commit any kind of credentials into source repositories. This is a common mistake some developers do; they think that since they are using private GitHub repositories, only they have access, which is not true. When you commit your credentials to a private GitHub repository, even though it's private, those credentials are stored in outside servers in cleartext.

Backing Services

A backing service is any kind of service our application consumes during its normal operations. It can be a database, a caching implementation, LDAP server, message broker, external service endpoint, or any kind of an external service (see Figure 2-15). The *backing services* factor says that these backing services should be treated as attachable resources. In other words, they should be pluggable into our microservices implementation. We should be able to change the database, LDAP server, or any external end point, just by editing a configuration file or setting up an environment variable. This factor is very much related to the previous one.

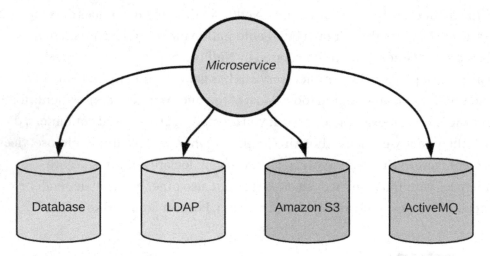

Figure 2-15. *Backing services*

Build, Release, Run

This is the fifth factor and it highlights the importance of having a clear separation among the build, release, and run phases of an application. Let's look at how Netflix builds its microservices[11]. They have a clear separation between these phases (see Figure 2-16). It starts with the developer who builds and locally tests using Nebula. Nebula is a build automation tool developed by Netflix; in fact it is a set of Gradle plugins. Then the changes are committed to the corresponding Git repository. Then a Jenkins job executes Nebula, which builds, tests, and packages the application for deployment. For those who are new to Jenkins, it is a leading open source automation server that facilitates continuous integration and deployment. Once the build is ready, it is baked into an Amazon Machine Image (AMI).

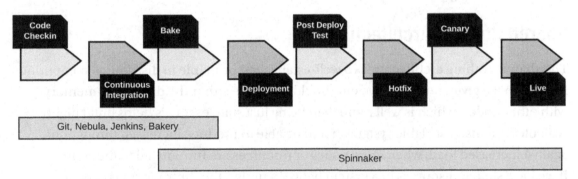

Figure 2-16. *Netflix build process*

Spinnaker is another tool used in Netflix's release process. It's in fact a continuous delivery platform for releasing software changes with high velocity and confidence, developed by Netflix, and later made open source. Once the AMI is ready to deploy, Spinnaker makes it available for deployment to tens, hundreds, or thousands of instances, and deploys it in the test environment. From there, the development teams will typically exercise the deployment using a set of automated integration tests.

---

[11]http://bit.ly/2tX3D1S

Processes

The sixth factor states that the processes should be stateless and should avoid using sticky sessions. Stateless means that an application should not assume any data to be in the memory before and after it executes an operation. Any microservices deployment compliant with the sixth factor should be designed in a way to be stateless. In a typical enterprise grade microservices deployment, you will find that multiple instances of a given microservice spin up and down based on the load it gets. If we are to maintain some kind of a state in memory in those microservices, it will be a cumbersome process to replicate the state across all the microservice instances and would add lot of complexity. Stateless microservices can be replicated on demand and no coordination is required between each during the bootstrap or even in the runtime, which leads us to the shared nothing architecture.

Shared Nothing Architecture

The shared nothing architecture is a well-established principle in distributed computing. It states that a given node in a system should not share either the disk or the memory with other nodes, which is well more than being just stateless. This helps build highly scalable systems. A scalable system should be able to produce increased throughput against increased load, when more nodes or resources are introduced to the system. If we have shared resources in a system between nodes, then introducing more nodes will introduce more load on to those shared resources, hence the impact on the total throughput will be less.

In a typical web application, the disk is shared between nodes for two main purposes. One is to share some common configuration files between the nodes and, in most of the cases, mounting a shared disk drive to each node does this. If use of a shared drive is not possible, we can build some kind of a replication mechanism between those nodes, possibly using a shared repository. One node may commit its changes to a shared Git or subversion repository, and the other nodes will periodically pull updates. There is another approach, which is quite common these days with the new advancements in DevOps engineering. We can use configuration management tools like Puppet[12] or Chef[13] to manage configurations centrally and automate the distribution between all the nodes

---

[12]https://puppet.com/
[13]https://www.chef.io/

in the system. In today's microservices deployment, we use a similar kind of approach with slight variations. No configuration changes are done on running servers; instead, a new container will be created with the new configuration using Puppet or Chef and will be deployed into the corresponding servers. This is the same approach Netflix follows.

The second purpose of having a shared disk is for the database. In a traditional web application as well as in a microservices deployment, we cannot totally eliminate the need for having a shared database. But to avoid the issues in scalability, we can have a separate database server, which can scale independently. Then again, even though we share the same database between different nodes of the same microservice, it is not encouraged to share the same database between different microservices. In Chapter 5, "Data Management", we talk about different data sharing strategies related to microservices.

Port Binding

The port binding factor highlights the need of having completely self-contained applications. If you take a traditional web application, let's say a Java EE application, it is deployed in some kind of Java EE container, for example a Tomcat, WebLogic, or WebSphere server, as a WAR (Web Application aRchive) file. The web application does not worry about how people (or systems) access it, under which transport (HTTP or HTTPS) or which port. Those decisions are made at the web container level (Tomcat, WebLogic, or WebSphere server configuration). A WAR file cannot exist on its own; it relies on the underneath container to do the transport/port bindings. They are not self-contained.

This seventh factor says your application itself has to do the port binding and expose it as a service, without relying on a third-party container. This is very common in microservice deployments. For example, Spring Boot[14], a popular Java-based microservices framework, lets you build microservices as self contained, self-executable JAR files. There are many other microservice frameworks (Dropwizard[15] and MSF4J[16]) out there that do the same. Chapter 4, "Developing Services" covers how to develop and deploy microservices with Spring Boot.

---

[14]https://projects.spring.io/spring-boot/
[15]http://www.dropwizard.io/
[16]https://github.com/wso2/msf4j

Concurrency

There are two ways an application can scale, either vertically or horizontally. To scale an application vertically, you add more resources to each node. For example, you add more CPU power or more memory. This method is becoming less popular these days, as people looking toward running software on commodity hardware. To scale an application horizontally, you need not to worry about the resources each node has, rather you increase the number of nodes in the system. The 7th factor, *concurrency*, says that an application should be able to horizontally scale or scale out.

The ability to dynamically scale (horizontally) is another important aspect of today's microservice deployments. The system, which controls the deployment, will spin up and spin down server instances as the load goes up and down to increase/decrease the throughput of the entire system. Unless each microservice instance can scale horizontally, dynamic scalability is not possible here.

Disposability

The 9th factor talks about the ability of an application to spin up fast and shut down gracefully when required. If we cannot spin up an application fast enough, then it's really hard to achieve dynamic scalability. Most of today's microservice deployments rely on containers and expect the startup time to be milliseconds. When you architect a microservice, you need to make sure that it adds less overhead to the server startup time. This is further encouraged by following one microservice per host (container) model, which we discuss in detail later in the book in Chapter 8. This is opposed to having multiple monolithic applications per server model, where each application contributes to the server startup time, which is usually in minutes (not even in seconds).

Everything at Google runs on containers. In 2014, Google spun up two billion containers per week. That means for every second Google was firing up on average some 3,300 containers[17].

---

[17]http://bit.ly/2pmOQIf

Dev/Prod Parity

The 10th factor states the importance of ensuring that the development, staging, and production environments stay identical, as much as possible. In reality many do have fewer resources on development servers, while making staging and production servers identical. When you do not have the same level of resources that you have in the staging and production environments as in the development environment, you sometimes need to wait until staging deployment to discover issues. We have noticed that some companies do not have a cluster in the development environment, and later waste hundreds of developer hours debugging state replication issues in the staging cluster.

It's not just the number of nodes or hardware resources; this is also applicable to the other services that your application relies on. For example, you should not have a MySQL database in your developer environment, if you plan to have Oracle in the production; don't have Java 1.6 in your developer environment if you plan to have Java 1.8 in the production. Most of the microservice deployments today rely on container-based (for example, Docker) deployments to avoid such mishaps, as all third-party dependencies are packaged in the container itself. One of the key fundamentals behind microservices is its rapid development and deployment. Early feedback cycle is extremely important and adhering to the 10th factor helps us get there.

Logs

The 11th factor says that you need to treat logs as event streams. Logs play two roles in an application. They help identify what is going on in the system and isolate any issues, and they can be used as audit trails. Most of the traditional applications push logs into files, and then these files are pushed into log management applications, like Splunk[18] and Kibana[19]. Managing logs in a microservices environment is challenging, as there are many instances of microservices. To cater to a single request, there can be multiple requests generated between these microservices. It is important to have the ability to trace and correlate a given request between all the microservices in the system.

---

[18]https://www.splunk.com/
[19]https://www.elastic.co/products/kibana

Log aggregation[20] is a common pattern followed by many microservice deployments. This pattern suggests introducing a centralized logging service, which aggregates logs from all the microservice instances in the environment. The administrators can search and analyze the logs from the central server and can also configure alerts that are triggered when certain messages appear in the logs. We can further improve this pattern by using a messaging system, as shown in Figure 2-17. This decouples the logging service from all the other microservices. Each microservice will publish a log event (with a correlation ID) to a message queue and the logging service will read from it.

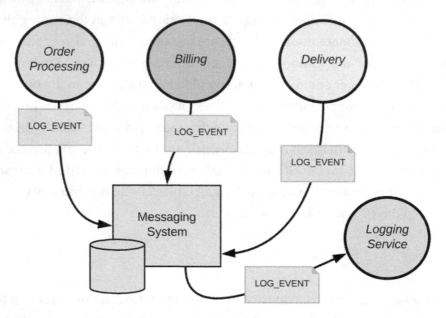

Figure 2-17. *Publishing logs from multiple microservices to a centralized logging server*

Even though the traditional applications use filesystem-based logging, it is quite discouraged in a microservices environment. Going by the ninth factor, a given microservice should be disposable at any given moment. This introduces the concept of *immutable servers*. An immutable server is never modified after it is first launched. If we are not modifying a server, then you cannot write anything to its filesystem. Following the immutable server pattern helps reproduce the same server instance from a configuration and dispose at any given time.

---

[20]http://microservices.io/patterns/observability/application-logging.html

Admin Processes

This 12th factor highlights the need for running administrative tasks as one-off processes. These tasks could be a database migration (due to a new version of the application) of a one-time script that needs to be run along with the application itself. The origin of this 12th factor seems to be little bias toward interpreted languages like Ruby, which support and encourage an interactive programming shell. Once the application is up, the developers can SSH into those servers and run certain scripts via these interactive programming consoles. If we adhere to the 12th factor, we should completely avoid such remotely done administrative tasks via SSH, rather introduce an admin process and make the admin tasks part of it. In a microservices deployment, just as you run your microservices in different containers, this admin process can also run from its own container.

Beyond the 12 Factor App

It is awesome to see how the original 12 factors introduced in 2012 (at a time when microservices were not mainstream and Docker was not even born) relate to the microservice deployments becoming mainstream today. In 2016, Kevin Hoffman from Pivotal introduced[21] three more factors to the original set, which we discuss next.

API First

Anyone coming from the SOA background must be familiar with the two approaches commonly used for service development: contract first and code first. With contract first, we first develop the service interface in a programming language independent manner. In the SOAP world, this produces a WSDL (Web Services Description Language), and in REST world, it could be an OpenAPI[22] document (formerly known as Swagger). The OpenAPI specification is a powerful definition format to describe RESTful APIs.

With this factor, Kevin highlights the need to start any application development following the API first approach, which is an extension to the contract first approach. In an environment where you have multiple development teams working on multiple microservices, under different schedules, having the API defined first for each microservice, helps all the teams build their microservices against APIs. This helps

---

[21]http://oreil.ly/2zjVXIa
[22]https://swagger.io/specification/

improve the productivity of the development process, without worrying too much about the implementation details of other microservices one has to integrate. If the implementation of a given microservice is not available at the time you are ready to test, you can simply mock it against the published API. There are many tools out there under different programming languages to create such mock instances.

Telemetry

According to Wikipedia, *telemetry* is an automated communications process by which measurements and other data are collected at remote or inaccessible points and transmitted to the receiving equipment for monitoring. When it comes to software, this is extremely useful to track the health of production servers and to identify any issues. Kevin Hoffman suggests a great analogy to highlight the need of telemetry for applications. Think of your applications like unmanned space shuttles launched into the space—this definition is so powerful and require no further explanation on the importance of telemetry.

Telemetry data can be categorized into three areas—application performance monitoring, domain specific, health and system logs. The number of HTTP requests, the number of database calls, and the time it takes to serve each request over the time are all recorded under the application performance monitoring category. The domain specific data category records data related to business functions. For example, the `Order Processing` microservice will push data related to orders being processed, including the number of new orders, open orders, and closed orders by date. The data related to server startup, shutdown, memory consumption and CPU utilization fall in the health and system logs category.

Security

This is a notable missing factor in the original 12 factors. Any application or microservice should worry about security from its early stages of design. There are multiple perspectives in securing microservices. The key driving force behind microservices is the speed to production (or the time to market). One should be able to introduce a change to a service, test it, and instantly deploy it in production. To make sure we do not introduce security vulnerabilities at the code level, we need to have a proper plan for static code analysis and dynamic testing—and most importantly those tests should be part of the continuous delivery (CD) process. Any vulnerability should be identified early in the development lifecycle and should have shorter feedback cycles.

There are multiple microservices deployment patterns (which we will discuss later in the book in Chapter 8), but the most commonly used one is service-per-host model. The host does not necessarily mean a physical machine—most probably it would be a container (Docker). We need to worry about container-level security here and worry about how to isolate a container from other containers and what level of isolation we have between the container and the host operating system.

And last, but not least, we need to worry about application-level security. The design of the microservice should talk about how we authenticate and access control users and how we secure the communication channels between microservices. We discuss microservices security in detail in Chapter 11, "Microservices Security Fundamentals" and Chapter 12, "Securing Microservices".

Summary

In this chapter we discussed the essential concepts related to the design of microservices. The chapter started with a discussion of domain-driven design principles, which are the key ingredients in modeling microservices from the business point of view. Then we delved deep into microservices design principles and finally concluded with the 12-factor app, which is a collection of best practices and guidelines to build and maintain much scalable, maintainable, and portable applications.

The external parties via messages consume any business functionality that is implemented as a microservice. Microservices can leverage messaging styles such as synchronous messaging and asynchronous messaging based on the business use cases. In the next chapter, we discuss messaging technologies and protocols in detail.

## CHAPTER 3

Inter-Service Communication

In the microservices architecture, services are autonomous and communicate over the network to cater a business use case. A collection of such services forms a *system* and the consumers often interact with those systems. Therefore, a microservices-based application can be considered a distributed system running multiple services on different network locations. A given service runs on its own process. So microservices interact using inter-process or inter-service communication styles.

In this chapter we discuss the microservice communication styles and the standard protocols that are used for microservice communication. The chapter compares and contrasts those protocols and styles. However, we will defer the discussion on integrating microservices, resilient inter-service communication, and service discovery. Those topics are discussed in detail in Chapter 6, "Microservices Governance" and Chapter 7, "Integrating Microservices".

Fundamentals of Microservices Communication

As discussed in the first chapter, services are business capability-oriented and the interactions between these services form a system or a product, which is related to a particular set of business use cases. Hence inter-service communication is a key factor to the success of the microservices architecture.

A microservices-based application consists of a suite of independent services that communicate with each other through messaging. Messaging is not a new concept in distributed systems. In monolithic applications, business functionalities of different processors/components are invoked using function calls or language-level method calls. In Service Oriented Architecture (SOA), this was shifted toward more loosely coupled

© Kasun Indrasiri and Prabath Siriwardena 2018
K. Indrasiri and P. Siriwardena, *Microservices for the Enterprise*, https://doi.org/10.1007/978-1-4842-3858-5_3

web service level messaging, which is primarily based on SOAP, on top of different protocols such as HTTP, message queuing, etc. Almost all of the service interactions are implemented at the centralized Enterprise Service Bus (ESB) layer.

In the context of microservices, there is no such restriction as with SOA/Web Services to use a specific communication pattern and message format. Rather, the microservices architecture favors selecting the appropriate service collaboration mechanism and message format that are used to exchange information, based on the use case.

Microservice communications styles are predominantly about how services send or receive data from one service to the other. The most common type of communication styles used in microservices are synchronous and asynchronous.

Synchronous Communication

In the synchronous communication style, the client sends a request and waits for a response from the service. Both parties have to keep the connection open until the client receives the response. The execution logic of the client cannot proceed without the response. Whereas in asynchronous communication, the client can send a message and be completely done with it without waiting for a response.

Note that synchronous and blocking communication are two different things. There are some textbooks and resources that interpret the synchronous communication as a pure blocking scenario in which the client thread basically blocks until it gets the response. That is not correct. We can use a non-blocking IO implementation, which registers a callback function once the service responds back, and the client thread can be returned without blocking on a particular response. Hence, the synchronous communication style can be built on top of a non-blocking asynchronous implementation.

REST

Representational State Transfer (REST) is an architectural style that builds distributed systems based on hypermedia. The REST model uses a navigational scheme to represent objects and services over a network. These are known as resources. A client can access the resource using the unique URI and a representation of the resource is returned. REST doesn't depend on any of the implementation protocols, but the most common implementation is the HTTP application protocol. While accessing RESTful resources with the HTTP protocol, the URL of the resource serves as the resource identifier and GET, PUT, DELETE, POST, and HEAD are the standard HTTP operations to be performed on that resource. The REST architecture style is inherently based on synchronous messaging.

To understand how we can use the REST architectural style in service development, let's consider the order-management scenario of the online retail application. We can model the order-management scenario as a RESTful service called Order Processing. As shown in Figure 3-1, you can define the resource *order* for this service.

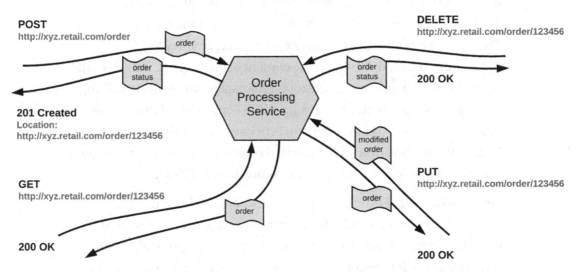

Figure 3-1. *Different operations that you can execute on the Order Processing RESTful service*

To place a new order, you can use the HTTP POST message with the content of the order, which is sent to the URL (http://xyz.retail.com/order). The response from the service contains an HTTP 201 Created message with the location header pointing to the newly created resource (http://xyz.retail.com/order/123456). Now you can retrieve the order details from that URL by sending an HTTP GET request. Similarly, you can update the order and delete the order using the appropriate HTTP methods.

Since REST is a style, when it comes to the realization of RESTful services, we need to make sure that our RESTful services are fully aligned with the core principles of REST. In fact, most of the RESTful services out there violate the core REST style concepts. To design a proper RESTful service, Leonard Richardson has defined[1] a maturity model for REST-based services.

Richardson Maturity Model

There are four levels in the *Richardson Maturity Model:*

- *Level 0 – Swamp of PoX*: A service at this level is in fact not considered RESTful at all. For example, suppose that there is a SOAP web service exposed over HTTP to implement online retail capabilities. This service has one URL (`http://xyz.retail.com/legacy/ RetailService`) and, based on the content of the request, it decides the operation (order processing, customer management, product search, etc.) that it needs to carry out. A single HTTP method (in most cases, `POST`) is used and no HTTP constructs or concepts are used for the logic of the service. Everything is based on the content of the message. The best example of a Level 0 service is any SOAP web service.

- *Level 1 – Resource URIs*: A service is considered to be at this level when it has individual URIs for each resource, but the message still contains operation details. For example, the retail application can have resources for /orders, /products, /customers, etc., but the CRUD (Create, Read, Update, Delete) operations for a given resource are still done through the content of the message. No HTTP methods or response status codes are used.

- *Level 2 – HTTP Verbs*: Instead of using the message content to determine the operation, we can use an HTTP verb instead. Hence, an HTTP `POST` message that is sent to the /order context can add a new order (order details are given in the message content but now we don't have operation details). Also, the proper HTTP status codes should be supported. For example, the response of an invalid request should be on status code 500. The example that we illustrated in

---

[1]`https://www.crummy.com/writing/speaking/2008-QCon/act3.html`

Figure 3-1 facilitates all these capabilities. A RESTful service, which is at Level 2 or higher, is considered to be a proper REST API.

- *Level 3 – Hypermedia Controls*: At level 3, the service responses have links that control the application state for the client. Often this concept is known as HATEOAS (Hypertext as The Engine of Application State). The hypermedia controls tell us what we can do next, and the URI of the resource we need to manipulate to do it. Rather than us having to know where to post our next request, the hypermedia in the response tell us how to do it.

Owing to the fact that REST is primarily implemented on top of HTTP (which is widely used, less complicated, and firewall friendly), REST is the most common form of microservice communication style adopted by microservices implementations. Let's consider some best practices when using RESTful microservices.

- RESTful HTTP-based microservices (REST is independent of the implementation protocol, but there are no non-HTTP RESTful services used in practice) are good for external facing microservices (or APIs) because it's easier to expose them through existing infrastructures, such as firewalls, reverse proxies, load balancers, etc.

- The resource scope should be fine-grained so that we can directly map it to an operation-related business capability (e.g., add order).

- Use the Richardson maturity models and other RESTful service best practices for designing services.

- Use versioning strategies when applicable. (Versioning is typically implemented at the API Gateway level when you decide to expose your service as APIs. We discuss this in detail in Chapter 7.)

As a lot of microservices frameworks use REST as their de-facto styles, you may be tempted to use it for all your microservices implementations. But you should use REST only if it's the most appropriate style for your use cases. (Be sure to consider the other suitable styles, which are discussed in this chapter.)

Try it out   You can try a RESTful web services sample in Chapter 4, "Developing Services".

---

gRPC

Remote Procedure Calls (RPC) was a popular inter-process communication technology for building client-server applications in distributed systems. It was quite popular before the advent of web services and RESTful services. The key objective of RPC is to make the process of executing code on a remote machine as simple and straightforward as calling a local function. Most conventional RPC implementations, such as CORBA, have drawbacks, such as the complexity involved in remote calls and using TCP as the transport protocol. Most conventional RPC technologies have lost their popularity. So you may wonder why we are talking about another RPC technology, gRPC.

gRPC[2] (gRPC Remote Procedure Calls) was originally developed by Google as an internal project called Stubby, which focused on high performance inter-service communication technology. Later it was open sourced as gRPC. There are alternatives such as Thrift, which is really fast. But Thrift-based communication required a lot of work from the developer side, as it exposed the low-level network details to the users (it exposes raw sockets), which made life harder for the developers. Also, being based on TCP is also a major limitation, as it's not suitable for modern web APIs and mobile devices.

gRPC enables the communication between applications built on top of heterogeneous technologies. It is based on the idea of defining a service and specifying the methods that can be called remotely with their parameters and return types. gRPC tries to overcome most of the limitations of the traditional RPC implementations.

By default, gRPC uses protocol buffers[3], Google's mature open source mechanism for serializing structured data (can be used with other data formats such as JSON). Protocol buffers are a flexible, efficient, automated mechanism for serializing structured data. gRPC uses protocol buffers, such as the Interface Definition Language (IDL), to describe both the service interface and the structure of the payload messages. Once a service is defined using the protocol buffer IDL, the service consumers can create a server skeleton and the client can create the stub to invoke the service in multiple programming languages.

---

[2]https://grpc.io/
[3]https://developers.google.com/protocol-buffers/

Using HTTP2 as the transport protocol is a key reason for the success and wide adaptation of gRPC. So, it's quite handy to understand the advantages that HTTP2 contains.

A Glimpse of HTTP2

Despite its wide adaptation, HTTP 1.1 has several limitations that hinder modern web scale computing. The main limitations of HTTP 1.1 are:

- *Head of line blocking*: Each connection can handle one request at a time. If the current request is blocked, then the next request will wait. Therefore, we have to maintain multiple connections between the client and server to support real use cases. HTTP1.1 defines a pipeline to overcome this, but it's not widely adopted.

- *HTTP 1.1 protocol overhead*: In HTTP 1.1, many headers are repeated across multiple requests. For example, headers such as User-Agent and Cookie are sent over and over, which is a waste of bandwidth. HTTP 1.1 defines the GZIP format to compress the payload, but that doesn't apply to the headers.

HTTP2 came up with solutions for most of these limitations. Most importantly, HTTP2 extends the HTTP capabilities, which makes it fully backward compatible with existing applications.

All communication between a client and server is performed over a single TCP connection that can carry any number of bidirectional *flows of bytes*. HTTP2 defines the concept of a *stream*, which is a bidirectional flow of bytes within an established connection, which may carry one or more messages. *Frame* is the smallest unit of communication in HTTP2, and each frame contains a frame header, which at a minimum identifies the stream to which the frame belongs. A *message* is a complete sequence of frames that map to a logical HTTP message, such as a request or response, which consists of one or more frames. So, based on this approach, the request and response can be fully multiplexed, by allowing the client and server to break down an HTTP message into independent frames, interleave them, and then reassemble them on the other end.

HTTP2 avoids header repetition and introduces header compression to optimize the use of bandwidth. It also introduces a new feature of sending server push messages without using the request-response style messages. HTTP2 is also a binary protocol, which boosts its performance. It also supports message priorities out of the box.

Inter-Service Communication with gRPC

By now you should have a good understanding of the advantages of HTTP2 and how it helps gRPC to perform better. Let's dive into a complete example that's implemented using gRPC. As illustrated in Figure 3-2, suppose that, in our online retail application example, there is a Returns service calling a Product Management service to update the product inventory with returned items. The Returns service is implemented using Java and the Product Management service is implemented using the Go language. The Product Management service is using gRPC and it exposes its contract via the ProductMgt.proto file.

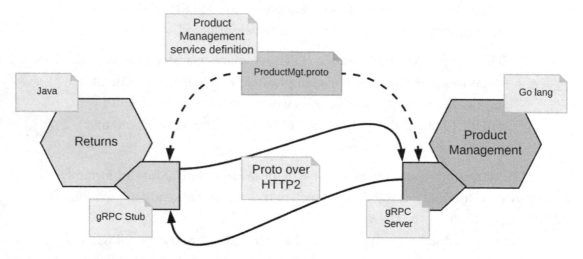

Figure 3-2. *gRPC communication*

So, the Product Management service developer will use the ProductMgt.proto file to generate the server-side skeleton in the Go language. Basically, the developer uses this in his project and complies it, so that it generates the service and client stubs. To implement the service, we can use the generated service stub and implement the required business logic of that service.

The consumer, which is the Returns service, can use the same ProductMgt.proto file to generate the client-side stub (in Java) and invoke the service. The Product Management service, which has an operation to add products, will have a ProductMgt. proto definition similar to the following.

```
// ProductMgt.proto
syntax = "proto3";
option java_multiple_files = true;
option java_package = "kasun.mfe.ecommerce";
option java_outer_classname = "EcommerceProto";
option objc_class_prefix = "HLW";
package ecommerce;
service ProductMgt {
  rpc AddProduct (ProductRequest) returns (ProductResponse) {}
}
message ProductRequest {
  string productID = 1;
  string name = 2;
  string description = 3;
}
message ProductResponse {
  string productID = 1;
  string status = 2;
}
```

Under the hood, when a client invokes the service, the client-side gRCP library uses the Proto Buf and marshals the remote function call, which is then sent over HTTP2. At the server side, the request is un-marshaled and the respective function invocation is executed using Proto Buf. The response follows a similar execution flow from the server to the client.

Try it out   You can try a gRPC service sample in Chapter 4, "Developing Services".

---

gRPC allows server streaming RPCs where the client sends a request to the server and gets a stream to read a sequence of messages back. The client reads from the returned stream until there are no more messages.

```
rpc productUpdate(ProdUpdateReq) returns (stream ProdUpdateStatues){
}
```

Similarly, you can use client-streaming RPCs where the client writes a sequence of messages and sends them over to the server as a stream. Once the client has finished writing the messages, it waits for the server to read them and returns its response.

```
rpc productUpdate(stream productUpdates) returns (ProdUpdateStatus) {
}
```

Bidirectional streaming RPCs are where both sides send a sequence of messages using a read-write stream. The two streams operate independently, so clients and servers can read and write in whatever order they like. For example, the server could wait to receive all the client messages before writing its responses, or it could alternately read a message and then write a message, or follow some other combination of reads and writes.

```
rpc productUpdate(stream productUpdates) returns (stream ProdUpdateStatuses)
{
}
```

Authentication mechanisms supported in gRPC are SSL/TLS and token-based authentications with Google.

Error Handling with gRPC

You can also implement various error-handling techniques with gRPC. If an error occurs, gRPC returns one of its error status codes and an optional string error message that provides further details of the error.

REST and gRPC are the most commonly used synchronous messaging protocols in microservices implementations. However, there are several other synchronous messaging technologies that are occasionally used for microservice implementations.

GraphQL

The RESTful services are built on the concept of resources, which are manipulated via HTTP methods. When the service you develop fits the resource-based architecture of REST, it works flawlessly. But as soon as it deviates from the RESTful style, the service fails to deliver the expected outcome.

Also, in some scenarios, the client needs data from multiple resources at the same time, which results in invocation of multiple resources via multiple service calls (or always sending large responses with redundant data).

GraphQL[4] addresses such concerns in a conventional REST-based service by providing a query language for APIs and a runtime for fulfilling those queries with your existing data. GraphQL provides a complete and understandable description of the data in your API, gives clients the power to ask for exactly what they need and nothing more, makes it easier to evolve APIs over time, and enables powerful developer tools.

The client can send a GraphQL query to the API and get exactly what the client needs, and the client has full control over the data it gets. The typical REST APIs require loading from multiple URLs, but GraphQL-based services get all the data your app needs in a single request.

For example, you may send the following query to a GraphQL-based service:

```
{
  hero {
    name
  }
}
```

And retrieve the result, which is shown here.

```
{
  "data": {
    "hero": {
      "name": "R2-D2"
    }
  }
}
```

The query has exactly the same shape as the result and the server knows exactly what fields the client requests.

The GraphQL server exposes a schema describing the API. This schema is made up of type definitions. Each type has one or more fields, which each take zero or more arguments and return a specific type. An example GraphQL schema is one for a book and an author of a book. Here we have defined the types for Book and Author, along with the operation name. In our previous example, we used a shorthand syntax where we omit both the query keyword and the query name, but in production apps, it's useful to

---

[4]https://graphql.org/

include these to make our code less ambiguous. So, in this example we have query as the operation type and latestBooks as the operation name:

```
type Book {
    isbn: ID
    title: String
    text: String
    category: String
    author: Author
}
type Author {
    id: ID
    name: String
    thumbnail: String
    books: [Book]
}
# The Root Query for the application
type Query {
    latestBooks(count: Int, offset: Int): [Book]!
}
# The Root Mutation for the application
type Mutation {
    addBook(id: String!, title: String!, text: String!, category: String,
    author: Author!) : Book!
}
```

The operation type is query, mutation, or subscription and it describes what type of operation you're intending to do. The operation type is required unless you're using the query shorthand syntax, in which case you can't supply a name or variable definition for your operation.

Every GraphQL service has a query type and may or may not have a mutation type. These types are the same as a regular object type, but they are special because they define the entry point of every GraphQL query. Similar to a query, you can define fields on the mutation type, and those are available as the root mutation fields you can call in your query. As a convention any operations that cause writes should be sent explicitly via a mutation.

> **Try it out**   You can try a GraphQL service sample in Chapter 4, "Developing Services".

WebSockets

WebSockets[5] protocol can simply be introduced as *TCP over the web*. It can be considered a transport protocol, which is fully duplex and asynchronous. So, you can overlay any messaging protocol on top of WebSockets.

The WebSockets protocol uses a single TCP connection for traffic in both directions and uses HTTP as the initial handshaking protocol, so that it can work with the existing infrastructure. It works on top of TCP for the initial handshake, and then it acts like raw TCP sockets. Figure 3-3 shows the interactions of a client and server that use WebSockets.

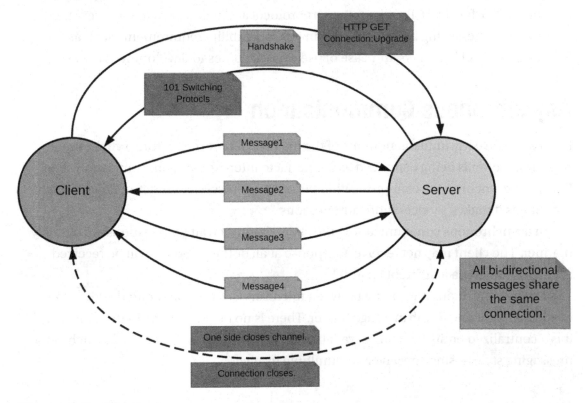

Figure 3-3. *WebSockets communication*

---

[5]https://tools.ietf.org/html/rfc6455

There are quite a few similarities with HTTP2 and WebSockets, such as using a single connection, bi-directional messaging, binary messages, etc. But the difference here is that WebSockets allows you to build your own messaging protocol on top of WebSockets (for instance, you can build MQTT or AMQP over WebSockets). The WebSockets architecture consists of a socket that is opened between the client and the server for full-duplex (bidirectional) communication. So, if your microservices require having such full-duplex communication and the ability to route the traffic via the web, then WebSockets is a great choice.

Thrift

Thrift[6] allows you to define data types and service interfaces in a simple definition file. Similar to gRPC, using the interface definition, the compiler generates code to be used to easily build RPC clients and servers that communicate seamlessly across programming languages. Thrift uses TCP as the transport protocol and it is known to have very high-performance messaging but it lacks certain interoperability requirements such as firewalls and load balancers and ease of use when it comes to developing services.

Asynchronous Communication

In most of the early implementations of the microservices architecture, synchronous communication is being embraced as the de-facto inter-service communication style. However, asynchronous communication between microservices is getting increasingly popular as it makes services more autonomous.

In asynchronous communication, the client does not wait for a response in a timely manner. The client may not receive a response at all or the response will be received asynchronously via a different channel.

The asynchronous messaging between microservices is implemented with the use of a lightweight and dumb message broker. There is no business logic in the broker and it is a centralized entity with high-availability. There are two main types of asynchronous messaging styles—single receiver and multiple receivers.

---

[6]https://thrift.apache.org/

Single Receiver

In single receiver mode, a given message is reliably delivered from a producer to exactly one consumer through a message broker (see Figure 3-4). Since this an asynchronous messaging style, the producer doesn't wait for a response from the consumer nor during the time of producing the message, and the consumer may or may not be available. This is useful when sending asynchronous message-based commands from one microservice to the other. Given that microservices can be implemented using different technologies, we must implement reliable message delivery between the producer and consumer microservices in a technology-agnostic manner.

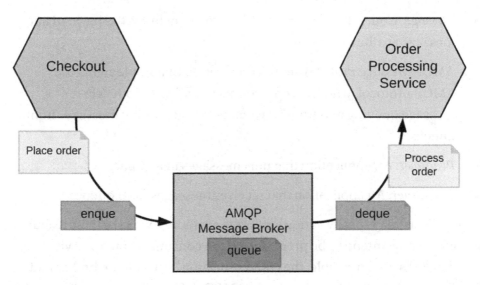

Figure 3-4. *Single receiver based asynchronous communication with AMQP*

The Advanced Message Queuing Protocol (AMQP) protocol is the most commonly used standard with single receiver-based communication.

AMQP

AMQP[7] is a messaging protocol that deals with publishers and consumers. The publishers produce the messages and the consumers pick them up and process them. It's the job of the message broker to ensure that the messages from a publisher go to

---

[7]https://www.amqp.org/

the right consumers. AMQP ensures reliability of message delivery, rapid and ensured delivery of messages, and message acknowledgements.

Let's take an example scenario from our online retail application use case. Suppose that the `Checkout` microservice places an order as an asynchronous command to the `Order Processing` microservice.

We can use an AMQP message broker (such as RabbitMQ[8] or ActiveMQ[9]) as the dumb messaging infrastructure and the `Checkout` microservice can produce a message to the specific queue in the broker. On an independent channel, the `Order Processing` microservice can subscribe to the queue as a consumer, and it receives messages in asynchronous fashion. For this use case, we can identify the following key components.

- *Message*: Content of data transferred, which includes the payload and message attributes.

- *AMQP Message Broker* A central application that implements the AMQP protocol, which accepts connections from producers for message queuing and from consumers for consuming messages from queues.

- *Producer*: An application that puts messages in a queue.

- *Consumer*: An application that receives messages from queues.

The producers may specify various message attributes, which can be useful to the broker or which only intend to be processed by the consuming microservice.

Since networks are unreliable, the communication between the broker and microservices may fail to process messages. AMQP defines a concept called *message acknowledgements*, which is useful in implementing reliable delivery of the messages. When a message is delivered to a consumer, the consumer notifies the broker, either automatically or when the application code decides to do so. In message acknowledgements mode, the broker will only completely remove a message from a queue when it receives a notification for that message (or group of messages). Also, since we are using a queue, we can ensure the ordered delivery and processing of the messages. There is a set of reliability mechanisms introduced by AMQP.

The failures can occur between the network interactions of broker, publisher, and consumer or the runtime of broker and client applications can fail.

---

[8]`https://www.rabbitmq.com/`
[9]`http://activemq.apache.org/`

Acknowledgements allow the consumer to indicate to the server that it has received the message successfully. Similarly, the broker can use acknowledgements to inform the producer that it has successfully received the message (e.g., confirms in RabbitMQ). Therefore, an acknowledgement signals the receipt of a message and a transfer of ownership, whereby the receiver assumes full responsibility for it.

AMQP 0-9-1 offers a *heartbeat* feature to ensure that the application layer promptly finds out about disrupted connections and completely unresponsive peers. Heartbeats also work with network equipment, which may terminate idle TCP connections.

- *Broker failures*: In order to handle broker failures, the AMQP standard defines a concept of durability for exchanges, queues, and persistent messages, requiring that a durable object or persistent message survive a restart. Enable clustering for the broker that you are using.

- *Producer failures*: When producing messages to the broker, the producers should retransmit any messages for which an acknowledgement has not been received from the broker. There is a possibility of message duplication here, because the broker might have sent a confirmation that never reached the producer (due to network failures, etc.). Therefore, consumer applications will need to perform de-duplication or handle incoming messages in an idempotent manner (i.e. internal state doesn't change even if we process the same message multiple times).

In the event of network failure (or a runtime crashing), messages can be duplicated, and consumers must be prepared to handle them. If possible, the simplest way to handle this is to ensure that your consumers handle messages in an idempotent way rather than explicitly deal with de-duplication.

In failure conditions, when a message cannot be routed, messages may be returned to publishers, dropped, or, if the broker implements an extension, placed into a so-called "dead letter queue". Publishers can decide how to handle such situations by publishing messages using certain parameters.

There are several open source message broker solutions out there and RabbitMQ could possibly be the most popular and widely used one. Apache ActiveMQ, ActiveMQ Artemis, and Apache Qpid are also popular.

There are multiple versions of the AMQP specification and v0-9-1 is the most commonly used one. The latest version is 1.0, which is yet to be fully adopted across the industry. From the microservices architecture perspective, we don't have to learn the details of the AMQP protocol; having a foundation level knowledge of the capabilities and messaging patterns it offers will be sufficient. AMQP also defines other message exchanging styles than single receiver-based exchanging, such as fan-out, topic, and header-based exchanging.

Important   AMQP message brokers are usually developed as monolithic runtimes and are not intended to be used only in the microservices architecture. Hence, most brokers come with various features that allow you to put business logic inside the broker (such as routing). So, we have to be extra cautious when using these brokers and we must only use them as dumb brokers. All the asynchronous messaging smarts should lie on our service logic only.

We discuss a development use case similar to the one described here in Chapter 4.

Multiple Receivers

When the asynchronous messages produced by one producer should go to more than one consumer, the publisher-subscriber or multiple receiver style communication will be useful.

As an example use case, suppose that there is a `Product Management` service, which produces the information on the price updates of the products. That information has to be propagated to multiple microservices, such as `Shopping Cart`, `Fraud Detection`, `Subscriptions`, etc. As shown in Figure 3-5, we can use an event bus as the communication infrastructure and the `Product Management` service can publish the price update events to a particular topic. The services that are interested in receiving price update events should subscribe to the same topic. The interested services will receive events on subscribed topics only if they are available at the time of the event broadcasting by the event bus. If the underlying event bus implementation supports it, the subscriber may have the option of subscribing as a durable subscriber, in which it will receive all the events despite being offline at the time of the event broadcasting.

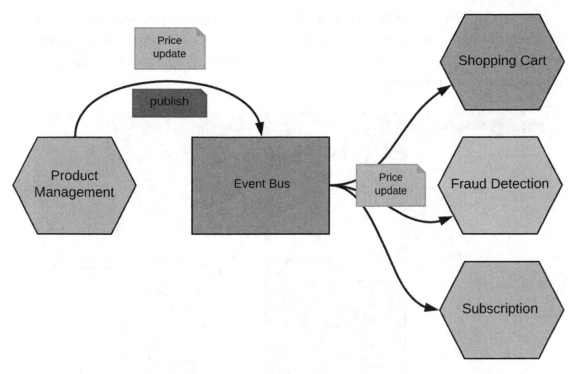

Figure 3-5. *Multiple receivers (pub-sub) based asynchronous communication*

There are multiple messaging protocols that support pub-sub messaging. Most of the AMQP-based brokers support pub-sub, but Kafka (which has its own messaging protocol) is the most widely used message broker for multiple receiver/pub-sub type messaging between microservices. Let's take a closer look at Kafka and revisit this implementation with Kafka.

Kafka

Apache Kafka[10] is a distributed publish/subscribe messaging system. It is often described as a *distributed commit log,* as the data within Kafka is stored durably, in order, and can be read deterministically. Also, data is distributed within the Kafka system for failover and scalability.

Let's take a closer look at how we can implement a publisher-subscriber scenario using Kafka. As illustrated in Figure 3-6, we can use Kafka as the distributed pub-sub messaging system to build multiple microservice asynchronous messaging scenarios.

---

[10]https://kafka.apache.org/

The unit of data used in Kafka is known as a *message* (an array of bytes). Unlike other messaging protocols, the data contained within it does not have a specific format or meaning to Kafka. Messages can also contain metadata, which can be helpful in publishing or consuming messages.

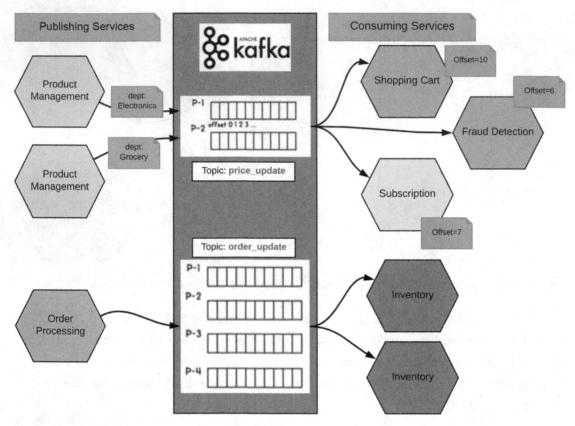

Figure 3-6. *Multiple receivers (pub-sub) based asynchronous communication with Kafka*

These messages in Kafka are categorized into *topics*. A given topic can optionally be split into multiple *partitions*. A partition is a logical and physical componentization of a given topic, in which the producer can decide to which partition it wants to write. This is typically done using the message metadata known as *key*. Kafka generates a hash of the key and maps it to a specific partition (i.e., all messages produced with a given key reside on the same partition). Partitions are the primary mechanism in Kafka for parallelizing consumption and scaling a topic beyond the throughput limits of a single node. Each partition can be hosted in different nodes.

Each message is written to a partition with the offset number. The *offset* is an incrementally numbered position that starts at 0 at the beginning of the partition.

The *producers* write the messages to a specific topic. By default, the producer does not care what partition a specific message is written to and will distribute messages over all partitions of a topic evenly. In some cases, the producer will direct messages to specific partitions using the message metadata, *key*.

The *consumers* subscribe to one or more topics and read the messages in the order in which they were produced. The consumer keeps track of which messages it has already consumed by keeping track of the *offset* of messages. Each message in a given partition has a unique offset. By storing the offset of the last consumed message for each partition (in Zookeeper or in Kafka), a consumer can stop and restart without losing its place.

Consumers work as part of a *consumer group*, where one or more consumers work together to consume a topic. The group ensure that one consumer group member only consumes message from each partition. However, a given consumer group member can consume from multiple partitions. Obliviously, the concept of a consumer group is useful when we have to horizontally scale the consumption of a topic with a high message volume.

Now let's try to take these concepts further with the scenario shown in Figure 3-6. In the following multiple-receiver messaging scenario, which is based on Kafka, there are two topics created in Kafka: `price_update` and `order_update`.

There are two `Product Management` producers (microservices from different departments) publishing product price update information (the producer can explicitly write to a given partition or the load can be distributed among the partitions evenly). For the `price_update` topic, there are three different consumers (from three consumer groups). They will independently read messages from Kafka and will maintain their own offset. For instance, suppose that there is an outage of `Subscription` services so that it was not able to receive the price updates during certain time. When the `Subscription` service starts again, it can check the currently persisted offset and pull all the events it received when it was offline.

The order-processing scenario with the `order_update` topic is slightly different. In that scenario, we can assume that we have a high load coming through the order update channels and we need to scale the consumer side to process them more efficiently. Hence, we use a consumer group with two consumers, so that they can parallel-process the order update events from multiple partitions.

A single Kafka server is known as a *broker*, and it serves message publishing and consuming. Multiple Kafka brokers can operate as a single cluster. From the multiple brokers in a cluster, there is a single broker, which functions as the cluster controller and takes care of the cluster administrative operations such as assigning partitions to brokers and detecting brokers failures. A partition is assigned to multiple brokers and there is a leader broker for each partition. Therefore, Kafka messaging has high availability because of the replication of the partitions across multiple brokers and the ability to appoint a new leader if the existing partition leader is not available (Kafka uses Zookeeper for most of the coordination tasks).

With clustering, Kafka is becoming even more powerful, so that you can massively scale your asynchronous messaging capabilities.

Tip   Can we do exactly-once delivery with Kafka? There is an interesting article[11] on how we can implement exactly-once delivery with Kafka. Most of the concepts start from the key Kafka principles that we discussed in this chapter, and you can easily build the same level of guaranteed delivery with your microservices.

We've only discussed a selected subset of capabilities of Kafka that are useful in building the multiple receiver asynchronous messaging scenarios, and there are a lot of other technical details that are not included in the scope of this book.

There are several other brokers, such as ActiveMQ and RabbitMQ, that can offer you the same set of pub-sub messaging capabilities for simple-to-medium scale asynchronous messaging scenarios. However, if you need a fully distributed and scalable asynchronous messaging infrastructure, then Kafka is a good choice. There are various asynchronous messaging and event stream processing solutions that are built on top of Kafka such as Confluent Open Source Platform, which may give you some additional capabilities for your microservices implementation.

Other Asynchronous Communication Protocols

There are quite a few asynchronous messaging protocols that we haven't discussed. MQTT[12], STOMP[13], and CoAP[14] are also quite popular. If you think you have the expertise and that one of these is the best technology choice for your microservices messaging,

---

[11]https://medium.com/@jaykreps/exactly-once-support-in-apache-kafka-55e1fdd0a35f
[12]http://mqtt.org/
[13]https://stomp.github.io/
[14]http://coap.technology/

then go for it. We do not cover those protocols in detail, as they don't have any explicit characteristics that are important in the microservices context.

Synchronous versus Asynchronous Communication

At this point, you should have a solid understanding of the synchronous and asynchronous messaging techniques. It's very important to understand when to use those communication styles in your microservices architecture implementation.

The main difference between synchronous and asynchronous communication is that there are scenarios in which it is not possible to keep a connection open between a client and a server. A durable one-way communication is more practical in those scenarios. Synchronous communication is more suitable in scenarios where you need to build services that provide request-response style interactions. If the messages are event-driven and the client doesn't expect a response immediately, asynchronous communication is more suitable.

However, in many books and articles, it is emphasized that synchronous communication is evil, and we should only use asynchronous communication for microservices as it enables the service autonomy. In many cases, the comparison between synchronous and asynchronous communication is being interpreted in such a way that, in synchronous communication a given thread will be blocked until it waits for a response. This is completely false, because most synchronous messaging implementations are based on fully non-blocking messaging architectures. (That is, the client-side sender sends the request and registers a callback, and the thread is returned. When the response is received, it is correlated with the original request and the response is processed.)

So, coming back to the pragmatic use of these communication styles, we need to select the communication style based on our use case.

In scenarios where short-running interactions require a client and service to communicate in the request-response style, the synchronous communication is mandatory. For example, in our online retail use case, a product search service is communicated in a synchronous fashion, because you want to submit a search query and want to see the search results immediately. Scenarios such as order placing or processing are inherently asynchronous. Hence, the asynchronous messaging style is the best fit for such scenarios.

Tip   Embracing only synchronous (e.g. REST) or asynchronous messaging between microservices is a complete myth. When adopting microservices to your enterprise scenarios, you may be required to use a mix or a hybrid of both of those communication styles.

Message Formats/Types

We have discussed about several communication styles and protocols that are commonly used in the microservices architecture. The information exchange between the microservices is based on exchanging messages. Determining which message formats to use in those scenarios is important.

JSON and XML

In most of the REST-based microservices implementations, JSON is the de-facto message interchange format, owing to its simplicity, readability, and performance. However, there are some services based on XML (not SOAP). However, they lack some important features, such as robust type handling and compatibility between schema versions. In most of the scenarios where your services are exposed to the external consumers, we heavily use JSON as the message type, while usage of XML is quite limited to specific use cases. As part of the service development, the service has to process the incoming JSON or XML messages and map them to types that are used in the service code.

Protocol Buffers

With a communication style such as gRPC, the message formats are well-defined and use a dedicated data interchange format such as protocol buffers. The service developer doesn't need to worry about processing the messages in a given message format. During marshaling and un-marshaling all the required type mapping is done and users only deal with the well-defined types. Owing to the flexible, efficient, automated mechanism of data serialization and deserialization, protocol buffers are ideal for high throughput synchronous messaging between internal services. Currently, the application of protocol buffers in microservices communication is heavily done using gRPC-based services.

Avro

Apache Avro[15] addresses the key limitations of most of the conventional data interchange formats such as JSON and XML. Avro is a data serialization system that provides rich data structures for data representations, a compact format, great bindings for a wide variety of programming languages, direct mapping to and from JSON, and an extensible schema language defined in pure JSON.

Therefore, Avro is heavily used in most of the asynchronous messaging scenarios in microservices implementations. For example, most of the Kafka-based messaging systems leverage Avro to define the schema for producing and consuming messages.

Service Definitions and Contracts

When you have a business capability that's implemented as a service, you need to define and publish the service contract. In traditional monolithic applications, we rarely have such features to define the business capabilities of an application. In SOA/web services world, WSDL is used to define the service contract, but as we all know, WSDL is not the ideal solution for defining a microservices contract, as WSDL is insanely complex and tightly coupled to SOAP.

Since we build microservices on top of the REST architectural style, we can use the same REST API definition techniques to define the contract of the microservices. Therefore, microservices use the standard REST API definition languages such as OpenAPIs[16] to define the service contracts. For services that don't fit the resource-based architecture, we can leverage GraphQL schemas.

As you saw in the gRPC section, protocol buffer definitions of your service are the service definition and contracts for your gRPC-based service (the same applies to other RPC styles such as Thrift). Service definitions are applicable to synchronous communication; there is no standard way of defining a service contract for asynchronous event-based communication.

---

[15]https://avro.apache.org/
[16]https://www.openapis.org/

Summary

In this chapter, we discussed the inter-service communication patterns and protocols that are used to implement those patterns in a microservices context. We took a closer look at the fundamentals of REST and gRPC, which are most commonly used in synchronous messaging between microservices. As asynchronous messaging styles, we learned about the AMQP protocol, which is a common choice for single consumer/point-to-point asynchronous messaging with reliability. For publisher-subscriber/multiple receiver type communication, Kafka is commonly used as the messaging infrastructure.

However, we haven't discussed the details of how we can implement service interactions, compositions, orchestration, or choreography. Chapter 7 is dedicated to those topics and further discusses the commodity features of service interactions, such as resilient communication with circuit breakers, timeouts, etc. In addition, we have dedicated chapters on service governance (Chapter 6) and service definitions and APIs (Chapter 10, "APIs, Events, and Streams").

CHAPTER 4

Developing Services

Netflix has taken three steps to build an anti-fragile organization[1]. The first step is to treat every developer as an operator of the corresponding service. The second is to treat each failure as an opportunity to learn and the third is to foster a blameless culture. These three little steps have helped Netflix become the top-leading organization in the microservices world. Many look to Netflix to learn how things are being done and for best practices. Netflix in fact optimized everything for the speed of delivery. As we already discussed in the book, at its core of any microservices design, time to production, scalability, complexity localization, and resiliency are key elements. Developer experience is one of the most important factors to reach these goals. The experience of a developer in a microservices environment is quite different from engineering a monolithic application. As rightly identified by Netflix, the developer's task does not end after pushing the code into a source repository and expecting a DevOps engineer to build and push the changes to production, or a support engineer to take on any issues that happen in the production environment. A microservices development environment demands a broader skillset from the developer.

Note　All Netflix developers are given SSH keys to access their production servers, where in most of the traditional application deployments, developers have no access from staging onward.

Over the past few years there have been many tools and frameworks developed to assist and speed up microservices development. Most of the popular tools and frameworks are open source. In this chapter, we discuss different options available for a microservices developer and see how to build a microservice from the ground up.

---

[1]https://queue.acm.org/detail.cfm?id=2499552

© Kasun Indrasiri and Prabath Siriwardena 2018
K. Indrasiri and P. Siriwardena, *Microservices for the Enterprise*, https://doi.org/10.1007/978-1-4842-3858-5_4

Developer Tooling and Frameworks

There are multiple tools and frameworks available for microservice developers under different categories. There are a few key elements we believe one should take into consideration before picking the right microservices framework. One of the very basic requirements is to have good support for RESTful services. In the Java world, most developers look for the level of support for JAX-RS[2]. Most of the Java-based frameworks do support JAX-RS based annotations, but to extend that functionality, they have introduced their own.

The seventh factor of the 12-factor app (which we discussed in Chapter 2, "Designing Microservices") says that your application has to do the port binding and expose itself as a service, without relying upon a third-party application server. This is another common requirement for any microservices framework. Without relying on any heavyweight application servers, which eat resources and take seconds (or minutes) to boot up, one should be able to spin up a microservice in a self-contained manner in just a few milliseconds.

Most of the microservice deployments follow the service per host model. In other words, only one microservice is deployed in one host, wherein most cases, the host is a container. It's a key aspect that everyone looks for in a microservice framework to be container friendly. What container friendly (or container native) means is discussed in detail in Chapter 8, "Deploying and Running Microservices". The level of security support that the language provides is another key differentiator in picking a microservice framework. There are multiple ways to secure a microservice and provide the service-to-service communication between microservices. We discuss microservices security in Chapter 11, "Microservices Security Fundamentals".

The first class language support for telemetry and observability is another important aspect in a microservice framework. It's extremely useful to track the health of the production servers and to identify any issues. We discuss observability in Chapter 13, "Observability". Another two important aspects of a microservice framework is its support for transactions and asynchronous messaging. Asynchronous messaging was discussed in Chapter 3, "Inter-Service Communication," and in Chapter 5, "Data Management," we discuss how transactions are handled in a microservices environment.

---

[2]The Java API for RESTful Web Services proposed in JSR 339.

The following sections explain the most popular microservice frameworks and tools. Later in the chapter, we go through a set of examples developed with Spring Boot, which is the most popular microservice development framework for Java developers.

Netflix OSS

As we already discussed in this chapter, Netflix is playing a leading role in the microservices domain, and its influence on making microservices mainstream and widely adopted is significant. The beauty of Netflix is its commitment toward open source. The Netflix Open Source Software[3] (OSS) initiative has around 40 open source projects under different categories (see Figure 4-1). The following sections explain some of the common tools under Netflix OSS that are related to microservices development.

Nebula

Nebula[4] is a collection of Gradle plugins built for Netflix engineers to eliminate boilerplate build logic and provide sane conventions. The goal of Nebula is to simplify common build, release, testing, and packaging tasks needed for projects at Netflix. They picked Gradle over Maven as the build tool, as they believe it's the best out there for Java applications.

Spinnaker

Spinnaker[5] is a multi-cloud continuous delivery platform for releasing software changes with high velocity and confidence. It combines a powerful and flexible pipeline management system with integration with the major cloud providers, which include AWS EC2, Kubernetes, Google Compute Engine, Google Kubernetes Engine, Google App Engine, Microsoft Azure, and OpenStack.

---

[3]https://netflix.github.io/
[4]https://nebula-plugins.github.io
[5]https://www.spinnaker.io/

Eureka

Eureka[6] is a RESTful service that is primarily used in the AWS cloud for locating services for the purpose of load balancing and failover of middle-tier servers. In a microservices deployment, Eureka can be used as a service registry to discover endpoints.

Archaius

Archaius[7] includes a set of configuration management APIs used by Netflix. It allows configurations to change dynamically at runtime, which enables production systems to get configuration changes without having to restart. To provide fast and thread-safe access to the properties, Archaius adds a cache layer that contains desired properties on top of the configuration. It also creates a hierarchy of configurations and determines the final property value in a simple, fast, and thread-safe manner.

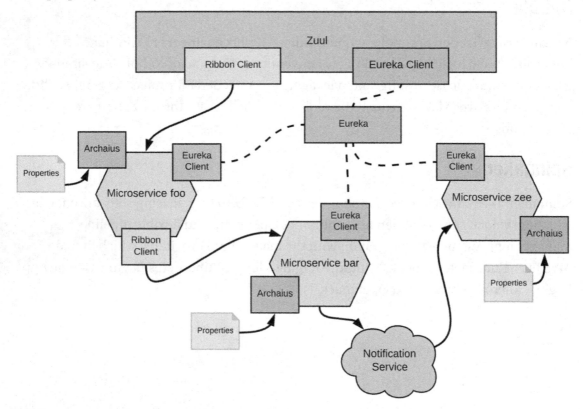

Figure 4-1. *Netflix OSS deployment*

---

[6]https://github.com/Netflix/eureka
[7]http://netflix.github.io/archaius/

Ribbon

Ribbon[8] is an Inter-Process Communication (remote procedure calls) library with a built-in software load balancer (which is mostly used for client-side load balancing). Primarily it is used for REST calls with various serialization scheme support.

Hystrix

Hystrix[9] is a latency and fault-tolerance library designed to isolate points of access to remote systems, services, and third-party libraries, stop cascading failure, and enable resilience in complex distributed systems where failure is inevitable. Hystrix implements many resiliency patterns discussed in Chapter 2. It uses the *bulkhead* pattern to isolate dependencies from each other and to limit concurrent access to any one of them, and the *circuit breaker* pattern to proactively avoid talking to faulty endpoints. Hystrix reports successes, failures, rejections, and timeouts to the circuit breaker, which maintains a rolling set of counters that calculate statistics. It uses these stats to determine when the circuit should "trip," at which point it short-circuits any subsequent requests until a recovery period elapses, upon which it closes the circuit again after doing certain health checks[10].

Zuul

Zuul[11] is a gateway service that provides dynamic routing, monitoring, resiliency, security, and more. It acts as the front door to Netflix's server infrastructure, handling traffic from all Netflix users around the world. It also routes requests, supports developer testing and debugging, provides deep insight into Netflix's overall service health, protects it from attacks, and channels traffic to other cloud regions when an AWS region is in trouble.

---

[8]https://github.com/Netflix/ribbon
[9]https://github.com/Netflix/hystrix
[10]https://github.com/Netflix/Hystrix/wiki/How-it-Works
[11]https://github.com/Netflix/zuul

Spring Boot

Spring Boot[12] is the most popular microservices development framework for Java developers. To be precise, Spring Boot offers an opinionated[13] runtime for Spring, which takes out a lot of the complexities. Even though Spring Boot is opinionated, it also allows developers to override many of its defaults picks. Due to the fact that many Java developers are familiar with Spring, and the ease of development is a key success factor in the microservices world, and many adopted Spring Boot. Even for Java developers who are not using Spring, it is a household name. If you have worked on Spring, surely would have worried about how painful it was to deal with large, chunky XML configuration files. Unlike Spring, Spring Boot thoroughly believes in convention over configuration—no more XML hell!

Note   *Convention over configuration* (also known as coding by convention) is a software design paradigm used by software frameworks that attempts to decrease the number of decisions that a developer using the framework is required to make without necessarily losing flexibility.[14]

Spring Cloud[15] came after Spring Boot in March 2015. It provides tools for developers to quickly build some of the common patterns in distributed systems. Spring Cloud, along with Spring Boot, provides a great development environment for microservices developers. Another feature of Spring Cloud is that it provides Netflix OSS integrations for Spring Boot apps through auto-configuration and binding to the Spring environment and other Spring programming model idioms. With a few simple annotations, you can enable and configure the common patterns inside your application and build large distributed systems with Netflix OSS components. The patterns provided include service discovery with Eureka, circuit breaker with Hystrix, intelligent routing with Zuul, and client-side load balancing with Ribbon. We'll use Spring Boot and Spring Cloud for the code examples we discuss later in this chapter.

---

[12]https://projects.spring.io/spring-boot/

[13]An *opinionated framework* locks or guides its developers into its own way of doing things.

[14]https://en.wikipedia.org/wiki/Convention_over_configuration

[15]http://projects.spring.io/spring-cloud/

Note   Convention over configuration was first introduced by David Heinemeier Hansson to describe the philosophy of the Ruby on Rails web framework. Apache Maven, the popular build automation tool, follows the same philosophy.

Istio

Istio is an open platform that provides a uniform way to connect, manage, and secure microservices. It supports managing traffic flows between microservices, enforcing access policies, and aggregating telemetry data, all without requiring changes to the microservice code. With a strong backing from Google, IBM, Lyft, and many others, Istio is one of the leading *service mesh* products in the microservices domain. We'll be discussing service mesh in detail in Chapter 9, "Service Mesh". For the time being, service mesh is a component in microservice architecture, which facilitates service-to-service communication along with routing rules, adhering to the resiliency patterns we discussed in Chapter 2, such as retries, timeouts, circuit breaker, and bulkheads. It also does performance monitoring and tracing. In most cases, the service mesh acts as a sidecar (Chapter 2), which will take the responsibility of handling the crosscutting features from the core microservice implementation. More details about Istio are covered in Chapter 9.

Dropwizard

Dropwizard is a widely used framework for developing microservices in Java. It's well known as a little bit of opinionated glue code, which bangs together a set of libraries. Dropwizard includes Jetty to serve HTTP requests. Jetty[16] provides a web server and `javax.servlet` container, plus support for HTTP/2, WebSockets, OSGi, JMX, JNDI, JAAS,[17] and many other integrations. Support for REST and JAX-RS (JSR 311 and JSR 339) in Dropwizard is brought in with Jersey. Jersey[18] is the JAX-RS reference implementation. It also integrates Jackson[19] for JSON parsing and building, and Logback[20] for logging. Logback is a successor to the popular log4j project.

---

[16]http://www.eclipse.org/jetty/

[17]If you are a Java developer, you should already be familiar with these terms.

[18]https://jersey.github.io/

[19]https://github.com/FasterXML/jackson

[20]https://logback.qos.ch/

Support for metrics is a key feature in any microservice framework, and Dropwizard embeds Metrics[21] Java library to gather telemetric data related to a running application. Dropwizard also embeds Liquibase[22], which is an open source database-independent library for tracking, managing, and applying database schema changes. It allows easier tracking of database changes, especially in an Agile software development environment. The database integration with Dropwizard is done with Jdbi and Hibernate. Jdbi[23] is built on top of JDBC to improve JDBC's rough interface, providing a more natural Java database interface that is easy to bind to your domain data types. Unlike an ORM (Object Relational Mapping), it does not aim to provide a complete object relational mapping framework—instead of that hidden complexity, it provides building blocks to construct the mapping between relations and objects as appropriate for your application. Hibernate[24] is the most popular ORM framework used by Java developers.

Dropwizard has a longer history than Spring Boot. In fact, Spring Boot was motivated by the success of Dropwizard. It was first released by Coda Hale[25] in late 2011 while he was at Yammer. However, with better developer experience, strong community support, and the backing from Pivotal, Spring Boot is now a better option than Dropwizard.

Vert.x

Vert.x[26] is toolkit for building reactive[27] applications on the JVM (Java Virtual Machine), which supports multiple languages, including Java, JavaScript, Groovy, Ruby, Ceylon, Scala, and Kotlin. It started as an open source project under the Eclipse Foundation in 2012 by Tim Fox. Even before microservices became mainstream, Vert.x had a powerful stack to build microservices. Unlike Dropwizard, Vert.x is an unopinionated toolkit. In other words, it is not a restrictive framework or container, which preaches developers a specific way to write applications. Instead, Vert.x provides a lot of useful bricks and lets developers create their own apps the way they want to.

---

[21]http://metrics.dropwizard.io/

[22]https://www.liquibase.org/

[23]http://jdbi.org/

[24]http://hibernate.org/orm/

[25]https://www.linkedin.com/in/codahale/

[26]https://vertx.io

[27]Reactive programming is a programming paradigm that deals with asynchronous data streams.

Like in Dropwizard, Vert.x also supports integrating Metrics, to gather telemetric data related to a running application. Further, it also supports integrating with Hawkular[28], which is a set of open source projects designed to be a generic solution for common monitoring problems. For service discovery, Vert.x integrates HashiCorp Consul[29]. Consul makes it simple for services to register themselves and to discover other services via a DNS or HTTP interface. Vert.x supports integrating with multiple message brokers—for example with Apache Kafka and RabbitMQ—and multiple messaging protocols—for example AMQP, MQTT, JMS, and STOMP.

Overall Vert.x is has a powerful ecosystem to build microservices, but yet Spring Boot, with the strong support from the Spring community, has the edge.

Lagom

Lagom[30] is an open source opinionated framework for building microservice systems in Java or Scala based on reactive principles[31]. Lagom is a Swedish word, which means just right or sufficient. It is built on top of the Akka[32] and Play[33] framework. Akka is a toolkit for building highly concurrent, distributed, and resilient message-driven applications for Java and Scala. Play is a high-productivity Java and Scala web application framework that integrates the components and APIs one needs for modern web application development. In Lagom, microservices are based on the following:

- *Akka Actors*—providing isolation through a shared nothing architecture based on the *Actor Model*

- *Akka Cluster*—providing resilience, sharding, replication, scalability, and load-balancing of the groups of individual isolated service instances making up a microservice

- *ConductR*—providing isolation down to the metal and runtime management of the microservice instances[34].

---

[28]https://www.hawkular.org/

[29]https://www.consul.io/

[30]https://www.lagomframework.com/

[31]https://www.reactivemanifesto.org/

[32]https://akka.io/

[33]https://www.playframework.com/

[34]https://www.infoq.com/news/2016/03/lagom-microservices-framework

Lagom is based on three design principles: message driven and asynchronous communication, distributed persistence, and developer productivity. It makes asynchronous communication the default, and the default persistence model is using event sourcing and CQRS (discussed in Chapter 10, "APIs, Events, and Streams")—using Akka Persistence and Cassandra, which is very scalable and easy to replicate and to make fully resilient.

Lagom is a promising, but relatively new, framework for microservices.

Getting Started with Spring Boot

In this section, we see how we can develop microservices using Spring Boot from scratch. We also see how to implement some of the design concepts we learned so far, as we go on. To run the examples, you will need Java 8[35] or latest, Maven 3.2[36] or latest, and a Git client. Once you have successfully installed them, run the following two commands in the command line to make sure everything is working fine. If you'd like some help in setting up Java or Maven, there are plenty of online resources out there.

```
\>java -version
java version "1.8.0_121" Java(TM) SE Runtime Environment
(build 1.8.0_121-b13)
Java HotSpot(TM) 64-Bit Server VM (build 25.121-b13, mixed mode)
\>mvn -version
Apache Maven 3.5.0 (ff8f5e7444045639af65f6095c62210b5713f426;
2017-04-03T12:39:06-07:00)
Maven home: /usr/local/Cellar/maven/3.5.0/libexec
Java version: 1.8.0_121, vendor: Oracle Corporation
Java home: /Library/Java/JavaVirtualMachines/jdk1.8.0_121.jdk/Contents/
Home/jre Default locale: en_US, platform encoding: UTF-8 OS name:
"mac os x", version: "10.12.6", arch: "x86_64", family: "mac
```

All the samples used in this book are available at the https://github.com/ microservices-for-enterprise/samples.git Git repository. Use the following git command to clone it. All the samples related to this chapter are inside the ch04 directory.

---

[35]https://bit.ly/1fVVnjC
[36]https://maven.apache.org/download.cgi

```
\> git clone https://github.com/microservices-for-enterprise/samples.git
\> cd samples/ch04
```

For anyone who loves Maven, the best way to get started with a Spring Boot project would be with a Maven archetype. Unfortunately, it is no longer supported. One option we have is to create a template project via https://start.spring.io/, which is known as the *Spring Initializer*. There you can pick which type of project you want to create, choose project dependencies, give it a name, and download a Maven project as a ZIP file. The other option is to use the Spring Tool Suite (STS)[37]. It's an IDE (integrated development environment) built on top of the Eclipse platform, with many useful plugins to create Spring projects. However, in this book, we are going to provide you with all the fully coded samples in the Git[38] repository.

Note   If you find any issues in building or running the samples given in this book, please refer to the README file under the corresponding chapter in the Git repository: https://github.com/microservices-for-enterprise/ samples.git. We will update the samples and the corresponding README files in the Git repository to reflect any changes or updates related to the tools, libraries, and frameworks used in this book.

Hello World!

This is the simplest microservice ever. You can find the code inside the ch04/sample01 directory. To build the project with Maven, use the following command:

```
\> cd sample01
\> mvn clean install
```

Before we delve deep into the code, let's look at some of the notable Maven dependencies and plugins added to ch04/sample01/pom.xml

---

[37]https://spring.io/tools
[38]https://github.com/microservices-for-enterprise/samples.git

Spring Boot comes with different `starter` dependencies to integrate with different Spring modules. The `spring-boot-starter-web` dependency brings in Tomcat and Spring MVC and does all the wiring between the components, keeping the developer's work to a minimum. The `spring-boot-starter-actuator` dependency brings in production-ready features to help you monitor and manage your application.

```
<dependency>
    <groupId>org.springframework.boot</groupId>
    <artifactId>spring-boot-starter-web</artifactId>
</dependency>
<dependency>
    <groupId>org.springframework.boot</groupId>
    <artifactId>spring-boot-starter-actuator</artifactId>
</dependency>
```

In the `pom.xml` file, we also have the `spring-boot-maven-plugin` plugin, which lets you start the Spring Boot service from Maven.

```
<plugin>
    <groupId>org.springframework.boot</groupId>
    <artifactId>spring-boot-maven-plugin</artifactId>
</plugin>
```

Now let's look at the `checkOrderStatus` method in the class file `src/main/java/com/apress/ch04/sample01/service/OrderProcessing.java`. This method accepts an order ID and returns the status of the order. There are three notable annotations used in the following code. The `@RestController` is a class-level annotation that marks the corresponding class as a REST endpoint, which accepts and produces JSON payloads. The `@RequestMapping` annotation can be defined both at the class level and the method level. The `value` attribute at the class-level annotation defines the path under which the corresponding endpoint is registered. The same at the method level appends to the class-level path. Anything defined in curly braces is a placeholder for any variable value in the path. For example, a `GET` request on `/order/101` and `/order/102` (where 101 and 102 are the order IDs) hits the method `checkOrderStatus`. In fact, the value of the `value` attribute is a URI template[39]. The annotation `@PathVariable` extracts the provided

---

[39]`https://tools.ietf.org/html/rfc6570`

variable from the URI template defined under the value attribute of the @Request Mapping annotation and binds it to the variable defined in the method signature.

```
@RestController
@RequestMapping(value = "/order")
public class OrderProcessing {
    @RequestMapping(value = "/{id}", method = RequestMethod.GET)
    public String checkOrderStatus
        (@PathVariable("id") String orderId)
    {
        return ResponseEntity.ok("{'status' : 'shipped'}");
    }
}
```

There is another important class file at src/main/java/com/apress/ch04/ sample01/OrderProcessingApp.java worth looking at. This is the class that spins up our microservice in its own application server, in this case the embedded Tomcat. By default, it starts on port 8080, and you can change the port by adding, say for example, server. port = 9000 to the src/main/resources/application.properties file. This will set the server port to 9000. The following shows the code snippet from that OrderProcessingApp class, which spins up our microservice. The @SpringBootApplication annotation, which is defined at the class level, is being used as a shortcut for four other annotations defined in Spring: @Configuration, @EnableAutoConfiguration, @EnableWebMvc, and @ ComponentScan.

```
@SpringBootApplication
public class OrderProcessingApp {
    public static void main(String[] args) {
        SpringApplication.run(OrderProcessingApp.class, args);
    }
}
```

Now, let's see how to run our microservice and talk to it with a cURL client. The following command executed from the ch04/sample01 directory shows how to start our Spring Boot application with Maven.

```
\> mvn spring-boot:run
```

To test the microservice with a cURL client, use the following command from a different command console. It will print the output as shown here, after the initial command.

```
\> curl http://localhost:8080/order/11
{"customer_id":"101021","order_id":"11","payment_method":{"card_type":"V
ISA","expiration":"01/22","name":"John Doe","billing_address":"201, 1st
Street, San Jose, CA"},"items": [{"code":"101","qty":1},{"code":"103","qty"
:5}],"shipping_address":"201, 1st Street, San Jose, CA"}
```

Spring Boot Actuator

Gathering telemetric data about a running microservice is extremely important. This is discussed in detail in Chapter 13. In this section, we explore some of the monitoring capabilities provided in Spring Boot out-of-the-box via the `actuator` endpoint[40]. There are multiple services running behind the `actuator` endpoint, and most of them are enabled by default. As discussed in the previous section, we only need to add a dependency to `spring-boot-starter-actuator` to enable it. Let's keep the Spring Boot application from the previous example up and running and execute a set of cURL commands.

The following cURL command, which does a GET to the `actuator/health` endpoint, returns the server status.

```
\> curl http://localhost:8080/actuator/health
{"status":"UP"}
```

Spring Boot exposes telemetric data over HTTP and JMX. Due to security reasons, not all of them are exposed via HTTP, only the `health` and `info` services. At our own risk, let's see how to enable the `httptrace` endpoint over HTTP. You need to add the following to the `src/main/resources/application.properties` file and reboot the Spring Boot application.

```
management.endpoints.web.exposure.include = health,info,httptrace
```

---

[40]https://bit.ly/2GiRbez

Now let's hit our microservice a few times.

```
\> curl http://localhost:8080/order/11
\> curl http://localhost:8080/order/11
\> curl http://localhost:8080/order/11
```

The following cURL command will invoke the httptrace endpoint, which will return the HTTP trace information.

```
\> curl http://localhost:8080/actuator/httptrace
{
    "traces":[
        {
            "timestamp":"2018-03-29T16:42:46.235Z",
            "principal":null,
            "session":null,
            "request":{
                "method":"GET",
                "uri":"http://localhost:8080/order/11",
                "headers":{
                    "host":[
                        "localhost:8080"
                    ],
                    "user-agent":[
                        "curl/7.54.0"
                    ],
                    "accept":[
                        "*/*"
                    ]
                },
                "remoteAddress":null
            },
            "response":{
                "status":200,
                "headers":{
                    "Content-Type":[
                        "text/plain;charset=UTF-8"
```

```
        ],
        "Content-Length":[
          "7"
        ],
        "Date":[
          "Thu, 29 Mar 2018 16:42:46 GMT"
        ]
      }
    },
    "timeTaken":14
  }
 ]
}
```

Configuration Server

In Chapter 2, under the 12-factor app, we discussed that the *configuration* factor emphasizes the need to decouple environment-specific settings from the code to configuration. For example, the connection URL of the LDAP or the database server are environment-specific parameters and certificates. Spring Boot provides a way to share the configuration between microservices via a configuration server. Multiple instances of microservices can connect to this server and, over HTTP, load the configuration. The configuration server can either maintain the configuration in its own local filesystem or load from Git. Loading from Git would be the ideal approach. The configuration server itself is another Spring Boot application. You can find the code for the configuration server inside ch04/sample02.

Let's look at some of the additional notable Maven dependencies added to ch04/sample02/pom.xml. The spring-cloud-config-server dependency brings all the components to turn a Spring Boot application into a configuration server.

```
<dependency>
    <groupId>org.springframework.cloud</groupId>
    <artifactId>spring-cloud-config-server</artifactId>
</dependency>
```

To turn a Spring Boot application into a configuration server, you only need to add one class-level annotation to src/main/java/com/apress/ch04/sample02/ ConfigServerApp.java, as shown in the following code snippet. The @EnableCon figServer annotation will do all the internal wiring between the Spring modules to expose the Spring Boot application as a configuration server. This is the only code we need.

```
@SpringBootApplication
@EnableConfigServer
public class ConfigServerApp {
    public static void main(String[] args) {
        SpringApplication.run(ConfigServerApp.class, args);
    }
}
```

In this example, the configuration server loads the configuration from the local filesystem. You will find that the following two properties are added to the src/main/ resources/application.properties file to change server port to 9000 and to use the native profile for the configuration server. When the native profile is used, the configurations are loaded from the local filesystem, not from Git.

```
server.port=9000
spring.profiles.active=native
```

Now we can create property files inside the src/main/resources directory for each microservice. You will find the following content in the src/main/resources/sample01. properties file, which can be used to define all the configuration parameters required for a given microservice.

```
database.connection = jdbc:mysql://localhost:3306/sample01
```

Now, let's start our configuration server with the following commands. First we build the project, and then launch the server via the Maven plugin.

```
\> cd sample02
\> mvn clean install
\> mvn spring-boot:run
```

Use the following cURL command to load all the configurations related to the sample01 microservice.

```
\> curl http://localhost:9000/sample01/default
{
    "name":"sample01",
    "profiles":[
        "default"
    ],
    "label":null,
    "version":null,
    "state":null,
    "propertySources":[
        {
            "name":"classpath:/sample01.properties",
            "source":{
                "database.connection":"jdbc:mysql://localhost:3306/sample01"
            }
        }
    ]
}
```

Consuming Configurations

In this section, we see how to consume a property loaded from an external configuration within another microservice. You can find the code for this microservice inside ch04/ sample03. It is in fact a slightly modified version of sample01. Let's start by looking at ch04/sample03/pom.xml for the additional notable Maven dependencies. The spring-cloud-starter-config dependency brings all the components required to bind the property values read from the remote configuration server to local variables.

```
<dependency>
    <groupId>org.springframework.cloud</groupId>
    <artifactId>spring-cloud-starter-config</artifactId>
</dependency>
```

The following code snippet shows the modified sample03/src/main/java/com/apress/ch04/sample03/service/OrderProcessing.java class, where the dbUrl variable is bound to the database.connection property (via @Value annotation) and is read from the configuration server. The properties are loaded from the configuration server at the startup, so we need to make sure the configuration server is up and running before we start this microservice.

```
@RestController
@RequestMapping(value = "/order")
public class OrderProcessing {
    @Value("${database.connection}")
    String dbUrl;
    @RequestMapping(value = "/{id}", method = RequestMethod.GET)
    public ResponseEntity<?> checkOrderStatus
            (@PathVariable("id") String orderId) {
        // print the value of the dbUrl
        // loaded from configuration server
        System.out.println("DB Url: " + dbUrl);
        return ResponseEntity.ok("{'status' : 'shipped'}");
    }
}
```

To set a value for the configuration server URL, we need to add the following property to src/main/resources/bootstrap.properties.

```
spring.cloud.config.uri=http://localhost:9000
```

We also need to add the spring.application.name property to src/main/resources/application.properties with a value corresponding to a property filename in the configuration server.

```
spring.application.name=sample03
```

Now, let's start our configuration client with the following commands. First we build the project, and then we launch the server via the Maven plugin. Also, we need to make sure that we already have the configuration service running, which we discussed in the previous section.

```
\> cd sample03
\> mvn clean install
\> mvn spring-boot:run
```

Use the following cURL command to load all the configurations related to the sample03 microservice.

```
\> curl http://localhost:8080/order/11
```

If it all works fine, you will find the following output in the command console, which runs the Spring Boot service (sample03).

```
DB Url: jdbc:mysql://localhost:3306/sample03
```

Service-to-Service Communication

In this section, we see how one microservice directly talks to another microservice over HTTP. We extend our domain-driven design example from Chapter 2. As per Figure 4-2, the Order Processing microservice (sample01) talks directly to the Inventory microservice (sample04) over HTTP to update the inventory.

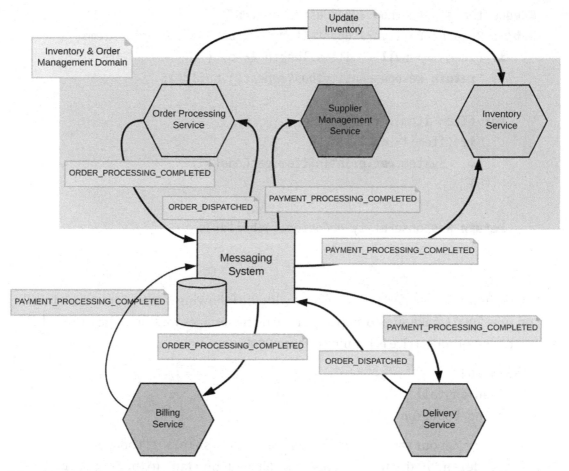

Figure 4-2. *Communication between microservices*

First, let's get the `Inventory` microservice up and running. You can find the code for this microservice inside `ch04/sample04`. It's another Spring Boot application, and there isn't anything new from what we have discussed so far. Let's look at the `updateItems` method in the `src/main/java/com/apress/ch04/sample04/service/Inventory.java` class. This method simply accepts an array of items, iterates through them, and prints the item code. Later in this section, the `Order Processing` microservice (`sample01`) will invoke this method to update the inventory.

```
@RestController
@RequestMapping(value = "/inventory")
public class Inventory {
```

```java
@RequestMapping(method = RequestMethod.PUT)
public ResponseEntity<?> updateItems(@RequestBody Item[] items) {
    if (items == null || items.length == 0) {
        return ResponseEntity.badRequest().build();
    }
    for (Item item : items) {
        if (item != null) {
            System.out.println(item.getCode());
        }
    }
    return ResponseEntity.noContent().build();
    }
}
```

Let's spin up the sample04 microservice with the following Maven command. It will start on port 9000 (make sure to stop any of the microservices we started before, and ensure that no other service is running on port 9000).

```
\> cd sample04
\> mvn clean install
\> mvn spring-boot:run
```

Now let's revisit our sample01 code, which is at ch04/sample01. There we have the createOrder method, which accepts an order, and then talks to the Inventory microservice (sample04). You can find the corresponding code inside the src/main/java/com/apress/ch04/sample01/service/OrderProcessing.java class.

```java
@RequestMapping(method = RequestMethod.POST)
public ResponseEntity<?> createOrder(@RequestBody Order order) {
    if (order != null) {
        RestTemplate restTemplate = new RestTemplate();
        URI uri = URI.create("http://localhost:9000/inventory");
        restTemplate.put(uri, order.getItems());
        order.setOrderId(UUID.randomUUID().toString());
        URI location = ServletUriComponentsBuilder
            .fromCurrentRequest().path("/{id}")
            .buildAndExpand(order.getOrderId())
            .toUri();
```

```
    return ResponseEntity.created(location).build();
  }
  return ResponseEntity.status(HttpStatus.BAD_REQUEST).build();
}
```

Let's spin up the sample01 microservice with the following Maven command. It will start on port 8080.

```
\> cd sample01
\> mvn clean install
\> mvn spring-boot:run
```

To test the completed end-to-end flow, let's use the following command.

```
\> curl -v -H "Content-Type: application/json" -d
'{"customer_id":"101021","payment_method":{"card_type":"VISA","expiration":
"01/22","name":"John Doe","billing_address":"201, 1st Street, San Jose, CA"},
"items":[{"code":"101","qty":1},{"code":"103","qty":5}],"shipping_address":
"201, 1st Street, San Jose, CA"}' http://localhost:8080/order


HTTP/1.1 201
Location: http://localhost:8080/order/b3a28d20-c086-4469-aab8-befcf2ba3345
```

You will also notice that the item codes are printed on the console where the sample04 microservice is running.

Getting Started with gRPC

In Chapter 3, we discussed the fundamentals of gRPC. In this section, we see how one microservice communicates with another microservice via gRPC. In the previous section, we saw how the Order Processing microservice (sample01) talks directly to the Inventory microservice (sample04) over HTTP to update inventory. Here we have modified the sample01 and sample04 microservices and built two new microservices, sample06 and sample05. The sample05 or the Inventory microservice acts as a gRPC server and the sample06 or the Order Processing microservice acts as a gRPC client. Source code for these two microservices is available under ch04/sample05 and ch04/sample06. Figure 4-3 shows the setup for this exercise.

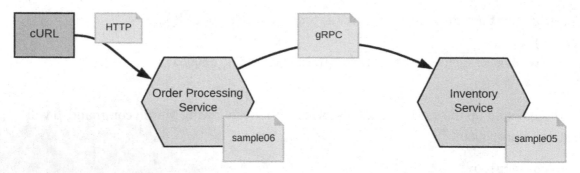

Figure 4-3. *Communication between microservices via gRPC*

Building the gRPC Service

First we need to create an IDL (Interface Definition Language). You can find it under
sample05/src/main/proto/InventoryService.proto. Later we will use a Maven plugin
to build the Java classes from this IDL file, and it will by default look for the location
sample05/src/main/proto/. Unless you want to change the plugin configuration, make
sure the IDL file is in this location. The following code shows the contents of the IDL file.

```
syntax = "proto3";

option java_multiple_files = true;
package com.apress.ch04.sample05.service;

message Item {
    string code = 1;
    int32 qty = 2;
}
message ItemList {
    repeated Item item = 1;
}
message UpdateItemsResp {
        string code = 1;
}
service InventoryService {
    rpc updateItems(ItemList) returns (UpdateItemsResp);
}
```

Now let's see what is new in our Maven `pom.xml` file. There are multiple dependencies added, but the only notable dependency is the `grpc-spring-boot-starter`. This takes care of the `@GRpcService` annotation in the `sample05/src/main/java/com/apress/ch04/sample05/service/Inventory.java` class, which spins up the Spring Boot application and exposes our microservice over gRPC.

```
<dependency>
    <groupId>org.lognet</groupId>
    <artifactId>grpc-spring-boot-starter</artifactId>
    <version>0.0.6</version>
</dependency>
```

We also need to add one new extension and a new Maven plugin to the `pom.xml` file. The `os-maven-plugin` extension will determine the operating system of the current setup and pass that information to the `protobuf-maven-plugin` plugin. The `protobuf-maven-plugin` plugin is used to generate the Java classes from the IDL.

```
........................................
<extension>
    <groupId>kr.motd.maven</groupId>
    <artifactId>os-maven-plugin</artifactId>
    <version>1.4.1.Final</version>
</extension>
........................................
<plugin>
    <groupId>org.xolstice.maven.plugins</groupId>
    <artifactId>protobuf-maven-plugin</artifactId>
    <version>0.5.0</version>

        ........................................
</plugin
```

The following Maven command can be used to create the Java classes from the IDL. By default they are created under the `target/generated-sources/protobuf/grpc-java` and `target/generated-sources/protobuf/java` directories.

```
\> cd sample05
\> mvn package
```

Now let's look at our service code. The Inventory (sample05/src/main/
java/com/apress/ch04/sample05/services/Inventory.java) class extends
InventoryServiceImplBase, which is a class generated by the Maven plugin. Once
the Order Processing microservice does a POST to the Inventory microservice, it will
simply print item codes and return.

```
@GRpcService
public class Inventory extends InventoryServiceImplBase{
    @Override
    public void updateItems(ItemList request,
                            StreamObserver<UpdateItemsResp>
                            responseObserver)
    {
        List<Item> items = request.getItemList();
        for (Item item : items) {
            System.out.println(item.getCode());
        }
        responseObserver.onNext(UpdateItemsResp.newBuilder()
                .setCode("success").build());
        responseObserver.onCompleted();
    }
}
```

To spin up the Inventory microservice and expose it over gRPC, use the following
Maven command.

```
\> cd sample05
\> mvn spring-boot:run
```

Once the server starts, it looks for the following line. By default it starts on 6565 and
you can change it by adding the property grpc.port to the application.properties
file and setting its value to the port number you need. In our case, we have set it to 7000
(grpc.port=7000).

```
gRPC Server started, listening on port 7000
```

Building the gRPC Client

Now let's see how to build a gRPC client application. In fact, in our case, the gRPC client we are building is another microservice. Just like in the gRPC service, first we need to create an IDL (Interface Definition Language). This is the same IDL we used for the gRPC service. You can find it under `sample06/src/main/proto/InventoryService.proto`. Later we will use a Maven plugin to build the Java classes from this IDL file, and it will by default look for the location `sample06/src/main/proto/`.

The only two additions to the client-side `pom.xml` are the `os-maven-plugin` extension and the `protobuf-maven-plugin` plugin. The `protobuf-maven-plugin` plugin is used to generate the Java classes from the IDL. Also, note that we do not need to add a dependency to `grpc-spring-boot-starter`. The following Maven command can be used to create the Java classes from the IDL. By default, they are created under the `target/generated-sources/protobuf/grpc-java` and `target/generated-sources/protobuf/java` directories.

```
\> cd sample06
\> mvn package
```

Now let's look at our client code. The `Order Processing` (`sample06/src/main/java/com/apress/ch04/sample06/service/OrderProcessing.java`) microservice calls the `Inventory` microservice, via the `InventoryClient` (`com/apress/ch04/sample06/InventoryClient.java`) class. The following shows the source code of the `InventoryClient`. It uses the `InventoryServiceBlockingStub`, which is a class generated from the IDL, to talk to the gRPC service.

```java
public class InventoryClient {
    ManagedChannel managedChannel;
    InventoryServiceBlockingStub stub;

    public void updateItems
            (com.apress.ch04.sample06.model.Item[] items) {

        ItemList itemList = null;
        for (int i = 0; i < items.length; i++) {
          Item item;
          item = Item.newBuilder().setCode(items[i].getCode())
                    .setQty(items[i].getQty()).build();
```

```java
        if (itemList != null
            && itemList.getItemList().size() > 0) {
        itemList = ItemList.newBuilder(itemList)
                    .addItem(i, item).build();
        } else {
        itemList = ItemList.newBuilder()
                .addItem(0, item).build();
        }
    }

    managedChannel = ManagedChannelBuilder
                    .forAddress("localhost", 7000)
                    .usePlaintext(true).build();
    stub = InventoryServiceGrpc
                    .newBlockingStub(managedChannel);
    stub.updateItems(itemList);
    }
}
```

To spin up the `Order Processing` microservice, which is also our gRPC client, use the following Maven command.

```
\> cd sample06
\> mvn spring-boot:run
```

To test the completed end-to-end flow, let's use the following command to create an order in the `Order Processing` microservice.

```
\> curl -v -H "Content-Type: application/json" -d '{"customer_id":"101021",
"payment_method":{"card_type":"VISA","expiration":"01/22","name":"John
Doe","billing_address":"201, 1st Street, San Jose, CA"},"items":[{"code":"
101","qty":1},{"code":"103","qty":5}],"shipping_address":"201, 1st Street,
San Jose, CA"}' http://localhost:8080/order


HTTP/1.1 201
Location: http://localhost:8080/order/17ff6fda-13b3-419f-9134-8abfec140e47
```

You will also notice that the item codes are printed on the console where the sample05 microservice is running.

Event-Driven Microservices with Kafka

In Chapter 3, we discussed the fundamentals of event-driven microservices and Kafka. In this section, we see how one microservice communicates with another microservice via asynchronous messaging. Going by the design we presented in Chapter 2, the Order Processing microservice (sample07) publishes an event to Kafka upon completing processing an order, and the Billing (sample08) microservice listens to the same event, consumes the message, and once billing is completed, publishes another event to Kafka. The sample07 or the Order Processing microservice acts as the event publisher (or the event source) and the sample08 or the Billing microservice acts as the event consumer (or the event sink). The source code of these two microservices is available under ch04/sample07 and ch04/sample08. Figure 4-4 shows the interactions between microservices and the message broker (Kafka).

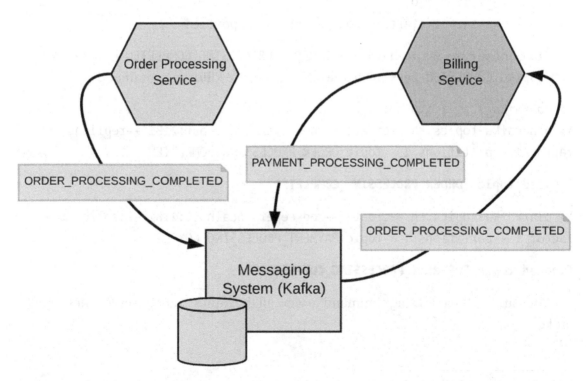

Figure 4-4. *Event-driven microservices with Kafka*

Setting Up a Kafka Message Broker

In this section we discuss how to set up a Kafka message broker. For the recommendations on a production deployment, always refer to the Kafka official documentation[41].

First we need to download the latest Kafka distribution. For the samples in the book, we are using version 2.11-1.1. Once the Kafka distribution is downloaded and unzipped, you can run the following command to start ZooKeeper[42]. Kafka uses ZooKeeper, so you need to first start a ZooKeeper server if you don't already have one. You can use the convenience script packaged with Kafka to get a quick-and-dirty single-node ZooKeeper instance.

```
\> cd kafka_2.11-1.1.0
\> bin/zookeeper-server-start.sh config/zookeeper.propertie
```

Now we can use the following command in a different console to start the Kafka server.

```
\> cd kafka_2.11-1.1.0
\> bin/kafka-server-start.sh config/server.properties
```

For our use case, we need two topics: ORDER_PROCESSING_COMPLETED and PAYMENT_PROCESSING_COMPLETED. Let's create the topics using the following commands.

```
\> cd kafka_2.11-1.1.0
\> bin/kafka-topics.sh --create --zookeeper localhost:2181 --replication-
factor 1 --partitions 1 --topic ORDER_PROCESSING_COMPLETED
```

Created topic "ORDER_PROCESSING_COMPLETED"

```
\> bin/kafka-topics.sh --create --zookeeper localhost:2181 --replication-
factor 1 --partitions 1 --topic PAYMENT_PROCESSING_COMPLETED
```

Created topic "PAYMENT_PROCESSING_COMPLETED"

You can use the following command to view all the topics available in the message broker.

---

[41]https://kafka.apache.org
[42]https://zookeeper.apache.org/

118

```
\> cd kafka_2.11-1.1.0
\> bin/kafka-topics.sh --list --zookeeper localhost:2181
```

ORDER_PROCESSING_COMPLETED
PAYMENT_PROCESSING_COMPLETED

Building Publisher (Event Source)

In this section, we discuss how to build the Order Processing microservice to publish events to the ORDER_PROCESSING_COMPLETED topic. Let's look at the notable dependencies added to the pom.xml file inside sample07. These two dependencies take care of the @EnableBinding annotation in the sample07/src/main/java/com/apress/ch04/sample07/OrderProcessingApp.java class and all the dependencies related to Kafka.

```
<dependency>
    <groupId>org.springframework.cloud</groupId>
    <artifactId>spring-cloud-stream</artifactId>
</dependency>
<dependency>
    <groupId>org.springframework.cloud</groupId>
    <artifactId>spring-cloud-starter-stream-kafka</artifactId>
</dependency>
```

Now let's look at the code, which publishes the event to the message broker. When the Order Processing (src/main/java/com/apress/ch04/sample07/service/OrderProcessing.java) microservice gets an order update, it talks to the OrderPublisher (src/main/java/com/apress/ch04/sample07/OrderPublisher.java) class to publish the event.

```
@Service
public class OrderPublisher {

    @Autowired
    private Source source;
    public void publish(Order order) {
        source.output().send(MessageBuilder.withPayload(order).build());
    }
}
```

The name of the topic and the message broker information are picked from the /src/main/resources/application.properties file.

```
spring.cloud.stream.bindings.output.destination:ORDER_PROCESSING_COMPLETED
spring.cloud.stream.bindings.output.content-type:application/json
spring.cloud.stream.kafka.binder.zkNodes:localhost
spring.cloud.stream.kafka.binder.zkNodes.brokers: localhost
```

Use the following Maven command to spin up the publisher microservice.

```
\> cd sample07
\> mvn spring-boot:run
```

Building Consumer (Event Sink)

In this section, we discuss how to build the Inventory microservice (sample08) to consume messages published to the ORDER_PROCESSING_COMPLETED topic. The Maven dependencies used in this example are the same as the ones before, and they cater the same purpose. Let's straightway look at the code, which consumes messages from the topic. The InventoryApp class (sample08/src/main/java/com/apress/ch04/sample08/InventoryApp.java) in the consumeOderUpdates method just reads from the topic and prints the order ID.

```java
@SpringBootApplication
@EnableBinding(Sink.class)
public class InventoryApp {
    public static void main(String[] args) {
        SpringApplication.run(InventoryApp.class, args);
    }
    @StreamListener(Sink.INPUT)
    public void consumeOderUpdates(Order order) {
        System.out.println(order.getOrderId());
    }
}
```

The name of the topic and the message broker information are picked from the sample08/src/main/resources/application.properties file.

```
server.port=9000
spring.cloud.stream.bindings.input.destination:ORDER_PROCESSING_COMPLETED
spring.cloud.stream.bindings.input.content-type:application/json
spring.cloud.stream.kafka.binder.zkNodes:localhost
spring.cloud.stream.kafka.binder.zkNodes.brokers: localhost
```

Use the following Maven command to spin up the consumer microservice.

```
\> cd sample08
\> mvn spring-boot:run
```

To test the complete end-to-end flow, let's use the following command to create an order via the Order Processing microservice.

```
\> curl -v -H "Content-Type: application/json" -d '{"customer_id":"101021",
"payment_method":{"card_type":"VISA","expiration":"01/22","name":"John
Doe","billing_address":"201, 1st Street, San Jose, CA"},"items":[{"code":"
101","qty":1},{"code":"103","qty":5}],"shipping_address":"201, 1st Street,
San Jose, CA"}' http://localhost:8080/order
```

```
HTTP/1.1 201
Location: http://localhost:8080/order/5f8ecb9c-8146-4021-aaad-b6b1d69fb80f
```

Now if you look at the console running the Inventory microservice (sample08), you find that the order ID is printed there.

You can also view the messages published to the ORDER_PROCESSING_COMPLETED topic with the following command.

```
\> cd kafka_2.11-1.1.0
\> bin/kafka-console-consumer.sh --bootstrap-server localhost:9092 --from-
beginning --topic ORDER_PROCESSING_COMPLETED
```

```
{"customer_id":"101021","order_id":"d203e371-2a8a-4a4c-a286-11e5b723f3d7",
"payment_method":{"card_type":"VISA","expiration":"01/22","name":"John
Doe","billing_address":"201, 1st Street, San Jose, CA"},"items":[{"code":"
101","qty":1},{"code":"103","qty":5}],"shipping_address":"201, 1st Street,
San Jose, CA2"}
```

Building GraphQL Services

In Chapter 3, we discussed how GraphQL is used in some synchronous messaging scenarios in which the RESTful service architecture won't fit. Let's try to build a GraphQL-based service using Spring Boot. You can find the complete code for this available under ch04/sample09.

By adding the graphql-spring-boot-starter[43] dependency to the project, you can get a GraphQL server running. Along with the GraphQL Java Tools library, you only need to write the code necessary for your service. First, we need to make sure that we have the following dependencies in our project.

```
<dependency>
    <groupId>com.graphql-java</groupId>
    <artifactId>graphql-spring-boot-starter</artifactId>
    <version>3.6.0</version>
</dependency>
<dependency>
    <groupId>com.graphql-java</groupId>
    <artifactId>graphql-java-tools</artifactId>
    <version>3.2.0</version>
</dependency>
```

Spring Boot will pick up the corresponding dependencies and set up the appropriate handlers to work automatically. This will expose the GraphQL service at the /graphql endpoint by default (configured in the /src/main/resources/application.properties file under sample09) and will accept POST requests containing GraphQL payloads. The GraphQL Tools library works by processing GraphQL schema files to build the correct structure and then wires special beans to this structure. The Spring Boot GraphQL Starter (graphql-spring-boot-starter) automatically finds these schema files. Those files need to be saved with the extension .graphqls and can be present anywhere in the classpath.

One mandatory requirement here is that there must be exactly one root query, and up to one root mutation. The root query needs to have special beans defined in the Spring context to handle various fields in it. The main requirements are that the beans implement the GraphQLQueryResolver interface and that every field in the root query from the schema have a method in one of those classes with the same name.

---

[43]https://github.com/graphql-java/graphql-spring-boot

```
public class Query implements GraphQLQueryResolver {
    private BookDao bookDao;
    public List<Book> getRecentBooks(int count, int offset) {
        return bookDao.getRecentBooks(count, offset);
    }
}
```

The method signature must have arguments corresponding to each parameter in the GraphQL schema. It should also return the correct return type for the type in the GraphQL schema. Any simple types—`String`, `Int`, `List`, etc.—can be used with the equivalent Java types, and the system just maps them automatically.

The `getRecentBooks` method in the previous code snippet handles any GraphQL queries for the `recentBooks` field in the schema defined earlier.

```
public class Book {
    private String id;
    private String title;
    private String category;
    private String authorId;
}
```

A Java bean represents every complex type in the GraphQL server. GraphQL also has a companion tool called *GraphiQL*[44]. This is a user interface (UI) that can communicate with any GraphQL server and execute queries and mutations against it. Fields inside the Java bean will directly map to the fields in the GraphQL response based on the name of the field. The instructions on how to run `sample09` is available in the README file under `ch04/sample09` directory, in the samples Git repository.

Summary

In this chapter, we discussed how to build microservices with Spring Boot. The chapter started with a discussion of the different tools and developer frameworks available for microservice developers. Then we delved deep into building microservices, with four different communication protocols—REST, gRPC, Kafka, and GraphQL. In the next chapter, we focus on the data management aspect of microservices.

---

[44]https://github.com/graphql/graphiql

CHAPTER 5

Data Management

In most business use cases, the service logic is built on top of an underlying persistent layer. Often a database is used as the persistent layer and it is acting as the system of record for a given service. As we've discussed, microservices are built as autonomous entities and should have control over the data layer that they operate on. This essentially means that microservices cannot depend on a data layer that is owned by or shared by another entity. So, in the process of building autonomous services, it is also required to have an isolated persistent layer for each microservice. In this chapter, we discuss the commonly used patterns and best practices for transforming centralized or shared database-based enterprise applications to microservices that are based on decentralized databases.

Monolithic Applications and Shared Databases

In the context of enterprise architecture, which is based on monolithic applications and services, often a single centralized database (or a few) is shared among multiple applications and services. For example, as depicted in Figure 5-1, all services of the retail system share a centralized database (Retail DB). So, all the information related to products, customers, orders, payments, and so on, are centrally managed through the Retail database.

© Kasun Indrasiri and Prabath Siriwardena 2018
K. Indrasiri and P. Siriwardena, *Microservices for the Enterprise*, https://doi.org/10.1007/978-1-4842-3858-5_5

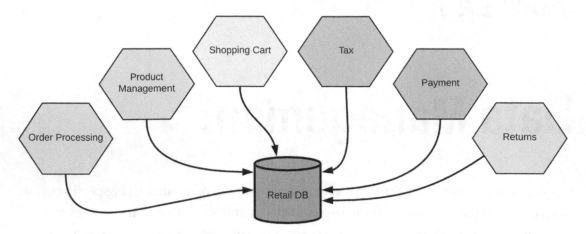

Figure 5-1. *The microservices of online retail application share a single database*

In fact, a centralized shared database makes it easier for the application to combine data from multiple tables and formulate different business representations. The powerful query languages like SQL innately support all the features required for sharing the data and building different data compositions. For example, using SQL we can join multiple tables on various complex conditions and create a composite view of different entities.

When working with shared business entities, implementing business interactions among them in transactional manner becomes quite important. A transaction is an atomic unit of work that either fails or succeeds. The key characteristics of transactions are known as ACID, which is an acronym for *atomicity* (all changes to the data are performed as if they are a single operation), *consistency* (data is in a consistent state when a transaction starts and when it ends), *isolation* (the intermediate state of a transaction is invisible to other transactions), and *durability* (after a transaction successfully completes, changes to data persist and are not undone, even in the event of a system failure).

A centralized database makes ACID transactions across multiple entities trivially easy. In a relational database, every SQL statement must execute in the scope of a transaction. Hence it's quite trivial to model a complex transactional scenario that involves multiple tables. Most Relational Database Management Systems (RDBMS) support such capabilities out of the box.

Despite the advantages of the centralized shared database architecture, it has drawbacks too. It is the single point of failure, creates a potential performance bottleneck due to heavy application traffic directed into a single database, and has tight dependencies between applications, as they share same database tables. So, you cannot build autonomous and independent microservices if you are using a shared persistent layer or database. Hence, with microservices you need to decentralize data management and each microservice has to fully own the data that it operates on.

A Database per Microservice

The microservices architecture encourages microservices to own the data that they operate on and databases shouldn't be shared with any other service. Therefore a given microservice will have an isolated datastore or use an isolated persistent service (e.g., from a cloud provider).

Having a database per microservice gives us a lot of freedom when it comes to microservices autonomy. For instance, microservices owners can modify the database schema as per the business requirements, without worrying about the external consumers of the database. There's nobody from the external applications who can access the database directly. This also gives the microservices developer the freedom to select the technology to be used as the persistent layer of microservices. Different microservices can use different persistent store technologies, such as RDBMS, NoSQL or other cloud services.

However, having a database per service introduces a new set of challenges. When it comes to the realization of any business scenario, sharing data between microservices and implementing transactions within and across service boundaries becomes quite challenging.

Sharing Data Between Microservices

In a monolithic database, it is quite easy to do any arbitrary data composition because we share a single monolithic database. However, in the microservices context, every piece of data is owned by a single service (single *system of record*). A system of record (or persistent layer) cannot be directly accessed from any other service or system. The only way to access the data owned by another microservice is through a service interface or API. Other systems, which access the data through the published API, possibly could use a read-only local cache to keep the data locally.

127

To cater to these requirements, we need to come up with suitable techniques to share data between microservices, as most business scenarios would require it.

Eliminating Shared Tables

Sharing tables between multiple services/applications is a quite common pattern in a monolithic database. As discussed earlier, when we share a table between two or more microservices, a change to the schema of that table could affect all dependent microservices. For example, as shown in Figure 5-2, the Order Processing and Shipping services share the same table TRACKING_INFO, which keeps track of the order status. Both services may read or write to the same table and the underlying central database provides all the required functionalities (such as ACID transactions). However, if we need to change the schema of the TRACKING_INFO table, then that'll affect both the Order Processing and Shipping services. Also, it is not possible to have service specific data (that service would not like to share) in the shared table. These types of shared table scenarios are not compatible with microservices data management fundamentals. The persistent store/database of a service should be independent and only one microservice should operate on it. Therefore, with a microservices architecture, we need to get rid of such shared tables.

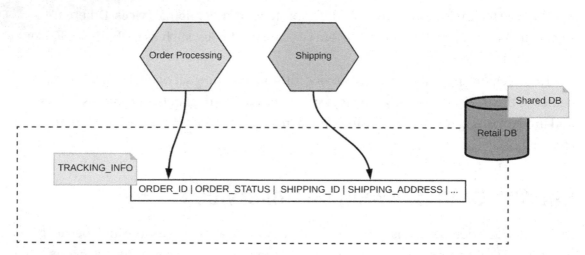

Figure 5-2. *Data management between two services using a shared table*

So, how do we get rid of shared tables? If you think in terms of microservice data handling principles that we have discussed earlier, a given piece of data must be owned by a single service. Hence, in this example (depicted in Figure 5-3), the tracking information should be split into two tables. One table should have the data, which is relevant to the `Order Processing` microservice and the other table should contain the data relevant to the `Shipping` microservice. There can be shared data duplicated on these two tables and services are responsible for keeping the data in-sync using the published APIs of those services (no direct database access). We discuss these synchronization techniques in detail later in this chapter.

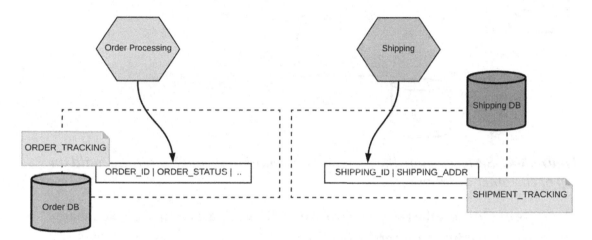

Figure 5-3. *Splitting shared data and managing it as independent entities*

Another variation of shared tables is when the shared data is represented as a separate business entity. In the previous example, the shared data (tracking information) doesn't represent a business entity. So, let's take a different example of sharing customer data between the `Order Processing` and `Product Management` services. In this case, both these services use data from a shared data table (`CUSTOMER` table) in their business logic. We can now identify that customer information is not just a table but also a completely different business entity. We can simply treat it as a business capability oriented entity and model that as a microservice. As shown in Figure 5-4, we can introduce the `Customer` microservice and let it own the customer data and the other services can consume customer data through an API exposed by the `Customer` service.

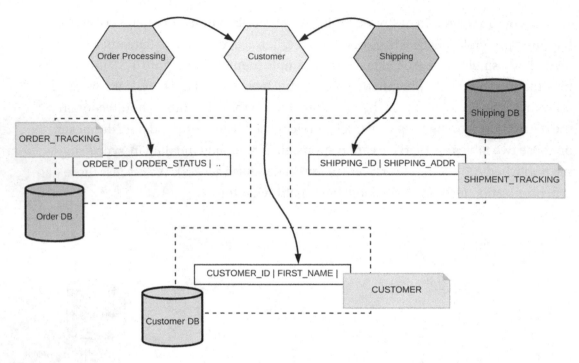

Figure 5-4. *Services share the customer information through a service build on top of customer database*

So, we can identify the key steps involved in eliminating data tables, which share data between multiple microservices.

1. Identify the shared table and identify the business capability of the data stored in that shared table.

2. Move the shared table to a dedicated database and, on top of that database, create a new service (business capability) identified in the previous step.

3. Remove all direct database access from other services and only allow them to access the data via the service's published API.

With this design, we need to have a dedicated owner of the newly created shared service that can modify the service interface or schema of that service. This also helps us discover the new business boundaries between these services, which will make our microservices-based application future-proof with any new requirements.

Shared Data

Storing data across multiple tables and connecting it through foreign keys (FK) is a very common technique in relational databases. A foreign key is a column or combination of columns that is used to establish and enforce a link between the data in two tables. You can create a foreign key by defining a FOREIGN KEY constraint when you create or modify a table. Foreign keys enable the referential integrity between the data stored in multiple tables, which means that if a foreign key contains a value, this value refers to an existing record in the related table.

For example, Figure 5-5 illustrates the Order Processing and Product Management services, which use the ORDER and PRODUCT tables. A given order contains multiple products and the order table refers to such products using a foreign key, which points to the primary key of the PRODUCT table. With the foreign keys constraint, you can only add a value to the foreign key of the ORDER table from an existing ORDER entity.

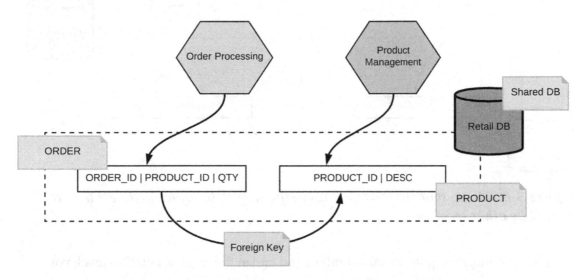

Figure 5-5. *Shared database - Foreign key relationship between tables*

With monolithic shared databases, using a foreign key and joining data is quite trivial. But when you want to have independent services and use a database per service, having this kind of link for referential integrity is virtually impossible. So, with a microservices architecture, we need to find different ways of handling this scenario. Let's take a look at some of the commonly used techniques to achieve these requirements.

Synchronous Lookups

When you have a dedicated database for each microservice, if one service needs to access the data of the other, it can simply access the published API of that microservice and retrieve the required data. For example, as shown in Figure 5-6, the order service keeps the required product IDs that are part of a given order. If the `Order Processing` service requires the detailed information of the products, then from it's application logic, it has to invoke the `Product Management` service and retrieve the product information.

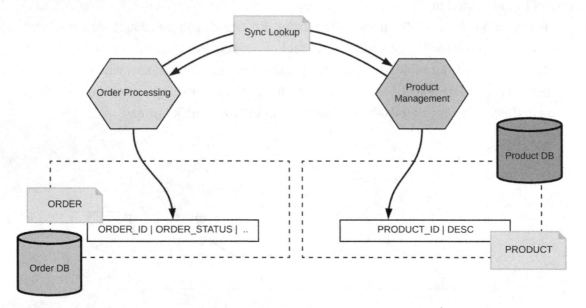

Figure 5-6. *Using synchronous lookups to the service interface to access the data owned by other services*

This technique is quite trivial to understand and at the implementation level, you need to write extra logic to do an external service call. We need to keep in mind that, unlike databases, we no longer have the referential integrity of a foreign key constraint. This means that the service developers have to take care of the consistency of data that they put into the table. For example, when you create an order you need to make sure (possibly by calling the product service) that the products that are referred from that order actually exist in the `PRODUCT` table.

Using Asynchronous Events

Sharing data using synchronous lookups from other microservices may be expensive in certain business scenarios. As an alternative, we can leverage the event-driven architecture (publisher-subscriber pattern) to share data between services. For example, for the same scenario of the `Order Processing` and `Product Management` services (see Figure 5-7), we can introduce an event-driven communication pattern, in which we have an event bus, which is used as the messaging infrastructure. If there is an update to a product, the `Product Management` service (publisher) updates its product table and publishes an event into the event bus. The `Order Processing` service (subscriber) has subscribed to the interested topic of product updates and, therefore, as the `Product Management` service publishes product update events to that topic, the `Order Processing` service will receive them. Then it can update its local cache of product information and use the cache to implement the business logic of the `Product Management` service.

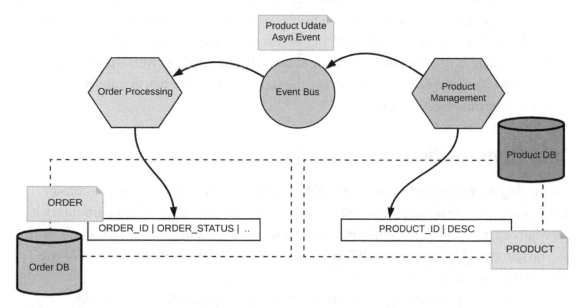

Figure 5-7. *Using asynchronous events to share data between microservices*

As the event bus you can select any asynchronous messaging technology (we discussed asynchronous messaging techniques in detail in Chapter 3, "Inter-Service Communication"), such as Kafka or AMQP Broker (such as RabbitMQ), and you can use different subscription techniques to ensure the delivery of the event to the subscriber (such as durable subscriptions).

With this approach, you can eliminate synchronous service calls from one service to the other, but since we are using a local cache, the data can be stale. Hence the asynchronous event-based data sharing is an eventual consistency model. Eventual consistency makes sure that the data of each service gets consistent eventually (you may get stale data for a certain amount of time). The time taken by the services to get consistent data may or may not be defined. Therefore, we need to use this pattern for use cases that are not affected by an eventual consistency nature.

Shared Static Data

When it comes to storing and sharing the immutable read-only metadata, conventional monolithic databases are often used and data is shared through a shared table. For example, data such as U.S. states, list of countries, etc., is often used as the shared static data. With a microservices approach, since we don't want to share the databases, we need to think about how to keep the shared static data.

One would think that having another microservices with the static data would solve this problem, but it is overkill to have a service just to get some static information that does not change over time. Hence, sharing static data is often done with shared libraries. For example, if a given service wants to use the static metadata, it has to import the shared library into the service code.

Data Composition

Composing data from multiple entities and creating different views is a very common requirement in data management. With monolithic databases (RDBMS in particular), it is trivially easy to build the composition of multiple tables using joins in SQL statements. So, you can seamlessly compose different data views out of the exiting entities and use them in your services.

However, in the microservices context, when you introduce the database per microservice method, building data compositions becomes very complex. You no longer can use the built-in constructs such as joins to compose data, which are dispersed among multiple databases owned by different services.

Let's take a closer look at some of the commonly used techniques to do data composition with microservices.

Composite Services or Client-Side Mashups

When you have to create join of data from multiple microservices, you are only allowed to access the service APIs. So, to create composition of data from multiple microservices, you can create a composite service on top of the existing microservices. The composite service is responsible for invoking the downstream services and does the runtime composition of the data retrieved via service calls.

For example, let's consider the example shown in Figure 5-8. Suppose that we need to create a composition of the orders placed and have the details of the customers who have placed those orders. Here we have two services—Order Processing and Customer—which have their own databases to hold the orders and customer information.

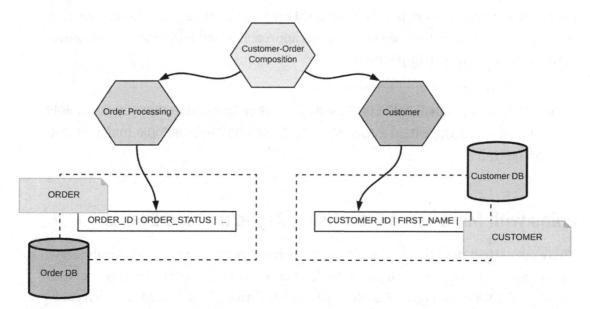

Figure 5-8. *Data composition using a composite service that calls the downstream services and aggregates the data*

The requirement that we have at hand is to create a join of the orders and customers. With the composite service approach, we can create a new service—the `Customer-Order` composite service—and call the `Order Processing` and `Customer` microservices from it. You need to implement the runtime data composition logic as well as the communication logic (for example, to invoke RESTful `Order Processing` and `Customer` microservices) inside the composite service.

One other alternative is to implement the same runtime data composition at the client side. Basically, rather having a composite service, the consumers/client applications can call the required downstream services and build the composition themselves. This is often known as a *client-side mashup*.

Composite services or client-side mashups are suitable when the data that you have joined is relatively small. Since this is a runtime composition, if you are going to load a lot of data into memory, the runtime of the composite service will require a lot of memory. Therefore, we need to select this approach based on the data composition scenario that we have to implement.

Tip   Data composition with composite services or client-side mashup is suitable for joins of 1:m type, where a row from one table can have multiple matching rows in another table.

Joins with Materialize View Using Asynchronous Events

There are certain data composition scenarios where you need to materialize the view with pre-joined data coming from multiple microservices. For example, consider the scenario illustrated in Figure 5-9. Here we have the `Order Processing` and `Customer` services, and we need to materialize the customer-order join/view. The materialized view will be used for a specific business function, which requires the join between orders and customers.

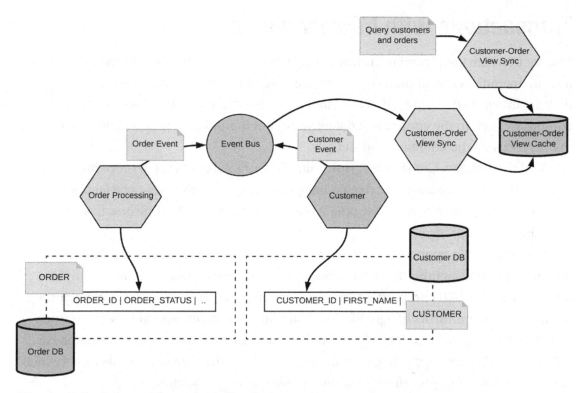

Figure 5-9. *Joins with materialized view using asynchronous events*

The Order Processing and Customer services publish order and customer update events to the event bus/broker. There is a service that has subscribed to those events and it then materializes the join of orders and customers. That service (Customer-Order-View-Sync) maintains a de-normalized join between the orders and customers, which is done ahead of time rather than in realtime. As shown in Figure 5-9, Customer-Order-View-Sync service also has a component that operates on the Customer-Order View Cache that serves all the external queries.

Tip   Data composition with materializing view is suitable for compositions with large numbers of rows (m:n joins with high cardinality) on each side.

The denormalized data can be kept in a cache or other such storage and it could be consumed by another microservices as a read-only datastore.

Transactions with Microservices

Transactions are an important concept in software applications. They allow you to group a set of operations that should be executed together in an all-or-none scenario (i.e., they are executed or are all rolled back in the event of a failure). Transactions are quite commonly used in the context of a database but not limited to it. In this chapter, we mainly focus on the database transactions.

ACID (Atomicity, Consistency, Isolation, and Durability) is a set of properties of database transactions intended to guarantee validity even in the event of a failure. Therefore, a sequence of database operations that satisfies the ACID properties can be considered a transaction.

The monolithic applications are often built on top of a single centralized relational database and transactions are used to keep data in a consistent state across multiple tables. Using the ACID properties in the application provides the capability of beginning a transaction to perform changes like insert, update, and delete and allows committing or rolling back the transaction. With monolithic applications and centralized databases, it is quite straightforward to begin a transaction, change the data in multiple rows (which can span across multiple tables), and finally commit the transaction.

With microservices, the business requirements related to transactions wouldn't change drastically. However, unlike a centralized database, microservices have their own database and the transactional boundaries that span across multiple services and databases. Therefore, implementation of such transactional scenarios is no longer straightforward as it is with monolithic applications and centralized databases.

Avoiding Distributed Transactions with Two-Phase Commit

Distributed transactions are built around the concept of using a centralized process called a *transaction manager* to orchestrate the steps of a transaction. The main algorithm that is used in implementing distributed transactions is known as *two-phase commit* (2PC). Let's look at the details of the two-phase commit protocol. The changes required by a transaction are sent to each participant and initially stored temporarily at each participant of the transaction. Then the transaction manager initiates the voting/commit-request phase.

Voting/Commit-Request Phase

- The transaction manager/coordinator sends a *prepare* request to all the services that participate in a given transaction.

- The transaction manager will wait until all services reply yes or no.

Commit Phase

- Based on the responses received in the first phase, if all the services have responded with a yes, then the transaction manager will commit the transaction.

- If any of the services respond with a no (or don't respond at all), then the transaction manager will invoke the rollback operations for all the participating services. Once the commit message is received, all the participant entities persist the temporarily stored changes.

The distributed transactions method addresses most of the transaction requirements that we discussed earlier, but it comes with inherent limitations that hinder the usage of distributed transactions with 2PC for most microservices transactional behaviors. Some of the limitations of the two-phase commit method are:

- The transaction manager is the single point of failure. All pending transactions will never complete.

- If a given participant fails to respond, then the entire transaction will be blocked.

- A commit can fail after voting. The 2PC protocol assumes that if a given participant has responded with a yes, then it can definitely commit the transaction too. This is not the case in most practical scenarios.

- Given the distributed and autonomous nature of microservices, using a distributed transactions/two-phase commit for implementing transactional business use cases is a complex, error-prone task that can hinder the scalability of the entire system.

Tip   Avoid using distributed transactions with two-phase commit for microservices transactions.

It is better if you can avoid using distributed transactions with two-phase commit when implementing transactions across multiple microservices. However, the requirement of building transactional business scenarios, which span multiple microservices, is still valid. There are several other alternatives you can use.

Publishing Events Using Local Transactions

Asynchronous event-based data management is quite common in microservices data management. There are certain transactional behaviors that you can implement in event-driven architecture that allow you to achieve atomicity. For example, suppose that the Order Processing service illustrated in Figure 5-10 is responsible for updating the ORDER table and publishing an event to the event bus in a transactional manner (i.e., update the order and publish the event at once).

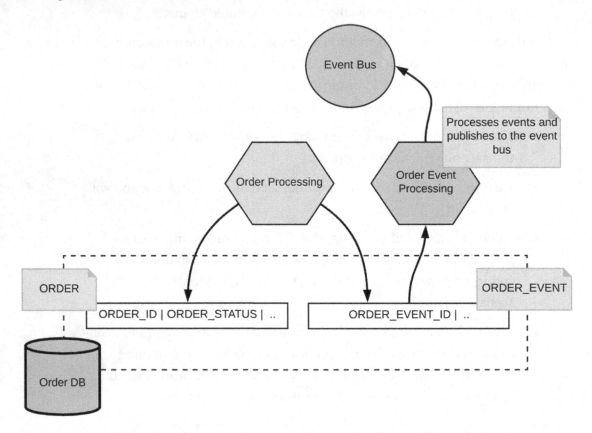

Figure 5-10. *Using local transactions to update a database table and create an event*

Here, we have used an event table to store the order update events. So, the Order Processing service can start a local transaction, which includes order update operations, and add an event to the ORDER_EVENT table. Both of these operations will be executed in the same local transaction boundary.

There is a dedicated service/process that is responsible for consuming the ORDER_ EVENT table and publishing the event to the event bus. It can also use local transactions to read the events, publish them to an event bus/message broker, and update the order event table. The event consumer service is responsible for reading events from the event bus and handling them in the transaction boundary of that service.

This approach avoids the usage of distributed transactions with 2PC, but it has some limitations, such as dependency on a database that supports transactions (i.e., most of the NoSQL databases do not support transactions).

Database Log Mining

When a service performs various database operations on top of the data owned by that service, all the transaction details are recorded in the database transactions or the commit log. Therefore, we can consider the database the single source-of-truth and extract data changes from its transaction or commit log. For example, as shown in Figure 5-11, the Order Processing service performs various database operations and they are recorded in the database transaction log. The DBTransactionLogProc application can mine the database transactions log of the Order database and create events that match each transaction. These events are then published into an event bus or a message broker.

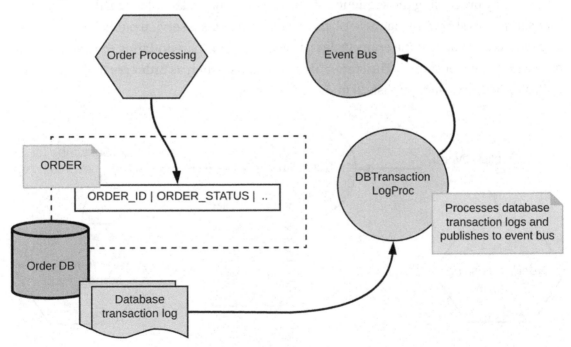

Figure 5-11. *Achieving atomicity by using a database transaction log and publishing events*

Other applications can consume these events and we can maintain eventual consistency between all services.

Data-management solutions such as *Change Data Capture* (CDC) leverage database transaction log processing techniques. For example, solutions such as Debezium or LinkedIn Databus use this technique to build CDC pipelines.

The transaction log mining technique is quite effective as we use the database as the single source of truth. Every successful database operation is recorded in the database transaction log. However, when it comes to the implementation and processing, the database transaction log drastically changes from one database to the other, because there is no standard format for transaction logs and each database has its own proprietary way to recording the transactions. Therefore, most of the data-management solutions based on database transaction log mining must have implementation for each and every database type.

Event Sourcing

By using the techniques that we discussed earlier (such as publishing events using local transactions), we can persist each state-changing event of an entity as a sequence of events. All such events are stored in an event bus and subscribers can derive the state of that entity by processing the sequence of the event that has taken place on that entity. For example, as shown in Figure 5-12, the Order Processing service publishes the changes taking place on the entity Order as events (rather than updating the database table with the order status). The state-changing events—such as order created, updated, paid, shipped, etc.—are published into the event bus.

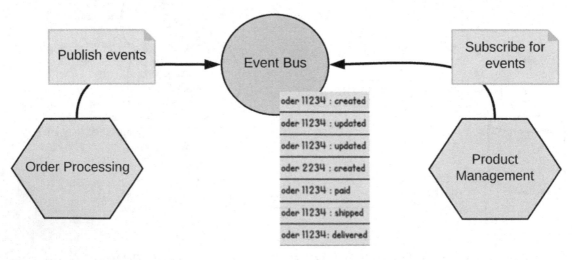

Figure 5-12. *Event sourcing*

The subscriber applications and services can recreate the status of an order by simply replaying the events that are taking place on an order. For example, it can retrieve all the events related to order11234 and derive the current state of that order.

Saga

So far, we have discussed several asynchronous event-driven architecture-based solutions that we can leverage to avoid distributed transactions with two-phase commit. For fully synchronous messaging scenarios, we can build transaction behavior across multiple services using *Sagas*.

Before we jump into the theoretical aspects of Saga, let's look at a real-world example of using Saga. (There[1] is also good conference talk by Caitie McCaffrey on how the Saga pattern is designed for real-world scenarios.) Consider a travel agent service (see Figure 5-13), which allows you to plan a vacation. The travel agent service takes the duration, location, and other details through the travel agent app and books flight, hotel, and car rental services. The booking of flight, hotel, and car rental service information has to be done in a transactional manner (book all three of them together or if a booking of one of those fails then cancel the rest). As we discussed earlier, if the travel agent service is built on top of a centralized database, the implementation of this scenario with transactions will be quite trivial.

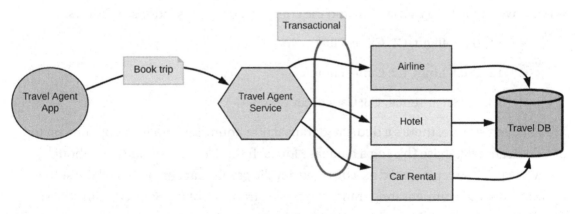

Figure 5-13. *Transactions on a centralized database*

---

[1]https://www.youtube.com/watch?v=xDuwrtwYHu8

With microservices, building this scenario requires us to have transactional safety across multiple service invocations. As you have seen in the previous sections, using distributed transactions with two-phase commit has inherent limitations and won't be a suitable approach to solve this problem.

Saga aims to solve the distributed transactions problem by grouping a given transaction into a sequence of sub-transactions and corresponding compensating transactions. All transactions in a Saga either complete successfully or, in the event of a failure, the compensating transactions are ran to roll back everything, which is done as part of the Saga.

Note   A *Saga* is a long-lived transaction that can be written as a sequence of transactions that can be interleaved. All transactions in a sequence complete successfully or the compensating transactions are executed to amend a partial execution. The Saga[2] pattern was introduced in a paper published in 1987 by Hector Garcia-Molina and Kenneth Salem.

Now, let's try to use the Saga pattern in our travel booking scenario. We can model (see Figure 5-14) this use case as a collection of sub-transactions—booking airline, booking hotel, and booking scar rental. Each of these sub-transactions operates on a single transaction boundary and each sub-transaction has an associated compensating transaction that can semantically undo the sub-transaction. For example, for each service, we can list the transaction and the compensating transactions as follows.

- T1: Book flight, C1: Cancel flight

- T2: Book hotel, C2: Cancel hotel

- T3: Book car rental, C3: Cancel car rental

For each service, there's a dedicated transaction boundary and it will operate on top of a dedicated database (having a database for each service is not mandatory though).

A Saga can be represented as a directed acyclic graph that consists of all the sub-transactions and compensating transactions. The travel-booking Saga contains the set of sub-transactions and compensating transactions. The travel agent service contains a component called Saga Execution Coordinator (SEC), which executes the book flight, book hotel, and book car rental transactions. If any of these operations fails at a

---

[2]https://www.cs.cornell.edu/andru/cs711/2002fa/reading/sagas.pdf

given step, then SEC rolls back the entire transaction by executing the corresponding compensating transactions.

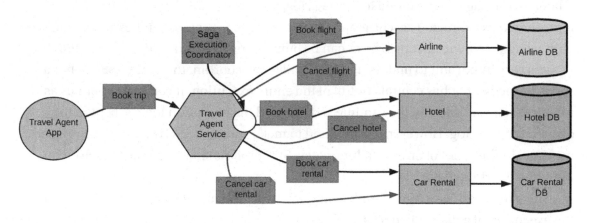

Figure 5-14. *Using Sagas*

Sagas at the conceptual level are quite trivial and most of the centralized workflow solutions, such as Business Process Model and Notation (BPMN) solutions, are in fact based on the same terminology. However, building a Saga pattern for a microservices-based system in a decentralized fashion is quite challenging. Therefore, let's take a closer look at how a Saga can be implemented in the microservices context.

The implementation of Saga requires a Saga log, which is a distributed log that the Saga Execution Coordinator interacts with.

Saga Log

The Saga log is a distributed log that's used to persist every transaction/operation during the execution of a given Saga. At a high level, the Saga log contains various state-changing operations, such as `Begin Saga`, `End Saga`, `Abort Saga`, `Begin T-i`, `End T-i`, `Begin C-i`, and `End C-i`.

The Saga log is often implemented using a distributed log and systems such as Kafka are commonly used for the implementation.

Saga Execution Coordinator (SEC)

The SEC is the main component that orchestrates the entire logic and is responsible for the execution of the Saga. All the steps in a given Saga are recorded in the Saga log and the SEC writes and interprets the records of the Saga log. It also executes the sub-transactions/operations (e.g., invoke the hotel service and make a reservation) and the corresponding compensating transactions when necessary. While the steps related to the Saga are recorded in the Saga log, the orchestration logic (which can be represented as a directed acyclic graph) is part of the SEC process (orchestration can be built using your own custom logic or can be built on top of a standard, such as BPMN).

It is very important to understand that, unlike the coordinator in 2PC, SEC is not a special process that has central control of the entire execution. It certainly operates as a centralized runtime, but the runtime is dumb and the execution logic is kept in the distributed Saga log. However, it is required to make sure that SEC is up and running all the time. In the event of an SEC failure, a new SEC process should be started based on the same distributed Saga log.

Since now you have a good understanding of the SEC and the Saga log, let's dive into the execution of a distributed Saga.

Executing a Distributed Saga

A distributed Saga is a Directed Acyclic Graph (DAG) and the SEC's primary task is to execute that DAG. Suppose that, in our travel-booking scenario (see Figure 5-15), we have the SEC built into the travel agent service.

The SEC can start processing the Saga, which is recorded in the distributed log.

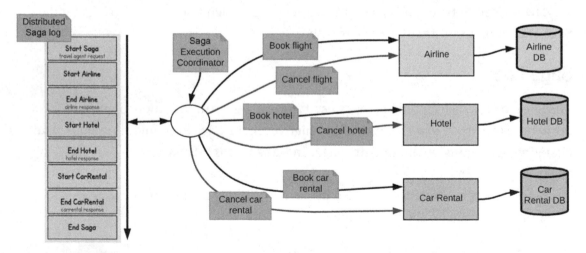

Figure 5-15. *Execution steps of a successful Saga*

Once the travel agent service gets a travel-booking request, SEC initiates a Saga by writing to the Saga log with a Start Saga instruction along with any other metadata required to process the Saga. Once the record is durably committed into the log, SEC can move into the next instruction.

Then, based on the DAG of the Saga, SEC can pick one of the airline, hotel, or car rental transactions (given that all three can work in parallel). Suppose that airline transactions are executed first. In that case, the SEC logs a Start Airline message to the Saga log. Then, the SEC executes the book flight operation.

Once the SEC receives the response from the airline service, it commits the End Airline message along with the response from the airline service, which we may need during the latter part of the Saga.

Similarly, the same set of steps continues until we have successfully executed all three operations on the airline, hotel, and car rental services.

Finally, since we have completed everything successfully, SEC commits the End Saga message into the Saga log. This is a successful Saga execution.

Now let's look at a Saga in a failure scenario. In Figure 5-16, we have the same set of steps that we discussed earlier, but in this case, the car rental process fails (imagine there are no cars available on the specified dates, for example).

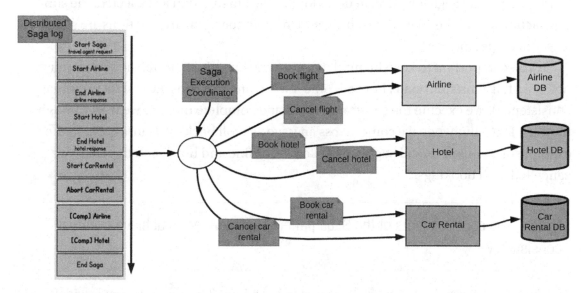

Figure 5-16. *Execution steps of an unsuccessful Saga*

Since we have detected a failure of a particular sub-transaction (i.e., the car reservation), we need to roll back all the other sub-transaction we made so far. So, in the Saga log you can find the `Start Car Rental` log and now the car reservation has failed. Now we have to walk through the inverted DAG of Saga that we executed so far and commit the rollback.

When the car rental service returns an error for the car reservation, the SEC commits the `Abort Car Rental` message to the Saga log.

Since this is a failure, the SEC has to initiate the rollback operations for the current Saga. The SEC can roll back the sub-transactions that are completed so far by inverting the DAG of this Saga and processing the Saga log backward.

So, the SEC looks for any records with car, hotel, and airline in the Saga log and it finds the records on the hotel and airline sub-transactions. The SEC will execute the compensating transactions for the hotel and airline. It can use the stored information on Saga logs, such as the reservation number, to execute the compensation transactions.

After a successful execution of the compensating transaction, the SEC commits the `[Comp] Airline` and `[Comp] Hotel` messages into the Saga log.

Finally, the SEC can commit the Saga completion into the Saga log.

SEC failures are relatively easier to handle, as we can recreate the DAG and the state by processing the Saga log. Also, in order for the Saga to function as expected, the sub-transaction should be sent at most once and the compensating transactions are sent at least once (idempotent).

It's also important to keep in mind that at any given point in time, the system may not be in full consistent state, but with time it will come to a consistent state (eventual consistency). We execute the sub-transactions and complete them as we walk through the Saga DAG. But when we come across an issue, we roll back the transaction. In the example of an unsuccessful Saga, we booked the airline and hotel, and then later we cancelled both bookings.

Note   The core concepts of the Saga pattern are intended to achieve eventual consistency.

The Saga pattern is not just for database transactions. The Saga concept is widely used in practice with solutions such as workflow, payment processing, financial systems, etc. Also, the Saga pattern is good for any use case that requires approval and human interaction.

The Saga pattern for microservices is supported in most workflow solutions that can operate in a microservices environment. In Chapter 7, "Integrating Microservices," we explore how such workflow and business processes are used in the context of a microservices architecture.

Polyglot Persistence

With decentralized data management, you can take advantage of using the most appropriate persistent technique for your use case. Based on your use case, one microservice can use a SQL database, while another service can leverage a NoSQL database.

For example, a microservices of a social media app may use a relational/SQL database to store its user information, while multimedia storage is based on a NoSQL database.

Caching

As part of the data-management techniques for microservices, caching plays a critical role as it improves availability, scalability, and performance of a given microservice. At each microservice level, we can cache the business entities that a given service operates on. Usually such business entities (or objects) do not frequently change (e.g., product information service caches the product name and details in a cache, which will be frequently used for product searching). Such data can usually be cached on-demand (when we first access the product information from the underlying datastore). Also, you can cache any service-level metadata (configurations or static data) during the service startup.

One of the most important aspects of caching is not to use a central caching layer that is shared between microservices. However, the instances of a given microservice will all have the same data requirements, so it makes sense to share a caching layer across these instances.

There are quite a few caching solutions out there, but Redis[3], Ehcache[4], Hazelcast[5], and Coherence[6] are some of the more popular caching implementations. Redis in particular has been widely used in open source and container-native microservice caching scenarios. Redis is an open source, in-memory data structure store, used as a database, cache, and message broker. It supports data structures such as strings, hashes, lists, sets, sorted sets with range queries, bitmaps, hyperloglogs, and geospatial indexes with radius queries. While Redis is mainly used for caching in the microservices context, it can also be used as a database or message broker (publisher-subscriber messaging).

Summary

In this chapter, we discussed the decentralized data-management techniques that we can leverage in a microservices architecture. The database per microservices pattern gives us a set of advantages and several challenges too. The conventional data sharing across multiple tables using SQL, dependencies between tables such as foreign key constraints, etc. are no longer applicable when each microservice can only operate on a single private database.

We discussed several techniques that we can use to share data between microservices, such as runtime lookups by accessing the service interface, asynchronous event-based data sharing using local caches, and maintaining a materialized view using event-driven communication.

Transactions are one of the main challenging aspects in distributed data management with microservices. You are no longer able to define transaction boundaries that span across multiple business services (multiple tables), as each service has a dedicated database and services are not allowed to access the external databases directly. Using distributed transaction with two-phase commit is not an option due to the inherent limitations related to scalability. Sagas provide an alternative approach to distributed transactions with two-phase commit. With the use of sub-transactions, which are associated with a corresponding compensating transaction, we can build transactional safe business scenarios that span over multiple microservices.

---

[3]https://redis.io/
[4]http://www.ehcache.org/
[5]https://hazelcast.org/
[6]http://www.oracle.com/technetwork/middleware/coherence/overview/index.html

CHAPTER 6

Microservices Governance

The microservices architecture inherently has to deal with dozens to hundreds or thousands of services. When you operate at that scale, you need to have some governance processes in place. However, using a strict centralized governance process will hinder the autonomy of the microservices architecture. Therefore, we need to rethink a strategy for microservices governance.

In this chapter, we walk through the requirements for microservices governance and delve deep into a few key aspects of it, such as *service registry* and *governance*. The rest of the governance topics are covered in the upcoming chapters.

Why Microservices Governance?

Service Oriented Architecture (SOA) governance was one of the key driving forces behind the operational success of SOA and it provides cooperation and coordination between different entities in an organization (development teams, service consumers, etc.). Although it defines a comprehensive set of theoretical concepts as part of SOA governance, only a handful of concepts are being actively used in practice.

When we shift into a microservices architecture, most of the useful governance concepts are also being discarded. The governance concept in microservices is just interpreted[1] as a decentralized process, which gives each team/entity the freedom to govern their own domain, in the way they prefer. Decentralized governance is applicable to the service development, deployment, and execution processes, but there's a lot more to it than that. Let's take a closer look at various aspects of microservices governance and see how we can implement them in practice.

---

[1]https://martinfowler.com/articles/microservices.html#DecentralizedGovernance

© Kasun Indrasiri and Prabath Siriwardena 2018
K. Indrasiri and P. Siriwardena, *Microservices for the Enterprise*, https://doi.org/10.1007/978-1-4842-3858-5_6

Aspects of Microservices Governance

Microservices governance comprises various practices that are coordinated together to realize a real-world scenario. Most of these concepts are not new but ones that we have successfully used in the SOA governance. They are equally applicable under the microservices architecture.

Service Definition

Any microservice that we develop must have enough information to uniquely identify itself, its functionality, and how a consumer should consume it. Therefore, it must have a mechanism to specify the service definition and it should be readily available to the service consumers.

There are several technologies (discussed in Chapter 3, "Inter-service Communication")—such as OpenAPI (Swagger), GrahQL schema, gRPC, and protocol buffer—that define service interfaces. These allow you to define the service identifiers, service interfaces (i.e., the available service functionalities), and service message models (schema or message format of the service requests and responses). Other service metadata, such as service ownership and service level agreements (SLAs), can also be part of the service definition.

Service definitions are often stored in a central repository, to which the consumers have access and the service owners can publish.

Service Registry and Discovery

The service registry is the place where you can store the service definitions, so that the service providers can make their services available and known to the consumers. Service consumers locate the services that they want to invoke using the service registry. The service metadata, which are part of the service definition (such as service URL, message models, supported functionalities, etc.), can be retrieved via the service registry.

The service registry defines an API to publish and access service definitions. When a service is created or updated, the service owners should publish the service definition to the service registry and the consumers can discover services during the runtime using a service discovery mechanism. Later in the chapter, we take a closer look at the most commonly used service registries and discovery mechanisms in the microservices architecture.

Service Lifecycle Management

Microservices have different lifecycle stages, which include *planning*, *designing*, *implementing*, *deploying*, *maintaining*, and *decommissioning*. Given the decentralized nature of microservices, often these tasks are owned by the team who owns each microservice. In most practical scenarios, it is common to have uniform lifecycle stages for your microservices irrespective of the business scope and the technologies that you use to develop them. The service lifecycle management techniques are centrally applied to your microservices architecture. This includes the deployment lifecycle management, how to version your services, etc. Most of these capabilities are implemented as part of API management or control planes in the service mesh. We discuss them in detail in Chapter 9, "Service Mesh," and Chapter 10, "APIs, Events, and Streams".

Quality of Service (QoS)

There are several Quality of Services (QoS) aspects that you need to consider prior to exposing a service to your consumers. The service may be exposed as a secured service, which leverages various security protocols and standards (starting from transport layer security, access tokens, etc.). Also you may control access to the service using rate-limiting and throttling. Caching and incorporating various hooks into monitoring and monetization are some other prominent QoS features. Most of these requirements are directly related to the governance of your microservices and often centrally controlled.

We cover the microservices security fundamentals and use cases in detail in Chapter 11, "Microservice Security Fundamentals," and Chapter 12, "Securing Microservices".

Service Observability

When your application interacts with multiple microservices, it is vital to have metrics, tracing, logging, visualization, and alerting capabilities for all your services, so that you will have a clear picture of their interactions and be able to troubleshoot when something goes wrong. All these requirements are consolidated under one concept, called *observability*.

With a microservices architecture, it is likely to have hundreds or thousands of services communicating with each other. The ability to get service metrics, trace messages and service interactions, get service logs, understanding runtime dependencies of services, troubleshoot in the event of a failure, and set alerting for anomalies can all be considered under the umbrella of observability.

Most of the observability tools operate as a centralized entity in which all services can push the required data, which are useful for metrics, tracing, logging, visualization, etc. It's up to the observability tools to analyze the data and process them so that they can derive the required observability related information. We discuss all the technologies and tools that are used for microservices observability in Chapter 13, "Observability".

With that, we have discussed most of the key aspects of microservices governance. Now it's time to take a look at how those concepts can be implemented in practice.

Implementing Microservice Governance

Microservice governance aspects, which we discussed in the previous sections, are implemented under four key categories (see Figure 6-1). While the design, development, and deployment of microservices are not centrally governed, these aspects are implemented as centralized and scalable entities.

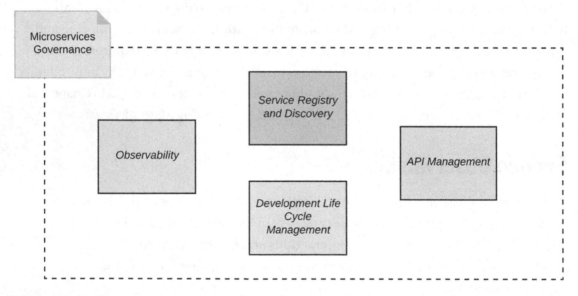

Figure 6-1. *Key components for the realization of microservices governance*

Let's revisit the governance aspects that we discussed in the previous sections and see how and where they are implemented with respect to these components.

Service Registry and Discovery

If we consider service definitions, the definition of service identifiers, message models, interfaces, etc., are the things that you can do without centralized governance. However, these service definitions must be published into a centralized service registry. The service registry is a centralized component, which will also define a canonical model to describe a service. All the service owners should publish their service definitions in that canonical form to the service registry. Even the services are implemented with drastically different technologies (e.g. OpenAPI vs gRPC), you can still find a common metadata for such services and add them to the service registry.

The service registry also comes with a service discovery protocol (or API), which can be used to retrieve service information during runtime. (We will discuss service registry and discovery in detail in the next section.)

Development Lifecycle Management

Service lifecycle management is often implemented at the service deployment level. For example, when a given service has to be deployed across multiple environments, the deployment process will address those requirements of replicating or moving the same service code across those environments. This also includes various DevOps-related deployment methodologies (blue-green, canary, AB testing, etc.) and describes how to manage different environments such as development (dev), test, quality assurance (QA), staging, production (prod), and so on.

API Management/API Gateway

API management plays a key role in the realization of several microservices governance aspects. As discussed in Chapter 1, "The Case for Microservices," the API management layer or API gateway is used to expose your microservices to your consumers as *managed* APIs. This includes all the quality of service aspects that we discussed in the previous sections as well as several other API management specific details, such as monetization. As part of API management, we can apply security, service versioning, throttling, caching, monetization, etc. for services during the runtime. It's important to understand that most of these capabilities have to be applied centrally for service invocations. Therefore, API gateways are centrally governed or managed and application of those capabilities can be either centralized or decentralized. Also, API gateways can be used for external or internal consumers. These capabilities can be equally applicable when microservices talk to each other via an internal API gateway.

API management solutions often work hand-in-hand with service registries to discover services as well as to use them as the API repository (i.e., the information related to APIs can be also published and discovered via a service registry). This is also quite useful when we use existing services and create new APIs out of them.

One other important aspect is that API management solutions provide a rich capability to discover and consume APIs. So, it is possible to leverage API management to manage all your microservices (rather than selecting the service that you want to expose externally).

We'll defer the detailed discussion on these topics to Chapter 10, "APIs, Events, and Streams".

Observability

Observability is something that is generically applicable to all your microservices. Each microservice can push data to any of those observability tools using the recommended observability agents. Observability tools offer a centralized view of all the interactions of your microservices and they operate as passive entities which would not intervene the original flow of business messages. The API management solution or API gateway also work hand-in-hand with observability tools. Most of the observability aspects that we discussed in the previous sections are often applicable to APIs as well.

There are specialized observability tools for each observability aspect, such as metrics, tracing, logging, service visualization, alerting, etc. We'll delve deep into microservices observability in Chapter 13.

Service Registry and Discovery

When you run hundreds or thousands of microservices, it is quite important to have a central place to get the details of services. That's where service registry and discovery come into the picture. In many resources that describe services registry and discovery in the context of microservices, it is explained as a mechanism to obtain the location of the microservice during execution. However, the service registry has a much broader meaning and can be used much more effectively.

Because you have so many services to deal with, it's very important to have a central place where you can obtain all service information. As we discussed in previous sections, service registry is that place where we store all the service definitions (not just the service URLs, as some microservices articles explain). Consumers can get all the service definitions by accessing the service registry. Then the service discovery defines a way to access the service registry. Service owners should register the service at the service registry so that the consumers can discover them. Also, the owners are responsible for updating and maintaining the information of services. The most commonly practiced use cases for service registry and discovery in a microservices architecture is to have addressable names for services that make them independent of the infrastructure that they are running on. For example, when we are doing a service call, we use a name with a logical reference to the service and the service discovery resolves that name to the actual endpoint address of the service. Therefore, external services or consumers do not need to change their code when there's a change in the actual endpoint address.

In general, we can consider service registry to be the repository to publish and retrieve canonical service definitions of all services in your microservices architecture. The mechanism, which we use to retrieve service definitions, is known as service discovery.

Let's discuss some of the commonly used patterns for service registry and discovery. As shown in Figure 6-2, let's take a scenario where we have a client that wants to call a service, but the service address is either not known or dynamically changes. In that case we can use a service registry to store service definitions. The client has to discover the service information by calling the API of the service registry and then use the information retrieved from the registry for the actual service calls. Often, most of the service registries offer a RESTful interface (or gRPC) along with dedicated client libraries to cater to this requirement. This mechanism is known as *client-side service discovery*.

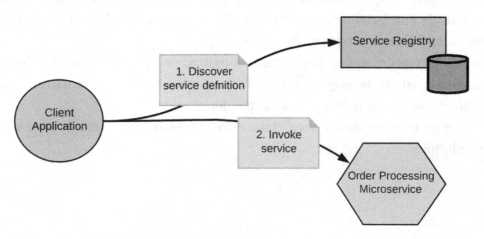

Figure 6-2. *Client-side service discovery*

The other pattern of service discovery (see Figure 6-3) is to offload the service discovery task to an intermediate component such as a load balancer. In this case, the client invokes the service with a predefined URL and the load balancer uses that as a key to resolve the actual URL of the service. In this pattern, the client is unaware of the existence of a service registry. This pattern is known as *server-side service discovery*.

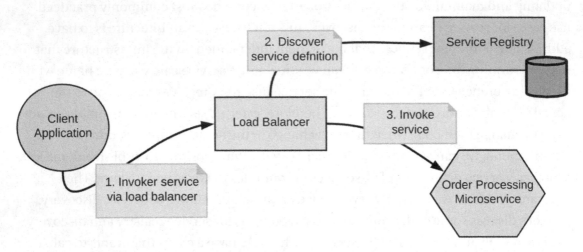

Figure 6-3. *Server-side service discovery*

Client-side discovery is commonly used when the client is fully aware of the existence of the service registry and client code contains the service discovery logic. Server-side discovery is often used with container management systems such as Kubernetes and Docker Swarm, where service discovery is transparent to the client side.

Service registry implementations are not dependent on any of the service discovery mechanisms. In fact, in both cases, either the client or an intermediate application (load balancer) uses the same service registry APIs.

The service registry is often used as the centralized component for service discovery and therefore it can be the single point of failure. Therefore, It's important to ensure high availability of the service registry as part of the deployment.

In the next couple of sections, we'll take a closer look at the commonly used service registry solutions.

Consul

Consul[2] is a distributed, highly available system that is designed for discovering and configuring services. It offers most of the service registry capabilities, so that services can publish service definitions, and clients can use Consul to discover a given service. Using either DNS or HTTP, applications can find the services they depend upon. In addition to the service registry and discovery capabilities, Consul also supports service health checking, a key-value store that can be used for dynamic configuration, feature flagging, coordination, leader election, and more.

Figure 6-4 illustrates the key components of the Consul architecture and how they communicate with each other. Let's next look at the key steps involved in services registry and discovery capabilities of Consul and the responsibility of each Consul components.

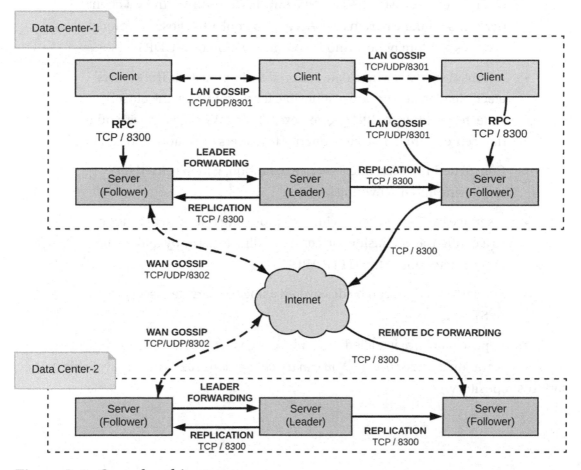

Figure 6-4. *Consul architecture*

---

[2]https://www.consul.io/

These are the key steps to using Consul as the service discovery solution:

- Every node that provides services to Consul should run a Consul agent.

- An agent is the long-running daemon on every member of the Consul cluster. It is started by running the Consul agent. The agent can run in client or server mode. However, an agent is not required for a client that discovers services.

- The agent is responsible for running health checks and keeping services in sync. The agents talk to one or more Consul servers.

- A Consul client is an agent that forwards all RPCs to a server. The client is relatively stateless and the only background activity a client performs is taking part in the LAN gossip pool. (The gossip protocol involves random node-to-node communication over UDP.)

- A Consul server is where data is stored and replicated. The servers elect a leader. Servers are responsible for maintaining the cluster state, responding to RPC queries, exchanging WAN gossip with other datacenters, and forwarding queries to leaders or remote datacenters.

- Consul defines a canonical service definition, which is used for registering and discovering services.

- A service can be registered either by providing a service definition as a configuration (inside the consul.d directory) or by making the appropriate calls to the HTTP API.

- Similarly, services can be discovered using the service discovery REST API.

Let's suppose you have installed[3] Consul. Let's go through the steps involved in service registration and discovery. (You can try ch06/sample01, which is available in the samples repository.)

---

[3]https://www.consul.io/intro/getting-started/install.html

Registering a Service

You can register a Consul service by using a configuration file created inside the consul.d directory and service definition can be placed in a new JSON file in the same directory. Suppose that we created consul/my_consul_config/consul.d and placed the order_service definition in the order_service.json file with the following service definition.

```
{"service": {"name": "order_service", "tags": ["order-mgt"], "port": 80}}
```

You can start Consul by pointing to the same configuration file using:

```
/consul agent -dev -config-dir= /my_home/my_consul_config/consul.d.
```

Alternatively, you can register the service via the catalog REST API[4].

Discovering a Service

Consul REST API provides a convenient way to retrieve the service definitions.

For example, from the client applications, you can get the service definition with a GET request sent to the specified service in the service catalog of Consul.

```
curl http://localhost:8500/v1/catalog/service/order_service
[
    {
        "ID": "b6de0d18-89ab-0d53-223f-1b8ac033265e",
        "Node": "Kasuns-MacBook-Pro.local",
        "Address": "127.0.0.1",
        "Datacenter": "dc1",
        "TaggedAddresses": {
            "lan": "127.0.0.1",
            "wan": "127.0.0.1"
        },
        "NodeMeta": {
            "consul-network-segment": ""
        },
        "ServiceID": "order_service",
```

---

[4]https://www.consul.io/api/catalog.html

```
    "ServiceName": "order_service",
    "ServiceTags": [
        "order-mgt"
    ],
    "ServiceAddress": "",
    "ServiceMeta": {},
    "ServicePort": 80,
    "ServiceEnableTagOverride": false,
    "CreateIndex": 6,
    "ModifyIndex": 6
  }
]
```

All these operations are also exposed via DNS interfaces. There is a wide range of other capabilities offered from Consul, which are not directly related to service registry, and which are not in the scope of this book. But just keep in mind that if you need some sort of key-value pair-based repository with coordination and high-availability support, Consul is a very good solution to incorporate into your microservice architecture.

Eureka

Eureka[5] is another service registry and discovery service, developed by Netflix. At Netflix, it was used in the AWS cloud for locating services for the purpose of load balancing and failover of middle-tier servers (a separate load balancer wraps Eureka to provide weighted load balancing based on several factors). Therefore, the Eureka server primarily functions as a service registry with an interface to discover the services. Eureka provides a REST API[6] and a Java client library, which can be used to register or discover the services. Figure 6-5 shows a high-level overview of the Eureka architecture.

---

[5]https://github.com/Netflix/eureka
[6]https://github.com/Netflix/eureka/wiki/Eureka-REST-operations

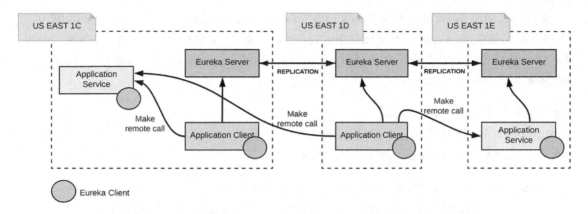

Figure 6-5. *Eureka architecture*

Eureka server is a web application that you can deploy into Tomcat. You can then connect to it via a Eureka client or the REST API. A Eureka client is a Java client that can be used to register heartbeats. As shown in Figure 6-5, you can embed the Eureka client as part of service code or client code. Application Services can use the Eureka client to register services, and application client can use it for discovering services. Services register with Eureka and then send heartbeats to renew their leases every 30 seconds. If the client cannot renew the lease, it is taken out of the server registry after about 90 seconds. The registration information and the renewals are replicated across all the Eureka nodes in the cluster.

There is one Eureka cluster per region (geographic locations such as us-east, us-west, etc.), which knows only about the instances in its region. There is at the least one Eureka server per zone (one region can have multiple zones, which can be considered isolated datacenters) to handle zone failures. The clients from any zone can look up the registry information (which happens every 30 seconds) to locate their services (which could be in any zone) and make remote calls.

Using Eureka with Spring Boot

Spring Boot offers native support for using Eureka as a service registry. Let's take a close look at how you can use Eureka in your Spring Boot applications and use service registry and discovery capabilities in practice.

With some annotations you can quickly enable and configure the service registry and discovery patterns inside your application with Eureka. Eureka instances can be registered, and clients can discover the instances using Spring-managed beans. An embedded Eureka server can be created with a declarative Java configuration.

163

First off, you need to have a Eureka server running. As shown in the sample code of ch06/sample02, you can spin up a Eureka service registry as an Spring application using the Spring Cloud's @EnableEurekaServer annotation. So, your application code looks as follows.

```
@EnableEurekaServer
@SpringBootApplication
public class EurekaServiceApplication {

    public static void main(String[] args) {
        SpringApplication.run(EurekaServiceApplication.class, args);
    }
}
```

This application will boot up a Eureka service registry instance and you can change various behaviors via the application.properties file.

Now let's try to register a service with the service registry from a different Spring Boot application. The application name is fetched from bootstrap.properties of your Spring Boot application.

```
@EnableDiscoveryClient
@SpringBootApplication
public class EurekaClientApplication {
    public static void main(String[] args) {
        SpringApplication.run(EurekaClientApplication.class, args);
    }
}
```

Now you can discover services using another Spring Boot application, which leverages the discovery client to discover the service.

```
@RestController
class ServiceInstanceRestController {

    @Autowired
    private DiscoveryClient discoveryClient;

    @RequestMapping("/service-instances/{applicationName}")
```

```
    public List<ServiceInstance> serviceInstancesByApplicationName(
            @PathVariable String applicationName) {
        return this.discoveryClient.getInstances(applicationName);
    }
}
```

This service retrieves the application name from the Eureka service registry and returns as part of the response.

Etcd

Etcd[7] is a general-purpose, distributed key-value store designed to reliably and quickly, preserve and provide access to critical data. It enables reliable distributed coordination through distributed locking, leader elections, and write-barriers. An etcd cluster is intended for high availability and permanent data storage and retrieval. Therefore, etcd is also being used as a service registry implementation. However, it offers a wide range of capabilities, which are beyond the service registration and discovery. etcd offers a CLI tool called etcdctl and a gRPC API to interact with it.

etcd v3 uses gRPC for its messaging protocol. The etcd project includes a gRPC-based Go client and a command-line utility, etcdctl, for communicating with an etcd cluster through gRPC. For languages with no gRPC support, etcd provides a JSON grpc-gateway. This gateway serves a RESTful proxy that translates HTTP/JSON requests into gRPC messages.

etcd is being widely used as part of most of the existing registry and deployment orchestrator solutions, such as Kubernetes.

Service Discovery with Kubernetes

In the Kubernetes environment, when you call one service from another, you don't need to worry about the actual location of your service. Kubernetes by default uses DNS names to discover the pods. Therefore, if you want to call the bar service from the foo service, in the foo service's code, you can just refer to http://bar:<port> as the service endpoint. Kubernetes will resolve and map the name to the actual endpoint. Kubernetes internally uses etcd as its distributed key-value store.

---

[7]https://coreos.com/etcd/

It's important to keep in mind that, although Kubernetes offers out-of-the-box capabilities to seamless discovery of a service, it is not meant to be used as the repository and interface for service developers or consumers to interact with. That's where you may want to manage such service definitions in an external service registry.

We discuss Kubernetes in detail in Chapter 8, "Deploying and Running Microservices," and will dive into a real-world example that uses service discovery inside Kubernetes.

Summary

In this chapter, we discussed microservices governance in a broad perspective. Rather than just abstracting it as a decentralized process, we took a detailed look at various aspects of microservices governance, such as service definitions, lifecycle management, registry and discovery, quality of service, and observability. While service design, development, and deployment can be done as a fully decentralized process, there are several concepts that you need to centrally apply to your microservices governance. In that context, we introduced key aspects of the implementation of microservices governance—service registry and discovery, development lifecycle management, API management, and observability. We set the foundation for most of these concepts in the context of microservice governance and we deferred a detailed discussion to the upcoming chapters that are dedicated to each of those topics.

We had a detailed discussion of service registry and discovery aspects of microservices governance in this chapter. We discussed the importance of service registry and discovery, and covered a couple of commonly used patterns. Then we discussed some of the most popular service registry solutions, such as Consul and Eureka, with real-world examples.

CHAPTER 7

Integrating Microservices

The microservices architecture fosters building a software application as a suite of independent services. When we have to realize a given business use case, we often need to have the communication and coordination between multiple microservices. Therefore, integrating microservices and building inter-service communication has become the one of the most challenging tasks needed to realize the microservices architecture.

In most of the existing books and other resources, the concepts of microservice integration is barely discussed or is explained in a very abstract manner. Therefore, in this chapter, we delve deep into the key challenges of integrating microservices, patterns for integrating microservices, and frameworks and languages that we can leverage.

Why We Have to Integrate Microservices

Microservices are designed to address specific fine-grained business functionality. Therefore, when you are building a software application using microservices, you have to build a communication structure between these services. As discussed in Chapter 1, "The Case for Microservices," when you are using SOA, you build a set of services (web services) and integrate them using a central bus known as an Enterprise Service Bus (ESB).

As shown in Figure 7-1, with the ESB-based approach, you build business logic as part of this centralized bus as well as various network communication functions such as resilient communication (circuit breaker and timeouts) and quality of service aspects (we discuss these capabilities in detail in the latter part of the chapter).

© Kasun Indrasiri and Prabath Siriwardena 2018
K. Indrasiri and P. Siriwardena, *Microservices for the Enterprise*, https://doi.org/10.1007/978-1-4842-3858-5_7

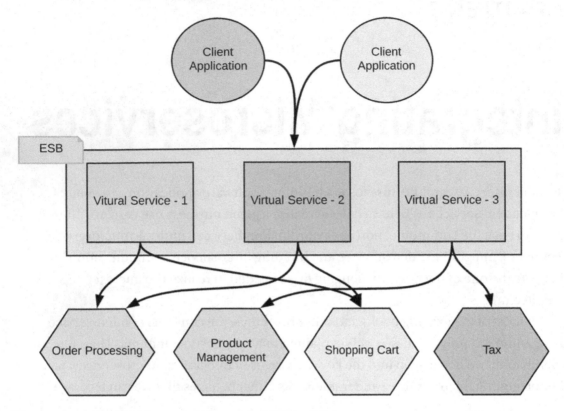

Figure 7-1. *Integrating services with ESB in SOA*

When you do service integration using an ESB, you will have a set of virtual services that are tightly coupled into the centralized ESB runtime. As the ESB layer grows with business and network communication logic, it becomes one gigantic monolithic application in most enterprises. This means it has all the limitations of a monolithic application that we discussed in Chapter 1.

When you move into microservices architecture, you will still need to integrate your microservices to build any meaningful business use cases. There are several important requirements in a microservices architecture that makes the microservice integration quite critical.

- *Microservice composition*: Creating a composite service out of the existing microservices and exposing that as a business functionality to the consumers is one of the most common use cases in microservices architecture. The composition can be built using synchronous communication (active) or using asynchronous (reactive) communication patterns.

- *Building resilient inter-service communication*: All microservice calls take place on the network and are prone to failures. Therefore, we need to implement the stability and resiliency patterns when we make inter-service calls.

- *Granular services and APIs*: Most microservices are too fine-grained to be published as a business functionality/API for the consumers.

- *Microservices in brownfield enterprises*: Microservices in enterprise applications need integration between existing legacy systems, proprietary systems (e.g., ERP systems), databases, and web APIs (e.g., Salesforce).

A microservices architecture favors an alternative approach to using a centralized ESB, which is known as *smart endpoints and dumb pipes.* All the requirements that we discussed above needs to be implement for microservices too. Let's have a closer look at the concept of smart endpoints and dumb pipes.

Smart Endpoints and Dumb Pipes

With the *smart endpoints and dumb pipes* approach, when we have to integrate microservices, we shouldn't be using a centralized monolithic ESB architecture but a fully decentralized approach of services communicating via a dumb messaging infrastructure. All the smarts live in the endpoints (services and consumers) and intermediate-messaging channels have no business or network communication logic. Therefore, as shown in Figure 7-2, integration of microservices is taken care by some other set of microservices. They are responsible for the integration logic as well as the network communication to invoke those services. These services may be built using different technologies and, unlike ESB, each integration service is autonomous.

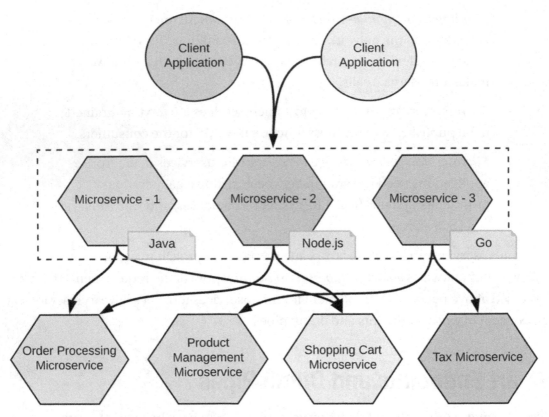

Figure 7-2. *Smart endpoints and dumb pipes: All smarts live in the endpoint (service) level while they communicate via a dumb messaging infrastructure*

Although this approach looks far more elegant than the conventional centralized ESB, there are several complexities that the developers have to deal with. First and foremost, we should clearly understand that this approach doesn't remove any of the complexities in business or network communication in the ESB approach. Which means that you need to implement all the capabilities that your service integration logic requires, as part of your service. For instance, microservice-1 should contain the composition of multiple data types from the `Order Processing` and `Shopping Cart` microservices and resilient communication to invoke those services (such as circuit breakers, failovers, etc.). It must also include any other cross-cutting capabilities that you will require (such as security and observability). Also, if you are using polyglot microservices technologies, it's more likely that you have to repeat the same implementation for commodity features such as resilient communication using multiple technologies.

It's crucial to take these requirements of microservice integration into consideration when picking technologies for implementation. We'll dive into the specifics of the requirements and the technologies that fit those requirements in the latter half of this chapter. But before that, it's important to discuss some of the common anti-patterns related to microservices integration that you should avoid.

Anti-Patterns of Microservice Integration

There are several anti-patterns in integrating microservices that we should be aware of. Most of these patterns have emerged because of the complexity of integrating microservices and trying to replicate the same set of features that a centralized ESB offers with the microservices architecture.

Monolithic API Gateway for Integrating Microservices

One common anti-pattern is to use an API gateway as the service integration (or composition) layer to expose business services to the consumers. For example, suppose you have developed several microservices and the business functionality that you want to expose needs to have some collaboration (or orchestration) between multiple services. What you need to build is a composite microservice that talks to a couple of downstream services and exposes the composite functionality. In many microservices implementations, we developed the integration logic as part of the API gateway, which is more or less a monolithic component. There are many real-world examples from the existing microservices implementations. For example, Figure 7-3 illustrates how the Netflix API gateway[1] was initially implemented.

---

[1] https://medium.com/netflix-techblog/engineering-trade-offs-and-the-netflix-api-re-architecture-64f122b277dd

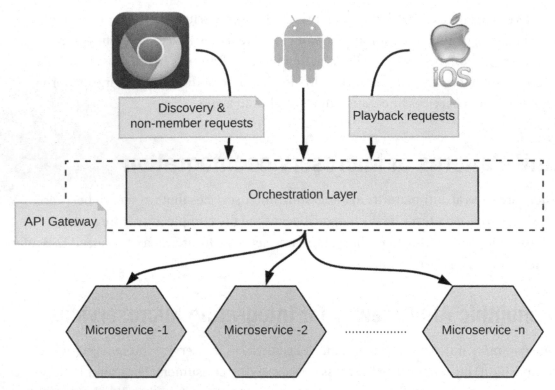

Figure 7-3. *Netflix API gateway: service integration is done at the API gateway level and multiple APIs are part of the monolithic API gateway layer*

Netflix is probably the most popular and successful microservices implementation out there. Netflix exposes their internal services through the Netflix API layer. They explain the functionality of the Netflix API as follows:

> *The Netflix API is the "front door" to the Netflix ecosystem of microservices. As requests come from devices, the API provides the logic of composing calls to all services that are required to construct a response. It gathers whatever information it needs from the backend services, in whatever order needed, formats and filters the data as necessary, and returns the response. So, at its core, the Netflix API is an orchestration service that exposes coarse-grained APIs by composing fined grained functionality provided by the microservices.*

You can clearly observe that the orchestration layer, which is a monolithic component, contains a significant portion of the business logic in this scenario. This leads to numerous trade-offs that are associated with monolithic applications that we discussed in earlier chapters (such as no failure isolation, can't scale independently, ownership issues, etc.).

Netflix has identified the drawbacks to the approach and introduced a new architecture for the very same scenario with a segregated API gateway layer, which is no longer monolithic. As shown in Figure 7-4, at the API gateway layer, each composition service is implemented as an independent entity.

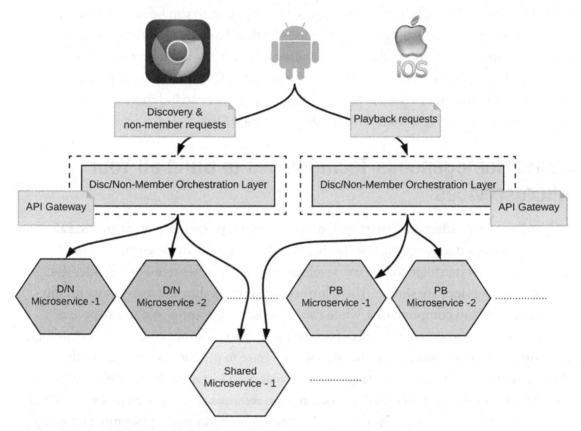

Figure 7-4. *Netflix API gateway with independent APIs that integrate microservices*

This approach is pretty much the same as introducing an integration service that is not part of a monolithic runtime and enforces the API gateway related functionality as part of the service runtime. They also tried another alternative of keeping the API gateway as dumb as possible and introducing a composite service where API gateway simply acts as a pass-through runtime.

The key takeaway from this use case is that you shouldn't be using an API gateway as a monolithic runtime to put the business logic. The service integration or composition logic must be part of another microservice (either at the API gateway layer or at the services layer).

Integrating Microservice with an ESB

There are some microservices implementations that bring in ESB back to a microservices architecture, by using ESB as a runtime to implement the service integration. In most cases, ESB is deployed in a container to serve the service integration of a specific use case. However, ESB has inherent limitations, such as too bulky to be run as a container, not so developer friendly because of the configuration-based integration, etc. In fact, there are some ESB vendors who try to promote this pattern, but this is something that you should avoid while integrating microservices. (There are also container friendly and lightweight versions of ESBs which can be used to independently integrate microservices, which is far better than using a central ESB.)

Using Homogeneous Technologies to Build all Your Microservices

We've discussed earlier that smart endpoints and dumb pipes literally means that all the cool features that we get out-of-the-box with ESBs now have to be implemented as part of our service logic. When we develop microservices, we need to consider that not all microservices are similar. There are certain services that will focus more on the business logic and computations, while some services are more about inter-service communications and network calls. If we stick to a single homogenous set of technologies to build all these microservices, and then we will have to put more effort into building the core components for integrating microservices than focusing on the business logic of the service. For example, service integration often requires service discover and resilient communication (such as circuit breakers). Some frameworks or programming languages offer these capabilities out-of-the-box while some don't. Therefore, your architecture should be flexible enough to pick the right technology for the job.

Organizing Microservices

Identifying different types of microservices based on their interactions and using the most appropriate technologies to build them is the key to building a successful microservices architecture. If we take a closer look at the microservices implementation, we can identify different types of services that we can categorize into a few different categories. Based on service functionalities and granularities, we can identify the following service categories.

Core Services

There are microservices that are fine-grained, self-contained (with no external service dependencies) and mostly consist of the business logic with little or no network communication logic. Given that these services do not have significant network communication functionalities, you are free to select any service implementation technology that can fulfill the service's business logic. Also, these services may have their own private databases that are leveraged to build the business logic. Such microservices can be categorized as *core* or *atomic* microservices.

Integration Services

Core microservices often cannot be directly mapped to business functionalities, as they are too fine-grained. And any realistic business capability would require the interactions or composition of multiple microservices. Such interactions or compositions are implemented as an *integration service* or a composite service. These services often have to support a significant portion of ESB functionalities such as routing, transformations, orchestration, resiliency and stability patterns etc., at the service level itself.

Integration services serve a composite business functionality, are independent from each other, and contain business logic (routing, what services to call, how to do data type mapping, etc.) and network communication logic (inter-service communication through various protocols and resiliency behaviors such as circuit breakers). Also, they may or may not have private databases associated with the business functionality of the service. These services can bridge the other legacy and proprietary systems (e.g., ERP systems), external web APIs (e.g., Salesforce), shared databases, etc. (often known as the anti-corruption layer).

It's very important to select the appropriate service development technology for building integration microservices. Since network communication is a critical part of integration services, you should select the most suitable technology for implementing these services. In the latter part of this chapter, we discuss the technologies and frameworks that are suitable for building these services.

API Services

You will expose a selected set of your composite services or even some core services as managed APIs using API services or edge services. These services are a special type of integration services, which apply basic routing capabilities, versioning of APIs, API security, throttling, monetization, API compositions, etc.

In most of these microservices implementations, API services are implemented as part of a monolithic API gateway runtime, and this violates the core microservices architectural concepts. However, most of the API gateway solutions are now moving toward a micro-gateway capability in which you can deploy your API services on an independent and lightweight runtime, while you manage them centrally. When it comes to implementation, the requirements are pretty similar to the integration services and we will require some additional features. We discuss API services and API management in a more broad way in Chapter 10, "APIs, Events, and Streams".

Since we have a good understanding of the different types of microservices, let's discuss some of the microservices integration patterns that we can commonly use.

Microservices Integration Patterns

We have found seams in different microservices categories, so now it's time to see how they can be used in real-world applications. When it comes to integrating microservices, we can identify a couple of integration patterns. Let's discuss them in detail and see the pros and cons along with when to use those patterns.

Active Composition or Orchestration

Microservice integration can be implemented in such a way that a given (integration) microservice actively calls several other services (can be core or composite service). The business logic and the network communication are built as part of the integration service. The integration microservice should formulate business functionality out of the composition that it does. For example, as illustrated in Figure 7-5, `microservice-1` calls `microservice-4` and `microservice-5` synchronously. The business capability that `microservice-1` offers is a composition of the capabilities of `microservice-4` and `microservice-5`. Also, the integration service that we develop can be exposed as an API via the API gateway layer.

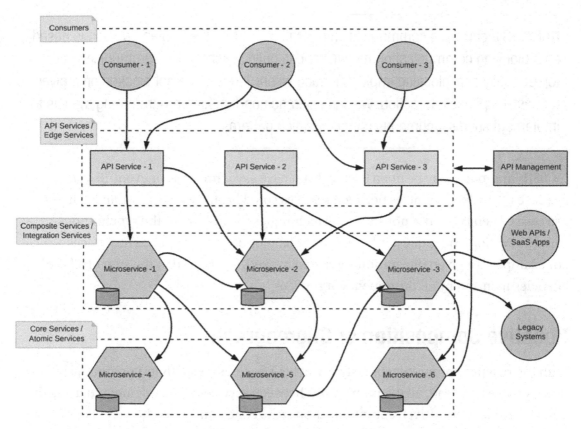

Figure 7-5. *Active composition of microservices: a given integration microservice calls multiple microservices and formulates a business capability*

The key concept here is that, with an active composition, we create an integration service that's dependent on some other set of microservices. If you consider the theoretical aspects that we discussed in the first few chapters, this seems like a violation of the microservices principles. But it's virtually impossible to build anything useful without depending on the other services and systems. What really important here is to understand the boundaries between these services and clearly define the capabilities.

Active compositions are commonly used when we need to control the service integration at a centralized service and when communication between dependent services is synchronous. Once you clearly define the business capability for an integration service, the business logic of it resides in a single service. That makes management and maintenance quite easier.

Note   Synchronous communication doesn't mean that the implementation is based on a blocking communication model. We can build synchronous communication on top of a fully non-blocking implementation where threads are not blocked on a given request-response interaction. We can leverage non-blocking programming models to implement such synchronous communication patterns.

This approach may be not a best fit if you have asynchronous or event-driven use cases. The dependencies between services could be an issue for certain business use cases. Even if you use non-blocking techniques to implement the synchronous communication, the request is bound to the latency of all the dependent services. For example, if a given integration service is invoked, it is bound to the sum of all the latencies incurred by all the dependent services.

Reactive Composition or Choreography

With the reactive communication style, we don't have a service that synchronously calls other services. Instead, all the interactions between services are implemented using the asynchronous event-driven communication style. For example, as shown in Figure 7-6, the communication between the microservices and the consumer application is done via event-driven asynchronous messaging. Therefore, we need to use an event bus as the messaging backbone. The event bus is a dumb messaging infrastructure and all the logic resides at the service level.

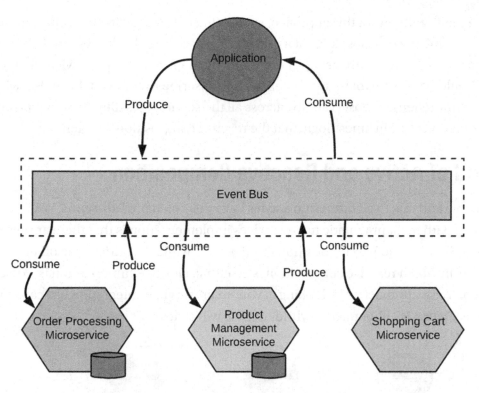

Figure 7-6. *Reactive compositions with asynchronous event-driven communication*

As discussed in Chapter 3, "Inter-Service Communication," the communication can be either queue-based (a single consumer) or pub-sub (multiple consumers). Based on your requirements, you can use Kafka, RabbitMQ, or ActiveMQ etc. as the event bus.

Reactive composition makes microservices inherently autonomous. Since we don't have a service that contains the centralized composition logic, these microservices are not dependent on each other. They only become active when a given event occurs and then it processes the message and completes the work once the result is published to the event bus.

Note   Event stream processing or complex event processing can be considered a more powerful way to process a stream of events. Here we only discussed the event-based messaging. We discuss event stream processing in detail in Chapter 10.

The main tradeoffs of this approach, such as the complexity in communication and not having the business logic at a centralized service, make the system really hard to understand. Since we are using an event bus/message bus, all the services that we write should have the capability to publish and subscribe to the event bus. Also, without having comprehensive observability, across all the services, it's difficult to understand the interactions and business logic that the reactive compositions implement.

Hybrid of Active and Reactive Composition

Both active and reactive composition styles have their own pros and cons. What we have seen with most pragmatic microservices implementation is that there are certain scenarios in which active composition is the best fit, while there are some other scenarios in which reactive composition is essential. Our recommendation is to use a hybrid of these approaches by looking at your microservices integration use cases. For instance, Figure 7-7 illustrates a hybrid of these two styles.

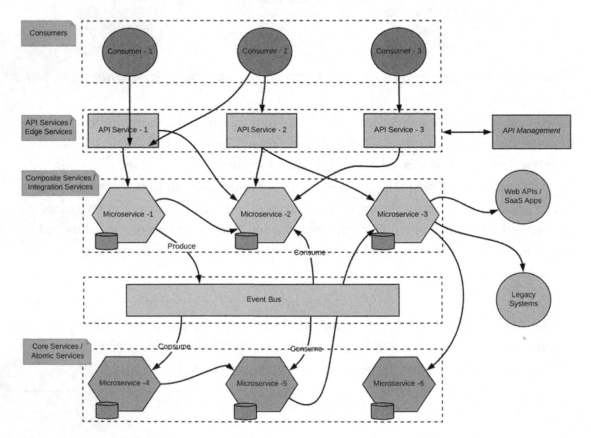

Figure 7-7. *Hybrid of an active and reactive microservices integration*

Often there are services that you would expose to the consumers as APIs that are fully synchronous. Such API calls will result in several other microservices calls where some invocations can be/should be done using a reactive approach. As discussed in Chapter 3, scenarios such as order placing and processing in a retail business use case are much more elegant when implemented with a reactive style. Hence, you have to pick and choose the style that you want to use, depending on your business use cases.

A hybrid composition is usually more pragmatic for most enterprise microservice integrations.

Anti-Corruption Layer

You can introduce a microservices architecture into an enterprise while some of its subsystems are still based on a monolithic architecture. We can build a façade or an adapter layer between the microservices and monolithic subsystems. In Chapter 2, "Designing Microservices," we discussed the anti-corruption layer, which allows you to independently develop either the microservices components or existing monolithic applications The applications built on top of these two different architectural styles can interact with each other via the anti-corruption layer. The technologies and standards that are used for the monolithic portion and the microservices portion may be drastically different. That's why building anti-corruption layer is often required when it comes to building microservices integrations.

For instance, in our hybrid composition use case that we discussed in Figure 7-7, `microservice-3` integrates the microservices subsystem with proprietary, legacy, and external web APIs, which are all part of the monolithic subsystem. That service is part of the anti-corruption layer. Typically, the technologies that you would use for building integration microservices can also be used for building services at the anti-corruption layer.

Strangler Façade

In the context of microservices in enterprises, you will often have to deal with the existing non-microservice subsystems. By introducing a microservices architecture, you will be gradually replacing most of the existing subsystems. However, this is not something that will happen overnight. The *strangler pattern* proposes an approach that helps you incrementally migrate a non-microservice subsystem by gradually replacing specific pieces of functionality with new microservices. If you are introducing microservices to an enterprise, you will build a strangler façade that will selectively route the traffic between the modern and legacy systems. Over time, you will entirely replace the legacy system with the new microservices and will get rid of the strangler layer.

Key Requirements of Integration Services

By now you have a good understanding of the importance of integration microservices and microservice integration patterns. Let's delve deep into the technologies that we can leverage to implement those patterns. However, before we do that, it will be beneficial to have a clear understanding of the specific requirements for building integration microservices.

Network Communication Abstractions

As we discussed in detail in Chapter 3, inter-microservice communication is absolutely essential to building a microservices-based application. Services are autonomous and the only way they interact and formulate business functionality is through inter-service communication. Therefore, for integration services, we must support different communication patterns such as synchronous and asynchronous communication and the associated network protocols.

In practice, for synchronous communication, RESTful services are heavily in use and native support for RESTful services and HTTP 1.1 is crucial. Also, many service implementation frameworks now leverage HTTP2 as the default communication protocol to benefit from all the new capabilities introduced in HTTP2.

Under the context of synchronous communication, gRPC services are proliferating and most of the microservice implementations use it as the de-facto standard for internal microservices communication. Given that gRPC and protocol buffers[2] cater to polyglot microservices implementations, they inherently cater to most of the inter-service communication requirements of microservices built with different languages.

Asynchronous service integrations are primarily built around queue-based communication (single receiver) and technologies such as AMQP are quite commonly used in practice. For pub-sub (event-driven multiple receiver communication), Kafka has become the de-facto standard for inter-service communication.

---

[2]https://developers.google.com/protocol-buffers/

What we have discussed so far covers the standards and the latest technologies that are commonly used for inter-microservice communication. How do we communicate with legacy or proprietary systems in our enterprise microservices ecosystem? In fact, microservices implementation technologies must cater to those legacy and proprietary integration use cases too. For instance, if you are using an ERP system in your enterprise, you can't build a useful application without interacting with it. Hence, if required, the microservice must be able to communicate with such legacy or proprietary systems. This leads us to think that microservices implementation technologies should be able to handle any of the network communication protocols that an ESB supports.

> *The things that you developed at the centralized ESB now must be implemented in your integration microservices. Microservices implementation technologies should cater to all of the capabilities that an ESB offers.*

In addition to the primitive network communication protocols, microservices often need to integrate with web APIs such as Twitter, Salesforce, Google Docs, PayPal, Twilio, etc. While there are SaaS applications that offer network accessible APIs, most of the integration products such as ESBs have high-level abstractions that allow you to integrate with these systems with minimal effort. Ultimately, the integration microservices implementation technologies need to have a certain set of abstractions to integrate with such web APIs. (For example, libararies or connectors to access web APIs such as Twitter API, PayPal API etc.)

Resiliency Patterns

As discussed in Chapter 2, one of the key fallacies of distributed computing is that the network be reliable. Inter-microservice communication or integration microservices must always worry about microservices communication over unreliable networks.

> *Now and forever, networks will always be unreliable.*
>
> —*Michael Nygard, "Release It"*

Michael Nygard discusses several patterns related to inter-application communication over unreliable network in his book, *Release It*. In this chapter, we take a closer look at the behavior of those patterns, in order to try to understand them using real-world use cases and look at some of the implementation details.

Timeout

When we are using synchronous inter-service communication, one service (caller) sends a request and waits for a response in a timely manner. Timeout is all about deciding when to stop waiting for a response at the caller service level. When you call another service or a system using a specific protocol (i.e., HTTP), you can specify a timeout, and if that timeout is reached, you can define a specific logic to handle such events.

It's important to keep in mind that a timeout is an application level thing and shouldn't be confused with any similar implementations at the protocol level. For instance, when a given integration microservice calls two microservice A and B, the integration microservice can define a timeout value for service A and B separately. Timeouts help services isolate failures. A misbehavior or an anomaly of another system or service does not have to become your service's problem. When you place a timeout while calling an external service and have specific logic to handle such events, this makes it easier to isolate failures as well as handle failures gracefully.

Circuit Breaker

When you are invoking external services or systems, they may fail due to various errors. In such cases you might want to wrap that invocation with an object that monitors and prevents further damage to the system. Circuit breakers are such wrapper objects and we can use them when invoking external services and systems. The main idea behind using a circuit breaker is, if the service invocation fails and reaches a certain threshold, then the circuit breaker wrapper prevents any further invocation of the external service. Rather it immediately returns from the circuit breaker with an error. Figure 7-8 shows the behavior of the circuit breaker when it is in the closed and open states.

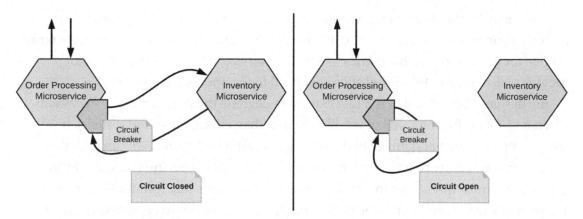

Figure 7-8. *Behavior of circuit breaker. When the circuit is closed, the circuit breaker wrapper object allows the service calls to go through to the external service. When the circuit is open, it prevents the invocations of the external service and returns immediately.*

When there is an invocation failure, a circuit breaker keeps that state and updates the threshold count and, based on the threshold count or frequency of the failure count, it opens the circuit. When the circuit is open, the real invocation of the external service is prevented, and the circuit breaker generates an error and returns immediately.

When the circuit is in an open state for a certain period of time, we can apply a self-resetting behavior by trying the service invocation again (for a new request) after a suitable interval and resetting the breaker should it succeed. This time interval is known as circuit reset timeout. With this behavior, we can identify three different states in the circuit breaker, which are depicted in Figure 7-9.

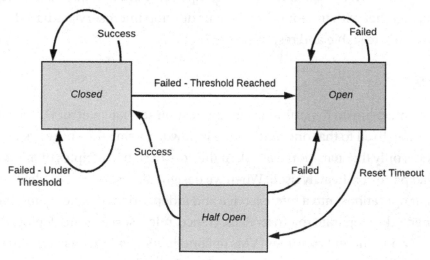

Figure 7-9. *Circuit breaker's states*

We can consider that when the reset timeout is reached, the circuit state is changed to the half-open state, where the circuit breaker allows another invocation of the external service for a new request that comes to the microservice. If it succeeds, the circuit breaker will change to the closed state again and to the open state otherwise.

By design, circuit breaker is a mechanism to degrade the performance of a system when it is not performing well or is failing (rather than failing the entire system). It will prevent any further damage to the system or cascading failures. We can tune the circuit breaker with various backoff mechanisms, timeouts, reset intervals, and error codes that it must directly go into open states, or error codes that it should ignore, etc. These behaviors are implemented at different levels with different complexities using various circuit breaker implementations. It is important to keep in mind that the circuit breaker behavior has a closer relationship with the business requirements of a particular microservices based application.

Fail Fast

In the fail fast pattern, the key objective is to detect a failure as quickly as possible. It is built around the concept that a failure response is much better than a slow failure response. Hence, detecting a failure at the early stages is an important factor during inter-service communication. We can detect failures at different stages of the inter-service communication. In certain situations, just by looking at the contents of the request/message, we can decide that this request is not a valid one. In other cases, we can check for the system resources (such as thread pools, connections, socket limits, and databases) and the state of the downstream components of the request lifecycle.

Fail fast, together with timeouts, will help us develop microservices based applications that are stable and responsive.

Bulkhead

Bulkhead is a mechanism to partition your application so that an error that occurs in a partition is localized to that one partition only. It won't bring the entire system to an unstable state; only that partition will fail. At the core design principles of microservices, the bulkhead pattern is heavily used. When we design microservices, we deliberately group similar operations into a microservice and independent business functionalities are implemented as separate microservices. Hence, microservices are deployed independently on different runtimes (VMs or containers), which means a failure of a given functionality would not affect the other functionalities.

However, for some reason, if you have to implement two or more business functionalities inside a single service, you need to take precautions to partition your service so that failure of a certain set of business operations will not affect the rest of the operations. In general, it is recommended to identify such independent operations and covert them to microservices if possible. However, if you can't split them into services, there are certain techniques to implements bulkheads within a single service/application. For example, we can have a dedicated resource (such as a thread pool, storage, or database) to handle different partitions of a service.

Load Balancing and Failover

The key ideas behind load balancing and failover are quite simple. Load balancing is used to distribute the load across multiple microservice instances, while failover is used to reroute requests to alternate services if a given service fails. In the conventional middleware implementation such as ESBs, these functionalities are also implemented as part of the service logic. However, with the advancement of containers and container management systems such as Kubernetes, most of these functionalities are now built into the deployment ecosystem itself. Also, most of the cloud infrastructure vendors, such as Amazon Web Services (AWS), Google Cloud, and Azure offer these capabilities as part of their infrastructure as a service (IaaS) offerings. We discuss containers and Kubernetes in detail in Chapter 8, "Deploying and Running Microservices".

Active or Reactive Composition

As we discussed in the section on microservices integration patterns, building active or reactive service compositions is absolutely vital to any real-world microservices implementation. Therefore, microservice integration technologies should support building active and reactive compositions. At the implementation level this means the ability to invoke services through different protocols, use supporting components such as circuit breakers, and create composite business logic. For active compositions, support for synchronous service invocations (implemented on top of non-blocking threads with callbacks) is quite important. For reactive compositions, support for messaging styles such as pub-sub and queue-based messaging is required along with seamless integration with messaging backbones such as Kafka or RabbitMQ. Also, different message exchange patterns need to be implemented at the service level—the ability to mix and match such patterns is required. For example, the inbound request may be an asynchronous message, while the external (outbound) service invocations are synchronous. Therefore, we should be able to mix and match these message-exchange patterns.

Data Formats

When we are building compositions, we must create compositions out of different data formats. For instance, a given microservice will be exposed via a given data format (for inbound requests), while it invokes other services (outbound), for which use different data formats. When we create compositions of these services, we must do type matching between these data formats and implement our service in a type-safe manner. Therefore, service implementation technologies that we are using should worry about all the different data formats and should provide a convenient way to handle those formats. Data formats such as JSON, Avro, CSV, XML, protocol buffers, are widely used in practice.

Container-Native and DevOps Ready

Microservices development technologies that we use should be cloud-native and container-native. The same applies to integration services. When you are building an integration service, the development technologies that you use have to be cloud- and container-native. When we were discussing the anti-patterns for microservices integration, using ESB for integrating microservices was heavily discouraged. The primary reason behind that is that almost all the ESB technologies are NOT cloud- or container-native.

For a technology to be cloud- or container-native, the runtime should start within a few seconds (or less), the memory footprint, CPU consumption and storage required must be extremely low. Therefore, when selecting a technology for microservice integration, we should consider all these aspects.

In addition to the container-native aspects of the runtime, the integration microservice development technologies have to worry about native integrations with containers and container management systems such as Kubernetes. What this means is how easily you can create a container out of the applications or services that you develop. Having support to configure and create the container-related artifacts with your service development technology will vastly improve the agility of your microservices development process. We cover the details of containers, Docker, and Kubernetes in Chapter 8.

Governance of Integration Services

We covered governance aspects of microservices in Chapter 6, "Microservices Governance". Some governance aspects, such as observability, are extremely crucial when we build microservice integrations. For instance, let's revisit the hybrid composition scenario that we discussed earlier (see Figure 7-10).

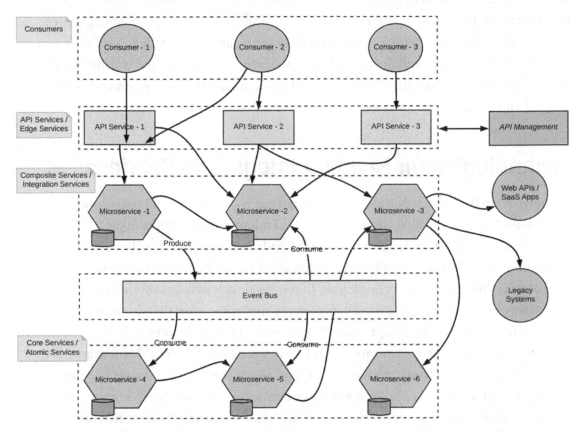

Figure 7-10. *Observability is mandatory with complex microservice integrations*

Figure 7-10 shows that you can clearly see all the interaction between microservices and we can get a clear idea about all the business use cases. However, just think about how these interactions look at the operational level. We will not have this kind of a view if we don't have a proper observability mechanism in place. As part of the integration service development technology, we need to have a seamless way to integrate existing observability tools to get the metrics, tracing, logging, service visualization, and alerting for your integration services.

Stateless, Stateful, or Long-Running Services

Microservices design favors stateless immutable services and most of the use cases can be realized with the use of such stateless services. However, there are many use cases, such as business processes, workflows, and so on, that require stateful and long-running services. In the context of conventional integration middleware, such requirements are implemented and supported at the ESB or business process solution level. With microservices, these requirements have to built from the ground up, so having native support at the integration microservice level for such capabilities will be useful.

The ability to build workflows, business processes, and distributed transactions with SAGAs (which is discussed in Chapter 5, "Data Management") is a key requirement of stateful and long-running services.

Technologies for Building Integration Services

From what we have discussed so far in this chapter, it should be clear that there is no silver-bullet technology that we can use to build microservices. There are different types of microservices and each microservice addresses a drastically different set of requirements. Hence, to realize such microservices, we need to leverage polyglot microservice development technologies. In this section, we discuss some of the most commonly used microservices development technologies; ones that are more suitable for building microservice compositions or integration microservices.

There are microservices frameworks that are built on top of generic programming languages such as Java and provide abstractions via different technologies to cater to microservice composition. Integration frameworks, on the other hand, are not solely targeted to build microservices (rather they are built to address the generic enterprise integration requirements), but still they can be used to integrate microservices. Also, there are certain programming languages that cater to such microservice integration needs out-of-the-box.

Let's take a closer look at some of the microservice development frameworks, integration frameworks, and generic programming languages that are commonly used in practice.

Note   If you find any issues in building or running the examples given in this book, refer to the README file under the corresponding chapter in the Git repository: `https://github.com/microservices-for-enterprise/ samples.git`. We will update the examples and the corresponding README files in the Git repository to reflect any changes related to the tools, libraries, and frameworks used in this book.

Spring Boot

Spring Boot is a microservice framework built on top of the Spring platform by taking an opinionated view of the Spring platform and third-party libraries, so that you can get started with minimum fuss. Spring Boot makes it easy to create standalone, production-grade Spring based applications that you can *just run*. You can write most of the Spring Boot microservices with no or minimal spring configuration. Spring Boot tries to make microservices implementation trivial by offering the following capabilities:

- Create stand-alone Spring applications.

- Embed Tomcat, Jetty, or Undertow directly (no need to deploy WAR files).

- Provide opinionated *starter* POMs to simplify your Maven configuration.

- Automatically configure Spring whenever possible.

- Provide production-ready features such as metrics, health checks, and externalized configuration.

- Absolutely no code generation and no requirement for XML configuration.

Let's discuss some of the key features that are essential for integrating microservices offered by Spring Boot.

RESTful Services

You can build composition microservices using Spring Boot's service development features. For example, you can build a simple RESTful service using Spring Boot as follows.

Suppose that you need to build an HTTP RESTful service that handles GET requests for a /greeting endpoint, optionally with a name parameter in the query string. The GET request should return a 200 OK response with a JSON payload in the body that represents a greeting. As the first step, to model the greeting, you need to define a representation for the greeting as follows.

```
package com.apress.ch07;

public class Greeting {

    private final long id;
    private final String content;

    public Greeting(long id, String content) {
        this.id = id;
        this.content = content;
    }

    public long getId() {
        return id;
    }

    public String getContent() {
        return content;
    }
}
```

Then you can create the service and resource that will serve the greeting requests. In Spring's approach to building RESTful web services, we have a controller to handle HTTP requests. These components are easily identified by the @RestController annotation, and the GreetingController class handles the GET requests for the /greeting endpoint (context) by returning a new instance of the Greeting class:

```
package com.apress.ch07;

import java.util.concurrent.atomic.AtomicLong;
import org.springframework.web.bind.annotation.RequestMapping;
import org.springframework.web.bind.annotation.RequestParam;
import org.springframework.web.bind.annotation.RestController;

@RestController
public class GreetingController {

    private static final String template = "Hello, %s!";
    private final AtomicLong counter = new AtomicLong();

    @RequestMapping("/greeting")
    public Greeting greeting(@RequestParam(value="name",
                    defaultValue="World") String name) {
        return new Greeting(counter.incrementAndGet(),
                            String.format(template, name));
    }
}
```

Since the response format is a POJO, it is explicitly converted to a JSON. If you want to control it, you can do this with @GetMapping(path = "/hello", produces=MediaType. APPLICATION_JSON_VALUE) at the request-mapping level.

You can try this example from our examples in ch07/sample01.

Network Communication Abstractions

Consuming and producing data over the network is supported in Spring Boot via numerous abstractions, as discussed next.

HTTP

You can consume a RESTful service with Spring REST templates. Here we have specified the POJO that we need to convert the response to. The getForObject retrieves a representation by doing a GET on the URL. The response (if any) is converted and returned.

```
RestTemplate restTemplate = new RestTemplate();
        Quote quote = restTemplate.getForObject("http://gturnquist-quoters.
        cfapps.io/api/random", Quote.class);
        log.info(quote.toString());
```

Similarly, `RestTemplate` also supports other HTTP verbs such as POST, PUT, and DELETE. When it comes to create a service that exposes a RESTful service, you can use Spring's support for embedding the Tomcat servlet container as the HTTP runtime, instead of deploying to an external instance. You can try this example from our examples in ch07/sample02.

JMS

Spring Boot also provides abstractions to integrate with other network communication protocols and systems. For example, you can create a service that consumes messages via JMS as follows:

```
@JmsListener(destination = "mailbox", containerFactory = "myFactory")
public void receiveMessage(Email email) {
  System.out.println("Received <" + email + ">");
}
```

The `JmsListener` annotation defines the name of the `Destination` that this method should listen to and the reference to the `JmsListenerContainerFactory` is used to create the underlying message listener container. Passing a value to the `containerFactory` attribute is not necessary unless you need to customize the way the container is built, as Spring Boot registers a default factory if necessary.

The messages can be produced using `JMSTemplates`.

```
public class JmsQueueSender {

    private JmsTemplate jmsTemplate;
    private Queue queue;

    public void setConnectionFactory(ConnectionFactory cf) {
        this.jmsTemplate = new JmsTemplate(cf);
    }

    public void setQueue(Queue queue) {
        this.queue = queue;
    }

    public void simpleSend() {
        this.jmsTemplate.send(this.queue, new MessageCreator() {
```

```
    public Message createMessage(Session session) throws JMSException {
        return session.createTextMessage("hello queue world");
    }
  });
  }
}
```

The `JmsTemplate` contains many convenience methods to send a message. There are send methods that specify the destination using a `javax.jms.Destination` object and those that specify the destination using a string for use in a JNDI lookup. You can try this example from our examples in `ch07/sample03`.

Databases/JDBC

For integrating your microservices with databases via JDBC, Spring provides a template class called `JdbcTemplate` that makes it easy to work with SQL relational databases and JDBC. Most generic JDBC code is full of resource acquisition, connection management, exception handling, and general error checking that is wholly unrelated to what the code is meant to achieve. The `JdbcTemplate` takes care of all of that for you.

```
jdbcTemplate.query(
            "SELECT id, first_name, last_name FROM customers WHERE
            first_name = ?", new Object[] { "Josh" },
            (rs, rowNum) -> new Customer(rs.getLong("id"),
            rs.getString("first_name"), rs.getString("last_name"))
    ).forEach(customer -> log.info(customer.toString()));
```

You can try this example from our examples in `ch07/sample04`. In addition to what we have mentioned, Spring provides the ability to integrate with numerous other network protocols.

Web APIs: Twitter

Integrating with web APIs such as Twitter is something that is supported by Spring Boot's libraries dedicated to each web API. For instance, connecting and tweeting from your Spring Boot microservice is pretty straightforward. You just need to initiate `TwitterTemplate` and call the required operations of it. You can try this example from our examples in `ch07/sample05`.

```
Twitter twitter = new TwitterTemplate(consumerKey, consumerSecret);
twitter.timelineOperations().updateStatus("Microservices for Enterprise.!")
```

As you can see, Spring Boot offers one of the most comprehensive set of capabilities to integrate your microservices with other systems and APIs.

Resiliency Patterns

Spring Boot leverages libraries such as Netflix Hystrix to allow resilient microservices communication. Spring Cloud Netflix Hystrix implementation looks for any method annotated with the @HystrixCommand annotation and wraps that method in a proxy connected to a circuit breaker so that Hystrix can monitor it. For example, in the following code snippet, the method that invokes the external RESTful service is annotated with the @HystrixCommand annotation.

```java
package hello;

import com.netflix.hystrix.contrib.javanica.annotation.HystrixCommand;
import org.springframework.stereotype.Service;
import org.springframework.web.client.RestTemplate;
import java.net.URI;

@Service
public class BookService {

  private final RestTemplate restTemplate;

  public BookService(RestTemplate rest) {
    this.restTemplate = rest;
  }

  @HystrixCommand(fallbackMethod = "reliable")
  public String readingList() {
    URI uri = URI.create("http://localhost:8090/recommended");
    return this.restTemplate.getForObject(uri, String.class);
  }
```

```
public String reliable() {
  return "Microservices for Enterprise (APress)";
  }
}
```

We've applied @HystrixCommand to our original readingList() method. We also have a new method here, called reliable(). The @HystrixCommand annotation has reliable as its fallbackMethod, so if, for some reason, Hystrix opens the circuit on readingList(), we'll have a default result to be shown. You can try this example from our examples in ch07/sample06.

Data Formats

Spring Boot allows you to write your microservices so that they can produce, consume, and transform multiple data formats, by primarily using Jackson[3] data processing tools.

```
// Java Object to JSON
ObjectMapper objectMapper = new ObjectMapper();
Car car = new Car("yellow", "renault");
objectMapper.writeValue(new File("target/car.json"), car);

// JSON to Java Object
String json = "{ \"color\" : \"Black\", \"type\" : \"BMW\" }";
Car car = objectMapper.readValue(json, Car.class);
```

Jackson provides a comprehensive set of data processing capabilities for a diverse set of data types, including the flagship streaming JSON parser/generator library, matching data-binding library (POJOs to and from JSON), and additional data format modules to process data encoded in Avro, BSON, CBOR, CSV, Smile, (Java) Properties, Protobuf, XML or YAML. It even provides a large set of data format modules to support data types of widely used data types such as Guava, Joda, Pcollections, and many, many others. You can try this example from our examples in ch07/sample07.

---

[3]https://github.com/FasterXML/jackson

Observability

You can enable metrics, logging, and distributed tracing for your Spring Boot microservices applications. It requires minimal changes in your microservices application to make your Spring Boot integration microservices observable. When we delve deep into observability concepts in Chapter 13, "Observability," we discuss these capabilities in detail.

Dropwizard

Dropwizard is another popular microservice development framework. The main objective of Dropwizard is to provide performant, reliable implementations of everything a production-ready web application needs. Because this functionality is extracted into a reusable library, your application remains lean and focused, reducing both time-to-market and maintenance burdens.

Dropwizard uses the Jetty HTTP library to embed a tuned HTTP server directly into your project. Jersey is used as the RESTful web application development engine, while Jackson handles the data formats. There are several other libraries that are bundled with Dropwizard by default. However, unlike Spring Boot, for certain microservice integrations that require integration with multiple network protocols and web APIs, there's a limited set of features offered from it out-of-the-box.

Apache Camel and Spring Integration

Apache Camel is a conventional integration framework designed to address the centralized integration/ESB needs. The key objectives of the Apache Camel integration framework is to provide an easy-to-use mechanism for implementing Enterprise Integration Patterns-EIPs such as content-based routing, transformations, protocol switching, scatter-gather, etc., in a trivial way with a small footprint and overhead, embeddable in your existing microservices.

Given its Domain Specific Language (DSL) capabilities to work with multiple languages such as Java, Scala, etc., and lightweight integration framework nature, there are quite a few microservices use cases that Apache Camel can address. Apache Camel has components that can consume and produce messages via almost all the popular network protocols, web APIs, and systems. You can build a Camel based self-contained runtime that can run on a container. (In fact, there are on going efforts on building a container native runtime that natively runs on Kubernetes, called Camel-K). For example, in the following example, you can find a Camel DSL of an integration use case that involves multiple EIPs.

```
public void configure() {
  from("direct:cafe")
    .split().method("orderSplitter")
    .to("direct:drink");

  from("direct:drink").recipientList().method("drinkRouter");

  from("seda:coldDrinks?concurrentConsumers=2")
    .to("bean:barista?method=prepareColdDrink")
    .to("direct:deliveries");
  from("seda:hotDrinks?concurrentConsumers=3")
    .to("bean:barista?method=prepareHotDrink")
    .to("direct:deliveries");

  from("direct:deliveries")
    .aggregate(new CafeAggregationStrategy())
      .method("waiter", "checkOrder").completionTimeout(5 * 1000L)
    .to("bean:waiter?method=prepareDelivery")
    .to("bean:waiter?method=deliverCafes");

}
```

Also, Apache Camel offers seamless integration with Spring Boot, which makes a powerful combination to facilitate microservice integration. You can try this example from our examples in ch07/sample08.

Spring Integration is quite similar to Apache Camel and it extends the Spring programming model to support well-known EIPs. Spring Integration enables lightweight messaging within Spring-based applications and supports integration with external systems via declarative adapters. Those adapters provide a higher level of abstraction over Spring's support for remoting, messaging, and scheduling. Spring Integration's primary goal is to provide a simple model for building enterprise integration solutions while maintaining the separation of concerns that is essential for producing maintainable, testable code.

The following code is an example DSL of a Spring Integration-based use case, which is similar to what we have seen with Camel.

```java
@MessagingGateway
public interface Cafe {
    @Gateway(requestChannel = "orders.input")
    void placeOrder(Order order);
}

private AtomicInteger hotDrinkCounter = new AtomicInteger();
private AtomicInteger coldDrinkCounter = new AtomicInteger();

@Bean(name = PollerMetadata.DEFAULT_POLLER)
public PollerMetadata poller() {
    return Pollers.fixedDelay(1000).get();
}

@Bean
public IntegrationFlow orders() {
    return f -> f
        .split(Order.class, Order::getItems)
        .channel(c -> c.executor(Executors.newCachedThreadPool()))
        .<OrderItem, Boolean>route(OrderItem::isIced, mapping -> mapping
          .subFlowMapping("true", sf -> sf
            .channel(c -> c.queue(10))
            .publishSubscribeChannel(c -> c
              .subscribe(s ->
                s.handle(m -> sleepUninterruptibly(1, TimeUnit.SECONDS)))
...
```

If you compare and contrast Camel and Spring Integration, you may find that Spring Integration DSL exposes the lower-level EIPs (e.g., channels, gateways, etc.), whereas the Camel DSL focuses more on the high-level integration abstractions.

With either Camel or Spring Integration, you can build your microservices integration based on a well defined DSL. However, keep in mind that you are constrained by this DSL and you will have to do a lot of tweaks when you are building real programming logic on top of a DSL.

Also, both these DSLs can become pretty clunky in substantially complex integration scenarios. One could argue that for microservices integration, we can completely omit the usage of EIPs and rather implement them as part of the service code from scratch. So, if your use case needs to use most of the existing EIPs and connectors to various systems, then Camel or Spring Integration is a good choice.

Vert.x

Eclipse Vert.x is event driven, non-blocking, reactive and polyglot software development toolkit, which you can use to build microservices and integrate them. Vert.x is not a restrictive framework (an unopinionated toolkit) and it doesn't force you to write an application a certain way. You can use Vert.x with multiple languages, including Java, JavaScript, Groovy, Ruby, Ceylon, Scala, and Kotlin.

Vert.x offers a rich set of capabilities for microservices integration. It has several key components and each component addresses a specific set of requirements. Vert.x core provides a fairly low-level set of functionalities for handling HTTP, and for some applications that will be sufficient. However, for microservices that leverage RESTful services concepts in depth, you will need the Vert.x web component. Vert.x-Web builds on top of Vert.x core to provide a richer set of functionalities for building web applications, more easily.

```
HttpServer server = vertx.createHttpServer();
Router router = Router.router(vertx);
router.route().handler(routingContext -> {

  // This handler will be called for every request
  HttpServerResponse response = routingContext.response();
  response.putHeader("content-type", "text/plain");

  // Write to the response and end it
  response.end("Hello World from Vert.x-Web!");
});

server.requestHandler(router::accept).listen(8080);
```

We create an HTTP server and a router. Once we've done that, we create a simple route with no matching criteria so it will match all requests that arrive on the server. We then specify a handler for that route. That handler will be called for all the requests that arrive on the server. You can further add routing logic, which captures the path parameters and HTTP methods etc. (You can try this example from our examples in ch07/sample09.)

```
Route route = router.route(HttpMethod.POST, "/catalogue/products/:productty
pe/:productid/");

route.handler(routingContext -> {
  String productType = routingContext.request().getParam("producttype");
  String productID = routingContext.request().getParam("productid");
  // Do something with them...
});
```

The client-side code is also trivial as Vet.x provides quite a few abstractions to interact with the clients. (You can try this example from our examples in ch07/sample10.)

```
WebClient client = WebClient.create(vertx);
client
  .post(8080, "myserver.mycompany.com", "/some-uri")
  .sendJsonObject(new JsonObject()
    .put("firstName", "Dale")
    .put("lastName", "Cooper"), ar -> {
    if (ar.succeeded()) {
      // Ok
    }
  });
```

Vert.x-Web API Contract brings two features to help you to develop your APIs, HTTP Request validation, and OpenAPI 3 support with automatic requests validation. Vert.x also provides different asynchronous clients for accessing various datastores from your microservice. (You can try this example from our examples in ch07/sample11.)

```
SQLClient client = JDBCClient.createNonShared(vertx, config);
client.getConnection(res -> {
  if (res.succeeded()) {
    SQLConnection connection = res.result();
    connection.query("SELECT * FROM some_table", res2 -> {
      if (res2.succeeded()) {
        ResultSet rs = res2.result();
        // Do something with results
        connection.close();
      }
    });
  } else {
    // Failed to get connection - deal with it
  }
});
```

Similarly, we can also connect your services with Redis, MongoDB, MySQL, and many more using Vet.x. For microservices integration, resilient inter-service communication capabilities such as circuit breaker are also included as part of Vert.x. (You can try this example from our examples in ch07/sample12.)

```
CircuitBreaker breaker = CircuitBreaker.create("my-circuit-breaker", vertx,
    new CircuitBreakerOptions().setMaxFailures(5).setTimeout(2000)
);

breaker.<String>execute(future -> {
  vertx.createHttpClient().getNow(8080, "localhost", "/", response -> {
    if (response.statusCode() != 200) {
      future.fail("HTTP error");
    } else {
      response
          .exceptionHandler(future::fail)
          .bodyHandler(buffer -> {
            future.complete(buffer.toString());
          });
    }
  });
});
```

```
}).setHandler(ar -> {
  // Do something with the result
});
```

Vet.x integration capacities also include gRPC, Kafka, AMQP-based on RabbitMQ, MQTT, STOMP, authentication and authorization, service discovery, and so on. In addition to functional components, all the ecosystem-related capabilities—such as testing, clustering, DevOps, integrating with Docker, observability with metrics and health checks, etc.—absolutely make Vet.x one of the comprehensive microservices and integration frameworks out there.

Akka

Akka is a set of open source libraries for designing scalable, resilient systems that span processor cores and networks. Akka is fully based on the actor model, which is a mathematical model of concurrent computation that treats *actors* as the universal primitives of concurrent computation. In response to a message that it receives, an actor can make local decisions, create more actors, send more messages, and determine how to respond to the next message received. Actors may modify their own private state but can only affect each other through messages; it avoids the need for any locks.

Akka aims to provide your microservices a multi-threaded behavior without the use of low-level concurrency constructs like atomics or locks—relieving you from even thinking about memory visibility issues, a transparent remote communication between systems and their components, and a clustered, high-availability architecture that is elastic and scales in or out on demand.

You can leverage the Akka HTTP modules to implement HTTP-based services, and it provides a full server and client-side HTTP stack on top of Akka-actor and Akka-stream. It's not a web-framework but rather a more general toolkit for providing and consuming HTTP-based services.

On top of the Akka HTTP, Akka provides a DSL to describe HTTP *routes* and how they should be handled. Each route is composed of one or more levels of directives that narrow down to handling one specific type of request.

For example, one route might start by matching the path of the request only if it finds a match to /order, then narrowing it down only to handle HTTP GET requests and then complete those with a string literal, which will be sent back as an HTTP OK with a string as the response body. The *route* created using the Route DSL is then bound to a port to start serving HTTP requests. JSON support is possible in Akka-http by using Jackson.

In the following use case, we have two separate Akka routes. The first route queries an asynchronous database and marshals the CompletionStage<Optional<Item>> result into a JSON response. The second unmarshalls an Order from the incoming request, saves it to the database, and replies with an OK when done. (You can try this example from our examples in ch07/sample13.)

```java
public class JacksonExampleTest extends AllDirectives {

  public static void main(String[] args) throws Exception {
    ActorSystem system = ActorSystem.create("routes");
    final Http http = Http.get(system);
    final ActorMaterializer materializer = ActorMaterializer.
    create(system);
    JacksonExampleTest app = new JacksonExampleTest();
    final Flow<HttpRequest, HttpResponse, NotUsed> routeFlow = app.
    createRoute().flow(system, materializer);
    final CompletionStage<ServerBinding> binding = http.
    bindAndHandle(routeFlow,
      ConnectHttp.toHost("localhost", 8080), materializer);

    binding
      .thenCompose(ServerBinding::unbind) // trigger unbinding from the port
      .thenAccept(unbound -> system.terminate()); // and shutdown when done
  }

  private CompletionStage<Optional<Item>> fetchItem(long itemId) {
    return CompletableFuture.completedFuture(Optional.of(new Item("foo",
    itemId)));
  }

  private CompletionStage<Done> saveOrder(final Order order) {
    return CompletableFuture.completedFuture(Done.getInstance());
  }

  private Route createRoute() {

    return route(
      get(() ->
```

```
        pathPrefix("item", () ->
          path(longSegment(), (Long id) -> {
            final CompletionStage<Optional<Item>> futureMaybeItem =
            fetchItem(id);
            return onSuccess(futureMaybeItem, maybeItem ->
              maybeItem.map(item -> completeOK(item, Jackson.marshaller()))
                .orElseGet(() -> complete(StatusCodes.NOT_FOUND, "Not Found"))
            );
          }))),
      post(() ->
        path("create-order", () ->
          entity(Jackson.unmarshaller(Order.class), order -> {
            CompletionStage<Done> futureSaved = saveOrder(order);
            return onSuccess(futureSaved, done ->
              complete("order created")
            );
          })))
    );
  }
}
```

Akka caters to the specific integration requirements of microservices and other types of integrations via Alpakka initiative. Alpakka enables Akka-based integration of various Akka Streams connectors, integration patterns, and data transformations for integration use cases. Alpakka provides numerous connectors, such as HTTP, Kafka, File, AMQP, JMS, CSV, web APIs (AWS S3, GCP pub-sub, and Slack), MongoDB, etc.

In the following example, you can find a sample AMQP producer and consumer written using Alpakka. (You can try this example from our examples in ch07/sample14.)

```
// AMQP Producer
final Sink<ByteString, CompletionStage<Done>> amqpSink = AmqpSink.createSimple(
    AmqpSinkSettings.create(connectionProvider)
        .withRoutingKey(queueName)
        .withDeclarations(queueDeclaration)
);
```

```
// AMQP Consumer
final Integer bufferSize = 10;
final Source<IncomingMessage, NotUsed> amqpSource = AmqpSource.
atMostOnceSource(
    NamedQueueSourceSettings.create(
        connectionProvider,
        queueName
    ).withDeclarations(queueDeclaration),
    bufferSize
);
```

Here, AmqpSink is a collection of factory methods that facilitates creation of sinks and sources allowing you to fetch messages from AMQP.

Node, Go, Rust, and Python

Node.js is an open source, cross-platform JavaScript runtime environment that executes JavaScript code server-side. Node.js supports building RESTful services out-of-the-box and you can build your service on a full non-blocking I/O model, which leverages the event loop. (When Node.js starts, it initializes the event loop, processes the provided input script—which may make async API calls, schedules timers, or calls `process.nextTick()`—and then begins processing the event loop.)

The following code shows a simple `Echo` service built with Node.js. (You can try this example from our examples in `ch07/sample15`.)

```
const http = require('http');

http.createServer((request, response) => {
  if (request.method === 'POST' && request.url === '/echo') {
    let body = [];
    request.on('data', (chunk) => {
      body.push(chunk);
    }).on('end', () => {
      body = Buffer.concat(body).toString();
      response.end(body);
    });
  } else {
```

```
    response.statusCode = 404;
    response.end();
  }
}).listen(8080);
```

In addition to the standard set of features, Node.js has a diverse ecosystem that allows you to integrate a microservice based on Node.js with almost any of the other network protocols, databases, web APIs, and other systems.

There are multiple frameworks built on top of Node.js, such as Restify, which is a web services framework optimized for building semantically correct RESTful web services ready for production use at scale. Similarly, there are numerous libraries and packages available for Node.js on NPM (NPM is a package manager for Node.js packages.). For example, you can find NPM packages for Kafka integration (kafka-node), AMQP (node-amqp), circuit breaker, and instrumentation libraries for most of the popular observability tools.

Go[4] is also quite commonly used for microservices development and offers a rich set of packages for network communication.

Similarly, other programing languages, such as Rust and Python, offer quite a few out-of-the-box capabilities to build microservices and integrate microservices. For Rust, we have Rocket, a web framework that makes it simple to write fast web applications without sacrificing flexibility or type safety. The Rust ecosystem components address most of the integration of Rust applications with other network protocols, data, web APIs, and other systems. However, some developers claim that Rust is too low level to be a microservices development lanauge. So, we recommend you to give it a try with some use cases prior to fully adopting it.

Similarly, Python has a broad community of production ready frameworks, such as Flask, for microservice development and integration.

Ballerina

Ballerina[5] is an emerging integration technology which is built as a programming language, and it aims to fill the gap between integration products and general-purpose programming languages by making it easy to write programs that integrate and orchestrate across distributed microservices and endpoints in a type-safe and resilient manner.

---

[4]https://golang.org/pkg/
[5]ballerina.io

At the time this book was written, Ballerina is in 0.981 version. Most of the programming constructs are final but some are subjected to change and the language is yet to be widely adopted across the microservices communities.

Disclaimer   The authors of this book have contributed to the design and development of Ballerina. As we thrive to keep the contents of this book technology and vendor neutral, we will not compare and contrast Ballerina with other similar technologies. We highly encourage the readers to select the most appropriate technology after doing a thorough evaluation of their use cases and the potential technologies to realize those use cases.

Both the code and the graphical syntax in Ballerina are inspired from how the independent parties communicate via interactions in a sequence diagram.

In the graphical syntax, Ballerina represents clients, workers, and remote systems as different actors in the sequence diagram. For example, as shown in Figure 7-11, the interaction between the client/caller, service, worker, and another external endpoints can be represented using a sequence diagram. Each endpoint is represented as an actor in the sequence diagram and actions are represented as interactions between those actors.

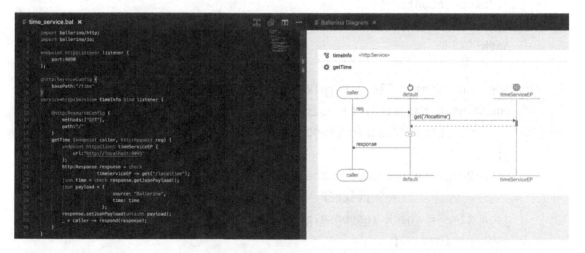

Figure 7-11. *Ballerina graphical syntax and source syntax is based on a sequence diagram metaphor*

In the code, the remote endpoints are interfaced via endpoints that offer type-safe actions and worker's logic is written as sequential code inside a resource or a function. You can define a service and bind it to a server endpoint (for example, an HTTP server endpoint can listen on a given HTTP port). Each service contains one or more resources that we write to the sequential code related to a worker and run by a dedicated worker thread.

The following code snippet shows a simple HTTP service that accepts an HTTP GET request, and then invokes another external service to retrieve some information and send it back to the client. (You can try this from our examples in ch07/sample16.)

```
import ballerina/http;
import ballerina/io;

endpoint http:Listener listener {
    port:9090
};

@http:ServiceConfig {
    basePath:"/time"
}
service<http:Service> timeInfo bind listener {

    @http:ResourceConfig {
        methods:["GET"],
        path:"/"
    }
    getTime (endpoint caller, http:Request req) {
        endpoint http:Client timeServiceEP {
            url:"http://localhost:9095"
        };
        http:Response response = check
                    timeServiceEP -> get("/localtime");
        json time = check response.getJsonPayload();
        json payload = {
                        source: "Ballerina",
                        time: time
                };
```

```
        response.setJsonPayload(untaint payload);
        _ = caller -> respond(response);
    }
}
```

Network-Aware Abstractions

Ballerina is designed for integration of disparate services, systems, and data. Hence,
Ballerina provides native network-aware constructs that provide abstraction for
interaction with endpoints via disparate network protocols. Ballerina offers out-of-the-
box support for most of the standard network communication protocols.

```
endpoint http:Client timeServiceEP {
        url:"http://localhost:9095"
};

...
http:Response response = check
                    timeServiceEP -> get("/localtime");

endpoint mysql:Client testDB {
    host: "localhost",
    port: 3306,
    name: "testdb",
    username: "root",
    password: "root",
    poolOptions: { maximumPoolSize: 5 },
    dbOptions: { useSSL: false }
};
...
var selectRet = testDB->select("SELECT * FROM student", ());

// Kafka producer endpoint
endpoint kafka:SimpleProducer kafkaProducer {
    bootstrapServers: "localhost:9092",
    clientID:"basic-producer",
    acks:"all",
    noRetries:3
};
```

...

```
 // Produce the message and publish it to the Kafka topic
kafkaProducer->send(serializedMsg, "product-price", partition = 0);
```

As in the previous case, you can leverage server connectors to receive messages via those protocols and bind them to the service that intends to consume those messages. Most of the implementation details of consuming messages via a given protocol are transparent to the developer.

```
// Server endpoint configuration.
endpoint grpc:Listener ep {
   host:"localhost",
   port:9090
};

// The gRPC service that binds to the server endpoint.
service SamplegRPCService bind ep {
   // A resource that accepts a string message.
   receiveMessage (endpoint caller, string name) {
       // Print the received message.         foreach record in records {
           blob serializedMsg = record.value;
           // Convert the serialized message to string message
           string msg = serializedMsg.toString("UTF-8");
           log:printInfo("New message received from the product admin");

...
endpoint jms:SimpleQueueReceiver consumer {
    initialContextFactory:"bmbInitialContextFactory",
    providerUrl:"amqp://admin:admin@carbon/carbon"
               + "?brokerlist='tcp://localhost:5672'",
    acknowledgementMode:"AUTO_ACKNOWLEDGE",
    queueName:"MyQueue"
};
```

```
service<jms:Consumer> jmsListener bind consumer {

    onMessage(endpoint consumer, jms:Message message) {
        match (message.getTextMessageContent()) {
            string messageText => log:printInfo("Message : " + messageText);
```

Resilient and Safe Integration

The integration microservices you write using Ballerina are inherently resilient. You can make invocations of an external endpoint in a resilient and type-safe manner.

For example, when you invoke an external endpoint that may be unreliable, you can circumvent such interactions with a circuit breaker for the specific protocol that you are using. This is as trivial as passing a few additional parameters to your client endpoint code.

```
// circuit breaker example
endpoint http:Client backendClientEP {
    circuitBreaker: {
        rollingWindow: { // failure calculation window
            timeWindowMillis:10000,
            bucketSizeMillis:2000
        },
        failureThreshold:0.2, // failure percentage threshold to open the
        circuit
        resetTimeMillis:10000, // time it takes to bring the circuit from
        open to half-close state
        statusCodes:[400, 404, 500] // HTTP status codes that are
        considered as failures
    }
    url: "http://localhost:8080",
    timeoutMillis:2000,
};
```

By design, Ballerina code you write will not require specific tools for checking for vulnerabilities or best practices. For example, a common issue in building distributed systems is that data coming over the wire cannot be trusted not to include injection attacks. Ballerina assumes that all data coming over the wire is tainted. And compilation-time checks prevent code that requires untainted data from accessing tainted data. Ballerina offers such capabilities as the built-in construct of the language, so that the programmer is enforced to write secure code.

Data Formats

Ballerina has a structural type system with primitive, record, object, tuple, and union types. This type-safe model incorporates type inference at assignment and provides numerous compile-time integrity checks for connectors, logic, and network-bound payloads.

The code that integrates services and systems often has to deal with complex distributed errors. Ballerina has error-handling capabilities based on union types. Union types explicitly capture the semantics without requiring developers to create unnecessary *wrapper* types. When you decide to pass the errors back to the caller, you can use the check operator.

For example, when you have a JSON data received over a message, you can cast it to a type that you have defined as part of your logic. Then you can safely cast the two types by handling the possible error as part of a match clause written against that union type.

```
// this is a simple structured object definition in Ballerina
// it can be automatically mapped into JSON and back again
type Payment {
    string name,
    string cardnumber,
    int month,
    int year,
    int cvc;
};

...
json payload = check request.getJsonPayload();
        // The next line shows typesafe parsing of JSON into an object
        Payment|error p = <Payment>payload;
        match p {
            Payment x => {
                io:println(x);
                res.statusCode = 200;
```

```
        // return the JSON that has been created
        res.setJsonPayload(check <json>x);
    }
    error e => {
        res.statusCode = 400 ;
        // return the error message if the JSON failed to parse
        res.setStringPayload(e.message);
    }
    _ = caller -> respond (res);
```

Observablity

Monitoring, logging, and distributed tracing are key methods that reveal the internal state of the Ballerina code to provide the observability. Ballerina provides out-of-the-box capabilities to work with observability tools, such as Prometheus, Grafana, Jeager, and Elastic Stack, all with minimal configuration.

Workflow Engine Solutions

We conclude our discussion of microservice integration technologies with technologies that are specifically designed for microservices that require workflows (i.e., long-running stateful processes that may also need some human interactions). Building workflows in a microservices architecture is a special case of integration requirements. There are quite a few new and existing solutions morphing into the microservices workflow domain. Zeebe, Netflix Conductor, Apache Nifi, AWS Step Functions, Spring Cloud Data Flow, and Microsoft Logic Apps are good examples.

Zeebe[6] supports the stateful orchestration of workers and microservices using visual workflows (developed by Camunda, which is a popular open source Business Process Model and Notation—BPMN—solution). It allows users to define orchestration flows visually using BPMN 2.0 or YAML. Zeebe ensures that, once started, flows are always carried out fully, retrying steps in case of failures. Along the way, Zeebe maintains a complete audit log, so that the progress of flows can be monitored and tracked. Zeebe is a Big Data system and scales seamlessly with growing transaction volumes. (You can try a Zeebe example from our examples in ch07/sample17.)

---

[6]https://zeebe.io/

Netflix Conductor[7] is an open source workflow engine that uses a JSON DSL to define a workflow. Conductor allows creating complex process/business flows in which an individual task is implemented by a microservice.

Apache NiFi[8] is a conventional integration framework that supports powerful and scalable directed graphs of data routing, transformation, and system mediation logic.

Inception of the Service Mesh

What we have seen so far in this chapter is that microservices have to work with other microservices, data, web APIs, and other systems. Since we don't use a centralized ESB as a bus to connect all these services and systems, the inter-services communication is now part of the service developer. Although many microservices frameworks address most of such needs, it's still a daunting task for the service developer to take care of all the requirements of integrating microservices.

To overcome this problem, architects identify that some of the inter-service communication functionalities can be treated as commodity features and the service code can be made independent from them. The core concept of a Service Mesh is to identify the commodity network communication functionalities such as circuit breaker, timeouts, basic routing, service discovery, secure communication, observability, etc. and implement them at a component called a *sidecar*, which you run alongside the microservices you develop. These sidecars are controlled by a central management called a *control plane*.

With the advent of the Service Mesh, the microservice developers get more freedom when it comes to polyglot service development technologies and they focus less on the inter-service communication. They can focus more on the business capabilities of a service that they develop.

We discuss the Service Mesh in detail in Chapter 9, "Service Mesh," and delve deep into some of the existing service mesh implementations.

---

[7]https://netflix.github.io/conductor/
[8]https://nifi.apache.org/

Summary

In this chapter, we took an in-depth analysis of the microservices integration challenges. With the omission of ESB, we need to practice the smart endpoints and dumb client philosophy when we develop services. With this approach, most of the ESB capabilities now need to be supported at the microservices that we develop. We identified some of the commonly used microservice integration patterns: active compositions/ orchestrations, reactive compositions/choreography, and a hybrid approach. It is more pragmatic to stick to a hybrid approach of integrating microservices and select the integration patterns based on your use cases.

In order to facilitate microservices integration, the microservices development frameworks need to have a unique set of capabilities such as built-in network communication abstractions, support for resiliency patterns, native support to data types, ability to govern integration microservices, cloud and container native nature, etc. With respect to those requirements, we had a detailed discussion of some of the key microservice implementation technologies. With the inception of the Service Mesh, some of the microservice integration requirement can be offloaded to a distributed network communication abstraction, which is executed as a sidecar alongside each service and controlled by a centralized control plane. In the next chapter, we discuss how to deploy and run microservices.

CHAPTER 8

Deploying and Running Microservices

The two main objectives of a microservices architecture is the speed to production and the capability of the application to evolve. Unlike a monolithic application, a microservices deployment includes many individual (and independent) deployments. Instead of one single deployment, now we have hundreds of deployments. Unless we have an automated build system, managing such a deployment is a nightmare. An automated build system will help to streamline the deployment process, but will not solve all the issues in a large-scale deployment. We also need to worry about making a microservice portable, along with all its dependencies, so that the environment the developer tests will not be different from the test and production environments. This helps identify any issues very early in the development cycle and the chances are quite minimal that there will be issues in production. In this chapter we talk about different microservices deployment patterns, containers, container orchestration, container native microservices frameworks, and finally continuous delivery.

Containers and Microservices

The primary goal of a container is to provide a containerized environment for the applications it runs. A containerized environment is an isolated environment. One or more containers can run on the same physical host machine. But one container does not know about the processes running in other containers. For example, if you run your microservice in a container, it has its own view of the filesystem, network interfaces, processes, and hostname. Let's say a *foo* microservice, which is running in the *foo* container, can refer to any other service running in the same container with the

© Kasun Indrasiri and Prabath Siriwardena 2018
K. Indrasiri and P. Siriwardena, *Microservices for the Enterprise*, https://doi.org/10.1007/978-1-4842-3858-5_8

hostname *localhost*, while a *bar* microservice, which is running in the *bar* container, can refer to any other service running in the same container with the hostname *localhost*, while both *foo* and *bar* containers running on the same host machine[1].

The concept of containers was made popular a few years back with Docker. But it has a long history. In 1979, with chroot system call in UNIX V7, users were able to change the root directory of a running process, so it will not be able to access any part of the filesystem, beyond the root. This was added to BSD in 1982, and even today, chroot is considered a best practice among sys-admins, when you run any process that's not in a containerized environment. A couple of decades later in 2000, FreeBSD introduced a new concept called FreeBSD Jails. With Jails, the same host environment can be partitioned into multiple isolated environments, where each environment can have its own IP address. In 2001, Linux VServer introduced a similar concept like FreeBSD Jails. With Linux VServer, the host environment can be partitioned by the filesystem, network, and the memory. Solaris came up with the Solaris Containers in 2004, which introduced another variation of process isolation. Google launched Process Containers in 2006, which was designed to build isolation over CPU, disk I/O, memory and the network. A year later this was renamed to control groups and merged into the Linux kernel 2.6.24.

Linux *cgroups* and *namespaces* are the foundation of the containers we see today. LXC (Linux Containers) in 2008 implemented the Linux Container Manager using cgroups and namespaces. CloudFoundry, in 2011, came up with a container implementation based on LXC, called Warden, but later changed it to its own implementation. Docker was born in 2013, and just like Warden, it too was built on top of LXC. Docker made container technologies much more usable and in the next sections, we'll talk about Docker in detail.

Introduction to Docker

As we discussed, the containerization provided by Docker is built on top of Linux control groups and namespaces. The Linux namespaces build isolation in a way that each process sees its own view of the system: file, process, network interfaces, hostname, and many more. Control groups, also known as *cgroups*, limit the number of resources each process can consume. The combination of these two can build an isolated environment on the same host machine, sharing the same CPU, memory, network and the filesystem, with no impact on others.

---

[1]This is just an example. It is not recommended to run multiple microservices in the same container.

The level of isolation that Docker introduces is quite different from what we see in virtual machines. Before Docker became popular, virtual machines were used to replicate similar operating environments, with all the dependencies. If you have really done it, you probably know the pain in doing it! A virtual machine image is quite bulky. It packs everything you need, from the operating system to application-level binary dependencies. Portability is a major concern. Figure 8-1 shows how a virtual machine creates isolation.

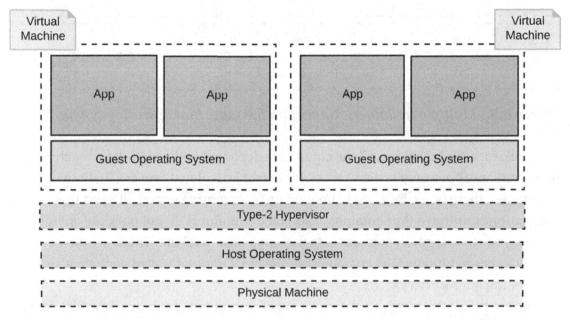

Figure 8-1. *High-level virtual machine architecture with a type-2 hypervisor*

A virtual machine runs on a hypervisor. There are two types of hypervisors. The type-1 hypervisor does not need a host operating system, while the type-2 hypervisor runs on a host operating system. Each virtual machine carries its own operating system. To run multiple virtual machines on the same host operating system, you need to have a good, powerful computer. To use one virtual machine per microservice to build an isolated environment is an overkill and a waste of resources. If you are familiar with virtual machines, you can think of a container as a lightweight virtual machine. Each container provides an isolated environment, yet they share the same operating system kernel with the host machine. Figure 8-2 shows how a container creates isolation.

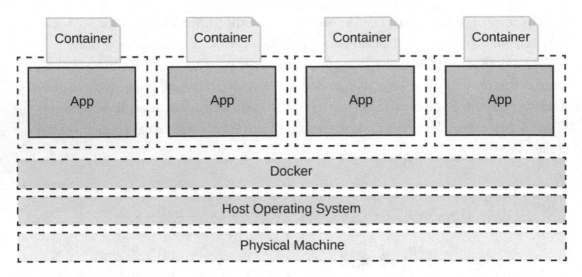

Figure 8-2. *Multiple containers running on the same host operating system*

Unlike a virtual machine, all the containers deployed in the same host machine share the same operating system kernel. It's in fact an isolated process. To boot up a container, there is no overhead in booting up an operating system; it's just the application running in the container. Also, since containers do not pack the operating system, you can run many containers in the same host machine. These are the key driving forces behind picking containers as the most popular way of deploying and distributing microservices.

Docker builds the process isolation on top of control groups and namespaces come with the Linux kernel. Even without Docker, we could still do the same with the Linux kernel. So, why has Docker become the most popular container technology? Docker adds several new features, apart from process isolation to make it more attractive to the developer community. Making containers portable, building an ecosystem around Docker Hub, exposing an API for container management and building tooling around that, and making container images reusable are some of these features. We discuss each of them in detail in this chapter.

Installing Docker

Docker follows a client-server architecture model, where you have a Docker client and a Docker host (which is also known as the *Docker Engine*). When you install Docker locally in your machine, you will get both the client and the host installed. All the instructions on how to install Docker based on your platform are available from the Docker website[2]. At the time of writing the book, Docker is available on MacOS, Windows, CentOS, Debian, Fedora, and Ubuntu. The following command will help to test the Docker installation. If the installation is successful, this will return the related system information.

```
:\> docker info
```

The following command will also return the versions related to the Docker client and the engine.

```
:\> docker version
Client:
 Version: 18.03.1-ce
 API version: 1.37
 Go version: go1.9.5
 Git commit: 9ee9f40
 Built: Thu Apr 26 07:13:02 2018
 OS/Arch: darwin/amd64
 Experimental: false
 Orchestrator: swarm
Server:
 Engine:
  Version: 18.03.1-ce
  API version: 1.37 (minimum version 1.08)
  Go version: go1.9.5
  Git commit: 9ee9f40
  Built: Thu Apr 26 07:22:38 2018
  OS/Arch: linux/amd64
  Experimental: true
```

---

[2]https://docs.docker.com/install/#supported-platforms

Docker Architecture

Figure 8-3 shows the high-level Docker architecture where we have the Docker client, Docker host, or the engine and the registry. The Docker client is the command-line tool that we are going to interact with. The Docker Daemon running on the Docker host listens to the requests coming from the client and acts accordingly. The client can communicate with the daemon using a REST API, over UNIX sockets, or a network interface. In the following sections, we explain how exactly the communication happens and the sequence of events.

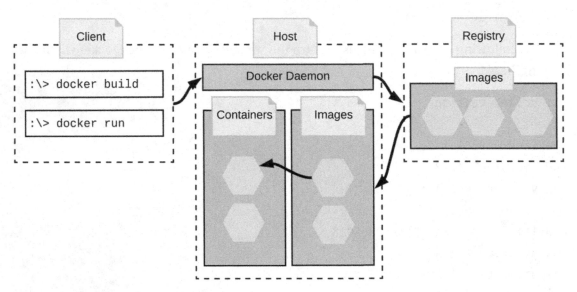

Figure 8-3. *High-level Docker architecture*

Docker Images

A Docker image is a package that includes your microservice (or your application) along with all its dependencies. Your application will see only the dependencies that you pack in your Docker image. You define the filesystem for your image, and it will not have access to the host filesystem. A Docker image is created using a Dockerfile. The Dockerfile defines all the dependencies to build a Docker image.

Note   For readers who are keen on exploring more on Docker concepts, we recommend following the Docker documentation[3].

The following code shows the contents from a sample Dockerfile. The first line says start building this new image using the base image called openjdk:8-jdk-alpine. When we build the Docker image from this Dockerfile with the tooling provided by Docker, it first loads the openjdk:8-jdk-alpine image. First the Docker engine will see whether the image is in the local registry of images, and if not, it will load from a remote registry (for example, the Docker Hub). Also, if the openjdk:8-jdk-alpine image has dependencies on other Docker images, those will also be pulled and stored in the local registry.

```
FROM openjdk:8-jdk-alpine
ADD target/sample01-1.0.0.jar /sample01-1.0.0.jar
ENTRYPOINT ["java", "-jar", "sample01-1.0.0.jar"]
```

The second line says to copy sample01-1.0.0.jar from the target directory under the current location of the filesystem (this is in fact our host filesystem, which we use to create a Docker image) to the root of the filesystem of the image we want to create. The third line defines the entry point or the command to execute when someone runs this Docker image.

To build a Docker image from a Dockerfile, we use the following command. We go through this later in the chapter, so you do not need to try it out now. This command will produce a Docker image and, by default, it will be stored in the local image registry. This is in fact the Docker client. Once we execute the command, the Docker daemon running on the Docker engine will make sure all the dependent images are loaded locally and the new image is created.

```
:\> docker build -t sample01 .
```

Docker Registry

If you are familiar with Maven, you may already know how Maven repositories work. The Docker registries follow a similar concept. A Docker registry is a repository of Docker images. They operate at different levels. The Docker Hub is a public Docker registry where anyone can push and pull images. Later in the chapter, we explain how to publish

---

[3]https://docs.docker.com/get-started/#docker-concepts

and retrieve images to and from the Docker Hub. Having a centralized registry of all the images helps you share and reuse them. It is also becoming a popular way of distributing software. If your organization needs a restricted Docker registry just for its employees, that can be done too.

The following command will list all the Docker images stored in your local machine. This will include all the images you built locally as well as pulled from a Docker registry.

```
:\> docker image ls
```

The following command will list all the containers available in the host machine and their status. In the next section, we discuss the difference between images and containers.

```
:\> docker ps
```

Containers

A container is a running instance of a Docker image. In fact, images become containers when they run on a Docker engine. There can be many images in your local machine, but not all of them are running all the time, unless you explicitly make them to run. A container is in fact a regular Linux container defined by namespaces and control groups. We use the following command to start a Docker container from a Docker image. Here, sample01 is the image name. This command will first check whether sample01 image and all the other base images are in the local Docker registry, and if not, it will pull all the missing images from a remote registry. Finally, once all the images are there, the container will start and execute the program or the command, set as the ENTRYPOINT in the corresponding Dockerfile.

```
:\> docker run sample01
```

Deploying Microservices with Docker

In this section, we see how to create a Docker image with a microservice, run it, and then finally publish it to the Docker Hub. First, we need to have our microservice running locally. Once you download all the examples from the Git repository of the book, you can find the source code related to this sample available in the ch08/sample01 directory. Let's build the sample with the following command, run from the ch08/sample01 directory.

```
:\> mvn clean install
```

This will result in the `target/sample01-1.0.0.jar` file. This is our microservice, and now we need to create a Docker image with it.

Note   To run the examples in this chapter, you need Java 8 or latest, Maven 3.2 or latest, and a Git client. Once you have successfully installed those tools, you need to clone the Git repo: `https://github.com/microservices-for-enterprise/samples.git`. The chapter samples are in the `ch08` directory.

`:\> git clone https://github.com/microservices-for-enterprise/samples.git`

Creating a Docker Image with a Microservice

To create Docker image, first we need to create a Dockerfile. As we discussed in previous sections, this file defines all the other dependent images, other binary dependencies, and the command to start our microservice. The following code lists the contents of the Dockerfile, created in the `ch08/sample01` directory. Since we use Spring Boot to build the microservice, we need to have Java in our image. There are two options. One is to get Java binary and install it to our image from scratch and the other approach is to find a Docker container already existing with a Java environment and reuse it. The second approach is the recommended one and we use it here. We use `openjdk:8-jdk-alpine` as the base image, which will be pulled from the Docker Hub at the time we build our image.

```
FROM openjdk:8-jdk-alpine
ADD target/sample01-1.0.0.jar /sample01-1.0.0.jar
ENTRYPOINT ["java", "-jar", "sample01-1.0.0.jar"]
```

Let's use the following command from `ch08/sample01` directory to build a Docker image with the name (`-t` in the command) `sample01`. The output you see may be slightly different from what is shown here, if you do not have the `openjdk:8-jdk-alpine` image already loaded into your Docker engine.

```
:\> docker build -t sample01 .
Sending build context to Docker daemon 17.45MB
Step 1/3: FROM openjdk:8-jdk-alpine
 ---> 83621aae5e20
Step 2/3: ADD target/sample01-1.0.0.jar /sample01-1.0.0.jar
 ---> f3448272e3a9
```

```
Step 3/3: ENTRYPOINT ["java", "-jar", "sample01-1.0.0.jar"]
 ---> Running in ec9a9f91c950
Removing intermediate container ec9a9f91c950
 ---> 35188a2bfb00
Successfully built 35188a2bfb00
Successfully tagged sample01:latest
```

There is one important thing to learn from this output. There you can see Docker engine performs the operation in three steps. There is a step corresponding to each line in the Dockerfile. Docker builds images as layers. Each step in this operation creates a layer. These layers are read-only and reusable between multiple containers. Let's revisit this concept, later in this chapter, once we better understand the behavior of containers.

To list all the images in the Docker engine, we can use the following command.

```
:\> docker image ls
```

Running a Microservice as a Docker Container

Once we have the Docker image available for our microservice, we can use the following command to spin up a Docker container with it.

```
:\> docker run -p 9000:9000 sample01
```

This command instructs the Docker engine to spin up a new Docker container from the sample01 image and map port 9000 of the host machine to port 9000 of the Docker container. We picked 9000 here, because our microservice in the container starts on port 9000. Unless we map the container port to a host machine port, we won't be able to communicate with our microservice running in a container.

When you run this command, you can see that the output from the microservice running in the container is printed on the console of the host machine. And also if you use Ctrl+C, it will kill the container. That is because, in the way we executed this command, the container is attached to the host machine's terminal. With the -d option used in the docker run command, we can de-attach the container from the host machine terminal. This will return the container ID corresponding to the one we just started.

```
:\> docker run -d -p 9000:9000 sample01
9a5cd90b714fc5a27281f94622c1a0d8f1dd1a344f4f4fcc6609413db39de000
```

To test our microservice running in the container, use the following command from the host machine.

```
:\> curl http://localhost:9000/order/11
{"customer_id":"101021","order_id":"11","payment_method":{"card_type":
"VISA","expiration":"01/22","name":"John Doe","billing_address":"201,
1st Street, San Jose, CA"},"items":[{"code":"101","qty":1},{"code":"103",
"qty":5}],"shipping_address":"201, 1st Street, San Jose, CA"}>
```

Hint   If we want to see all the containers running on our Docker engine, we can use the docker ps command. To stop a running container, we need to use the docker stop <container id> command. Also if you want remove a container, use the docker rm <container id> command. Once you remove the container, you can delete the corresponding Docker image from your local registry with the docker rmi <image name> command.

Publishing a Docker Image to the Docker Hub

Docker Hub is a public Docker registry available to anyone to push Docker images and pull from. First, we need to create a Docker ID from https://hub.docker.com/. For example, we use the Docker ID prabath in the following example. Once you create a Docker ID, with a password, use the following command to register your Docker ID with the Docker client running locally.

```
:\> docker login --username=prabath
```

This command will prompt you to enter the password, and the Docker client will store your credentials in the keychain. Next, use the following command to find the image ID of the Docker image we created before and copy the value of IMAGE ID field corresponding to the sample01 image; for example, 35188a2bfb00.

```
:\> docker images
```

Now we need to tag our image with the Docker ID from the Docker Hub, as shown in the following command. Tagging helps create a more meaningful name for an image and since we plan to publish this image to the Docker Hub, make sure the tag follows the convention, where it starts with your Docker Hub account name. You would need to replace prabath from your Docker Hub account name.

```
:\> docker tag 35188a2bfb00 prabath/sample01
```

Finally, use the following command to push the image to the Docker Hub, and it should appear under your Docker Hub account once published.

```
:\> docker push prabath/sample01
```

Now, anyone can pull this image from anywhere, using the following command.

```
:\> docker pull prabath/sample01
```

Docker Compose

In practice, in a microservices deployment we have more than one service, where each service has its own container. For example, in Figure 8-4 the Order Processing microservice talks to the Inventory microservice. Also, there can be cases where one microservice depends on other services like a database. The database will be another container, but still part of the same application. The Docker Compose helps define and manage such multi-container environments. It's another tool that we have to install apart from the Docker client and the Docker engine (host).

Note   Compose is a tool for defining and running multi-container Docker applications. With Compose, you use a YAML file to configure your application's services. Then, with a single command, you create and start all the services from your configuration[4]. You can refer to the Docker documentation[5] for more details. It's quite straightforward.

---

[4]https://docs.docker.com/compose/overview/
[5]https://docs.docker.com/compose/install/#install-compose

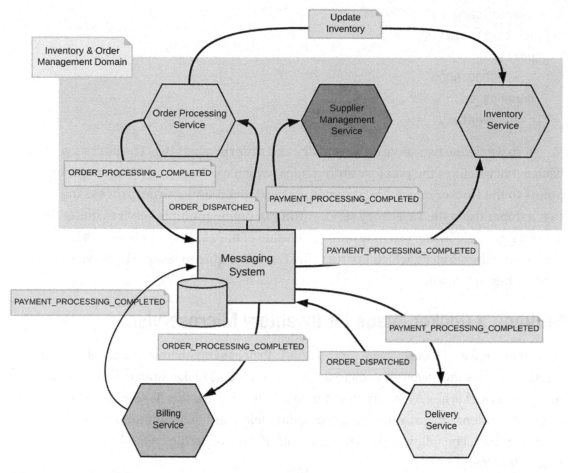

Figure 8-4. *Multi-container microservices deployment*

Docker Compose uses a YAML file to define the configuration of an application. The following is an example YAML file that's named docker-compose.yml, and it brings up the Order Processing(sample01) and Inventory(sample02) microservices. You can find the complete file in the ch08/sample02 directory.

```
version: '3.3'

services:
  inventory:
    image: sample02
    ports:
      - "9090:9090"
    restart: always
  orderprocessing:
```

```
image: sample01
restart: always
ports:
  - "9000:9000"
depends_on:
  - inventory
```

Here we define two services, inventory and orderprocessing. The ports tag under each service defines the port forwarding rules (which we discussed). The image tag points to the Docker image. The depends_on tag defined under orderprocessing states that it depends on the inventory service. You can define multiple services under the depends_on tag. Finally, you may notice the value of the restart tag is set to always, under both the services, which instructs the Docker engine to restart the services always, in case they are down.

Building a Docker Image for Inventory Microservice

We already have a Docker image for the Order Processing microservice. Let's create another one for the Inventory microservice. To create a Docker image, first we need to create a Dockerfile. As we discussed in previous sections, this file defines all the other dependent images, other binary dependencies, and the command to start our microservices. The following lists the contents of the Dockerfile created in the ch08/sample02 directory.

```
FROM openjdk:8-jdk-alpine
ADD target/sample02-1.0.0.jar /sample02-1.0.0.jar
ENTRYPOINT ["java", "-jar", "sample02-1.0.0.jar"]
```

Let's use the following command from the ch08/sample02 directory to build the Docker image with the name sample02. Before running this command, make sure you have built the sample with Maven.

```
:\> docker build -t sample02 .
```

Now, let's push this image to the Docker Hub. This may not be useful for this example, but later in the book, we'll refer directly to the image from the Docker Hub. Use the following command to find the image ID of the Docker image we created before and copy the value of IMAGE ID field corresponding to the sample02 image; for example, 35199a2bfb00.

```
:\> docker images
```

Now we need to tag our image with the Docker ID from the Docker Hub, as shown in the following command. Finally, use the following command to push the image to the Docker Hub, and it should appear under your Docker Hub account once published. Also make sure that you are logged into the Docker Hub with the docker login command, prior to executing the docker push command.

```
:\> docker tag 35199a2bfb00 prabath/sample02
:\> docker push prabath/sample02
```

If you are already running the Order Processing microservice, stop the running container. To find all the containers running in the Docker host, use the following command and it will return the container ID of all the containers. Find the container ID (for example e1039667db1a) related to the sample01 image.

```
:\> docker ps
```

To remove a running container, we have to stop it first, and then remove it.

```
:\> docker container stop e1039667db1a
:\> docker container rm e1039667db1a
```

Launching the Application with Docker Compose

We are all set to launch our application with Docker Compose. Run the following command from ch08/sample02. This is where we have docker-compose.yml, which we created before.

```
:\> docker-compose up
```

Since we are launching docker-compose here in the attached mode (with no -d) you will be able to see the output from both the containers on your terminal. Also you will notice that each log from both the microservices is tagged with the corresponding service name defined in the docker-compose.yml file.

Testing the Application with cURL

Now we have all our microservices running with Docker Compose. Let's first try to test the Order Processing microservice with the following cURL command. This call only hits the Order Processing microservice and returns the result.

```
:\> curl http://localhost:9000/order/11
{"customer_id":"101021","order_id":"11","payment_method":{"card_type":
"VISA","expiration":"01/22","name":"John Doe","billing_address":"201,
1st Street, San Jose, CA"},"items":[{"code":"101","qty":1},{"code":"103",
"qty":5}],"shipping_address":"201, 1st Street, San Jose, CA"}>
```

Let's try another request to the Order Processing microservice, which also invokes the Inventory microservice. The request goes to Order Processing microservice and it invokes the Inventory microservice. Here we are posting a JSON request to the Order Processing microservice.

```
:\> curl -v -H "Content-Type: application/json" -d '{"customer_id":"101021",
"payment_method":{"card_type":"VISA","expiration":"01/22","name":"John Doe",
"billing_address":"201, 1st Street, San Jose, CA"},"items":[{"code":"101","qty":1},
{"code":"103","qty":5}],"shipping_address":"201, 1st Street, San Jose, CA"}'
http://localhost:9000/order
```

Now if you look at the terminal attached to both containers, you will find the following output, which confirms that the request has hit the Inventory microservice.

```
inventory_1 | 101
inventory_1 | 103
```

How Does the Communication Happen Between Containers?

To see how exactly the two microservices are wired in our previous example, we need to look at the source code of the Order Processing microservice, which available at ch08/sample01/ src/main/java/com/apress/ch08/sample01/service/OrderProcessing.java. There you can see that, instead of an IP address or a hostname, we use the service name (as defined in the docker-compose.yml) of the Inventory microservice: http://inventory:9090/inventory.

```
@RequestMapping(method = RequestMethod.POST)
public ResponseEntity<?> createOrder(@RequestBody Order order) {
```

```
if (order != null) {
    RestTemplate restTemplate = new RestTemplate();
    URI uri = URI.create(
        "http://inventory:9090/inventory");
    restTemplate.put(uri, order.getItems());
    order.setOrderId(UUID.randomUUID().toString());
    URI location = ServletUriComponentsBuilder
            .fromCurrentRequest().path("/{id}")
            .buildAndExpand(order.getOrderId())
            .toUri();
    return ResponseEntity.created(location).build();
}
return ResponseEntity.status(
        HttpStatus.BAD_REQUEST).build();
}
```

Note   By default, Compose sets up a single network for your app. Each container for a service joins the default network and is both reachable by other containers on that network, as well as discoverable by them at a hostname identical to the container name[6].

Container Orchestration

Containers and Docker took most of the pain out of working on microservices. If not for Docker, microservices wouldn't be popular today. Then again, containers only solve one part of the problem in a large-scale microservices deployment. How about managing the lifecycle of a container from the point it is born to the point it is terminated? How about scheduling containers to run on different physical machines in a network, tracking their running status, and load balancing between multiple containers of a given cluster? How about autoscaling containers to meet varying requests or the load on the containers? These are the issues addressed in a container orchestration framework. Kubernetes and

---

[6]https://docs.docker.com/compose/networking/

Apache Mesos are the most popular container orchestration frameworks. In this chapter, we only focus on Kubernetes.

Introduction to Kubernetes

In short, Docker abstracts the machine (or the computer), while Kubernetes abstracts the network. Google introduced Kubernetes to the public in 2014 as an open source project. Before Kubernetes, for many years, Google worked on a project called Borg, to help their internal developers and system administrators manage thousands of applications/ services deployed over large datacenters. Kubernetes is the next phase of Borg.

Kubernetes lets you deploy and scale an application of any type, running on a container, to thousands of nodes effortlessly. For example, in a deployment descriptor (which is understood by Kubernetes), you can specify how many instances of the Order Processing microservice you need to have.

Kubernetes Architecture

Just like in Docker, Kubernetes too follows a client-server based architecture. There is one Kubernetes master node and a set of worker nodes connected to it. The master node is also known as the Kubernetes control plane, which controls the complete Kubernetes cluster. There are four main components in a Kubernetes control plane: the API server, scheduler, controller manager, and etcd. The API server exposes a set of APIs to all the worker nodes and also to the other components in the control plane itself. The scheduler assigns a worker node to each deployment unit of your application. The applications are actually running on a worker node.

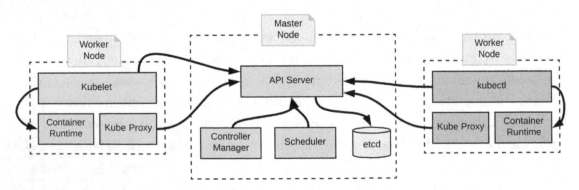

Figure 8-5. *High-level Kubernetes architecture (a Kubernetes cluster)*

The controller manager is responsible for managing and tracking all the nodes in the Kubernetes deployment. It makes sure components are replicated properly and autoscaled, the failures are handled gracefully, as well as performs many other tasks. The etcd is a highly available, consistent datastore, which stores the Kubernetes cluster configuration.

A worker node consists of three components—a kubelet, a container runtime, and a kube-proxy. The container runtime can be based on Docker or rkt. Even though the Kubernetes container runtime was initially tied to Docker and rkt, it can now be extended to support any Open Container Initiative (OCI)-based container runtimes via the Container Runtime Interface (CRI). The responsibility of the kubelet is to manage the node by communicating with the API server running on the master node. It is running on each worker node and acts as a node agent to the master node. Kube-proxy or the Kubernetes network proxy does simple TCP and UDP stream forwarding or round-robin TCP and UDP forwarding across a set of backends.

Installing Kubectl

The Kubernetes master node can run anywhere. To interact with the master node, we need to have kubectl installed locally in our machine. The kubectl installation instructions are available at `https://kubernetes.io/docs/tasks/tools/install-kubectl/`. Make sure that the version of kubectl is within one minor version difference of your cluster.

Installing Minikube

Minikube is the best way to get started with Kubernetes in your local machine. Unlike a production Kubernetes cluster, Minikube only supports one-node Kubernetes cluster. In this chapter, we use Minikube to set up a Kubernetes cluster. Minikube installation details are available at `https://kubernetes.io/docs/tasks/tools/install-minikube/`. You will never use Minikube in a production environment, but the Kubernetes concepts that you learn with Minikube are still valid across any type of a Kubernetes distribution.

Test the Kubernetes Setup

Once you have installed both the kubectl and Minikube in your local machine, we need to start the Minikube server with the following command.

```
:\> minikube start
minikube config set WantUpdateNotification false
Starting local Kubernetes v1.9.0 cluster...
Starting VM...
Getting VM IP address...
Moving files into cluster...
Setting up certs...
Connecting to cluster...
Setting up kubeconfig...
Starting cluster components...
Kubectl is now configured to use the cluster.
Loading cached images from config file.
```

Once Minikube starts, run the following command to verify the communication between kubectl and the Kubernetes cluster. This prints the version of both the kubectl client and the Kubernetes cluster.

```
:\> kubectl version
Client Version: version.Info{Major:"1", Minor:"11", GitVersion:"v1.11.0",
GitCommit:"91e7b4fd31fcd3d5f436da26c980becec37ceefe", GitTreeState:"clean",
BuildDate:"2018-06-27T22:30:22Z", GoVersion:"go1.10.3", Compiler:"gc",
Platform:"darwin/amd64"}
Server Version: version.Info{Major:"", Minor:"", GitVersion:"v1.9.0", Git
Commit:"925c127ec6b946659ad0fd596fa959be43f0cc05", GitTreeState:"clean",
BuildDate:"2018-01-26T19:04:38Z", GoVersion:"go1.9.1", Compiler:"gc",
Platform:"linux/amd64"}
```

Also, with the following command, we can determine where the Kubernetes cluster is running.

```
:\> kubectl cluster-info
Kubernetes master is running at https://192.168.99.100:8443
```

Now we can use following command to see all the nodes in our Kubernetes cluster. Since we are running Minikube, you will only find one node.

```
:\> kubectl get nodes
NAME        STATUS    ROLES      AGE       VERSION
minikube    Ready     <none>     24d       v1.9.0
```

To find more details about a given node, use the following command. This will return a whole lot of metadata related to the node.

```
:\> kubectl describe nodes minikube
```

Kubernetes Core Concepts

In this section, we discuss fundamental concepts associated with Kubernetes. Before we get there, let's look at how Kubernetes works with containers.

The first thing we need to do prior to a Kubernetes deployment is to identify and package our applications into container images, where at runtime, each application will have its own isolated container. Then we need to identify how we are going to group these containers. For example, there can be microservices that run always together, and only one microservice exposes the functionality to the outsiders. In all the other cases, communication between microservices is just internal. Another example is a database we have as a container, which is only used by one microservice. In that case, we can group the database container and the corresponding microservice together. Well, someone of course can argue this as an anti-pattern. We do not disagree. Let's revisit our example, after defining the term pod, within the context of Kubernetes.

Pod

In Kubernetes, we call a group of containers a pod. A *pod* is the smallest deployment unit in Kubernetes. You cannot just deploy containers. First we need to group one or more containers as a pod. Since the pod is the smallest deployment unit in Kubernetes, it can scale only the pods, not the containers. In other words, all the containers grouped as a pod must have the same scalability requirements. If we revisit our previous example, you can group a set of microservices together in a pod. If all of them have the same scalability requirements. But grouping a microservice with a database in a pod is not an ideal use case. Usually a database has different scalability requirements than a microservice.

One common use case for a pod is to have a sidecar proxy with the microservice itself (see Figure 8-6). Here, all the inbound and outbound requests to the microservice flow through the proxy. This model is discussed in detail in Chapter 9, "Service Mesh".

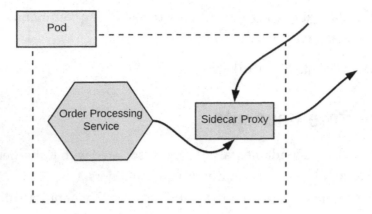

Figure 8-6. *Grouping a set of services into a pod*

Even though a pod can have multiple containers, all of them share the same network interface and storage. Containers within a pod can communicate with each other using localhost as the hostname, and none of the services by default are exposed outside the pod. Also, since all the containers in same pod share the same network interface, no two containers can spin up their services on the same port. When scheduling pods on worker nodes, Kubernetes makes sure that all the containers in the same pod are scheduled to run on the same physical machine (see Figure 8-7).

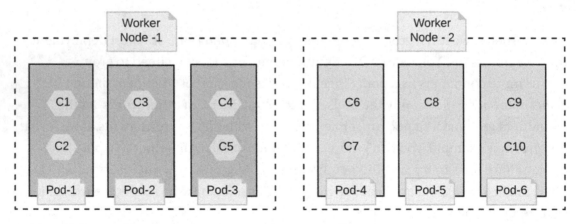

Figure 8-7. *Containers in the same pod are scheduled to run on the same physical machine*

Creating a Pod

Let's look at the following deployment descriptor, which is used to create a pod with the Order Processing microservice and the Inventory microservice. Here first we set the value of the kind attribute to Pod, and later under the spec attribute, we define the set of images need to be grouped into this pod.

Important   Here we made an assumption that both the Order Processing and Inventory microservices fit into a pod and both of them have the same scalability requirements. This is a mere assumption we made here to make the examples straightforward and explain the concepts.

```
apiVersion: v1
kind: Pod
metadata:
  name: ecomm-pod
  labels:
    app: ecommapp
spec:
  containers:
    - name: orderprocessing
      image: prabath/sample04
      ports:
        - containerPort : 9000
    - name: inventory
      image: prabath/sample02
      ports:
        - containerPort : 9090
```

Once the application developer comes up with the deployment descriptor, he or she will feed that into the Kubernetes control plane using kubectl, via the API server. Then the scheduler will schedule the pods on worker nodes, and the corresponding container runtime will pull the container images from the Docker registry.

Note   In the Kubernetes deployment descriptor we point to a slightly modified version of the `Order Processing` microservice (from what we discussed earlier) called `sample04`, instead of the `sample01`.

ReplicaSet

When you deploy a pod in a Kubernetes environment, you can specify how many instances of a given pod you want to keep running all the time. There can be many other scaling requirements as well, which we discuss later in the chapter with examples. It is the responsibility of the ReplicaSet[7] to monitor the number of running pods and make sure to maintain the expected number. If one pod goes down for some reason, the ReplicaSet will make sure to spin up a new one. Later in the chapter, we explain how ReplicaSet works.

Service

In a way, a service[8] in Kubernetes is a grouping of pods that provide the same functionality. These pods in fact are different instances of the same pod. For example, you may run five instances of the same `Order Processing` microservice as five pods to cater to high traffic. These pods are exposed to the outside world, via a service. A service has its own IP address and port, which will never change during its lifetime and it knows how to route traffic to the attached pods. None of the microservice client applications need worry about talking directly to a pod, but to a service. At the same time, based on the scalability requirements and other reasons, pods may come up and go down. Whenever a pod comes up and goes down, it may carry a different IP addresses and it is hard to make any connection from a client application to a pod. The service in Kubernetes solves this problem. There is an example later in the chapter that demonstrates how to create a service in Kubernetes.

---

[7]https://kubernetes.io/docs/concepts/workloads/controllers/replicaset/
[8]https://kubernetes.io/docs/concepts/services-networking/service/

Deployment

Deployment[9] is a higher-level construct that can be used to deploy and manage applications in a Kubernetes environment. It uses the ReplicaSet (which is a low-level construct) to create pods. We discuss how to use the deployment construct later in this chapter.

Figure 8-8 illustrates how the Pods, Services, ReplicaSets, and Deployments are related.

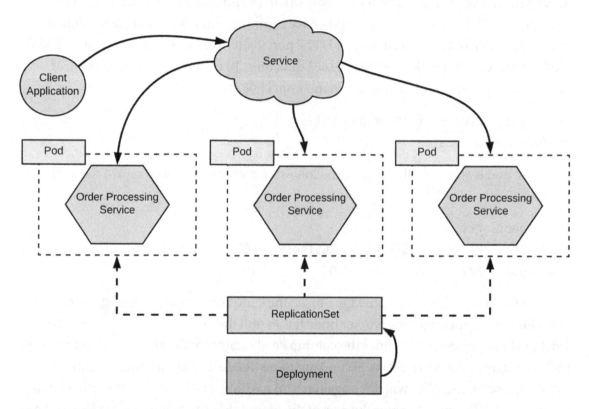

Figure 8-8. *Pods, Services, ReplicaSets, and Deployments*

Deploying Microservices in a Kubernetes Environment

In this section, we see how to create a pod with two microservices and invoke one microservice from the host machine using cURL while the two microservices communicate with each other, in the same pod.

---

[9]https://kubernetes.io/docs/concepts/workloads/controllers/deployment/

Creating a Pod with a YAML File

The first thing we need to do is to come up with a deployment descriptor for our pod. It's the same YAML file we discussed in the previous section. There we create a pod called `ecomm-pod`, with two container images called `prabath/sample04` and `prabath/sample02`. Previously in this chapter we created those two images and pushed to the Docker Hub (`sample04` is a slightly modified version of the `sample01`). Each container in the YAML configuration defines the port where the microservice is running. For example, the `Order Processing` microservice is running on HTTP port 9000, while the `Inventory` microservice is running on HTTP port 9090. You can find the complete YAML file (`ecomm-pod.yml`) in the `ch08/sample03` directory. To create a pod with this YAML configuration, run the following command from `ch08/sample03`.

```
:\> kubectl create -f ecomm-pod.yml
pod/ecomm-pod created
```

If the pod is successfully created, the following command should return the status of the pod.

```
:\> kubectl get pods
NAME            READY       STATUS      RESTARTS    AGE
ecomm-pod       2/2         Running     0           1m
```

The fist time, it may take some time to get the status updated to `Running`, as the container environment of the worker node has to pull the container images from the Docker Hub. The value 2/2 under the column `Ready` states that both containers in this pod are ready to accept requests. To find out more details about this pod, we can use the following command. This will once again return a whole lot of useful information about the given pod. Figure 8-9 shows the part of the output that lists all the events generated while booting up the pod.

```
:\> kubectl describe pod ecomm-pod
```

```
Type     Reason                Age   From                Message
----     ------                ----  ----                -------
Normal   Scheduled             4m    default-scheduler   Successfully assigned ecomm-pod to minikube
Normal   SuccessfulMountVolume 4m    kubelet, minikube   MountVolume.SetUp succeeded for volume "default-token-4jpwq"
Normal   Pulling               4m    kubelet, minikube   pulling image "prabath/sample01"
Normal   Pulled                4m    kubelet, minikube   Successfully pulled image "prabath/sample01"
Normal   Created               4m    kubelet, minikube   Created container
Normal   Started               4m    kubelet, minikube   Started container
Normal   Pulling               4m    kubelet, minikube   pulling image "prabath/sample02"
Normal   Pulled                4m    kubelet, minikube   Successfully pulled image "prabath/sample02"
Normal   Created               4m    kubelet, minikube   Created container
Normal   Started               4m    kubelet, minikube   Started container
```

Figure 8-9. *Events in starting up the ecomm-pod*

If you want to delete a pod, use the following command.

```
:\> kubectl delete -f ecomm-pod.yml
```

Creating a Service with a YAML File

Even though we have a running pod, none of the microservices running there are accessible outside the pod. To expose a microservice outside of a pod, we need to create a service. Once again to define a service, we need to have a service descriptor, a YAML file, as shown here. The complete YAML file (ecomm-service.yml) is available in the ch08/sample03 directory.

```
apiVersion: v1
kind: Service
metadata:
  name: ecomm-service
spec:
  selector:
    app: ecommapp
  ports:
    - port: 80
      targetPort: 9000
  type: NodePort
```

Here you can see the value of the kind attribute is set to Service, and under selector/app attribute, the value is set to the label of the ecomm-pod we created before. This service exposed to the outside world via HTTP port 80 and the traffic coming to it will be routed to port 9000 (targetPort), which is the port of the Order Processing microservice. Finally, another important attribute we cannot miss is the type, where the value is set to NodePort. When the value of the service type is set to NodePort, it exposes the service on each node's IP at a static port.

Let's run the following command from the ch08/sample03 directory to create the service.

```
:\> kubectl create -f ecomm-service.yml
service/ecomm-service created
```

If the service is successfully created, the following command should return the status of the service. There you can see that port 80 of the service is mapped to port 32179 of the Kubernetes master node.

```
:\> kubectl get svc
NAME              TYPE         CLUSTER-IP       EXTERNAL-IP    PORT(S)
ecomm-service     NodePort     10.97.200.207    <none>         80:32179/TCP
kubernetes        ClusterIP    10.96.0.1        <none>         443/TCP
```

If you want to delete a service, use the following command. This will only remove the service, not the corresponding pod.

```
:\> kubectl delete -f ecomm-service.yml
```

Testing the Pod with cURL

Now let's invoke the Order Processing service from the host machine. Here we use the IP address of Kubernetes cluster master node (which you can obtain from the kubectl cluster-info command).

```
:\> curl http://192.168.99.100:32179/order/11
{"customer_id":"101021","order_id":"11","payment_method":{"card_type":
"VISA","expiration":"01/22","name":"John Doe","billing_address":"201,
1st Street, San Jose, CA"},"items":[{"code":"101","qty":1},{"code":"103",
"qty":5}],"shipping_address":"201, 1st Street, San Jose, CA"}
```

This request only hits the Order Processing microservice and does not validate the communication between the two microservices. Let's use the following request to create an order via the Order Processing microservice, which will also then update the Inventory microservice.

```
curl -v -H "Content-Type: application/json" -d '{"customer_
id":"101021","payment_method":{"card_type":"VISA","expiration":"01/22",
"name":"John Doe","billing_address":"201, 1st Street, San Jose, CA"},
"items":[{"code":"101","qty":1},{"code":"103","qty":5}],"shipping_address":
"201, 1st Street, San Jose, CA"}'  http://192.168.99.100:32179/order
```

We can confirm whether our request hits the Inventory microservice by looking at its logs. The following command helps to get the logs from a container running in a pod. Here, ecomm-pod is the name of the pod, and inventory is the container name (as defined in the pod deployment descriptor YAML file). The logs from the Inventory microservice print the item codes from our order request.

```
:\> kubectl logs ecomm-pod -c inventory
101
103
```

How Does Communication Happen Between Containers in the Same Pod?

Within a pod, communication between microservices can happen in different ways. In this example, the Order Processing microservice uses localhost as the hostname to talk to the Inventory microservice, as per the following codebase available at ch08/ sample04/ src/main/java/com/apress/ch08/sample04/service/OrderProcessing. java. There you can see, instead of an IP address or a hostname, that we use *localhost* (http://*localhost*:9090/inventory).

```java
@RequestMapping(method = RequestMethod.POST)
public ResponseEntity<?> createOrder(@RequestBody Order order) {

    if (order != null) {
        RestTemplate restTemplate = new RestTemplate();
        URI uri = URI.create(
            "http://inventory:9090/inventory");
        restTemplate.put(uri, order.getItems());
        order.setOrderId(UUID.randomUUID().toString());
        URI location = ServletUriComponentsBuilder
                .fromCurrentRequest().path("/{id}")
                .buildAndExpand(order.getOrderId())
                .toUri();
```

```
        return ResponseEntity.created(location).build();
    }
    return ResponseEntity.status(
            HttpStatus.BAD_REQUEST).build();
}
```

In addition to using HTTP over localhost, there are two other popular options for inter-container communication within a single pod: using shared volumes and using inter-process communication (IPC). We recommend interested readers to refer to Kubernetes documentation[10] on those topics.

How Does Communication Happen Between Containers in Different Pods?

The containers in different pods communicate with each other using the pod IP address and the corresponding port. In a Kubernetes cluster, each pod has its own distinct IP address.

Deployments and Replica Sets

Even though we discussed creating a pod using a deployment descriptor, in practice you will never use it. You'll use a deployment instead. A *deployment* is an object type in Kubernetes (just like a pod) that helps us manage pods using ReplicaSets. A *ReplicaSet* is an essential component in a Kubernetes cluster where you can specify how you want to scale up and down a given pod. Before we create a deployment, let's do some clean up by deleting the pod we created and the corresponding service.

The following commands first delete the service and then the pod. You need to run these commands from the ch08/sample03 directory.

```
:\> kubectl delete -f ecomm-service.yml
:\> kubectl delete -f ecomm-pod.yml
```

Now, to create a deployment, we need to define our requirements in a deployment descriptor, which is a YAML file. The complete YAML file (ecomm-deployment.yml) is available in the ch08/sample03 directory. Here you can see that the value of the kind attribute is set to Deployment. The value of spec/replicas is set to 3, which means this

---

[10]https://kubernetes.io/docs/

deployment will create three instances of the pod defined under `template`. Just like in the deployment descriptor for the pod (which we used before), here too we define the container images those should be part of the pod, created under this deployment.

```
apiVersion: apps/v1beta1
kind: Deployment
metadata:
  name: ecomm-deployment
spec:
  replicas: 3
  template:
    metadata:
      labels:
        app: ecomm-deployment
    spec:
      containers:
        - name: orderprocessing
          image: prabath/sample04
          ports:
            - containerPort : 9000
        - name: inventory
          image: prabath/sample02
          ports:
            - containerPort : 9090
```

Let's use the following command from `ch08/sample03` to create a deployment.

```
:\> kubectl create -f ecomm-deployment.yml
deployment.apps/ecomm-deployment created
```

If the deployment is successfully created, the following command should return the status of it. The output says that three replicas of the pod defined under the corresponding deployment have been created and are ready to use.

```
:\> kubectl get deployments
NAME                DESIRED    CURRENT    UP-TO-DATE    AVAILABLE    AGE
ecomm-deployment    3          3          3             3            23m
```

The following command shows all the pods created by this deployment.

```
:\> kubectl get pods
NAME                                    READY  STATUS    RESTARTS AGE
ecomm-deployment-546f8c4d6b-67ttd       2/2    Running   1        24m
ecomm-deployment-546f8c4d6b-hldnf       2/2    Running   0        24m
ecomm-deployment-546f8c4d6b-m9vmt       2/2    Running   0        24m
```

Now we need to create a service pointing to this deployment, so the services running in the pods are accessible from the outside. Here we use `ecomm-dep-service.yml`, which is available in the `ch08/sample03` directory, to create the service. The only difference from the previous case is the value of `spec/select/app`, and it now points to the `labels/app` of the deployment.

```
apiVersion: v1
kind: Service
metadata:
  name: ecomm-service
spec:
  selector:
    app: ecomm-deployment
  ports:
    - port: 80
      targetPort: 9000
  type: NodePort
```

Let's use the following command from `ch08/sample03` to create the service.

```
:\> kubectl create -f ecomm-dep-service.yml
service/ecomm-service created
```

If the service is successfully created, the following command should return the status of the service. There you can see that port 80 of the service is mapped to port 31763 of the Kubernetes master node.

```
:\> kubectl get svc
NAME            TYPE        CLUSTER-IP      EXTERNAL-IP   PORT(S)
ecomm-service   NodePort    10.111.102.84   <none>        80:31763/TCP
kubernetes      ClusterIP   10.96.0.1       <none>        443/TCP
```

Now let's invoke the `Order Processing` service from the host machine.

```
:\> curl http://192.168.99.100:31763/order/11
{"customer_id":"101021","order_id":"11","payment_method":{"card_type":
"VISA","expiration":"01/22","name":"John Doe","billing_address":"201,
1st Street, San Jose, CA"},"items":[{"code":"101","qty":1},{"code":"103",
"qty":5}],"shipping_address":"201, 1st Street, San Jose, CA"}
```

Scaling a Deployment

In the previous section, we started our deployment with three replicas or three instances of the pod defined under the deployment descriptor. The following command shows how to scale the replicas to five. Here, `deployment.extensions/ecomm-deployment` is the name of our deployment.

```
:\> kubectl scale --replicas=5 deployment.extensions/ecomm-deployment
deployment.extensions/ecomm-deployment scaled
```

Immediately after this command, if you run the following, you will find that new two pods are created.

```
:\> kubectl get pods
```

NAME	READY	STATUS	RESTARTS
ecomm-deployment-546f8c4d6b-67ttd	2/2	Running	1
ecomm-deployment-546f8c4d6b-hldnf	2/2	Running	0
ecomm-deployment-546f8c4d6b-hsqnp	0/2	ContainerCreating	0
ecomm-deployment-546f8c4d6b-m9vmt	2/2	Running	0
ecomm-deployment-546f8c4d6b-vt624	0/2	ContainerCreating	0

If you run the same command again in a few seconds, you find that all the pods are successfully created.

NAME	READY	STATUS	RESTARTS
ecomm-deployment-546f8c4d6b-67ttd	2/2	Running	1
ecomm-deployment-546f8c4d6b-hldnf	2/2	Running	0
ecomm-deployment-546f8c4d6b-hsqnp	0/2	Running	0
ecomm-deployment-546f8c4d6b-m9vmt	2/2	Running	0
ecomm-deployment-546f8c4d6b-vt624	0/2	Running	0

Autoscaling a Deployment

Kubernetes also lets you autoscale a deployment based on certain parameters. For example, the following command sets the ecomm-deployment to autoscale based on the average CPU utilization. If the average CPU utilization across all the pods is over 50%, then the system should start scaling up to 10 replicas. At the same time, if the CPU utilization goes below 50%, the system should scale down to one replica.

```
:\> kubectl autoscale deployment ecomm-deployment --cpu-percent=50 --min=1
--max=10
horizontalpodautoscaler.autoscaling/ecomm-deployment autoscaled
```

Helm: Package Management with Kubernetes

Helm[11] is a package manager for Kubernetes, and it makes it possible to organize Kubernetes objects in a packaged application that anyone can download and install in one click or customize. Such packages are known as *charts* in Helm. Using Helm charts, you can define, install, and upgrade even the most complex Kubernetes applications.

A chart is a collection of files that describes a related set of Kubernetes resources. A single chart might be used to deploy something simple, like a memcached pod, or something complex, like a full web app stack with HTTP servers, databases, caches, and so on. Installing a chart is quite similar to installing a package using a package management tool such as Apt or Yum. Once you have Helm up and running, installing a package can be as simple as running helm install stable/mysql in the command line.

Helm charts describe even the most complex apps, provide repeatable application installation, and serve as a single point of authority. Also, you can build lifecycle management for your Kubernetes-based microservices as charts, which are easy to version, share, and host on public or private servers. You can also roll back to any specific version if required.

---

[11]https://helm.sh/

Microservices Deployment Patterns

Based on the business requirements, we find that there are multiple deployment patterns for microservices. Microservices were there a while, even before the containers became mainstream, and these deployment patterns have evolved over time. In the following sections, we weigh the pros and cons of each of these deployment patterns.

Multiple Services per Host

This model is useful when you have fewer microservices and do not expect each microservice to be isolated from the others. Here the host can be a physical machine or a virtual machine. This pattern will not scale when you have multiple microservices, and also will not help you in achieving the benefits of a microservices architecture.

Service per Host

With this model, the physical host machine isolates each microservice. This pattern will not scale when you have many microservices, even for something around 10. It will be a waste of resources and will be a maintenance nightmare. Also, it becomes harder and more time consuming to replicate the same operating environment across development, test, staging, and production setups.

Service per Virtual Machine

With this model, the virtual machine isolates each microservice. This pattern is better than the previous service per host model, but still will not scale when you have many microservices. A virtual machine carries a lot of overhead, and we need to have powerful hardware to run multiple virtual machines in a single physical host. Also, due to the increased size, the virtual machine images are less portable.

Service per Container

This is the most common and the recommended deployment model. Each microservice is deployed in its own container. This makes microservices more portable and scalable.

Container-Native Microservice Frameworks

Most of the microservices frameworks and programming languages that we use to build microservices are not designed to work with container management and orchestration technologies by default. Therefore, developers or DevOps have to put extra effort to create the artifacts/configurations that are required for deploying the applications as containers. There are certain technologies, such as Metaparticle.io, that try to build a uniform set of plugins to incorporate such container-native capabilities into the application's or microservice's code that you develop, as annotations. We discuss several of them next.

Metaparticle

Metaparticle[12] is getting some traction when it comes to microservice development as it provides some interesting features to harness your applications with containers and Kubernetes.

Metaparticle is a standard library for cloud-native applications on Kubernetes. The objective of Metaparticle is to democratize the development of distributed systems by providing simple, but powerful building blocks, built on top of containers and Kubernetes.

Metaparticle provides access to these primitives via familiar programming language interfaces. Developers no longer need to master multiple tools and file formats to harness the power of containers and Kubernetes. Metaparticle allows us to do the following:

- Containerize your applications.

- Deploy your applications to Kubernetes.

- Quickly develop replicated, load-balanced services.

- Handle synchronization like locking and master election between distributed replicas.

- Easily develop cloud-native patterns like sharded systems.

---

[12]https://metaparticle.io/tutorials/java/

For example, let's consider the following code snippet, which contains a simple Java code for a `hello world` HTTP service. You can find the complete code example in the `ch08/sample05` directory.

```
public class Main {
    private static final int port = 8080;

    public static void main(String[] args) {
    // Code of a simple HTTP service
    }
}
```

Here we use Metaparticle to containerize our Java microservices. You need to have the following Maven dependency to build a program with Metaparticle.

```
<dependency>
    <groupId>io.metaparticle</groupId>
    <artifactId>metaparticle-package</artifactId>
    <version>0.1-SNAPSHOT</version>
</dependency>
```

To harness your code with Docker and Kubernetes, you need to wrap the code of the HTTP service with Metaparticle constructs.

```
@Package(repository = "docker.io/your_docker_id",

jarFile = "target/metaparticle-hello-1.0-SNAPSHOT.jar")

public static void main(String[] args) {
    Containerize(() -> {
        try {
            HttpServer server = HttpServer.create(new
            InetSocketAddress(port), 0);
...
```

Here, we use the `@Package` annotation to describe how to package the application and specify the Docker Hub username. Also, we need to wrap the main function in the `Containerize` function, which triggers the Metaparticle code when we build our microservice application.

Now we can build your application with `mvn compile` and, once the build is successful, we can run it with `mvn exec:java -Dexec.mainClass=io.metaparticle.tutorial.Main`.

This will start the HTTP microservice as a container. To access this service externally, we need to expose the ports of our microservice application. To do this, we need to add a `@Runtime` annotation to supply the ports to expose.

...

```
    @Runtime(ports={port})
```

...

As a final step, consider the task of exposing a replicated service on the Internet. To do this, we need to expand our usage of the `@Runtime` and `@Package` annotations. The `@Package` annotation has its `publish` field added with a value set to `true`. This is necessary in order to push the built image to the Docker repository. Then, we add the `executor` field to the `@Runtime` annotation to set our execution environment to `metaparticle`, which will launch the service into the currently configured Kubernetes environment. Finally, we add a `replicas` field to the `@Runtime` annotation. This specifies the number of replicas to schedule.

...

```
    @Runtime(ports={port},
             replicas = 4,
             executor = "metaparticle")
    @Package(repository = "kasunindrasiri",
             jarFile = "target/metaparticle-package-tutorial-0.1-SNAPSHOT-
             jar-with-dependencies.jar",
             publish = true,
             verbose = true)
```

...

After we compile and run this, we can see that there are four pod replicas running behind a Kubernetes `ClusterIP` service.

Containerizing a Spring Boot Service

We can use Metaparticle to containerize an existing Spring Boot application by using the Metaparticle dependency and annotations. First we need to add the Metaparticle dependency to our project's pom file and add execute the `SpringApplicaiton.run` inside the `Containerize` function.

```
import static io.metaparticle.Metaparticle.Containerize;

@SpringBootApplication
public class BootDemoApplication {
    @Runtime(ports = {8080},
            replicas = 4,
            executor = "metaparticle")
    @Package(repository = "your-docker-user-goes-here",
            jarFile = "target/boot-demo-0.0.1-SNAPSHOT.jar",
            publish = true,
            verbose = true)
    public static void main(String[] args) {
        Containerize(() -> SpringApplication.run(BootDemoApplication.
        class, args));
    }
}

@RestController
class HelloController {
    @GetMapping("/")
    public String hello(HttpServletRequest request) {
        System.out.printf("[%s]%n", request.getRequestURL());
        return String.format("Hello containers [%s] from %s",
                request.getRequestURL(), System.getenv("HOSTNAME"));
    }
}
```

In addition to seamless containerization, it also offers other features such as distributed synchronization, sharding, etc. In addition to Metaparticle, languages such as Ballerina.io support such capabilities via the annotations. You can find the complete example in the ch08/sample06 directory.

Spring Boot and Docker Integration

Spring Boot is meant to be deployed and run on containers. It offers plugins that allow you to create docker images from the Spring Boot service that you develop. You can create the Docker image by creating the required Dockerfile and adding the `docker-file` Maven plugin to the project build phase. For example, the Dockerfile will look as follows:

```
FROM openjdk:8-jdk-alpine
VOLUME /tmp
ARG JAR_FILE
COPY ${JAR_FILE} app.jar
ENTRYPOINT ["java","-Djava.security.egd=file:/dev/./urandom","-jar","/app.jar"]
```

You can add the `docker-file` plugin[13] to your `pom` file of your project. The complete code example is in the `ch08/sample07` directory.

When it comes to Spring Boot runtime, it uses an embedded web server such as Tomcat to deploy and boot up your services. So you can easily start a microservice with its embedded Tomcat runtime. Although the startup time and memory footprint are relatively high (several seconds), still we can consider Spring Boot a container native technology.

Ballerina: Docker and Kubernetes Integration

We introduced Ballerina in Chapter 7, "Integrating Microservices," and it also offers some container-native capabilities as part of the language extensions. The developers can generate the deployment artifacts for the Ballerina code just by annotating code with suitable annotations of a deployment method of their choice. For example, in the following code snippet, we annotate code with Kubernetes annotations to generate deployment artifacts.

```
import ballerina/http;
import ballerinax/kubernetes;

@kubernetes:Deployment {
    enableLiveness: true,
    singleYAML: true
}
```

---

[13]https://github.com/spotify/dockerfile-maven

```
@kubernetes:Ingress {
    hostname: "abc.com"
}
@kubernetes:Service {name: "hello"}
endpoint http:Listener helloEP {
    port: 9090
};

@http:ServiceConfig {
    basePath: "/helloWorld"
}
service<http:Service> helloWorld bind helloEP {
    sayHello(endpoint outboundEP, http:Request request) {
        http:Response response = new;
        response.setTextPayload("Hello, World from service helloWorld ! \n");
        _ = outboundEP->respond(response);
    }
}
```

During the Ballerina build phase, it will generate Docker images and respective Kubernetes deployment artifacts. The complete code example is in the ch08/sample08 directory. Ballerina deployment choices are so diverse so that you can deploy it in a conventional virtual machine (VM) or bare metal servers, Docker, Kubernetes and on a service mesh, if you are using a Service Mesh such as Istio.

Continuous Integration, Delivery, and Deployment

One of the key rationales behind microservice architecture is less time to production and shorter feedback cycles. One cannot meet such goals without automation. A good microservices architecture will only look good on paper (or on a whiteboard), if not for the timely advancements in DevOps and tooling around automation. Microservices came as a good idea, as they have all the tooling support at the time they started to become mainstream, in the form of Docker, Ansible, Puppet, Chef, and many more. Tooling around automation can be divided into two broader categories—continuous integration tools and continuous deployment tools.

> **Note**   This article is a great source of information, and it includes ideas from different personalities on continuous integration, continuous deployment, and continuous delivery: `https://bit.ly/2wyBLNW`.

Continuous Integration

Continuous integration enables software development teams to work collaboratively, without stepping on each other's toes, by automating builds and source code integration to maintain source code integrity. It also integrates with DevOps tools to create an automated code delivery pipeline. Continuous integration helps development teams avoid *integration hell* where the software works on individual developers' machines, but it fails when all developers integrate their code. Forrester, one of the top analyst firms, in its latest report[14] on continuous integration tools, identified the top ten tools in the domain: Atlassian Bamboo, AWS CodeBuild, CircleCI, CloudBees Jenkins, Codeship, GitLab CI, IBM UrbanCode Build, JetBrains TeamCity, Microsoft VSTS, and Travis CI.

Continuous Delivery

The continuous delivery tools bundle applications, infrastructure, middleware, and their supporting installation processes and dependencies into release packages that transition across the lifecycle. The objective of this is to keep the code in a deployable state all the time. The latest Forrester report on continuous delivery and release automation highlighted 15 most significant vendors in the domain: Atlassian, CA Technologies, Chef Software, Clarive, CloudBees, Electric Cloud, Flexagon, Hewlett Packard Enterprise (HPE), IBM, Micro Focus, Microsoft, Puppet, Red Hat, VMware, and XebiaLabs.

---

[14]`http://bit.ly/2IBWhEz`

However, if we look at the continuous delivery tools that are primarily supporting Kubernetes, the tools such as Weave Cloud[15], Spinnaker[16] (by Netflix), Codefresh[17], Harness[18], and GoCD[19] are quite popular.

Continuous Deployment

Continuous deployment is a process that takes the artifacts produced by the continuous delivery process and deploys into a production setup, ideally every time a developer updates the code! Organizations that follow continuous deployment practices deploy code into production more than one hundred times a day. Blue-green, A/B testing, and canary releases are the three main approaches or practices people follow in continuous deployment.

Blue-Green Deployment

Blue-green deployment is a proven strategy for introducing changes into a running system. It's been around for almost a decade now, and it's successfully used by many large enterprises. Under the blue-green strategy we maintain two close-to-identical deployments; one is called blue and the other one is green. At a given time either blue or green takes the live traffic—let's say blue. Now, we have the green environment to deploy our changes and test. If all works fine, we redirect the live traffic from blue to green at the load balancer. Then green becomes the environment that takes live traffic, while blue becomes available to deploy new changes. If there is an issue, we can quite easily switch the environments, and therefore can automatically roll back the new changes.

Canary Releases

The concept behind the canary comes from a tactic used by coal miners. They used to bring canaries into the mines with them to monitor the level of carbon monoxide in the air. If a canary dies, that means the level of carbon monoxide in the air is high, so they leave the coalmine. With the canary releases, a build is first made available to a selected

---

[15]https://www.weave.works/product/cloud/

[16]https://www.spinnaker.io/concepts/

[17]https://codefresh.io/

[18]https://harness.io/

[19]https://www.gocd.org/

set of the audience (maybe 5% to 10% of the entire live traffic), and if it works well (or doesn't die), then it's made available to everyone. This minimizes the risk of introducing new changes, as the production roll out happens slowly, in smaller chunks.

A/B Testing

A/B testing is about evaluating the impact of a new change against the old system or evaluating the impact of two different changes simultaneously. This is mostly used to track user behavior due to some changes introduced to a website. For example, you may have one version of your website having enabled social login as an option for signup, and another without social login. Another example would be having different colors or placements for important messages on a website and seeing which one is clicked more. A/B testing is used to measure different competing functionalities of an application with live traffic. After some time only the winner stays and the other competing features will be rolled back.

Note   For readers who are interested in more details about continuous deployment, we recommend going through the "Canary Release" article[20] by Danilo Sato and "Blue Green Deployment" article[21] by Marin Fowler.

Summary

In this chapter, we discussed how to run microservices in a production deployment with containers. Containers and microservices are a match made in heaven and if not for containers, microservices wouldn't be mainstream. We discussed deploying microservices with Docker and later discussed how the container orchestration works with Kubernetes. We also looked at Metaparticle, one of the prominent cloud native microservices frameworks, which helps us incorporate container-native capabilities into the applications or microservices code that we develop as annotations. Finally we discussed continuous integration/delivery and deployment.

In the next chapter, we discuss one of the trending topics in microservices architecture and also a key ingredient in any microservices deployment: the Service Mesh.

---

[20]https://martinfowler.com/bliki/CanaryRelease.html

[21]https://martinfowler.com/bliki/BlueGreenDeployment.html

CHAPTER 9

Service Mesh

In Chapter 7, "Integrating Microservices," we discussed that microservices have to communicate with each other and inter-service communication is one of the key challenges in realizing the microservices architecture. In the conventional Service Oriented Architecture (SOA), the centralized Enterprise Service Bus (ESB) facilitated most of the inter-service communication requirements and with the shift to the *smart endpoints and dumb pipes with Microservices architecture*, now the service developers have to take care of all the complexities of inter-service communication. *Service Mesh* has immerged as a pattern to overcome most of these challenges. It does this by providing a generic distributed layer that encapsulates the commodity features of inter-service communication which are not part of the business logic of the service.

Note   Some of the concepts and examples in this chapter may require prior knowledge of Docker and Kubernetes. If you are new to either of these technologies, we recommend you read Chapter 8, "Deploying and Running Microservices" first.

In this chapter, we delve deep into the motivation and key concepts behind the Service Mesh pattern. Then we discuss some of the main Service Mesh implementations with real-world examples.

Why Service Mesh?

The main motivation behind the inception of Service Mesh is the challenges we started to encounter after the elimination of the centralized ESB architecture, which lead us to build smart endpoints and dumb pipes.

As with many emerging technologies, there is a lot of hype around the microservices architecture. Most people think that microservices architecture is the answer to all the problems they had with the previous SOA/ESB architecture. However, when we

© Kasun Indrasiri and Prabath Siriwardena 2018
K. Indrasiri and P. Siriwardena, *Microservices for the Enterprise*, https://doi.org/10.1007/978-1-4842-3858-5_9

observe the real-world microservices implementations, we can see that most of the functionalities that a centralized bus (ESB) supports are now implemented at the microservices level. We are more or less solving the same set of fundamental problems, but we are solving them at different dimensions with microservices.

For example, let's consider a scenario where you need to call multiple downstream services in a resilient manner and expose the functionality as an another microservice. As shown in Figure 9-1, with the ESB architecture, you can easily leverage the built-in capabilities of ESB, in order to build virtual/composite services and functionalities such as circuit breakers, timeouts, service discovery, etc., which are useful during inter-service communication, are already provided as out of the box capabilities of an ESB.

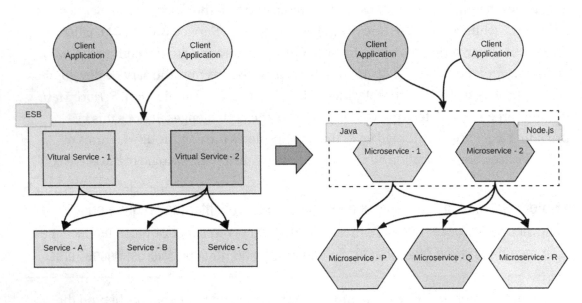

Figure 9-1. *From ESB to smart endpoints and dumb pipes*

When you implement the same scenario using microservices, you no longer have a centralized integration/ESB layer, but a set of microservices. You have to implement all these functionalities at the each microservice level.

Therefore, a microservice that communicates with other services embeds both the business logic and the network communication logic. As illustrated in Figure 9-2, each microservice contains a significant portion of its code related to network communication, which is independent from the service's business logic. From the perspective of the application level, `microservice-P` communicates with `microservice-Q` (denoted as a dashed-line) and the actual communication takes place over the network stack.

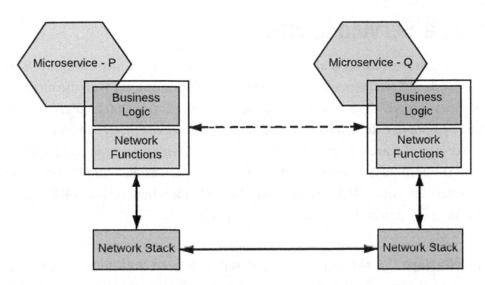

Figure 9-2. *Microservice components and service-to-service communication*

We can identify the key responsibilities of each of these layers as follows:

- *Business Logic* implements the business functionalities, computations, and service composition/integration logic.

- *Network Functions* take care of the inter-service communication mechanisms (basic service invocation through a given protocol, apply resiliency and stability patterns, service discovery, and instrumentation for observability). These network functions are built on top of the underlying operating system (OS) level network stack.

Now think about the effort involved in implementing such a microservice. Implementing the functionalities related to service-to-service communication from scratch is a nightmare. Rather than focusing on the business logic, you will have to spend a lot of time building service-to-service communication functionalities. This is even worse if you use multiple technologies to build microservices, because you need to duplicate the same efforts across different languages (e.g., the circuit breaker has to be implemented in Java, Node, Python, etc.).

Since most of the inter-service communication requirements are quite generic across all microservices implementations, we can think about offloading all such tasks to a different layer, so that we can keep the service code independent. That's where *Service Mesh* comes into the picture.

What Is a Service Mesh?

In a nutshell, a Service Mesh is an inter-service communication infrastructure. With A Service Mesh, a given microservice won't directly communicate with the other microservices. Rather, all service-to-service communications will take place on top of a software component called the *Service Mesh proxy* (or *sidecar proxy*). Sidecar or Service Mesh proxy is a software component that is co-located with the service in the same VM or pod (Kubernetes). The sidecar proxy layer is known as the *Data Plane*. All these sidecar proxies are controlled via a *Control Plane*. That is where all the configuration related to inter-service communications are applied.

Sidecar Pattern   A sidecar is a software component that is co-located with the primary application but runs on its own process or container, providing a network interface to connect to it, which makes it language-agnostic. All the core application functionalities are implemented as part of the main application logic, while other commodity crosscutting features, which are not related to the business logic, are facilitated from the sidecar. Usually all the inbound and outbound communication of the application take place via the sidecar proxy.

Service Mesh provides the built-in support for some network functions such as resiliency, service discovery, etc. Therefore, service developers can focus more on the business logic while most of the work related to the network communication is offloaded to the Service Mesh. For instance, you don't need to worry about circuit breaking anymore when your microservice calls another service. That comes as part of the Service Mesh.

Service Mesh is language-agnostic. The microservice to Service Mesh proxy communication always happens over standard protocols such as HTTP1.x/2.x, gRPC, etc. You can write your microservices from any technology and they will still work with the Service Mesh.

With the introduction of the Service Mesh, the way the services interact changes, as shown in Figure 9-3. For instance, `microservice-P` does not directly communicate with `microservice-Q` anymore. Rather, all inbound (ingress) and outbound (egress) traffic of a given service goes through the Service Mesh sidecar.

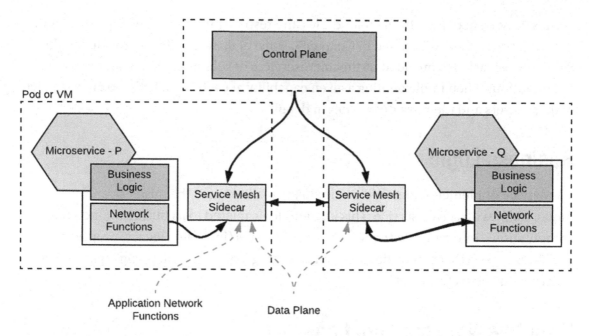

Figure 9-3. *Service-to-service communication with Service Mesh*

The service directly communicates with the sidecar proxy and it should therefore be capable of doing primitive network functions (such as calling an HTTP service), but should not need to take care of application-level network functions (circuit breakers, etc.).

Let's look further into the service interactions and responsibilities shown in Figure 9-4.

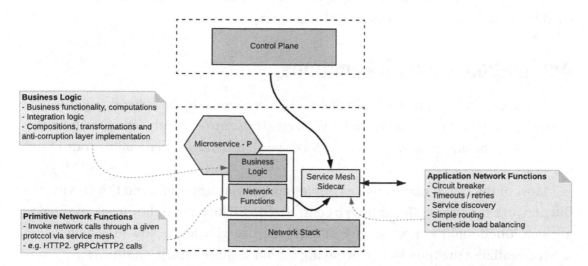

Figure 9-4. *Responsibilities of a Service Mesh sidecar and a microservice that is running alongside*

It's important to identify the boundaries and responsibilities between a service and a sidecar proxy. As we discussed in Chapter 7, some of the capabilities provided in the Service Mesh are also provided by the microservices development languages. We need to be cautious when implementing a given capability at each layer. Let's look next at each of these layers and their responsibilities in detail.

Business Logic

The service implementation should contain the realization of the business functionalities of a given service. This includes logic related to its business functions, computations, integration with other services/systems (including legacy, proprietary, and SaaS) or service compositions, complex routing logics, type mapping logic between different business entities, etc.

Primitive Network Functions

Although we offload most of the network functions to the Service Mesh, a given service must contain the basic high-level network interactions to connect with the Service Mesh sidecar proxy. Hence, a given service implementation will have to use some kind of a network library (unlike the ESB world, where you just have to use a very simple abstraction) to initiate network calls (to the Service Mesh proxy only). In most cases, microservices development frameworks embed the required network libraries to be used for these functions (e.g. basic HTTP transport).

Application Network Functions

There are application functionalities that are tightly coupled to the network, such as circuit breaking, timeouts, service discovery, etc. Those are explicitly separated from the service code/business logic, and Service Mesh facilitates those functionalities out-of-the-box.

Most of the initial microservices implementations simply ignored the gravity of the network functions offered from a centralized ESB layer, and they implemented all such functionalities from scratch at each microservice level. Now they have started realizing the importance of having a similar shared functionality as a distributed mesh.

Control Plane

All Service Mesh proxies are centrally managed by a control plane. This is quite useful when supporting Service Mesh capabilities such as access control, observability, service discovery, etc. All the changes you make at the control plane are pushed into sidecar proxies.

Functionalities of a Service Mesh

As we saw earlier, the Service Mesh offers a set of application network functions while the primitive network functions (such as calling the sidecar over the localhost network) are still implemented at the microservices level. There is no hard and fast rule on what functionalities should be offered from a Service Mesh. However, some of the commonly offered features by a Service Mesh are mentioned in the following sections.

Resiliency for Inter-Service Communications

The network communication capabilities, such as circuit-breaking, retries and timeouts, fault injection, fault handling, load balancing, and failover are supported as part of the Service Mesh. With microservices, we used to have such capabilities implemented as part of the service logic. With the Service Mesh in place, you will not have to build such network functions as part of your service code.

Service Discovery

The services that you run with the Service Mesh needed to be discovered via a logical naming scheme (no hardcoded hosts or ports). Therefore, Service Mesh works with a given service discovery tool to support service registration and discovery. Most Service Mesh implementations come with out-of-the-box capabilities to support service discovery. For example, Istio comes with built-in support for service discovery using the underlying Kubernetes and etcd[1]. If you already have a service discovery solution such as Consul[2], it can also be integrated with the Service Mesh.

---

[1]https://coreos.com/etcd/
[2]https://www.consul.io/

Routing

Some of the primitive routing capabilities, such as routing based on, certain headers, versions etc., are supported by Service Mesh. We have to be really careful about what we implement at the Service Mesh routing layer to not to have any business logic as part of the Service Mesh routing logic.

Observability

When you use Service Mesh, all your services are automatically becoming observable without any changes to your code. Metrics, monitoring, distributed logging, distributed tracing, and service visualizations are available out-of-the-box. Since all the traffic data is captured at the sidecar proxy level, sidecar proxy can publish those data to the relevant control plane components that are responsible to analyze are published to corresponding observability tools.

Security

Service Mesh supports transport level security (TLS) between service-to-service communication and Role-Based-Access Control (RBAC). Also, some of the existing Service Mesh implementations are constantly adding more security-related capabilities to the Service Mesh implementations.

Deployment

Almost all the Service Mesh implementations are closely integrated to container and container management systems. Docker and Kubernetes are the de-facto standards for deployment options with Service Meshes. However, running inside VMs is also possible.

Inter-Service Communication Protocols

Service Meshes support different communication protocols, such as HTTP1.x, HTTP2, and gRPC. The service has to communicate with the sidecar with the same protocol of the service that it would like to proxy to. Service Mesh takes care of most of the low-level communication details while your service code uses primitive network capabilities to invoke the sidecar. Now let's look at some of the popular Service Mesh implementations out there.

Istio

Istio[3] is an open platform to connect, manage, and secure microservices. It provides a communication infrastructure for inter-microservices communication, with resiliency, routing, load balancing, service-to-service authentication, observability, and more, without requiring any changes in your service code.

You can simply add your service to the Istio Service Mesh, by deploying the Istio sidecar proxy alongside your service. As we discussed earlier, the Istio sidecar proxy is responsible for all network communication between microservices, configured and managed using Istio control plane. Istio deployment is deeply married to Kubernetes, but deploying it on some of the other systems is also possible.

Istio Architecture

Figure 9-5 illustrates the high-level architecture of the Istio Service Mesh. Istio comprises two logical components, namely the data plane and control plane.

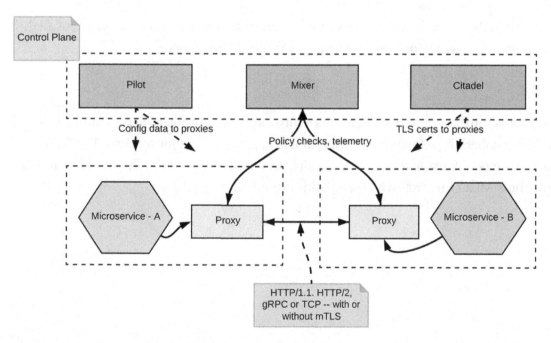

Figure 9-5. *Istio architecture[4]*

---

[3]http://istio.io

[4]https://istio.io/docs/concepts/what-is-istio/

- *Data plane*: The data plane is composed of a set of sidecar proxies that route and control all network communication between microservices. Istio's data plane is mainly composed of the Envoy proxy (which is developed by Lyft).

- *Control plane*: The control plane is responsible for managing and configuring sidecar proxies to change their network communication behaviors. Control plane is composed of Pilot, Mixer, and Citadel components.

Istio Proxy

In its data plane, Istio uses an enhanced version of the Envoy[5] proxy, which is a high-performance proxy developed in C++, to mediate all inbound and outbound traffic for all the services in the Service Mesh. Istio leverages Envoy's many built-in features such as dynamic service discovery, load balancing, TLS termination, HTTP/2 and gRPC proxying, circuit breakers, health checks, staged rollouts with percentage-based traffic split, fault injection, and rich metrics.

Envoy is deployed as a sidecar alongside your microservice and it takes care of all the ingress and egress network communication of your microservice.

Mixer

Mixer is responsible for enforcing access control and usage policies across the Service Mesh and collecting telemetry data from the Istio proxy and other services. The Istio proxy extracts request-level attributes, which are sent to Mixer for evaluation. Figure 9-6 shows how Mixer interacts with other Istio components.

---

[5]https://www.envoyproxy.io/

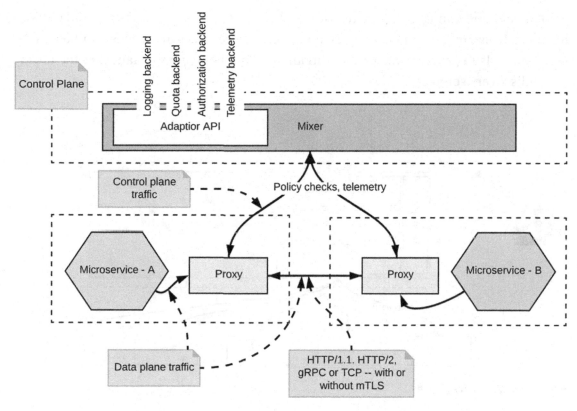

Figure 9-6. *Istio Mixer*

Mixer allows you to fully decouple your service/application code from policy decision-making, so that you can move policy decisions out of the application layer into the configuration instead, which is under operator control. The application code instead does a fairly simple integration with Mixer, and Mixer takes responsibility for interfacing with the backend systems.

Mixer provides three main capabilities in the Istio ecosystem. The Istio proxy sidecar logically calls Mixer before each request to perform precondition checks and after each request to report telemetry. The sidecar has local caching such that a large percentage of precondition checks can be performed with the cache. Additionally, the sidecar buffers outgoing telemetry so that it only calls Mixer infrequently.

Pilot

The core component used for traffic management in Istio is Pilot (see Figure 9-7), which manages and configures all the Istio proxy instances deployed in a particular Istio Service Mesh. Pilot lets you specify which rules you want to use to route traffic between

Istio proxies and configure failure recovery features such as timeouts, retries, and circuit breakers. It also maintains a canonical model of all the services in the mesh and uses this model to let Istio proxy instances know about the other Istio proxy instances in the mesh via its discovery service.

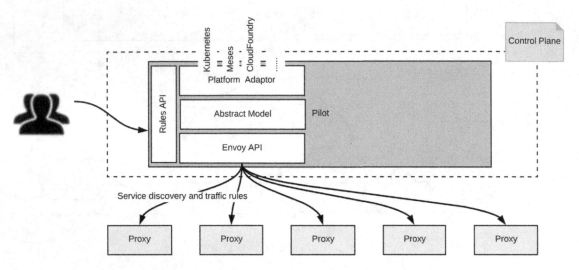

Figure 9-7. *Istio Pilot[6]*

Pilot maintains a canonical representation of services in the mesh that is independent of the underlying platform. Pilot abstracts platform-specific service discovery mechanisms and synthesizes them into a standard format consumable by any sidecar that conforms to the Envoy data plane APIs.

Citadel

Citadel provides strong service-to-service and end-user authentication using mutual TLS, with built-in identity and credential management. It can be used to upgrade unencrypted traffic in the Service Mesh and provide operators with the ability to enforce policies based on service identity rather than on network controls.

---

[6]https://istio.io/docs/

> **Note**   The scope of this book is to give an introduction to Istio as a Service Mesh implementation. For any low-level details and further information on Istio, we recommend you follow the Istio documentation[7] and recommend the book entitled *Introducing Istio Service Mesh for Microservices*[8] by Christian Posta and Burr Sutter.

Using Istio

In this section, we take a closer look at some of the capabilities of Istio with some use cases. We will only cover a selected set of commonly used microservices scenarios; for other scenarios, it is highly recommended that you refer to the Istio official documentation.

> **Note**   Istio examples are heavily dependent on Docker and Kubernetes. Therefore, it is recommended that you read Chapter 8 if you are not familiar with Docker or Kubernetes.

Running Your Services with Istio

Running your microservice with Istio is trivially easy. If you are running your service on Kubernetes, then as the first step you need to create the Docker image for your service. Once you have the Docker image, then you need to create the Kubernetes artifacts to deploy the service.

For example, suppose that you want to develop a simple `hello` service and you have created the Docker image and Kubernetes artifacts to deploy the service. What we have shown here is the generic Kubernetes deployment artifact for that service.

For example, in the following Kubernetes descriptor, you can find the configuration for Kubernetes service and deployment components. In addition, you need to include two Istio specific configurations, namely `VirtualService` and `Gateway`.

---

[7]https://istio.io/docs/

[8]https://developers.redhat.com/books/introducing-istio-service-mesh-microservices/

A `VirtualService` defines the rules that control how requests for a service are routed in an Istio Service Mesh. A `Gateway` configures a load balancer for HTTP/TCP traffic, most commonly operating at the edge of the mesh to enable ingress traffic for an application.

Figure 9-8 shows the request flow between the services and sidecars that you have in a simple communication scenario. Suppose that you are sending a request to `microservice-A` using an external client, and then you need to expose an Istio ingress gateway, which acts as the external interface to your service. When you create a virtual service for `microservice-A`, based on the rules that you specified in that virtual service, the message routing takes place. Similarly, when `microservice-A` calls `microservice-B`, then based on the virtual service configuration of `microservice-B`, the message routing rules will get applied (at the sidecar of the `microservice-A`).

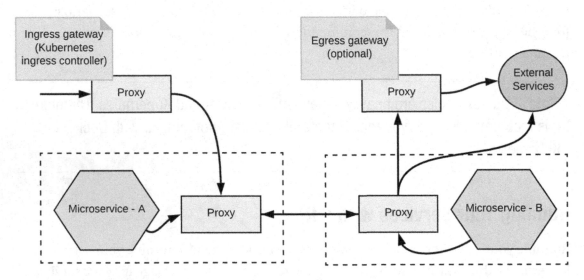

***Figure 9-8.** Request flow*

In this example, we define a gateway that is exposing our service at the edge so that external clients can invoke via the load balancer. The virtual service created for our `HelloWorld` service simply checks for the path `/hello` and routes it to the service.

```
# Helloworld.yaml
apiVersion: v1
kind: Service
metadata:
  name: helloworld
  labels:
    app: helloworld
```

```
spec:
  type: NodePort
  ports:
  - port: 5000
    name: http
  selector:
    app: helloworld
---
apiVersion: extensions/v1beta1
kind: Deployment
metadata:
  name: helloworld-v1
spec:
  replicas: 1
  template:
    metadata:
      labels:
        app: helloworld
        version: v1
    spec:
      containers:
      - name: helloworld
        image: kasunindrasiri/examples-helloworld-v1
        resources:
          requests:
            cpu: "100m"
        imagePullPolicy: IfNotPresent #Always
        ports:
        - containerPort: 5000
---
apiVersion: networking.istio.io/v1alpha3
kind: Gateway
metadata:
  name: helloworld-gateway
```

```
spec:
  selector:
    istio: ingressgateway # use istio default controller
  servers:
  - port:
      number: 80
      name: http
      protocol: HTTP
    hosts:
    - "*"
---
apiVersion: networking.istio.io/v1alpha3
kind: VirtualService
metadata:
  name: helloworld
spec:
  hosts:
  - "*"
  gateways:
  - helloworld-gateway
  http:
  - match:
    - uri:
        exact: /hello
    route:
    - destination:
        host: helloworld
        port:
          number: 5000
```

Now you want to deploy this service on Istio. To do that, you need to inject the Istio sidecar into your deployment. This can either be done as an automatic capability of Istio installation or as a manual process. To understand the behavior properly, let's use the manual sidecar injection.

You can inject the sidecar to your service deployment descriptors with the following:

```
istioctl kube-inject -f helloworld.yaml -o helloworld-istio.yaml
```

It modifies the deployment descriptor and adds the Istio proxy to the same pod that you are going to create. Therefore, the Istio proxy acts as a sidecar in this scenario. Once the sidecar injection is completed, you can simply deploy the modified deployment descriptor as follows:

```
kubectl create -f helloworld-istio.yaml
```

That's all you have to do. Now you can access your service via the Node port or an ingress (if any) and the traffic flows through the Istio Service Mesh. (If needed, you can verify this by enabling tracing at the Istio level. We discuss how to do that in the next couple of sections.)

Most of the Istio examples are based on the official use case[9] that Istio provided to showcase its capabilities. Hence, we will stick to the same example. What we have shown in Figure 9-9 is the BookInfo example deployed on Istio.

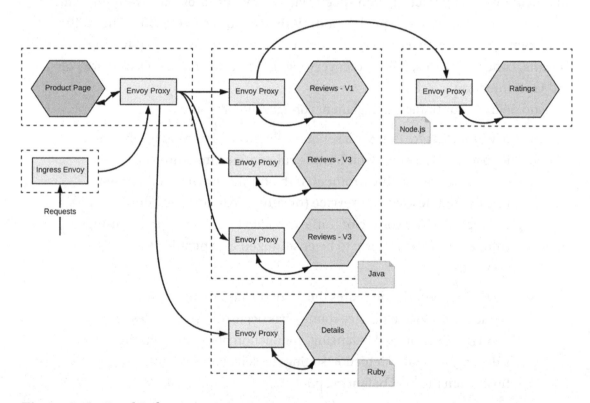

Figure 9-9. BookInfo use case on Istio

---

[9]https://istio.io/docs/examples/bookinfo/

The BookInfo use case is comprised of four polyglot services—Product Page, Reviews, Details, and Ratings. Now let's move on to some of the requirements of this use case in which we can leverage Istio.

Note   You can try most of the following Istio examples by following the guidelines given in the Istio documentation[10].

Traffic Management with Istio

When one service calls the other service or when a given service is exposed to external clients, you can apply Istio's traffic-management capabilities to route the traffic based on different mechanisms. It decouples the traffic flow and infrastructure scaling, letting you specify via Pilot what rules they want the traffic to follow rather than which specific pods/VMs should receive traffic. The traffic-management feature also includes dynamic request routing for A/B testing, gradual rollouts, canary releases, failure recovery using timeouts, retries, circuit breakers, and fault injection.

Istio defines four traffic-management configuration resources:

- A *VirtualService* defines a set of traffic routing rules to apply when a host is addressed. Each routing rule defines matching criteria for traffic of a specific protocol. If the traffic is matched, it is sent to a named destination service (or subset/version of it) defined in the registry. The source of traffic can also be matched in a routing rule. This allows routing to be customized for specific client contexts.

- A *DestinationRule* configures the set of policies to be applied to a request after VirtualService routing has occurred. These rules specify configuration for load balancing, connection pool size from the sidecar, and outlier detection settings to detect and evict unhealthy hosts from the load balancing pool.

---

[10]https://istio.io/docs/

- A *ServiceEntry* is commonly used to enable requests to services outside of an Istio Service Mesh.

- A *Gateway* configures a load balancer for HTTP/TCP traffic, most commonly operating at the edge of the mesh to enable ingress traffic for an application.

Request Routing

Let's try to build a simple request routing scenario using the Istio's BookInfo example. The Istio's BookInfo example consists of four separate microservices, each with multiple versions. Suppose that we need to apply a routing rule that routes all traffic to v1 (version 1) of the Ratings service.

You can implement this example by applying a virtual service and routing rules to each virtual service to route the traffic to v1 of the service. In the following code snippet, we have illustrated the rules for the Ratings and Reviews services. Similarly, you need to do this across all services that you have in the BookInfo example.

```
apiVersion: networking.istio.io/v1alpha3
kind: VirtualService
metadata:
  name: ratings
  ...
spec:
  hosts:
  - ratings
  http:
  - route:
    - destination:
        host: ratings
        subset: v1
---
apiVersion: networking.istio.io/v1alpha3
kind: VirtualService
metadata:
  name: reviews
  ...
```

```
spec:
  hosts:
  - reviews
  http:
  - route:
    - destination:
        host: reviews
        subset: v1
---
```

There can be certain scenarios that you need to do content-based routing on, based on the request. For example, the following virtual service configuration of the Reviews service illustrates an HTTP header-based routing scenario, in which it specifically looks for an HTTP header and routes the traffic to the v2 of the service.

```
apiVersion: networking.istio.io/v1alpha3
kind: VirtualService
metadata:
  name: reviews
  ...
spec:
  hosts:
  - reviews
  http:
  - match:
    - headers:
        end-user:
          exact: jason
    route:
    - destination:
        host: reviews
        subset: v2
  - route:
    - destination:
        host: reviews
        subset: v1
```

Resiliency

As part of resilient inter-service communication techniques, you can use *timeouts* when calling another service via the Istio sidecar proxy. For example, suppose that you want to apply a timeout when you call the Reviews service of the Istio Bookinfo example. Then you can include the timeout configuration as part of your virtual service created for the Reviews service.

The following configuration sets a timeout of 0.5 seconds when calling the Reviews service and calls are routed to version v2 of the service.

```
apiVersion: networking.istio.io/v1alpha3
kind: VirtualService
metadata:
  name: reviews
spec:
  hosts:
  - reviews
  http:
  - route:
    - destination:
        host: reviews
        subset: v2
    timeout: 0.5s
```

Circuit breaker configuration for invoking a specific service can be applied as a *DestinationRule* (which will be applied after the virtual service routing). For example, suppose that we need to apply a circuit breaker configuration when invoking the Httpbin service. Then we can apply the following *DestinationRule,* which includes rules to open the circuit if we exceed more than one connection and request concurrently.

```
apiVersion: networking.istio.io/v1alpha3
kind: DestinationRule
metadata:
  name: httpbin
```

```
spec:
  host: httpbin
  trafficPolicy:
    connectionPool:
      tcp:
        maxConnections: 1
      http:
        http1MaxPendingRequests: 1
        maxRequestsPerConnection: 1
    outlierDetection:
      consecutiveErrors: 1
      interval: 1s
      baseEjectionTime: 3m
      maxEjectionPercent: 100
```

Similarly, there are a number of other service resiliency related capabilities that you can apply when you invoke your services via Istio.

Fault Injection

A route rule can specify one or more faults to inject while forwarding HTTP requests to the rule's corresponding request destination. The faults can be either delays or aborts. In the following example, we inject an HTTP 400 response for all the requests that go to the v1 of the Ratings service.

```
apiVersion: networking.istio.io/v1alpha3
kind: VirtualService
metadata:
  name: ratings
spec:
  hosts:
  - ratings
  http:
  - fault:
      abort:
        percent: 10
        httpStatus: 400
```

```
route:
- destination:
    host: ratings
    subset: v1
```

Policy Enforcement

We introduced Istio Mixer earlier in this chapter as one of the main components of Istio, which is responsible for policy enforcement and telemetric collection. Let's look at how we can leverage policy enforcement with respect to rate limiting.

For example, suppose that you need to configure Istio to rate-limit traffic to the Product Page service based on the IP address of the originating client. You will use the X-Forwarded-For request header as the client IP address.

From the Istio side, you need to configure the memory quota (memquota) adapter to enable rate limiting (or use the Redis quota for production use cases). You can apply the memquota handler configuration, as shown here.

```
apiVersion: config.istio.io/v1alpha2
kind: memquota
metadata:
  name: handler
  namespace: istio-system
spec:
  quotas:
  - name: requestcount.quota.istio-system
    maxAmount: 500
    validDuration: 1s
    - dimensions:
        destination: reviews
      maxAmount: 1
      validDuration: 5s
    - dimensions:
        destination: productpage
      maxAmount: 2
      validDuration: 5s
```

This `memquota` handler defines three different rate-limit schemes. The default, if no overrides match, is 500 requests per one second (1s). The first is 1 request (`maxAmount`) every 5s (`validDuration`), if the destination is reviews.

The second is 2 requests every 5s, if the destination is the `Product Page` service.

```
apiVersion: config.istio.io/v1alpha2
kind: quota
metadata:
  name: requestcount
  namespace: istio-system
spec:
  dimensions:
    source: request.headers["x-forwarded-for"] | "unknown"
    destination: destination.labels["app"] | destination.service.host |
    "unknown"
    destinationVersion: destination.labels["version"] | "unknown"
```

The quota template defines three dimensions that are used by `memquota` or `redisquota` to set overrides on requests that match certain attributes. The destination will be set to the first non-empty value in `destination.labels["app"]`, `destination.service.host`, or `unknown`.

```
apiVersion: config.istio.io/v1alpha2
kind: rule
metadata:
  name: quota
  namespace: istio-system
spec:
  actions:
  - handler: handler.memquota
    instances:
    - requestcount.quota
```

This rule tells Mixer to invoke the `handler.memquota\handler.redisquota` handler and pass it the object constructed using the instance `requestcount.quota`. This maps the dimensions from the quota template to the `memquota` or `redisquota` handler.

```
apiVersion: config.istio.io/v1alpha2
kind: QuotaSpec
metadata:
  name: request-count
  namespace: istio-system
spec:
  rules:
  - quotas:
    - charge: "1"
      quota: requestcount:
```

This QuotaSpec defines the `requestcount` quota you created with a charge of 1.

```
kind: QuotaSpecBinding
metadata:
  name: request-count
  namespace: istio-system
spec:
  quotaSpecs:
  - name: request-count
    namespace: istio-system
  services:
  - name: productpage
    namespace: default
```

This `QuotaSpecBinding` binds the `QuotaSpec` you created to the services you want to apply it to. The `Product Page` service is explicitly bound to request-count. Note that you must define the namespace since it differs from the namespace of the `QuotaSpecBinding`.

Observability

When you are using Istio, making your services observable is trivially easy. For example, suppose that you want to enable distributed tracing for your microservices application. Then you need to install the corresponding add-on (such as Zipkin[11] or Jaeger[12]) into

---

[11]https://zipkin.io/
[12]https://www.jaegertracing.io/

your Istio installation. Now when you send requests to your microservices, they will go through the sidecar proxies. Sidecar proxies are capable of sending tracing spans automatically to either Zipkin or Jaeger.

Istio proxies can also automatically send spans. They need some hints to tie together the entire trace. Applications need to propagate the appropriate HTTP headers so that when the proxies send span information to Zipkin or Jaeger, the spans can be correlated correctly into a single trace.

Similarly, other aspects of observability can also be supported with no or minimal changes to your code. Refer to the Istio documentation[13] for more details on how you can make your services observable with Istio. We discuss observability in detail, with respect to microservices, in Chapter 13, "Observability".

Security

Istio's security capabilities are still evolving at a rapid rate. At the time this book was written, Istio offered the following security features:

- Mutual TLS (mTLS) authentication between services

- Whitelisting and blacklisting of services

- Access control with denials

- Role-Based Access Control (RBAC)

For further details on these security use cases, refer to the Istio documentation[14].

Since you had a closer look at Istio, let's look at another popular Service Mesh implementation, Linkerd.

Linkerd

Linkerd is an open source network proxy designed to be deployed as a Service Mesh: a dedicated layer for managing, controlling, and monitoring service-to-service communication within an application.

---

[13]https://istio.io/docs/tasks/telemetry/
[14]https://istio.io/docs/tasks/security/

Linkerd takes care of the difficult, error-prone parts of cross-service communication—including latency-aware load balancing, connection pooling, TLS, instrumentation, and request-level routing. Linkerd is built on top of Netty and Finagle.

Figure 9-10 shows how Linkerd is used as a Service Mesh to connect multiple microservices. You can find that it uses the standard Service Mesh pattern in a way pretty similar to Istio.

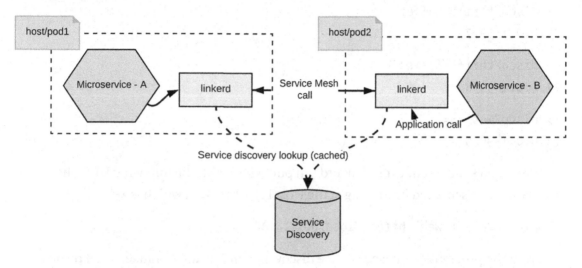

Figure 9-10. *Linkerd Service Mesh*

To get started (`https://linkerd.io/getting-started/locally/`) with Linkerd, you can run it in your local machine and run your service in the same machine (both runtimes on the same host). When you are running Linkerd, you can use the following Yaml configuration file to start your Service Mesh. Suppose that your microservice is running on port 9999 on HTTP. The following configuration starts Linkerd on HTTP port 4140.

```
#linkerd.yaml
routers:
- protocol: http
  dtab: |
    /svc => /#/io.l5d.fs
  servers:
  - ip: 0.0.0.0
    port: 4140
```

Linkerd uses a file-based service discovery mechanism by default. With the configuration that ships with Linkerd, the first place it looks when it needs to resolve a service endpoint is the disco/ directory. With this configuration, Linkerd looks for files with names corresponding to the concrete name of a destination, and it expects these files to contain a newline-delimited list of addresses in host port form.

```
 head disco/*
==> disco/thrift-buffered <==
127.0.0.1 9997

==> disco/thrift-framed <==
127.0.0.1 9998

==> disco/web <==
127.0.0.1 9999
```

When you send a request to Linkerd (on port 4140) with the following URL, the destination is discovered by looking at the Host HTTP header, which is web.

```
$ curl -H "Host: web" http://localhost:4140/
```

From the previous file-based service discovery configuration, Linkerd can resolve the host and port (9999) for the service web.

We can extend the same configuration to have resilient calls to the backend microservice by using Linkerd's failureAccrual configuration.

```
- protocol: http
  label: io.l5d.consecutiveFailures
  dtab: /svc => /#/io.l5d.fs/service2;
  client:
    failureAccrual:
      kind: io.l5d.consecutiveFailures
      failures: 5
      backoff:
        kind: constant
        ms: 10000
  servers:
  - port: 4142
    ip: 0.0.0.0
```

```
service:
  responseClassifier:
    kind: io.l5d.http.nonRetryable5XX
```

`failureAccrual` is configured in Linkerd's configuration under the client section, so any failure related to the backend reside on that route and are subjected to the client, which is resilient.

Should We Use Service Mesh?

At the time this book was written, there was a lot of traction toward using Service Mesh. However, production usage of Service Mesh was rare at this time. Therefore, we don't have sufficient understanding of the real pros and cons yet. Let's look at some of the key areas that we need to be mindful about when using Service Mesh.

Pros

Service Mesh certainly has the capability to revolutionize the way we develop container-native services and applications. Given that the complexity that microservices architecture brings in, in the context of inter-service communication, Service Mesh provides some promising advantages:

- *Developers can focus more on business functionality than on inter-service communication*: Most of the commodity features are implemented outside microservice code and are reusable.

- *Observability out of the box*: Services are innately observable via the sidecar. Hence, distributed tracing, logging, metrics, etc. require no additional effort from the service developer.

- *Polyglot-services friendly*: More freedom when it comes to selecting a microservices implementation language. You don't need to worry about whether a given language supports or has libraries to build network application functions.

- *Centrally managed decentralized system:* Most of the capabilities can be managed centrally via the control plane and pushed into decentralized sidecar runtimes.

If you are already running Kubernetes in your enterprise, adopting Service Mesh into your architecture is quite straightforward.

Cons

- *Complexity*: Having a Service Mesh drastically increases the number of runtime instances that you have in a given microservices implementation.

- *Adding extra hops*: Each service call has to go through an extra hop (through the Service Mesh sidecar proxy).

- *Service Meshes address a subset of problems*: Service Mesh only addresses a subset of inter-service communication problems, and there are a lot of complex problems it doesn't address, such as complex routing, transformation/type mapping, and integrating with other services and systems. These must be solved by your microservice's business logic.

- *Immature*: Service Mesh technologies are relatively new to be declared as full production ready for the large-scale deployments.

Summary

In this chapter, we took a detailed look at the concept of a Service Mesh and the key reason behind its inception. Service Mesh tries to simplify some of the inter-service communication complexities and service governance requirements. When we use a Service Mesh, the developers don't need to worry about the inter-service communication and most of the other crosscutting features of a service such as security, observability, etc. Each microservice runs with a co-located sidecar, which is controlled by a central control plan. The sidecars are controlled using a predefined configuration, which is pushed via the control plane. Istio is one of the most commonly used implementations of the Service Mesh. The Service Mesh concept is relatively new and yet to be fully battle-tested. So, we need to be very aware of its pros and cons.

CHAPTER 10

APIs, Events, and Streams

In this chapter, we focus on how microservices can connect with external services, systems and data using APIs, Events and Streams.

As discussed in previous chapters, any of the microservices applications that you develop have to expose the business capabilities to consumers in such a way that you can create, manage, secure, analyze, and scale those capabilities. Therefore, such capabilities are exposed to consumers as APIs, which are governed by a process commonly known as API management. Similarly, Microservices can consume external APIs via invoking API calls. APIs more or less follow a synchronous and request-response messaging type communication.

Microservices can also build on top Event-driven architecture, where applications are fully decoupled from each other and communicate via asynchronous events or messages. An event can be emitted by a given service or a system and some other service can act on it. Microservices have to cater to various event-driven communication styles, with internal as well as external service boundaries.

A stream is an unbounded set of events that a service processes continuously. The consumer service of a given stream keeps processing that stream and can emit the resulting events based on the stream processing logic.

The business capabilities of your microservices based applications can be exposed using APIs, events or stream and they can also connect and consume external APIs, events and streams.

Let's delve deeply into each of these areas and see how we can leverage them when building a microservices architecture.

© Kasun Indrasiri and Prabath Siriwardena 2018
K. Indrasiri and P. Siriwardena, *Microservices for the Enterprise*, https://doi.org/10.1007/978-1-4842-3858-5_10

APIs and API Management

Any business capability that you want to expose to a consumer (internal or external) can be considered an API. Exposing such business capabilities in a way that you can create, manage, secure, analyze, and scale them, is known as *API management*. By using API management solutions, you can enable policy and key validation, service versioning, quota management, primitive transformations, authorization and access control, observability, self-service capabilities, ratings, and so on, for your microservices.

When it comes to API management, there are several main components that should be part of any API management solution. They are:

- API Publisher

- API Developer Portal/Store

- API Gateway

- API Analytics/Observability

- API Monetization

- API Quality of service (security, throttling, caching, etc.)

It's important to understand that most of these components are generic and not tightly coupled to the microservices architecture. Therefore, exposing a microservice as an API and exposing an API for a monolithic system is pretty much the same. (There is a certain set of components that you will make decentralized with the introduction of the microservices architecture. We discuss them in the next few sections of this chapter.)

Figure 10-1 illustrates these key API management components and shows how they interact.

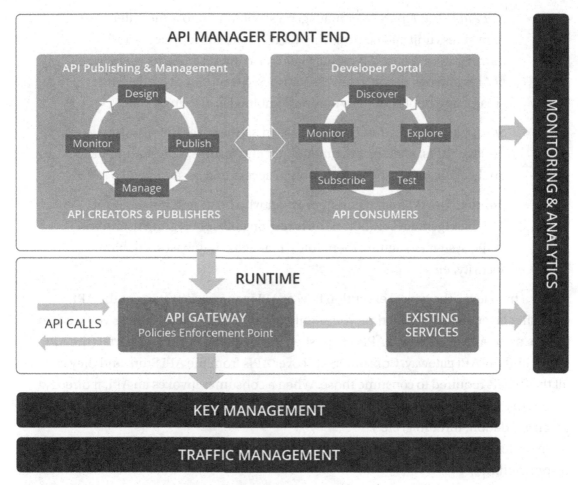

Figure 10-1. Components of API management

Prior to going into detail about the responsibilities of each of these components, we can also identify some of the different roles that are associated with API management. They are:

- *API Creator/API Developer*: A creator is a person in a technical role who understands the technical aspects of the API (interfaces, documentation, versions, etc.) and uses the API Publisher to provision APIs into the API store. The creator uses the API Store to consult ratings and feedback provided by API users. The creator can add APIs to the store but cannot manage their lifecycle.

- *API Publisher*: A publisher manages a set of APIs across the enterprise or business unit and controls the API lifecycle, subscriptions, and monetization aspects. The publisher is also interested in usage patterns of APIs and has access to all API statistics. (In certain cases, the API creator and publisher roles may be combined into a single role.)

- *Subscriber/Application Developer*: A subscriber uses the API store to discover APIs, read the documentation and forums, rate/comment on the APIs, subscribe to APIs, obtain access tokens, and invoke APIs.

- *Admin*: The API management provider who hosts and manages the API management solution. S/he is responsible for creating user roles in the system, assigning them roles, managing databases, enabling security, etc.

At a high level, the typical execution flow of API management starts at the API Publisher layer. In fact, at that time you should decide which microservices you want to expose as an API. The created APIs are pushed into both the developer portal (the API Store) and the API gateway. Consumers discover APIs from the API Store and they can find all the details required to consume those. When a consumer invokes an API, it directly comes to the API gateway. The gateway is responsible for doing QoS validations (security token validation, throttling, etc.).

Now let's take a closer look at each of these components and learn about their responsibilities.

API Publisher/API Lifecycle Manager

When you develop microservices, you design them around business capabilities. You may also integrate multiple microservices and form a composition to build them. If you need to expose this capability as a managed capability to the consumers, you will have to create an API for doing so.

API providers or creators are responsible for designing, developing, publishing, deploying, versioning, governing, monitoring availability, and measuring performance. The API Publisher/Lifecycle Manager component of an API management solution is responsible for this.

The API Publisher or API Lifecycle Manager allows you to develop, document, scale, and version APIs. It also provides API Lifecycle Management-related tasks, such as publishing an API, monetization, analyzing statistics, and promoting.

We can identify some of the key steps that are related to each lifecycle state of the API lifecycle manager:

- *Develop phase*: Identifying and developing business capabilities that we should expose as managed APIs. This task may involve combining multiple microservices and creating composite functionalities, as well as exposing existing microservices as an API.

- *Publish phase*: Once we implement the API's functionality, then we need to publish that API so that it will be visible on the API developer portal/store. We also associate SLAs (Service Level Agreements) and other QoS (Quality of Service) related (security, throttling) functions to the APIs that we publish.

- *Manage phase*: API versioning strategy that manages lifecycle states of an API.

- *Observability phase*: When APIs are consumed by the consumers, all the data related to metrics, tracing, and logging are captured by the API gateway component. The API providers should use this data to enhance, change, or monetize their API consumption.

API Gateway

When you publish an API from the API Publisher, the API definition is pushed into the API gateway component. API gateway secures, protects, manages, and scales API calls. All the requests that the API consumers send are intercepted by the API gateway. It applies policies such as throttling and security, using handlers, publishes data for API observability and other API governance tasks. Also, in certain cases, we may implement composition of multiple business functionalities at the API gateway level. However, you need to be cautious about what type of compositions you do at the API gateway level and must avoid the monolithic gateway antipattern discussed in Chapter 7, "Integrating Microservices".

> **Note**   We discussed the Monolithic API Gateway anti-pattern in Chapter 7, where you develop certain microservices composition at a monolithic gateway level. (Refer to the section entitled "Monolithic API Gateway for Integrating Microservices" in Chapter 7.)
>
> The best approach to avoid this is to create a composite service on top of the microservices that you want to integrate and then expose that at the API gateway. If you want to do compositions at the API gateway, your API gateway needs to have the ability to function as a micro-gateway, in which you will have independent runtimes for each and every API that you deploy at the API gateway.

Most of the API management solution vendors often call their entire solution an API gateway. You should keep in mind that all the other functionalities of the other components may get baked into a single solution.

API Micro-Gateway

Most of the API gateways are initially built as monolithic runtimes. However, with the advent of the microservices architecture, most API management solutions now offer micro-gateway capability too. The key idea behind a micro-gateway is that we develop the APIs and deploy them independently on a container-native gateway runtime, which is managed/governed by a centralized API publisher/lifecycle manager.

> **Note**   We will further analyze how you can morph your entire microservices architecture around the API micro-gateway concept when we discuss the microservice reference architecture with APIs, streams, and events.

API Store/Developer Portal

When API providers publish APIs through an API Publisher, those APIs are pushed into the corresponding API Store or developer portal. API developers self-service, discover, evaluate, subscribe to, and use secured, protected, authenticated APIs via the API Store. Let's look at some of the lifecycle activities related to an API Store.

- *Discover phase*: Find out the APIs that match the API developer's business capability.

- *Explore phase*: View ratings and comments for the API, read documentation, and try out some of the capabilities.

- *Subscribe phase*: Register an application and subscribe to APIs, obtain the required security tokens, etc., to invoke the API and subscribe to notifications about API lifecycle changes.

- *Evaluate phase*: Once we start consuming an API, we can rate, comment, and give feedback on it.

API Analytics/Observability

API analytics or observability is a critical factor from both the technical and business perspectives. Therefore, API management solutions provide various API analytics capabilities out of the box. This includes metrics on API invocation, API subscribers, top APIs, top developers, slow/fast APIs, API invocation errors, trending APIs, and so on. Also, the ability to trace the API traffic is a critical factor for troubleshooting and identifying bottlenecks. It is also required to have conventional runtime monitoring capabilities and logging. Some other solutions, such API monetization, are built on top of the API analytic data.

API QoS

API Quality of Service (QoS) has multiple perspectives such as security, caching, throttling, and other SLAs (Service Level Agreements). We have two dedicated chapters (Chapter 11, "Microservices Security Fundamentals" and Chapter 12, "Securing Microservices") covering microservices security fundamentals and we cover API security as part of them. Other QoS aspects, such as caching, throttling, etc. are pretty straightforward to implement with any API management solutions (and they have no special notion in the context of a microservice). Most of the QoS-related enforcements are done at the API gateway level and offload the actual decision making (e.g., security token validation) to an external entity.

API Monetization

APIs are all about your business capabilities and you can generate revenue by exposing them to your customers/partners. API management solutions provide such capabilities out-of-the-box to build a monetary ecosystem around your API management solution.

API Definition with OpenAPI

The key idea of designing an API for a microservice is to hide the implementation details and only expose the interface that addresses a specific business functionality. The OpenAPI specification (OAS), which is formerly known as Swagger, defines a standard programming language-agnostic interface description for REST APIs. It allows both humans and computers to discover and understand the capabilities of a service without requiring access to source code, additional documentation, or inspection of network traffic.

OpenAPI documents describe an API's services and are represented in either YAML or JSON formats. These documents may be produced and served statically or be generated dynamically from an application.

You can either start by designing the API first (contract first) and then implement the API (may be using code-generation plugins) or you can first implement the API and derive the OpenAPI definition for your service. However, it's important to keep in mind that OpenAPI is not intended to cover all possible styles of RESTful service design. You can learn about building an OpenAPI-based API definition by referring to OpenAPI samples[1].

A Query Language for Your APIs: GraphQL

As discussed in Chapter 3, "Inter-Service Communication," GraphQL provides a query language for APIs, which are not necessarily based on the REST architecture. We can still implement API management on top of GraphQL-based services and expose them as managed APIs. An API based on GraphQL can be more powerful than a conventional RESTful API, as it provides a complete and understandable description of the data in your API, gives clients the power to ask for exactly what they need and nothing more, makes it easier to evolve APIs over time, and enables powerful developer tools.

---

[1]https://github.com/OAI/OpenAPI-Specification/tree/master/examples/v3.0

API Management and Service Mesh

API gateways/management solutions and service mesh have similar characteristics, which confuses some in the community. In order to differentiate an API gateway from a service mesh, let's take a closer look at the key characteristics of both. It's important to understand the users who interact with the management of API gateways and service mesh.

- *API management*: The users who interact with the API management are creating and managing business functionalities that they want to expose as APIs.

- *Service Mesh management*: The users interact with the service mesh are primarily responsible for managing the non-business logic aspects of the communication between microservices. More or less, they manage the inter-service communication infrastructure of the services.

With this distinction, Figure 10-2 shows how you can use API management along with a service mesh.

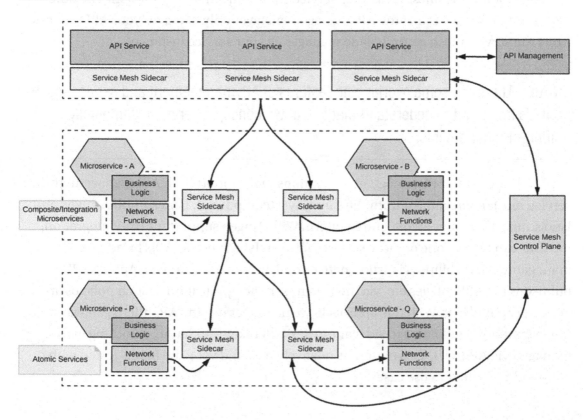

Figure 10-2. *Service-to-service communication with service mesh and the API gateway*

The API/edge services that we develop at the API gateway layer serve a specific business functionality. They call the downstream microservices and may contain some business logic that creates compositions/mashups of multiple services. API services also need to call the downstream services in a resilient manner and apply various stability patterns, such as circuit breakers, timeouts, and load balancing/failover. They can offload such functionalities to the service mesh. Therefore, there will be a service mesh sidecar proxy running alongside each API service. (Although most of the API gateway solutions out there have these features built in, they can still offload such functionalities to the service mesh.) Since the service mesh is the network communication infrastructure, and it allows you to decouple and offload most of the application network functions from your service code, you will have a separate control plane to manage such capabilities. There can be certain overlapping features such as observability of a given API service, which is available from both service mesh and API management observability capabilities. We can still keep them as two different things, as the API management layer is designed for business capabilities, while the service mesh layer is designed for non-business logic inter-service communication requirements. Another important difference is that the API management layer only manages your API services, while the service mesh control plane manages all your service instances.

Note   There are some overlapping features of API management and service mesh, but it's important to understand that these two concepts serve fundamentally different requirements.

There are some API management solutions that support both API management and service mesh management from the same layer/component. For example, Apigee and Istio support a similar architecture pattern. With Apigee support for Istio integration, the user can expose one or more services from an Istio mesh as APIs by adding API management capabilities via Istio's native configuration mechanism. Apigee APIM publishes the API policies etc. via the Istio mixer and application of such policies are done at each sidecar. With this approach, we no longer use the API micro gateways but everything is offloaded to sidecar proxies. API token validation, throttling can be managed via APIM UI. This pattern is relatively new and yet to be battle-tested with real-world production use cases.

Implementing API Management

Implementation of comprehensive API management for your microservices requires catering all the API management aspects that we discussed earlier. There are quite a few solutions, which have drastically cut down the API management features and promote them as an API gateway for microservices. You need to be cautious when selecting an API management solution and make sure you can facilitate all your API management requirements. Also, if you have fully embraced a container-native architecture, the components such as API gateway must be container-native too (i.e., they must support a micro-gateway architecture).

There are quite a few API management solutions out there, such as Apigee, WSO2 API Manager, Kong, MuleSoft, etc. We don't focus on comparing and contrasting them or recommending a specific solution. We want to give full freedom to the readers to evaluate them and select the most suitable technology. You can find couple of API Management use cases built with such API Management solutions in the samples of chapter 10.

Events

Event-driven architecture (EDA) is a widely used architectural paradigm in software applications in which a given application executes some form of code/logic in response to a one or more event notifications. EDA makes applications/services more autonomous than the client-server architecture, where the party that sends the notification waits or depends on the consumer who consumes the event.

In the context of microservices, we already discussed multiple forms of EDA under the asynchronous communication style (Chapter 2, "Designing Microservices") and reactive compositions/choreography (Chapter 7). Basically, we can design microservices so that they operate in a full event-driven model and asynchronous message passing allows them to be more autonomous. In this chapter, we explore some of the commonly used event-driven patterns in a microservices architecture.

Event Notifications

Event notification is a common form of EDA where a service sends events to notify other services of a change in its domain. Often the event receiver must have the autonomy to carry out the task, if it wishes to do so. An event needs not carry much data on it; often a reference to where the updated information can be retrieved is sufficient.

For example, as shown in Figure 10-3, suppose we have two microservices, called Customer and Shipping. When there is a change in customer information, such as a customer's address, we can send an event notification to the Shipping service. The event itself may not have all the details of the change, but includes a reference to where the information related to the change can be obtained. As discussed in Chapter 3, the asynchronous event-based communication can be used to realize such scenarios; we can use queue-based communication or topic-based communication to do this.

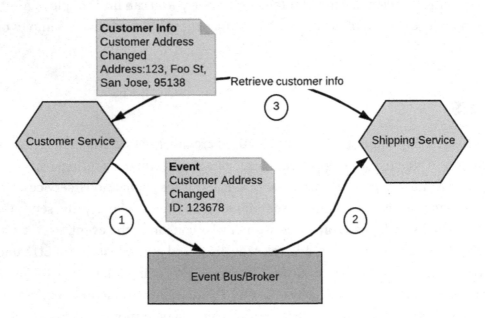

Figure 10-3. *Event notifications*

Obviously, most of the message/event broker solutions can be used as the backbone to implement this pattern and Kafka, RabbitMQ, and ActiveMQ are most commonly used in this domain.

It is an anti-pattern to have logic flow that runs as part of event notifications. For example, if your event publisher expects the receivers to do a certain tasks upcon the receipt of your event. then there is a logic flow between the event publisher and receiver.

Some of the mere theoretical microservices books and other resources suggest that every integration/composition of microservices must be done using asynchronous event-driven communication. That literally means having logic flows across your microservices that run via event notifications.

Having these kinds of logic flows is not a practical approach because they are extremely hard to manage and troubleshoot. Maybe the only way that you can derive such a logic flow is via observability (tracing). Therefore, you need to be cautious when applying an event-notification pattern to a scenario where you need to pass commands (you expect the receiver would do a definite task upon the receipt of your event).

Event-Carried State Transfer

This is a subtle variation of the event notification pattern. When an event is trigged, the subscribers are notified with events that contain details of the data that changed. So, the recipient services don't need to access or refer to any other systems or services. The data is already being received as part of the event. Figure 10-4 shows the same scenario that we discussed in the previous section, which is now modified with an event-carried state transfer.

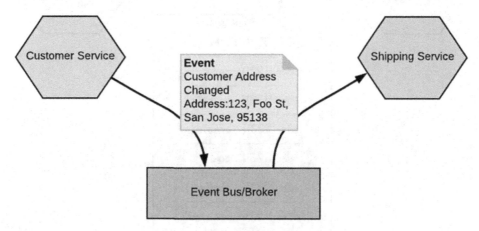

Figure 10-4. *Event-carried state transfer*

One of the possible downsides of this approach is the duplication of data across multiple services, because all the subscribers will receive the same data. The implementation technology can be similar to event notifications. On the flip side, there is also decreased network traffic, because in this approach, the shipping service would not need to make a request to the customer service to get the updated address.

Event Sourcing

By using asynchronous messaging techniques, we can persist each state-changing event of an entity as a sequence of events. All such events are stored in an event bus or event log and subscribers can derive the state of that entity by processing the sequence of events that has taken place on that entity. For example, as shown in Figure 10-5, the Order Processing service publishes the changes taken place on the Order entity as events. The state-changing events such as order created, updated, paid, shipped, etc. are published to the event bus. With event sourcing, since we have all the state changing events in the event log, multiple consumers can materialize different view of the same data and those consumers can discard the application state completely and rebuild it by re-running the events from the event log on an empty application. Also, we can determine the application state at any point in time as the events are recorded sequentially. If we need to replay the events executed previously (maybe with some modifications to those events), we can also do that using the event log.

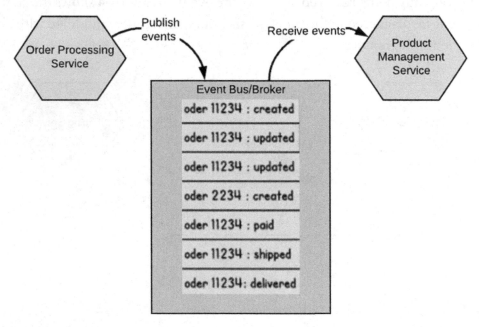

Figure 10-5. *Event sourcing*

The subscriber applications and services can recreate the status of an order by just replaying the events that are taking place on an order. For example, it can retrieve all the events related to order 11234 and derive the current state of the order.

Command Query Responsibility Segregation (CQRS)

Most of the conventional services or applications are developed with the assumption that we *create* new records, *read* records, *update* existing records, and *delete* records when we're done with them. These are known as CRUD (Create, Read, Update, and Delete) operations and all these operations are executed on top of a common model. This approach is known as the *CRUD model*.

However, with the microservices and modern sophisticated enterprise requirements having a common data model for all, such operations are not always feasible. For example, suppose that you have two functionalities of a given service, one to search and read records from the table and the other one to update records in the table. In most cases, these two functionalities are drastically different and using a common data model often complicates the implementation. In such cases, we can split the common data model into a query model and a command model. This is the fundamental concept behind CQRS.

In CQRS (see Figure 10-6), the query model is primarily used for reading data from the datastore, while the command model is used for managing records in the datastore.

These models may operate on the same database but often have dedicated databases with significant advantages. If we assume that we use two dedicated databases for each model, then we need some sort of event-driven messaging mechanism to keep the data in sync. In most cases, eventual consistency (we discuss this in detail in Chapter 5) is sufficient for CQRS scenarios, hence the event-driven messaging techniques that we discussed earlier can be used to build CQRS.

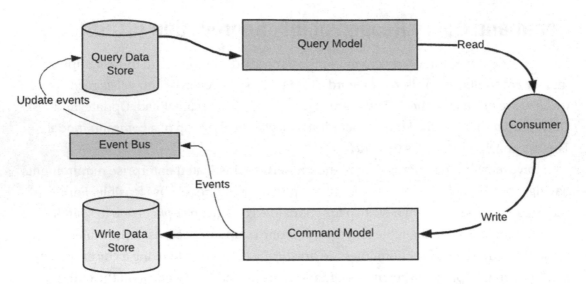

Figure 10-6. *CQRS involves splitting the data model into two and operating them on top of dedicated databases, which are eventually consistent via events*

In the context of microservices, we can consider that each query and command model are part of two different microservices. Since they have dedicated databases and well-defined functionalities, they are adhering to most of the microservice data management techniques. The complete decoupling of query and command model allows us to use two completely different persistent layers (databases) for command and query services. For example, we can use a database that is optimized for reads in the query model while we use a write-optimized database for command model. While CQRS has several advantages, such as independent scaling and management of read and write components of your application, we should use it when it is absolutely necessary to have the separation between the command and query models, because it comes with added complexity related to synchronizing the same data across multiple datastores/caches. For most commons use cases, the CRUD model fits elegantly.

Streams

A *stream* is a sequence of events/data elements made available over time. A series of events over time is quite common in modern enterprise applications, where continuous streams are generated with regard to many use cases, such as financial trading systems, weather data, traffic information, etc. The seams between the event-driven architecture and streams are pretty hard to determine, if you don't delve deep into the concept of stream processing.

Stream Processing

The software components that receive and send data streams and execute the business logic are called *stream processors*. Unlike conventional event-driven architecture, the processing logic of a stream is written against not one event but across multiple.

In the context of microservices, some of the input to your microservice can come from streams or microservices, which have to publish to a given stream. Therefore, the ability to integrate stream processing along with your service is a common requirement.

Programmatic Stream Processing

Stream processing can be done by writing code to process events sequentially from a source event stream. As shown in Figure 10-7, an *actor* or *agent* that accepts an event, processes the event and produces new events. A stream processor allows you to write logic for each actor, which takes care of most of the heavy lifting tasks such as collecting data, delivering to each actor, ordering, results collection, scaling, and error handling.

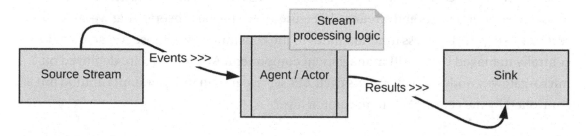

Figure 10-7. *Stream processing with code*

There are quite a few stream processor solutions out there, including Apache Storm[2], Apache Flink[3], and Kafka Streams[4], and they are based on a coding approach to stream processing.

---

[2]http://storm.apache.org/
[3]https://flink.apache.org/
[4]https://kafka.apache.org/documentation/streams/

Streaming SQL

Rather writing code to do stream processing, we can use SQL-like syntax to process streams. This is known as streaming SQL. With *streaming SQL*, you don't need to write code to build your stream processing use cases. Rather most of the essential functionalities can be abstracted into a streaming SQL engine.

Therefore, streaming SQL enables us to manipulate streaming data declaratively without having to write code. There are many stream-processing solutions, such as Apache Flink, Kafka (KSQL), that now offer streaming SQL support.

A Microservices Architecture with APIs, Events, and Streams

A pragmatic microservices architecture is often built on top of APIs, events, and streams. We discussed in Chapter 6, "Microservices Governance," how to organize services around core services, integration services, and API services. You can extend the same model to support events and streams. In Figure 10-8, you can observe that we used API services to expose business functionalities to the consumers and those API services are centrally managed by the API management component. API services are deployed on micro-gateway nodes, which means each API service has an independent runtime but is controlled by the central API management layer.

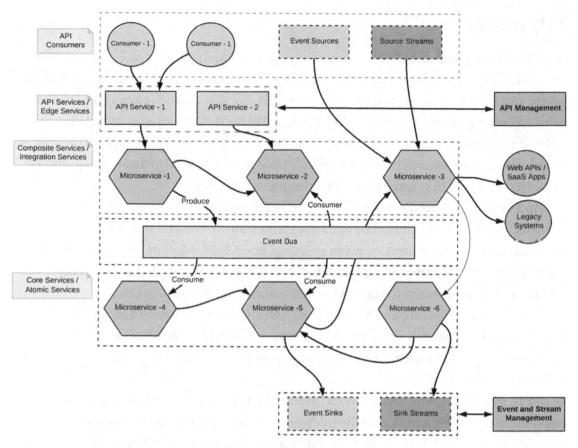

Figure 10-8. *Microservices reference architecture with APIs, events, and streams*

Microservices are integrated using active/orchestration and reactive (choreography) patterns and the event bus is used as the messaging backbone.

Microservices can receive events from external event sources and each consumer service has the business logic of processing those events. Similarly, stream-processing logic is also part of the services that consume the source streams. They can either implement using streaming SQL runtimes or programmatically process the event streams. Unlike API management, the consumption of events and streams is managed when services publish events to the consumers. If required, the events and stream-sinking services can be managed via an event and stream-management layer when we sink events or streams. Similar to the API management ecosystem, we can build an event and stream management layer, so that we can fully manage the event sinking or stream sinking (publishing) channels of our microservices implementation.

Summary

In this chapter, you learned about how to expose your microservices as managed APIs. The API management layer is the primary entry point to your microservices consumers where you expose business functionalities as APIs. We discussed the key components of an API management solution—API Gateway, API Store/Developer portal, API Publisher/Lifecycle Manager, API Analytics/Observability, and API Security solutions. We identified the differences between the API Gateway and service mesh proxy, and we discussed how API management and service mesh can coexist.

An event-driven architecture is quite useful for making services autonomous. We discussed the commonly used pattern for an event-driven architecture—event notification, event state transfer, event sourcing, and CQRS. Most of the event-driven communication patterns are implemented with the technologies that are used in messaging queuing and publisher-subscriber messaging infrastructures.

Streams are a special case of an event-driven architecture, where a sequence of events are processed over time. Stream processing is often done using a dedicated query language called streaming SQL, while some solutions are based on a pure coding approach to process streams.

APIs, events, and streams act as the front door to your enterprise's microservices implementation. You can extend the microservices reference architecture with APIs, events, and streams by connecting the external systems with the internal microservices.

CHAPTER 11

Microservices Security Fundamentals

The microservices architecture expands the attack surface with multiple microservices communicating with each other remotely. Instead of having one or two entry points, now we have hundreds of entry points to worry about. It's a common principle in security that the strength of a given system is only as strong as the strength of its weakest link. The more entry points we have, the broader the attack surface, and the higher the risk of being attacked. Unlike in a monolithic application, the depth and breadth we need to worry about in securing a microservice is much higher. There are multiple perspectives in securing microservices: secure development lifecycle and test automation, security in DevOps, and application level security.

Note   In 2010, it was discovered that since 2006, a gang of robbers equipped with a powerful vacuum cleaner had stolen more than 600,000 euros from the Monoprix supermarket chain in France. The most interesting thing was the way they did it. They found out the weakest link in the system and attacked it. To transfer money directly into the store's cash coffers, cashiers slid tubes filled with money through pneumatic suction pipes. The robbers realized that it was sufficient to drill a hole in the pipe near the trunk and then connect a vacuum cleaner to capture the money. They didn't have to deal with the coffer shield.

The key driving force behind the microservices architecture is the speed to production (or the time to market). One should be able to introduce a change to a service, test it, and instantly deploy it into production. A proper secure development lifecycle and test automation strategy needs to be there to make sure that we do not introduce security vulnerabilities at the code level. We need to have a proper plan for

© Kasun Indrasiri and Prabath Siriwardena 2018
K. Indrasiri and P. Siriwardena, *Microservices for the Enterprise*, https://doi.org/10.1007/978-1-4842-3858-5_11

static code analysis and dynamic testing—and most importantly those tests should be part of the continuous delivery (CD) process. Any vulnerability should be identified early in the development lifecycle and should have shorter feedback cycles.

There are multiple microservices deployment patterns—but the most commonly used one is service-per-host model. The host does not necessarily mean a physical machine—most probably it would be a container (Docker). The DevOps security needs to worry about container-level security. How do we isolate a container from other containers and what level of isolation we have between the container and the host operating system? Apart from containers, Kubernetes as a container orchestration platform introduced another level of isolation, in the form of a *pod*. Now we need to worry about securing the communication between containers as well as between pods. In Chapter 8, "Deploying and Running Microservices," we discussed containers and security in detail. Another important pattern with respect to microservices deployment is the *Service Mesh*, which we discussed in detail in Chapter 9, "Service Mesh". In a typical containerized deployment in Kubernetes, the communication between pods always happens through a Service Mesh, to be precise, through the Service Mesh proxy. The Service Mesh proxy is now responsible for applying and enforcing security between two microservices.

How do we authenticate and access control users to microservices and how do we secure the communication channels between microservices? All this falls under application-level security. This chapter covers security fundamentals with a set of patterns to address the challenges we face in securing microservices at the application level. What does it mean to secure a microservice? How does securing a microservice differ from securing any other service? What's so special about microservices? All these questions will be addressed in this chapter. Security at the development time and in the deployment process (with Docker and Kubernetes) is out of the scope of this book. We encourage the readers who are keen on knowing all the aspects in microservices security to refer to a book specifically focusing on microservices security.

Monolith versus Microservices

In a monolithic application, where all the services are deployed in the same application server, the application server itself provides session management features. The interactions between services happen over local calls and all the services can share the user's login status. Each service (or the component) needs not to authenticate the user independently. Authentication will be done centrally at an interceptor, which intercepts all the service calls. Once the authentication is completed, it passes the login context of the user between the services (or components) and that process varies from one platform to another. Figure 11-1 shows the interactions between multiple components in a monolithic application. The monolithic application is deployed in a single application container, probably on a bare metal host machine or on a virtual machine.

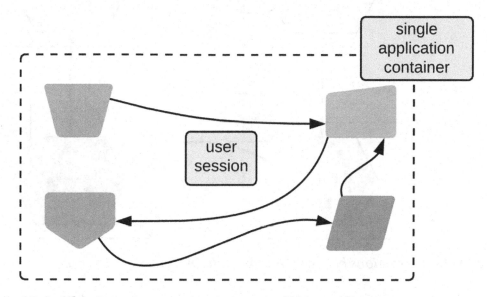

Figure 11-1. *Sharing a user session in a monolithic application*

In a Java EE environment, the interceptor can be a servlet filter. This servlet filter will intercept all the requests coming to its registered contexts and will enforce authentication. The service invoker should either carry valid credentials or a session token that can be mapped to a user. Once the servlet filter finds the user, it can create a login context and pass it to the downstream components. Each downstream component can identify the user from the login context to do any authorization.

Security becomes challenging in a microservices environment. In the microservices world, the services are scoped and deployed in multiple containers in a distributed setup. The service interactions are no more local, but remote, mostly over HTTP. Figure 11-2 shows the interactions between multiple microservices.

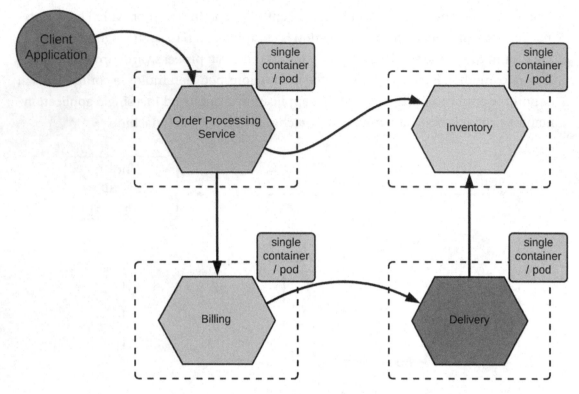

Figure 11-2. *Interactions between multiple microservices*

The challenge here is how we authenticate the user and then pass the login context between microservices in a symmetric manner, and then how does each microservice authenticate to each other and authorize the user. The following section explains the different techniques to secure service-to-service communication in the microservices architecture, both for authentication and authorization, and also to propagate user context across different microservices.

Securing Service-to-Service Communication

Service-to-service communication can happen synchronously via HTTP or asynchronously via event-driven messaging. In Chapter 3, "Inter-Service Communication," we discussed both synchronous and asynchronous messaging between microservices. There are two common approaches to secure service-to-service communication. One is based on JSON Web Token (JWT) and the other is based on Transport Layer Security (TLS) mutual authentication. In the following section, we look at the role of JWT in securing service-to-service communication in the microservices architecture.

JSON Web Token (JWT)

JWT (JSON Web Token) defines a container to transport data between interested parties (see Figure 11-3). It became an IETF standard in May 2015 with the RFC 7519[1]. A JWT can be used to:

- Propagate one's identity information between interested parties. For example, user attributes such as first name, last name, email address, phone number, etc.

- Propagate one's entitlements between interested parties. The entitlements define what the user is capable of doing at a target system.

- Transfer data securely between interested parties over an unsecured channel. A JWT can be used to transfer signed and/or encrypted messages.

- Assert one's identity, given that the recipient of the JWT trusts the asserting party (the token issuer). For example, the issuer of a JWT can sign the payload with its private key, which makes it protected for integrity, so that no one in the middle can alter the message. The recipient can validate the signature of the JWT, by verifying it with the corresponding public key of the issuer. If the recipient trusts the public key known to it, it also trusts the issuer of the JWT.

---

[1]https://tools.ietf.org/html/rfc7519

Figure 11-3. Transporting data between interested parties via a JWT

A JWT can be signed or encrypted or both. A signed JWT is known as a JWS[2] (JSON Web Signature) and an encrypted JWT is known as a JWE[3] (JSON Web Encryption). In fact a JWT does not exist itself—either it has to be a JWS or a JWE. It's like an abstract class—the JWS and JWE are the concrete implementations. Let me be little precise here. JWS and JWE have a broader meaning beyond JWT. JWS defines how to serialize (or represent) any signed message payload; it can be JSON, XML, or can be in any format. In the same way, JWE defines how to serialize an encrypted payload. Both JWS and JWE support two types of serializations: *compact serialization* and *JSON serialization*. We call a JWS or JWE, a JWT only if it follows the compact serialization. Any JWT must follow compact serialization. In other words a JWS or JWE token, which follows JSON serialization, cannot be called a JWT.

Note   Further details on JWS and JWE are out of the scope of this book. Any interested readers who want a detailed walk-through of JWS and JWE should refer to this blog: "JWT, JWS and JWE for Not So Dummies!" at `https://medium.facilelogin.com/jwt-jws-and-jwe-for-not-so-dummies-b63310d201a3`.

---

[2]`https://tools.ietf.org/html/rfc7515`
[3]`https://tools.ietf.org/html/rfc7516`

Let's take a closer look at the following sample JWT:

eyJhbGciOiJSUzI1NiIsImtpZCI6Ijc4YjRjZjIzNjU2ZGMzOTUzNjRmMWI2YzAyOTA3NjkxZj
JjZGZmZTEifQ.**eyJpc3MiOiJhY2NvdW50cy5nb29nbGUuY29tIiwic3ViIjoiMTEwNTAyMjUxMT
U4OTIwMTQ3NzMyIiwiYXpwIjoiODI1MjQ5ODM1NjU5LXRlOHFnbDcwMWtnMnNub21ucDRhcmcXY3
ZXJodTEyMTFzLmFwcHMuZ29vZ2xldXNlcmNvbnRlbnQuY29tIiwiZW1haWwiOiJwcmFiYXRoQH
dzbzIuY29tIiwiYXRfaGFzaCI6InpmODZ2TnVscc0xCOGdGYXFSd2R6WWciLCJlbWFpbF92ZXJp
ZmllZCI6dHJ1ZSwiYXVkIjoiODI1MjQ5ODM1NjU5LXRlOHFnbDcwMWtnMnNub21ucDRhcmcXZX
JodTEyMTFzLmFwcHMuZ29vZ2xldXNlcmNvbnRlbnQuY29tIiwiaGQiOiJ3c28yLmNvbSIsImlhd
CI6MTQwMTkwODI3MSwiZXhwIjoxNDAxOTEyMTcxfQ.**TVKv-pdyvk2gW8sGsCbsnkqsrSOT-H0Oxn
Y6ETkIfgIxfotvFn5IwKm3xyBMpyOFFeORb5Ht8AEJV6PdWyxz8rMgX2HROWqSo_RfEfUpBb4iO
sq4W28KftW5HOIA44VmNZ6zU4YTqPSt4TPhyFC9fP2D_Hg7JQozpQRUfbWTJI

This looks gibberish until you break it by periods (.) and *base64url-decode* each part. There are two periods in it, which break the whole string into three parts (see Figure 11-4). Once you base64url-decode the fist part, it appears like so:

```
{"alg":"RS256","kid":"78b4cf23656dc395364f1b6c02907691f2cdffe1"}
```

Figure 11-4. *JWS (compact serializing, representing a JWT)*

This first part (once parted by the periods) of the JWT is known as the JOSE header. JOSE stands for JavaScript Object Signing and Encryption—and it's the name of the IETF working group[4] that works on standardizing the representation of integrity-protected data using JSON data structures.

The JOSE header indicates that it's a signed message with the provided algorithm under the `alg` parameter. The token issuer asserts the identity of the end user by signing the JWT, which carries data related to the user's identity. Both the `alg` and `kid` elements there are not defined in the JWT specification, but in the JSON Web Signature (JWS) specification. The JWT specification only defines two elements (`typ` and `cty`) in the JOSE header and both the JWS and JWE specifications extend it to add more appropriate elements.

---

[4]https://datatracker.ietf.org/wg/jose/about/

Note   Both JWS and JWE compact serialization use base64url encoding. It is a slight variation of the popular base64 encoding. The base64 encoding defines how to represent binary data in an ASCII string format. Its objective is to transmit binary data such as keys or digital certificates in a printable format. This type of encoding is needed if these objects are transported as part of an email body, a web page, an XML document, or a JSON document.

To do base64 encoding, first the binary data is grouped into 24-bit groups. Then each 24-bit group is divided into four 6-bit groups. A printable character can represent each 6-bit group based on its bit value in decimal. For example, the decimal value of the 6-bit group 000111 is 7. As per Figure 11-5 the character H represents this 6-bit group. Apart from the characters shown in Figure 11-5, the character = is used to specify a special processing function, which is to pad. If the length of the original binary data is not an exact multiple of 24, then we need padding. Let's say the length is 232, which is not a multiple of 24. Now we need to pad this binary data to make its length equal to the very next multiple of the 24, which is 240. In other words, we need to pad this binary data by 8 to make its length 240. In this case, padding is done by adding eight 0s to the end of the binary data. Now, when we divide 240 bits by 6 to build 6-bit groups, the last 6-bit group will be all zeros, and this complete group will be represented by the padding character =.

One issue with base64 encoding is that it does not work quite well with URLs. The + and / characters in base64 encoding (see Figure 11-5) have a special meaning when used within a URL. If we try to send a base64 encoded image as a URL query parameter and if the base64 encoded string carries either of these two characters, the browser will interpret the URL incorrectly. The base64url encoding was introduced to address this problem. It works exactly the same as base64 encoding other than two exceptions: the character - is used in base64url encoding instead of the character + and the character _ is used in base64url encoding instead of the character /.

0	A	16	Q	32	g	48	w
1	B	17	R	33	h	49	x
2	C	18	S	34	I	50	y
3	D	19	T	35	j	51	z
4	E	20	U	36	k	52	0
5	F	21	V	37	l	53	1
6	G	22	W	38	m	54	2
7	H	23	X	39	n	55	3
8	I	24	Y	40	o	56	4
9	J	25	Z	41	p	57	5
10	K	26	a	42	q	58	6
11	L	27	b	43	r	59	7
12	M	28	c	44	s	60	8
13	N	29	d	45	t	61	9
14	O	30	e	46	u	62	+
15	P	31	f	47	v	63	/

Figure 11-5. *Base64 encoding*

The second part of the JWT, as shown in Figure 11-4, is known as the JWT claim set (see Figure 11-6). Whitespace can be explicitly retained while building the JWT claim set—no canonicalization is required before base64url encoding or decoding. Canonicalization is the process of converting different forms of a message into a single standard form. This is used mostly before signing XML messages.

```
{ ⊟
    "iss":"accounts.google.com",
    "sub":"110502251158920147732",
    "azp":"825249835659-np4sqv7erhu1211s.apps.googleusercontent.com",
    "email":"prabath@wso2.com",
    "at_hash":"zf86vNulsLB8gFaqRwdzYg",
    "email_verified":true,
    "aud":"825249835659-np4sqv7erhu1211s.apps.googleusercontent.com",
    "hd":"wso2.com",
    "iat":1401908271,
    "exp":1401912171
}
```

Figure 11-6. *JWT claim set*

The JWT claim set represents a JSON object whose members are the claims asserted by the JWT issuer. Each claim name within a JWT must be unique. If there are duplicate claim names, then the JWT parser will either return a parsing error or just return the claims set with the very last duplicate claim. JWT specification does not explicitly define which claims are mandatory and which are optional. It's up to the each application of JWT to define mandatory and optional claims. For example, the OpenID Connect specification defines the mandatory and optional claims. According to the OpenID Connect core specification, `iss`, `sub`, `add`, `exp`, and `iat` are treated as mandatory elements, while `auth_time`, `nonce`, `acr`, `amr`, and `azp` are optional elements. In addition to the mandatory and optional claims, which are defined in the specification, the token issuer can include additional elements into the JWT claim set.

The third part of the JWT (shown in Figure 11-4) is the signature, which is also base64url encoded. The cryptographic elements related to the signature are defined in the JOSE header. In this particular example, the token issued uses RSASSA-PKCS1-V1_5 with the SHA-256 hashing algorithm, which is expressed by the value of the `alg` element in the JOSE header: RS256. The signature is calculated against the first two parts in the JWS—the JOSE header and the JWT claim set.

Propagating Trust and User Identity

The user context from one microservice to another can be passed along with a JWS (see Figure 11-7). Since a key known to the calling microservice signs the JWS, it will carry both the end user identity (as claimed in the JWT) and the identity of the calling microservice (via the signature). In other words, the calling microservice itself is the issuer of the JWS. To accept the JWS, the recipient microservice first needs to validate the signature of the JWS against the public key embedded in the JWS itself or retrieved via any other mechanism. That's not just enough—then it needs to check whether it can trust that key or not. Trust between microservices can be established in multiple ways. One way is to provision the trusted certificates, by service, to each microservice. It's a no brainer to realize that this would not scale in a microservices deployment. The approach we would like to suggest is to build a private certificate authority (CA) and use intermediate certificate authorities by different microservices teams, if the need arises. Now, rather than trusting every individual certificate, the recipient microservices will only trust either the root certificate authority or an intermediary. That will vastly reduce the overhead in certificate provisioning.

Note   Trust bootstrap is a harder problem to solve. The Secure Production Identity Framework For Everyone (SPIFFE)[5] project builds an interesting solution around this, which can be used to bootstrap trust between different nodes in a microservices deployment. With SPIFFE, each node will get an identifier and a key pair, which can be used to authenticate to other nodes it communicates with.

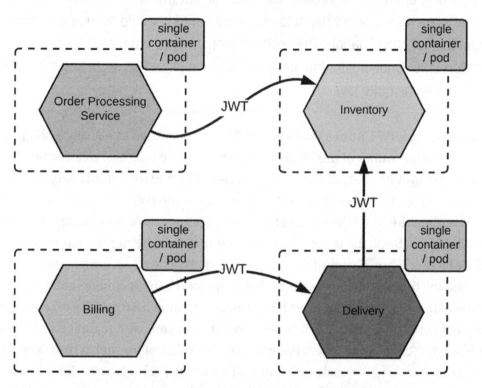

Figure 11-7.   Passing user context as a JWT between microservices

In the JWT, the public key corresponding to the key used to sign the token represents the caller (or the calling microservice). How does the recipient microservice find the end user information? The JWT carries a parameter called sub in its claim set, which represents the subject or the user who owns the JWT. If any microservice needs to identify the user during its operations, this is the attribute it should look into. The value of the sub attribute is unique only for a given issuer. If you have a microservice, which

---

[5]https://spiffe.io/

accepts tokens from multiple issuers, then the uniqueness of the user should be decided as a combination of the issuer and the sub attribute. In addition to the subject identifier, the JWT can also carry user attributes such as first_name, last_name, email, and so on.

Note   When we pass user context between microservices via a JWT, each microservice has to bear the cost of JWT validation, which also includes a cryptographic operation to validate the token signature. Caching the JWT at the microservices level against the data extracted out of it would reduce the impact of repetitive token validation. The cache expiration time must match the JWT expiration time. Once again, the impact of caching would be quite low if the JWT expiration time is quite low.

When issuing a JWT from a token issuer, it has to be issued to a given audience. The audience is the consumer of the token. For example, if the microservice foo wants to talk to the microservice bar, then the token is issued by foo (or a third party issuer), and the audience of the token is bar. The aud parameter in the JWT claim set specifies the intended audience of the token. It can be a single recipient or a set of recipients. Prior to any validation check, the token recipient must first see whether the particular JWT is issued for its use. If not, it should reject it immediately. The token issuer should know, prior to issuing the token, who the intended recipient (or the recipients) of the token is. The value of the aud parameter must be a pre-agreed value between the token issuer and the recipients. In a microservices environment, we can use a regular expression to validate the audience of the token. For example, the value of the aud in the token can be *.facilelogin.com, while each recipient under the facilelogin.com domain can have its own aud values: foo.facilelogin.com, bar.facilelogin.com, and so on.

Transport Layer Security (TLS) Mutual Authentication

Transport Layer Security (TLS) mutual authentication, also known as client authentication or two-way Secure Socket Layer (SSL), is part of the TLS handshake process. In one-way TLS, only the server proves its identity to the client; this is mostly used in e-commerce to win consumer confidence by guaranteeing the legitimacy of the e-commerce vendor. In contrast, mutual authentication authenticates both parties—the client and the server. In a microservices environment, TLS mutual authentication can be used between microservices to authenticate each other.

Both in TLS mutual authentication and with the JWT-based approach, each microservice needs to have its own certificates. The difference between the two approaches is that, in JWT-based authentication, the JWS can carry the end user identity as well as the upstream service identity. With TLS mutual authentication, the end user identity has to be passed at the application level—probably as an HTTP header.

Certificate Revocation

Both in TLS mutual authentication and with the JWT based approach, the certificate revocation is bit tricky. It is a harder problem to solve—though there are multiple options available: CRL (Certification Revocation List/RFC 2459), OCSP (Online Certificate Status Protocol / RFC 2560), OCSP Stapling (RFC 6066), and OCSP Stapling Required.

With CRL, the certificate authority (CA) has to maintain a list of revoked certificates. The client who initiates the TLS handshake has to get the long list of revoked certificates from the corresponding certificate authority and then check whether the server certificate is in the revoked certificate list. Instead of doing that for each request, the client can cache the CRL locally. Then you run into the problem that the security decisions are made based on stale data. When TLS mutual authentication is used, the server also has to do the same certificate verification against the client. The CRL is a not more often used technique. Eventually people recognized that CRLs are not going to work and started building something new, which is the OCSP.

In the OCSP world, the things are little bit better than CRL. The TLS client can check the status of a specific certificate without downloading the whole list of revoked certificates from the certificate authority. In other words, each time the client talks to a new downstream microservice, it has to talk to the corresponding OCSP responder[6] to validate the status of the server (or the service) certificate—and the server has to do the same against the client certificate. That creates some extensive traffic on the OCSP responder. Once again clients still can cache the OCSP decision, but then again it will lead to the same old problem of making decisions on stale data.

With OCSP stapling, the client does not need to go to the OCSP responder each time it talks to a downstream microservice. The downstream microservice will get the OCSP response from the corresponding OCSP responder and staple or attach the response to the certificate. Since the corresponding certificate authority signs the OCSP response,

---

[6]An OCSP responder is an endpoint hosted by the certificate authority to respond to certificate validation requests by client applications.

the client can accept it by validating the signature. This makes things little better. Instead of the client, the service has to talk to the OCSP responder. But in a mutual TLS authentication model, this won't bring any additional benefits when compared to the plain OCSP.

With OCSP must stapling, the service (downstream microservice) gives a guarantee to the client (upstream microservice) that the OCSP response is attached to the service certificate it receives during the TLS handshake. In case the OCSP response is not attached to the certificate, rather than doing a soft failure, the client must immediately reject the connection.

Short-Lived Certificates

From the end user perspective the short-lived certificates behave the same way as the normal certificates work today, they just have a very short expiration. The TLS client needs not to worry about doing CRL or OCSP validations against short-lived certificates and rather sticks to the expiration time, stamped on the certificate itself.

The challenge in short-lived certificates mostly lies in their deployment and maintenance. Automation is the goddess of rescue! Netflix suggests using a layered approach (see Figure 11-8) to build a short-lived certificate deployment. You would have a system identity or long-lived credential that resides in a TPM (Trusted Platform Module) or an SGX (Software Guard Extension) having lot of security on it. Then use that credential to get a short-lived certificate. Then use the short-lived certificate for your microservice, which would be consumed by another microservice. Each microservice can refresh the short-lived certificates regularly using its long-lived credentials. Having the short-lived certificate is not enough—the underlying platform, which hosts the service (or the TLS terminator), should support dynamic updates to the server certificate. A lot of TLS terminators out there support dynamically reloading the server certificates, but not with zero downtime in most cases.

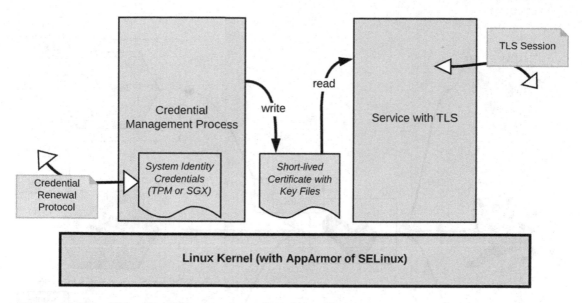

Figure 11-8. *How Netflix uses short-lived certificates*

The Edge Security

In Chapter 7, "Integrating Microservices" and Chapter 10, "APIs, Events, and Streams," we discussed different techniques for exposing microservices to the rest of the world. One common approach discussed there was to use the *API gateway* pattern. With the API gateway pattern (see Figure 11-9)—the microservices, which need to be exposed outside, would have a corresponding API in the API gateway. Not all the microservices need to be exposed from the API gateway.

The end user's access to the microservices (via an API) should be validated at the edge—or at the API gateway. The most common way of securing APIs is OAuth 2.0. Over time, OAuth 2.0 has become the de-facto standard for API security.

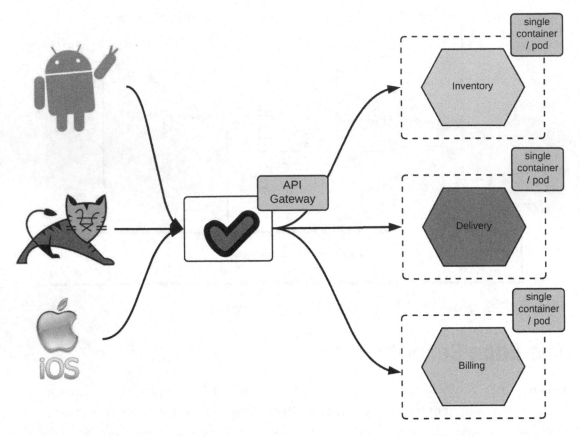

Figure 11-9. *The API gateway pattern*

OAuth 2.0

OAuth 2.0 is a framework for access delegation. It lets someone do something on behalf of someone else. There are four main characters in an OAuth 2.0 flow: the client, the authorization server, the resource server, and the resource owner. Let's say you build a web application that lets users export their Flickr photos into it. In that case, your web application has to access the Flickr API to export photos on behalf of the users who actually own the photos. There the web application is the OAuth 2.0 client, Flickr is the resource server (which holds its users' photos), and the Flickr user who wants to export photos to the web application is the resource owner. For your application to access Flickr API on behalf of the Flickr user, it needs some sort of an authorization grant. The authorization server issues the authorization grant, and in this case it'll be Flickr itself. But, in practice there can be many cases where the authorization server and the resource server are two different entities. OAuth 2.0 does not couple those two together.

Note   An OAuth 2.0 client can be a web application, a native mobile application, a single page application, or even a desktop application. Whoever the client is, it should be known to the authorization server. Each OAuth client has an identifier, which is known as a *client ID*, given to it by the authorization server. Whenever a client communicates with authorization server, it has to pass its client ID. In some cases, client has to use some kind of credentials to prove who it is. The most popular form of credentials is the *client secret*. It is like a password. But it is always recommended that OAuth clients use stronger credentials, like certificates or JWTs.

OAuth 2.0 introduces multiple grant types. A grant type in OAuth 2.0 explains the protocol; the client should get the resource owner's consent to access a resource on his behalf. Also, there are some grant types that define a protocol to get a token, just on behalf of himself (`client_credentials`)—in other words, the client is also the resource owner. Figure 11-10 illustrates OAuth 2.0 protocol at a very high-level. It describes the interactions between the OAuth client, the resource owner, the authorization server, and the resource server.

Note   The OAuth 2.0 core specification (RFC 6749[7]) defines five grant types: authorization code, implicit, password, client credentials, and refresh. The authorization code grant type is the most popular grant type, used by more than 70% of the web applications. In fact, it is the recommended grant type for many of the use cases, whether you have a web application, a native mobile application, or even a single page application (SPA).

---

[7]https://tools.ietf.org/html/rfc6749

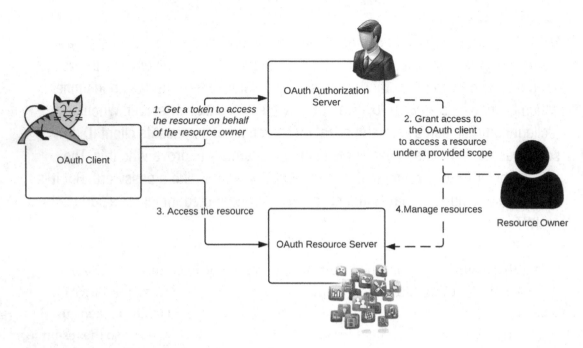

Figure 11-10. *The OAuth 2.0 protocol*

Whoever wants to access a microservice via the API gateway must get a valid OAuth token first (see Figure 11-11). A system can access a microservice, just by being itself—or on behalf of another user. For the latter case, an example would be when a user logs in to a web application and the web application accesses a microservice on behalf of the user who logged in. When a system wants to access an API on behalf of another user, authorization code is the recommended grant type. In other cases where a system accesses an API by being itself, we can use the client credentials grant type.

Note   There are two types of OAuth 2.0 access tokens: *reference* tokens and *self-contained* tokens. A reference token is an arbitrary string issued by the authorization server to the client application to be used against a resource server. It must have a proper length and should be unpredictable. Whenever a resource server sees a reference access token, it has to talk to the corresponding authorization server to validate it. A self-contained access token is a signed JWT (or a JWS). To validate a self-contained access token, the resource server does not need to talk to the authorization server. It can validate the token by validating its signature.

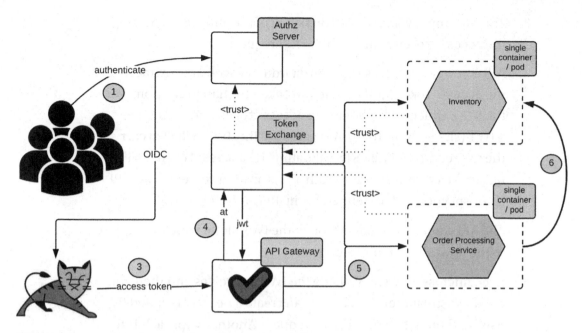

Figure 11-11. *End-to-end authentication flow*

Let's see how end-to-end communication works, as illustrated in Figure 11-11:

1. The user logs into the web app/mobile app via the identity provider, which the web app/mobile app trusts via OpenID Connect (this can be SAML 2.0 too). OpenID Connect is an identity federation protocol built on top of OAuth 2.0. SAML 2.0 is another similar identity federation protocol.

2. The web app gets an OAuth 2.0 access_token, a refresh_token, and an id_token. The id_token will identify the end user to the web app. OpenID Connect introduces the id_token to the OAuth flow. If SAML 2.0 is used, then the web app needs to talk to the token endpoint of the OAuth authorization server it trusts and exchange the SAML token to an OAuth access_token, following the SAML 2.0 grant type for OAuth 2.0. Each access_token has an expiration, and when the access_token is expired or close to expiration, the OAuth client can use the refresh_token to talk to the authorization (no need to have the end user) and get a new access_token.

3. The web app invokes an API on behalf of the end user—passing the `access_token` along with the API request.

4. API gateway intercepts the request from the web app, extracts the `access_token`, and talks to the Token Exchange endpoint (or the STS), which will validate the `access_token` and then issue a JWT (signed by it) to the API gateway. This JWT will also carry the user context. While STS validating the `access_token` it will talk to the corresponding OAuth authorization server via an API (Introspection API as defined by the RFC 7662[8]).

5. The API gateway will pass through the JWT along with the request to the downstream microservices.

6. Each microservice will validate the JWT it receives and then, for the downstream service calls, it can create a new JWT signed by itself and send it along with the request. Another approach is to use a nested JWT—so the new JWT will also carry the previous JWT. Also, there is third approach, where each microservice talks to the security token service and exchanges the token it got for a new token, to talk to the other downstream microservices.

Note   A detailed explanation of OAuth 2.0 and OpenID Connect is out of the scope of this book. We encourage interested readers to go through the book, *Advanced API Security*, written by one of the authors of this book and published by Apress.

With this approach, only the API calls coming from the external clients will go through the API gateway. When one microservice talks to another, that needs not to go through the gateway. Also, from a given microservice perspective, whether you get a request from an external client or another microservice, what you get is a JWT—so this is a symmetric security model.

---

[8]https://tools.ietf.org/html/rfc7662

Access Control

Authorization is a business function. Each microservice can determine the criteria to allow access to its operations. In the simplest form of authorization, we check whether a given user can perform a given action on a particular resource. The combination of an action and a resource is termed as the permission. An authorization check evaluates whether a given user has the minimum set of required permissions to access a given resource. The resource can define who can perform and which actions they can perform. The declaration of the required permissions for a given resource can be done in multiple ways. The most common way is to attach a policy or an access control list (ACL) to the resource. There are multiple policy languages being used to express these access control requirements. If you are familiar with Amazon Web Services (AWS), you might have noticed the quite simple, but strong, JSON-based policy language[9] used there, as shown here.

```
{
  "Version": "2012-10-17",
  "Statement": {
        "Effect": "Allow",
        "Action": "s3:ListBucket",
        "Resource": "arn:aws:s3:::example_bucket"
  }
}
```

Open Policy Agent[10] (OPA) introduces another policy language mostly targeting policy-based control for cloud native environments. The following shows a sample policy defined in OPA, which allows access to all HTTP requests.

```
package http.authz
allow = true
```

XACML (eXtensible Access Control Markup Language) provides another way of defining access control policies. It is so far the only standard (by OASIS) out there for a policy language. The following section delves deeply into XACML.

---

[9]https://docs.aws.amazon.com/IAM/latest/UserGuide/access_policies.html
[10]http://www.openpolicyagent.org/

XACML (eXtensible Access Control Markup Language)

XACML is the de-facto standard for fine-grained access control. It introduces a way to represent the required set of permissions to access a resource, in a very fine-grained manner in an XML-based domain-specific language (DSL).

XACML provides a reference architecture, a request response protocol, and a policy language. Under the reference architecture, it talks about a Policy Administration Point (PAP), a Policy Decision Point (PDP), a Policy Enforcement Point (PEP), and a Policy Information Point (PIP). This is a highly distributed architecture in which none of the components is tightly coupled. The PAP is the place where you author policies. The PDP is the place where policies are evaluated and decisions are made. While evaluating policies, if there is any missing information that can't be derived from the XACML request, the PDP calls the PIP. The role of the PIP is to feed the PDP any missing information, which can be user attributes or any other required details. The policy is enforced through a PEP, which sits between the client and the service and intercepts all requests. From the client request, it extracts certain attributes such as the subject, the resource, and the action; then it builds a standard XACML request and calls the PDP. Then it gets a XACML response from the PDP. That is defined under the XACML request/response model. The XACML policy language defines a schema to create XACML policies for access control.

Figure 11-12 shows the XACML component architecture. The policy administrator first needs to define XACML policies via the PAP (Policy Administration Point) and those policies will get stored in the policy store. To check whether a given entity has the permission to access a given resource, the PEP (Policy Enforcement Point) has to intercept the access request, create a XACML request, and send it to the XACML PDP (Policy Decision Point). The XACML request can carry any attributes that could help the decision-making process at the PDP.

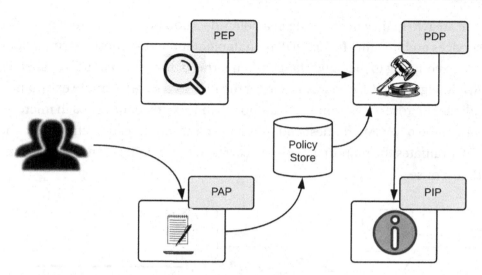

Figure 11-12. *XACML component architecture*

For example, it can include the subject identifier, the resource identifier, and the action the given subject is going to perform on the resource. The microservice that needs to authorize the user has to build a XACML request by extracting the relevant attributes from the JWT and talk to the PDP. The PIP (Policy Information Point) comes into the picture when the PDP finds that certain attributes required for policy evaluation are missing in the XACML request. Then the PDP will talk to the PIP to find the missing attributes. The PIP can connect to relevant datastores, find the attributes, and then feed those into the PDP.

Note   XACML is an XML-based open standard for policy-based access control developed under the OASIS XACML technical committee. The latest XACML 3.0 specification was standardized in January 2013. See `www.oasis-open.org/ committees/tc_home.php?wg_abbrev=xacml`.

There are two main ways to bring in a policy decision point (PDP) to the microservices architecture. In fact PDP is an implementation-agnostic term; it does not have a deep coupling to the policy language in terms of the architectural perspective. As shown in Figure 11-13, one way is to treat the PDP as a single, remote endpoint, where all the microservices connect to authorize the access requests. Each microservice will create its own XACML request and pass it over a communication channel to the PDP. PDP evaluates the request against the corresponding policies and sends back the XACML response.

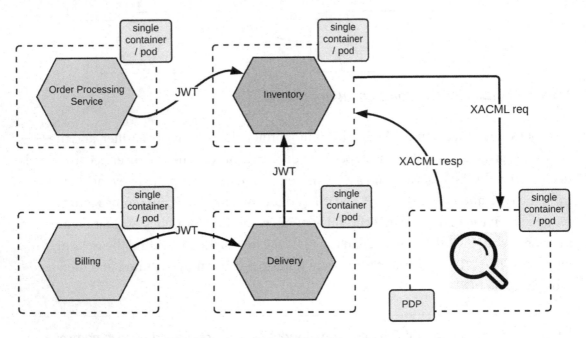

Figure 11-13. *Centralized/remote XACML PDP*

Figure 11-14 shows an example XACML request in JSON. Here we can assume that someone invokes the `bar` microservice to buy a beer. The `bar` microservice extracts the subject or the user who invokes the service from the JWT coming along with the request and builds the XACML request accordingly.

```
{ ⊟
   "Request":{ ⊟
      "Action":{ ⊟
         "Attribute":[ ⊟
            { ⊟
               "AttributeId":"urn:oasis:names:tc:xacml:1.0:action:action-id",
               "Value":"buy"
            }
         ]
      },
      "Resource":{ ⊟
         "Attribute":[ ⊟
            { ⊟
               "AttributeId":"urn:oasis:names:tc:xacml:1.0:resource:resource-id",
               "Value":"beer"
            }
         ]
      },
      "AccessSubject":{ ⊟
         "Attribute":[ ⊟
            { ⊟
               "AttributeId":"urn:oasis:names:tc:xacml:1.0:subject:subject-id",
               "Value":"peter"
            }
         ]
      }
   }
}
```

Figure 11-14. *XACML request in JSON*

Note   With the increasing popularity and adaptation of APIs, it becomes crucial for XACML to be easily understood in order to increase the likelihood that it will be adopted. XML is often considered too verbose. Developers increasingly prefer a lighter representation using JSON, the JavaScript Object notation. The profile "Request / Response Interface based on JSON and HTTP for XACML 3.0" aims at defining a JSON format for the XACML request and response.

See `https://www.oasis-open.org/committees/document.php?document_id=47775`.

Embedded PDP

There are certain drawbacks to the remote or the centralized PDP model that could easily violate base microservices principles:

- *Performance cost*: Each time we need to do an access control check, the corresponding microservice has to talk to the PDP over the wire. With decision caching at the client side, the transport cost and the cost of the policy evaluation can be cut down. But with caching, we will make security decisions based on stale data.

- *The ownership of policy information points (PIP)*: Each microservice should have the ownership of its PIPs, which know where to bring in the data required to do the access controlling. With this approach we are building a centralized PDP, which has all the PIPs corresponding to all the microservices.

- *Monolithic PDP*: The centralized PDP becomes another monolithic application. All the policies associated with all the microservices are stored centrally in the monolithic PDP. Introducing changes is hard as a change to one policy may have an impact on all the policies, since all the policies are evaluated under the same policy engine.

As illustrated in Figure 11-15, the embedded PDP will run along with each microservice. It follows an eventing model for policy distribution, where each microservice will subscribe to its interested topics to get the appropriate access control policies from the PAP and then update the embedded PDP. You can have PAPs by

338

microservices teams or one globally in a multi-tenanted mode. When a new policy is available or when there is a policy update, the PAP will publish an event to the corresponding topics. The embedded PDP model introduces a message broker to the microservices architecture.

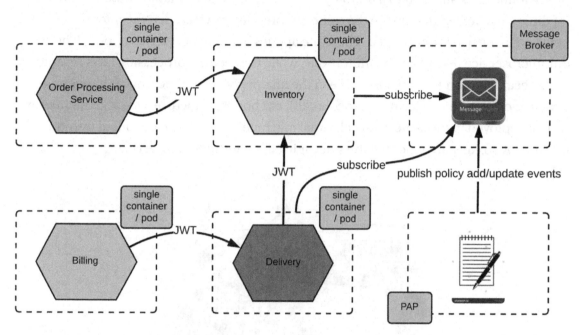

Figure 11-15. *Embedded XACML PDP*

This approach does not violate the immutable server concept in microservices. *Immutable server* means that you build servers or containers directly out of configuration loaded from a repository at the end of the continuous delivery process and you should be able to build the same container again and again with the same configuration. So, we would not expect anyone to log in to a server and do any configuration changes there. With the embedded PDP model—even though the server loads the corresponding policies while it's running—if we spin up a new container it too gets the same set of policies from the corresponding PAP.

There is an important question that's still unanswered. What is the role of the API gateway under the context of authorization? We can have two levels of policy enforcements. One is globally for all the requests going through the API gateway (which will act as the policy enforcement point or the PEP), and the other one is at the service level. The service-level policies must be enforced via some kind of an interceptor at the container or the service level.

Security Sidecar

We introduced the concept of sidecar in the Chapter 2, "Designing Microservices". Let's quickly recap. As shown in Figure 11-16, the sidecar pattern is derived from the vehicle where a sidecar is attached to a motorcycle. If you'd like you can attach different sidecars (of different colors or designs) to the same motorcycle, provided that the interface between those two is unchanged. The same applies in the microservices world, where our microservice resembles the motorcycle, while the security processing layer resembles the sidecar. The communication between the microservice and the sidecar happens over a remote channel (not a local, in-process call), but both the microservice and the sidecar will be deployed in the same physical/vitual machine, so it will not be routed over the network. Also, keep in mind that the sidecar itself is another microservice.

Figure 11-16. *Sidecar*

Note   As discussed in Chapter 9, Istio[11] introduces a sidecar proxy for supporting strong identity, powerful policy, transparent TLS encryption, and authentication, authorization, and audit (AAA) tools to protect your services and data. Istio Citadel provides strong service-to-service and end-user authentication with built-in identity and credential management, based on the sidecar and control plane architecture.

---

[11]https://istio.io/docs/concepts/security/

There are many benefits of implementing security as a sidecar in the microservices architecture. The following list explains some of them.

- The microservice implementation does not need to worry about the internals of the security implementation and those need not to be in the same programming language.

- When implemented as a sidecar, the security functionality can be reused by other microservices, without worrying about individual implementation details.

- The ownership of the security sidecar can be taken care by a different team that has expertise on the security domain, other than the microservices developers, who worry about domain-specific business functionalities.

Let's see how the security sidecar fits into the microservices architecture. As shown in Figure 11-17, there can be four main functionalities of a security sidecar: token validation (introspection), get user info (userinfo), token issuance (token), and authorize access requests (pdp). Each microservice should have its own interceptor that intercepts all the requests and talk to the token validation endpoint to check whether the provided token is good enough to access the corresponding microservice. To make the sidecar interoperable, it is recommended to expose the OAuth 2.0 introspection endpoint[12] to validate the tokens. This endpoint will accept a token in the request and will reply with a JSON payload, which includes information related to the provided token.

---

[12]https://tools.ietf.org/html/rfc7662

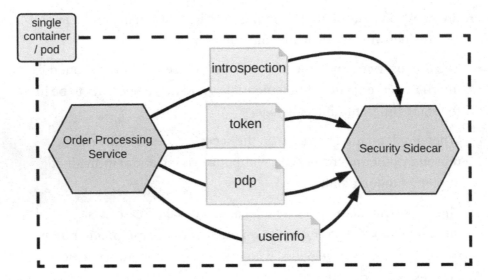

Figure 11-17. *Security sidecar*

The following text shows a request to the introspection endpoint and a response from it.

```
POST /introspect HTTP/1.1
Host: sidecar.local
Accept: application/json
Content-Type: application/x-www-form-urlencoded

token=2YotnFZFEjr1zCsicMWpAA
HTTP/1.1 200 OK
Content-Type: application/json

    {
     "active": true,
     "client_id": "l238j323ds-23ij4",
     "username": "jdoe",
     "scope": "read write dolphin",
     "sub": "jdoe",
     "aud": "https://foo.com",
     "iss": "https://issuer.example.com/",
     "exp": 1419356238,
     "iat": 1419350238
    }
```

Once the token is validated, if the microservice wants to find more information about the end user who invoked the microservice, it can talk to the userinfo endpoint exposed by the security sidecar. This is another standard endpoint defined in the OpenID Connect specification[13]. This endpoint accepts a request with a valid token and returns the associated user's information in a JSON message. The following text shows a request to the userinfo endpoint and a response from it.

```
GET /userinfo HTTP/1.1
Host: sidecar.local
Authorization: Bearer SlAV32hkKG
HTTP/1.1 200 OK
Content-Type: application/json

  {
   "sub": "jdoe",
   "name": "Jane Doe",
   "given_name": "Jane",
   "family_name": "Doe",
   "preferred_username": "j.doe",
   "email": "janedoe@example.com",
  }
```

The pdp endpoint can be called either by an interceptor or within the microservice itself to find out whether the incoming request is good enough to perform the action it is intended to perform. This can be standardized over the JSON profile for XACML[14] and the REST profile for XACML[15]. Even though we standardized the request and response over XACML, that does not necessarily mean that we have to maintain access control policies in the sidecar in XACML. It can be in any way we want. The following text shows a request to the pdp endpoint and the response from it.

---

[13]http://openid.net/specs/openid-connect-core-1_0.html#UserInfo
[14]http://docs.oasis-open.org/xacml/xacml-json-http/v1.0/xacml-json-http-v1.0.html
[15]http://docs.oasis-open.org/xacml/xacml-rest/v1.0/xacml-rest-v1.0.html

```
POST /pdp HTTP/1.1
Host: sidecar.local
Accept: application/json
Content-Type: application/x-www-form-urlencoded
[xacml request in json, see figure 11-4]
HTTP/1.1 200 OK
Content-Type: application/json
{
    "Response": [{
        "Decision": "Permit"
    ]]
}
```

The token endpoint exposed by the security sidecar can be called by the microservice to get a new token, which is good enough to talk to another downstream microservice. This endpoint can be standardized under the OAuth 2.0 token endpoint, with support for the OAuth 2.0 Token Exchange[16] profile. The request to the token endpoint will carry the original token and an identifier representing the downstream microservice it wants to talk to. In response we get a new token. The following text shows a request to the token endpoint and the response from it.

```
POST /token HTTP/1.1
Host: sidecar.local
Content-Type: application/x-www-form-urlencoded

grant_type=urn:ietf:params:oauth:grant-type:token-exchange
&resource=foo
&subject_token=SlAV32hkKG
&subject_token_type=urn:ietf:params:oauth:token-type:access_token
HTTP/1.1 200 OK
Content-Type: application/json
Cache-Control: no-cache, no-store
```

---

[16]https://tools.ietf.org/html/draft-ietf-oauth-token-exchange-10

```
{
    "access_token":"eyJhbGciOiJFUzI1NiIsImtpZCI6Ijllc",
    "issued_token_type": "urn:ietf:params:oauth:token-type:access_token",
    "token_type":"Bearer",
    "expires_in":60
}
```

Summary

In this chapter, we discussed the common patterns and fundamentals related to securing microservices. Securing service-to-service communication is the most critical part in securing microservices, where we have two options with JWT and certificates. Edge security is mostly handled by the API gateway with OAuth 2.0. There are two models in access controlling microservices: centralized PDP and embedded PDP. Toward the end of the chapter, we also discussed the value of a security sidecar in the microservice architecture. Understanding the fundamentals of securing microservices is a key to build a production-ready microservices deployment. In the next chapter, we discuss how to implement security for microservices using Spring Boot.

CHAPTER 12

Securing Microservices

In Chapter 11, "Microservices Security Fundamentals," we discussed the common patterns and fundamentals related to securing microservices. If you haven't gone through it, we strongly recommend you do that. In this chapter, we discuss how to implement security for microservices using Spring Boot. We explain how you can invoke a microservice directly, either as an end user or a system, secure the communication between two microservices, access controlling, and protecting access to the actuator endpoints.

Securing a Microservice with OAuth 2.0

In a typical microservices deployment, OAuth 2.0 is used for edge security (see Figure 12-1). A gateway sitting in front of a microservices deployment will validate the OAuth 2.0 access tokens and will issue its own tokens to the downstream microservices. This token can be another OAuth token issued by an internal security token service (STS), which is trusted by all the downstream microservices. If it is a self-contained access token (or JSON Web Token), then the microservice itself can validate the token by verifying its signature. If not, it has to talk to a token validation endpoint exposed by the security token service. In the examples in this chapter, we skip the gateway interactions, and the microservice, which receives the access token talks to the token issuer to validate it.

© Kasun Indrasiri and Prabath Siriwardena 2018
K. Indrasiri and P. Siriwardena, *Microservices for the Enterprise*, https://doi.org/10.1007/978-1-4842-3858-5_12

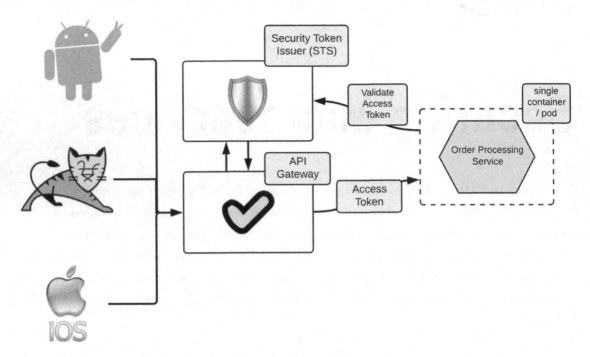

Figure 12-1. *Accessing a secured microservice via an API gateway*

Enable Transport Layer Security (TLS)

OAuth 2.0 tokens used in Figure 12-1 are bearer tokens. Bearer tokens are like cash. If someone steals ten bucks from you, no one can prevent him or her from using the stolen money at Starbucks to buy a cup of coffee. The cashier will never challenge the person to prove the ownership of money. In the same way, anyone who steals a bearer token can use it to impersonate the owner of it and can access the resource (or the microservice). Whenever we use bearer tokens, we must use them over a secured communication channel, hence we need to enable TLS for all the communication channels shown in Figure 12-1.

Note   To run the examples in this chapter, you need Java 8 or latest, Maven 3.2 or latest, and a Git client. Once you have successfully installed those tools, you need to clone the Git repo: `https://github.com/microservices-for-enterprise/samples.git`. The chapter samples are in the `ch12` directory.

`:\> git clone https://github.com/microservices-for-enterprise/samples.git`

To enable TLS, first we need to create a public/private key pair. The following command uses keytool, which comes with the default Java distribution, to generate a key pair and stores it in the keystore.jks file. This file is also known as a key store and it can be in different formats. Two most popular formats are Java Key Store (JKS) and PKCS#12. JKS is specific to Java, while PKCS#12 is a standard that belongs to the family of standards defined under Public-Key Cryptography Standards (PKCS). In the following command, we specify the key store type with the storetype argument, which is set to JKS.

```
\> keytool -genkey -alias spring -storetype JKS -keyalg RSA -keysize 2048
-keystore keystore.jks -validity 3650
```

The alias argument in this command specifies how to identify the generated keys stored in the key store. There can be multiple keys stored in a given key store, and the value of the corresponding alias must be unique. Here we use spring as the alias. The validity argument specifies that the generated keys are only valid for 10 years or 3650 days. The keysize and keystore arguments specify the length of the generated keys and the name of the key store where the keys are stored. The genkey option instructs the keytool to generate new keys; instead of genykey, you can also use the genkeypair option. Once this command is executed, it will prompt you to enter a key store password and will ask you to enter the data required to generate the certificate, as shown here.

```
Enter keystore password: XXXXXXXXX
Re-enter new password: XXXXXXXXX
What is your first and last name?
  [Unknown]:  foo
What is the name of your organizational unit?
  [Unknown]:  bar
What is the name of your organization?
  [Unknown]:  zee
What is the name of your City or Locality?
  [Unknown]:  sjc
What is the name of your State or Province?
  [Unknown]:  ca
What is the two-letter country code for this unit?
  [Unknown]:  us
Is CN=foo, OU=bar, O=zee, L=sjc, ST=ca, C=us correct?
  [no]:  yes
```

The certificate created in this example is known as a self-signed certificate. In other words, there is no certificate authority (CA). Typically in a production deployment, either you will use a public certificate authority or an enterprise-level certificate authority to sign the public certificate, so any client who trusts the certificate authority can verify it. If you are using certificates to secure service-to-service communication in a microservices deployment, you need not worry about having a public certificate authority. You can have your own certificate authority.

Note   For each of your microservices, you need to create a unique key store, along with a key pair. For convenience, in this chapter, we use the same key store for all our microservices.

To enable TLS for a Spring Boot microservice, copy the key store file created previously (keystore.jks) to the home directory of the sample (e.g., ch12/sample01/) and add the following to [SAMPLE_HOME]/src/main/resources/application. properties. The samples that you download from the samples Git repository already have these values. We are using springboot as the password for both the key store and the private key.

```
server.port: 8443
server.ssl.key-store: keystore.jks
server.ssl.key-store-password: springboot
server.ssl.keyAlias: spring
```

To validate that everything works fine, use the following command from the ch12/ sample01/ directory to spin up the TokenService microservice. Notice the line, which prints the HTTPS port.

```
\> mvn spring-boot:run
Tomcat started on port(s): 8443 (https) with context path "
```

Note   In the sections that follow, we assume the TLS is configured in all the examples, with the same key store we created here.

Setting Up an OAuth 2.0 Authorization Server

The responsibility of the authorization server is to issue tokens to its clients and respond to the validation requests from downstream microservices. This also plays the role of a security token service (STS), as shown in Figure 12-1. There are many open source OAuth 2.0 authorization servers out there: WSO2 Identity Server, Keycloak, Gluu, and many more. In a production deployment, you may use one of them, but for this example, we are setting up a simple OAuth 2.0 authorization server with Spring Boot. It is another microservice and quite useful in developer testing. The code corresponding to the authorization server is in the `ch12/sample01` directory.

Let's start by looking at `ch12/sample01/pom.xml` for the notable Maven dependencies. These dependencies introduce a new set of annotations (the `@EnableAuthorizationServer` annotation and `@EnableResourceServer` annotation) to turn a Spring Boot application to an OAuth 2.0 authorization server.

```
<dependency>
  <groupId>org.springframework.boot</groupId>
  <artifactId>spring-boot-starter-security</artifactId>
</dependency>
<dependency>
  <groupId>org.springframework.security.oauth</groupId>
  <artifactId>spring-security-oauth2</artifactId>
</dependency>
```

The `sample01/src/main/java/com/apress/ch12/sample01/TokenServiceApp.java` class carries the `@EnableAuthorizationServer` annotation, which turns the project into an OAuth 2.0 authorization server. We've added the `@EnableResourceServer` annotation to the same class, as it also has to act as a resource server to validate access tokens and return the user information. It's understandable that the terminology here is little confusing, but that's the easiest way to implement the token validation endpoint (in fact, the user info endpoint, which also indirectly does the token validation) in Spring Boot. When you use self-contained access tokens (JWTs), this token validation endpoint is not required.

The registration of clients with the Spring Boot authorization server can be done in multiple ways. This example registers clients in the code itself, in the `sample01/src/main/java/com/apress/ch12/sample01/config/` `AuthorizationServerConfig.java` file. The `AuthorizationServerConfig` class extends the AuthorizationServerConfigurerAdapter class to override its default behavior. Here we set the client ID to 10101010, client secret to 11110000, available scope values to foo and/or bar, authorized grant types to client_credentials, password, and refresh_token, and the validity period of an access token to 60 seconds. Most of the terminology we use here is from OAuth 2.0 and those we explained in Chapter 11.

```java
@Override
public void configure(ClientDetailsServiceConfigurer clients) throws
Exception {
        clients.inMemory().withClient("10101010")
            .secret("11110000").scopes("foo", "bar")
            .authorizedGrantTypes("client_credentials", "password",
                                "refresh_token")
            .accessTokenValiditySeconds(60);
}
```

To support password grant type, the authorization server has to connect to a user store. A user store can be a database or an LDAP server that stores user credentials and attributes. Spring Boot supports integration with multiple user stores, but once again, the most convenient one, which is just good enough for this example, is an in-memory user store. The following code from the sample01/src/main/java/com/apress/ch12/sample01/config/WebSecurityConguration.java file adds a user with the USER role to the system.

```java
@Override
public void configure(AuthenticationManagerBuilder auth) throws
Exception {
        auth.inMemoryAuthentication()
            .withUser("peter").password("peter123").roles("USER");
}
```

Once we define the in-memory user store in Spring Boot, we also need to engage that with the OAuth 2.0 authorization flow, as shown next, in the code sample01/src/main/java/com/apress/ch12/sample01/config/AuthorizationServerConfig.java.

```java
@Autowired
private AuthenticationManager authenticationManager;
@Override
```

```
public void configure(AuthorizationServerEndpointsConfigurer endpoints)
throws Exception {
        endpoints.authenticationManager(authenticationManager);
}
```

To start the authorization server, use the following command from the ch12/ sample01/ directory to spin up the TokenService microservice.

```
\> mvn spring-boot:run
```

To get an access token using the client credentials OAuth 2.0 grant type, use the following command. Make sure to replace the values of $CLIENTID and $CLIENTSECRET appropriately. The hard-coded value for the client ID and client secret used in our example are 10101010 and 11110000, respectively.

```
\> curl -v -X POST --basic -u $CLIENTID:$CLIENTSECRET -H "Content-Type:
application/x-www-form-urlencoded;charset=UTF-8" -k -d "grant_type=client_
credentials&scope=foo" https://localhost:8443/oauth/token
{"access_token":"81aad8c4-b021-4742-93a9-e25920587c94","token_
type":"bearer","expires_in":43199,"scope":"foo"}
```

Note   We use the −k option in the cURL command. Since we have self-signed (untrusted) certificates to secure our HTTPS endpoint, we need to pass the −k parameter to tell cURL to ignore the trust validation. You can find more details about the parameters used here from the OAuth 2.0 6749 RFC: `https://tools. ietf.org/html/rfc6749`.

To get an access token using the password OAuth 2.0 grant type, use the following command. Be sure to replace the values of $CLIENTID, $CLIENTSECRET, $USERNAME, and $PASSWORD appropriately. The hard-coded value for the client ID and client secret used in our example are 10101010 and 11110000 respectively; for username and password, we used peter and peter123.

```
\> curl -v -X POST --basic -u $CLIENTID:$CLIENTSECRET -H "Content-Type:
application/x-www-form-urlencoded;charset=UTF-8" -k -d "grant_type=password&
username=$USERNAME&password=$PASSWORD&scope=foo" https://localhost:8443/
oauth/token
```

{"access_token":"69ff86a8-eaa2-4490-adda-6ce0f10b9f8b","token_
type":"bearer","refresh_token":"ab3c797b-72e2-4a9a-a1c5-
c550b2775f93","expires_in":43199,"scope":"foo"}

Note   If you carefully observe the two responses we got for the OAuth 2.0 client
credentials grant type and the password grant type, you might have noticed that
there is no refresh token in the client credentials grant type flow. In OAuth 2.0,
the refresh token is used to obtain a new access token, when the access token
is expired. This is quite useful when the user is offline and the client application
has no access to his/her credentials to get a new access token. In that case, the
only way is to use a refresh token. For the client credentials grant type, there is
no user involved, and it always has access to its own credentials, so it can be
used any time it wants to get a new access token. Hence a refresh token is not
required.

Now let's see how to validate an access token by talking to the authorization server.
The resource server usually does this. An interceptor running on the resource server
intercepts the request, extracts the access token, and then talks to the authorization
server. We see in the next section how to configure a resource server (another
microservice protected with OAuth 2.0), and the following command shows how to
directly talk to the authorization server to validate the access token obtained in the
previous command. Be sure to replace the $TOKEN value with the corresponding access
token.

```
\> curl -k -X POST -H "Authorization: Bearer $TOKEN" -H "Content-Type:
application/json"   https://localhost:8443/user
{"details":{"remoteAddress":"0:0:0:0:0:0:0:1","sessionId":null,"tokenValue":
"9f3319a1-c6c4-4487-ac3b-51e9e479b4ff","tokenType":"Bearer","decodedDetails":
null},"authorities":[],"authenticated":true,"userAuthentication":null,
"credentials":"","oauth2Request":{"clientId":"10101010","scope":["bar"],
"requestParameters":{"grant_type":"client_credentials","scope":"bar"},
"resourceIds":[],"authorities":[],"approved":true,"refresh":false,
"redirectUri":null,"responseTypes":[],"extensions":{},"grantType":
"client_credentials","refreshTokenRequest":null},"clientOnly":true,
"principal":"10101010","name":"10101010"}
```

This command returns the metadata associated with the access token, if the token is valid. The response is built inside the user() method of the sample01/src/main/java/com/apress/ch12/sample01/TokenServiceApp.java class, as shown in the following code snippet. With the @RequestMapping annotation, we map the /user context (from the request) to the user() method.

```
@RequestMapping("/user")
public Principal user(Principal user) {
        return user;
}
```

Note   By default, with no extensions, Spring Boot stores issued tokens in memory. If you restart the server after issuing a token and then validate it, it will result in an error response.

Protecting a Microservice with OAuth 2.0

In this section, we see how to protect a Spring Boot microservice with OAuth 2.0. In OAuth terminology, it's a resource server. The code corresponding to the OAuth 2.0 protected Order Processing microservice is in the ch12/sample02 directory. To secure the microservice with OAuth 2.0, we add the @EnableResourceServer annotation to the sample02/src/main/java/com/apress/ch12/sample02/OrderProcessingApp.java class and point the security.oauth2.resource.user-info-uri property in the sample02/src/main/resources/application.properties file to the authorization server's user info endpoint. The following shows the application.properties file corresponding to sample02. Note that the security.oauth2.resource.jwt.keyUri property is commented out there by default; we'll discuss its usage later in the chapter.

```
server.port=9443
server.ssl.key-store: keystore.jks
server.ssl.key-store-password: springboot
server.ssl.keyAlias: spring
```

```
security.oauth2.resource.user-info-uri=https://localhost:8443/user
#security.oauth2.resource.jwt.keyUri:
https://localhost:8443/oauth/token_key
```

Since the `Order Processing` microservice calls the user info endpoint over HTTPS, and we use self-signed certificates to secure the authorization server, this call will result in a trust validation error. To overcome that, we need to export the public certificate of the authorization server from `ch12/sample01/keystore.jks` to a new key store and set it as the trust store of the `Order Processing` microservice.

Use the following `keytool` command to export the public certificate and store it in the `cert.crt` file. The password used to protect `keystore.jks` is `springboot`. Instead of the export argument, which instructs the `keytool` to export a certificate under the given alias, you can also use the `exportcert` argument.

```
\> keytool -export -keystore keystore.jks -alias spring -file cert.crt
```

Now use the following `keytool` command to create a new trust store with `cert.crt`. Here we use `authserver` as the alias to store the authorization server's public certificate in `trust-store.jks` and copy the trust store to the `ch12/sample02` directory (by default, you will find all the key stores and trust stores required to run the samples under the corresponding directories, when you clone the code from the sample Git repository). We use the same password, `springboot`, to protect `trust-store.jks` as well. Instead of the import argument, which instructs the `keytool` to import a certificate under the given alias, you can also use the `importcert` argument.

```
\> keytool -import -file cert.crt -alias authserver -keystore trust-store.jks
```

We also need to set the location of the trust store and its password as system parameters in the code. You will find the following code snippet in the `sample02/src/main/java/com/apress/ch12/sample02/OrderProcessingApp.java` class, which sets the system properties.

```
static {
  String path = System.getProperty("user.dir");
  System.setProperty("javax.net.ssl.trustStore", path
                          + File.separator + "trust-store.jks");
```

```
System.setProperty("javax.net.ssl.trustStorePassword", "springboot");

HttpsURLConnection.setDefaultHostnameVerifier(new HostnameVerifier()
{
    public boolean verify(String hostname, SSLSession session) {
            return true;
    }
});
}
```

In addition to setting up the trust store system properties, the last few lines of code in this code snippet do something else too. Apart from the trust validation, we could also face a potential other problem while making an HTTPS connection to the authorization server. When we do an HTTPS call to a server, the client usually checks whether the common name (CN) of the server certificate matches the hostname in our server URL. For example, when we use `localhost` as the hostname in `user-info-url` (which points to the authorization server), the authorization server's public certificate must have `localhost` as the common name. If not, it results in an error. This code disregards the hostname verification by overriding the `verify` function and returns `true`. Ideally in a production deployment you should use proper certificates and avoid such workarounds.

Let's use the following command from the `ch12/sample02/` directory to spin up the `Order Processing` microservice; it starts on HTTPS port 9443.

```
\> mvn spring-boot:run
```

First, let's try to invoke the service with the following cURL command with no valid access token, which should ideally return an error response.

```
\> curl -k https://localhost:9443/order/11
{"error":"unauthorized","error_description":"Full authentication is
required to access this resource"}
```

Now let's invoke the same service with a valid access token obtained from the OAuth 2.0 authorization server. Make sure the value of $TOKEN is replaced appropriately with a valid access token.

```
\> curl -k -H "Authorization: Bearer $TOKEN"
https://localhost:9443/order/11
```

```
{"customer_id":"101021","order_id":"11","payment_method":{"card_type":
"VISA","expiration":"01/22","name":"John Doe","billing_address":"201, 1st
Street, San Jose, CA"},"items":[{"code":"101","qty":1},{"code":"103","qty":
5}],"shipping_address":"201, 1st Street, San Jose, CA"}
```

If we see this response, then we've got our OAuth 2.0 authorization server and the OAuth 2.0 protected microservice running properly.

Securing a Microservice with Self-Contained Access Tokens (JWT)

In Chapter 11, we discussed JWT and its usage in detail. In this section, we are going to use a JWT issued from our OAuth 2.0 authorization server to access a secured microservice.

Setting Up an Authorization Server to Issue JWT

In this section, we see how to extend the authorization server we used in the previous section (ch12/sample01/) to support self-contained access tokens or JWTs. The first step is to create a new key pair along with a key store. This key is used to sign the JWTs issued from the authorization server. The following keytool command will create a new key store with a key pair.

```
\> keytool -genkey -alias jwtkey -keyalg RSA -keysize 2048 -dname
"CN=localhost" -keypass springboot -keystore jwt.jks -storepass springboot
```

This command creates a key store with the name jwt.jks, protected with the password springboot. We need to copy this key store to sample01/src/main/resources/. To generate self-contained access tokens, we need to set the value of the following properties in the sample01/src/main/resources/application.properties file.

```
spring.security.oauth.jwt: true
spring.security.oauth.jwt.keystore.password: springboot
spring.security.oauth.jwt.keystore.alias: jwtkey
spring.security.oauth.jwt.keystore.name: jwt.jks
```

The value of `spring.security.oauth.jwt` is set to `false` by default, and it has to be changed to `true` to issue JWTs. The other three properties are self-explanatory and you need to set them appropriately based on the values you used when creating the key store.

Let's go through the notable changes in the source code to support JWTs. First, in the `pom.xml` file, we need to add the following dependency, which takes care of building JWTs.

```xml
<dependency>
  <groupId>org.springframework.security</groupId>
  <artifactId>spring-security-jwt</artifactId>
</dependency>
```

In the `sample01/src/main/java/com/apress/ch12/sample01/config/AuthorizationServerConfig.java` class, we added the following method, which takes care of injecting the details about how to retrieve the private key from the key store. This private key is used to sign the JWT.

```java
@Bean
protected JwtAccessTokenConverter jwtConeverter() {
  String pwd = environment.getProperty(
                "spring.security.oauth.jwt.keystore.password");
  String alias = environment.getProperty(
                "spring.security.oauth.jwt.keystore.alias");
  String keystore = environment.getProperty(
                "spring.security.oauth.jwt.keystore.name");

  KeyStoreKeyFactory keyStoreKeyFactory = new KeyStoreKeyFactory(
                    new ClassPathResource(keystore),
                        pwd.toCharArray());
  JwtAccessTokenConverter converter = new JwtAccessTokenConverter();
  converter.setKeyPair(keyStoreKeyFactory.getKeyPair(alias));
  return converter;
}
```

In the same class file, we also set `JwtTokenStore` as the token store. The following function does it in a way, such that we set the `JwtTokenStore` as the token store only if the `spring.security.oauth.jwt` property is set to `true` in the `application.properties` file.

```
@Bean
public TokenStore tokenStore() {
  String useJwt = environment.getProperty("spring.security.oauth.jwt");
  if (useJwt != null && "true".equalsIgnoreCase(useJwt.trim())) {
      return new JwtTokenStore(jwtConeverter());
  } else {
      return new InMemoryTokenStore();
  }
}
```

Finally, we need to set the token store to
AuthorizationServerEndpointsConfigurer, which is done in the following function,
and once again, only if we want to use JWTs.

```
@Autowired
private AuthenticationManager authenticationManager;

@Override
public void configure(AuthorizationServerEndpointsConfigurer endpoints)
throws Exception {
  String useJwt = environment.getProperty("spring.security.oauth.jwt");
  if (useJwt != null && "true".equalsIgnoreCase(useJwt.trim())) {
      endpoints.tokenStore(tokenStore()).tokenEnhancer(jwtConeverter())
                            .authenticationManager(authenticationManager);
  } else {
      endpoints.authenticationManager(authenticationManager);
  }
}
```

To start the authorization server, use the following command from the ch12/
sample01/ directory to spin up the TokenService microservice, which now issues
self-contained access tokens (JWTs).

```
\> mvn spring-boot:run
```

To get an access token using the client credentials OAuth 2.0 grant type, use the
following command. Be sure to replace the values of $CLIENTID and $CLIENTSECRET
appropriately.

```
\> curl -v -X POST --basic -u $CLIENTID:$CLIENTSECRET -H "Content-Type:
application/x-www-form-urlencoded;charset=UTF-8" -k -d "grant_type=client_
credentials&scope=foo" https://localhost:8443/oauth/token
```

This command will return a base64-url-encoded JWT, and the following shows the decoded version.

```
{ "alg": "RS256", "typ": "JWT" }
{ "scope": [ "foo" ], "exp": 1524793284, "jti": "6e55840e-886c-46b2-bef7-
1a14b813dd0a", "client_id": "10101010" }
```

Only the decoded header and the payload are shown here; we are skipping the signature (which is the third part of the JWT). Since we used the client_credentials grant type, the JWT does not include a subject or username. It also includes the scope values associated with the token.

Protecting a Microservice with JWT

In this section, we see how to extend the Order Processing microservice we used in the previous section (ch12/sample02/) to support self-issued access tokens or JWTs. We only need to comment out the security.oauth2.resource.user-info-uri property and uncomment the security.oauth2.resource.jwt.keyUri property in the sample02/ src/main/resources/application.properties file. The complete application. properties file will look like the following.

```
#security.oauth2.resource.user-info-uri:https://localhost:8443/user
security.oauth2.resource.jwt.keyUri: https://localhost:8443/oauth/token_key
```

Here the value of security.oauth2.resource.jwt.keyUri points to the public key corresponding to the private key, which is used to sign the JWT by the authorization server. It's an endpoint hosted under the authorization server. If you just type https:// localhost:8443/oauth/token_key on the browser, you will find the public key, as shown here. This is the key the resource server, or in this case, the Order Processing microservice uses to verify the signature of the JWT included in the request.

```
{
   "alg":"SHA256withRSA",
   "value":"-----BEGIN PUBLIC KEY-----\
nMIIBIjANBgkqhkiG9w0BAQEFAAOCAQ8AMIIBCgKCAQEA+WcBjPsrFvGOwqVJd8vpV+
gNx5onTyLjYx864mtIvUxO8D4mwAaYpjXJgsre2dcXjQO3BOLJdcjY5Nc9Kclea09nhFIEJD
G3obwxm9gQw5Op1TShCP3OXqf8b7I738EHDFT6qABul7itIxSrz+AqUvj9LSUKEw/
cdXrJeu6b71qHd/YiElUIAOfjVwlFctbw7REbi3Sy3nWdm9yk7M3GIKka77jxw1MwIBg2klf
DJgnE72fPkPi3FmaJTJA4+9sKgfniFqdMNfkyLVbOi9E3DlaoGxEit6fKTI9GR1SWX4OFhh
gLdTyWdu2z9RS2BOp+3d9WFMTddab8+fd4L2mYCQIDAQAB\n-----END PUBLIC KEY-----"
}
```

Once we have a JWT access token obtained from the OAuth 2.0 authorization server, in the same as we did before, with the following cURL command, we can access the protected resource. Make sure the value of $TOKEN is replaced with a valid access token.

```
\> curl -k -H "Authorization: Bearer $TOKEN" https://localhost:9443/order/11
{"customer_id":"101021","order_id":"11","payment_method":{"card_type":"VISA",
"expiration":"01/22","name":"John Doe","billing_address":"201, 1st Street,
San Jose, CA"},"items":[{"code":"101","qty":1},{"code":"103","qty":5}],
"shipping_address":"201, 1st Street, San Jose, CA"}
```

Controlling Access to a Microservice

There are multiple ways to control access to microservices. In this section, we see how to control access to different operations in a microservice based on the scopes associated with the access token and the user's roles.

Scope-Based Access Control

Here we use self-contained access tokens (or JWTs) and first you need to have a valid JWT obtained from the OAuth 2.0 authorization server. The following command will get you a JWT access token with the scope foo. Make sure to replace the value of $CLIENTID and $CLIENTSECRET appropriately and keep the sample01 (which is our authorization server) running.

```
\> curl -v -X POST --basic -u $CLIENTID:$CLIENTSECRET -H "Content-Type:
application/x-www-form-urlencoded;charset=UTF-8" -k -d "grant_type=client_
credentials&scope=foo" https://localhost:8443/oauth/token
```

To enable scope-based access control for the Order Processing microservice (sample02), we need to add the @EnableGlobalMethodSecurity annotation to the sample02/src/main/java/com/apress/ch12/sample02/OrderProcessingApp.java class, as shown here.

```
@SpringBootApplication
@EnableGlobalMethodSecurity(prePostEnabled = true)
@EnableResourceServer
public class OrderProcessingApp {
}
```

Now let's use the @PreAuthorize annotation at the method level to enforce scope-based access control. The following method in the sample02/src/main/java/com/apress/ch12/sample02/service/OrderProcessing.java class requires the bar scope to access it.

```
@PreAuthorize("#oauth2.hasScope('bar')")
@RequestMapping(value = "/{id}", method= RequestMethod.GET)
public ResponseEntity<?> getOrder(@PathVariable("id") String orderId) {
}
```

Let's try run the following cURL command, with the previously obtained JWT access token, which only has the foo scope. The command should result in an error, since our token does not carry the required scope value.

```
\> curl -k -H "Authorization: Bearer $TOKEN" https://localhost:9443/
order/11
{"error":"access_denied","error_description":"Access is denied"}
```

Role-Based Access Control

Just like in the previous section, here we have to use self-contained access tokens (or JWTs) and first you need to have a valid JWT obtained from the OAuth 2.0 authorization server.

The following cURL command will give you a JWT access token using the `password` grant type. Be sure to replace the values of $CLIENTID, $CLIENTSECRET, $USERNAME, and $PASSWORD appropriately. Unlike in the scope-based scenario, the client credentials grant type won't work here, as by default, no roles are associated with clients (only with users).

```
\> curl -v -X POST --basic -u $CLIENTID:$CLIENTSECRET -H "Content-Type:
application/x-www-form-urlencoded;charset=UTF-8" -k -d "grant_type=passwor
d&username=$USERNAME&password=$PASSWORD&scope=foo" https://localhost:8443/
oauth/token
```

To enable role-based access control for the `Order Processing` microservice (sample02), we need to add the `@EnableGlobalMethodSecurity` annotation to the `sample02/src/main/java/com/apress/ch12/sample02/OrderProcessingApp.java` class, as shown here (this is the same step we did while setting up scope-based access control in the previous section).

```
@SpringBootApplication
@EnableGlobalMethodSecurity(prePostEnabled = true)
@EnableResourceServer
public class OrderProcessingApp {
}
```

Now let's use the `@PreAuthorize` annotation at the method level to enforce role-based access control. The following method in the `sample02/src/main/java/com/apress/ch12/sample02/service/OrderProcessing.java` class requires the USER role to access it. By default, we add the USER role to the user named `peter`, from our authorization server. Hence an access token issued to him should be good enough to access this operation.

```
@PreAuthorize("hasRole(USER)")
@RequestMapping(value = "/{id}", method= RequestMethod.GET)
public ResponseEntity<?> getOrder(@PathVariable("id") String orderId) {
}
```

Let's try to run the following cURL command, with the previously obtained JWT access token, which only has the `foo` scope. If it's issued to a user having the USER role it should result in a successful response.

```
\> curl -k -H "Authorization: Bearer $TOKEN" https://localhost:9443/order/11
```

Finally, if we want to control access to a method both by the scope and the role, we can use the following annotation against the corresponding method.

```
@PreAuthorize("#oauth2.hasScope('bar') and hasRole('USER')")
```

Securing Service-to-Service Communication

In the previous section, we discussed how to set up an OAuth 2.0 authorization and secure a microservice with OAuth 2.0. In this section, we see how to invoke one microservice from another securely. We follow two approaches here—one is based on JWT and the other is based on TLS mutual authentication.

Service-to-Service Communication Secured with JWT

In this section, we see how to invoke a microservice secured with OAuth 2.0 from another microservice by passing a JWT.

Figure 12-2 extends Figure 12-1 by introducing the Inventory microservices. Upon receiving an order, the Order Processing microservice talks to the Inventory microservice to update the inventory. Here, the Order Processing microservice passes the access token it gets to the Inventory microservice.

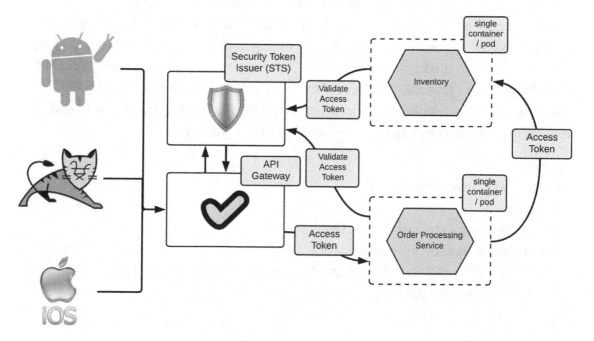

Figure 12-2. *Protecting service-to-service communication with OAuth 2.0*

The token validation step in Figure 12-2 will change if we use self-contained (JWT) access tokens. In that case, there is no validation call from the microservice to the authorization server (or the security token issuer). Each microservice will fetch the corresponding public key from the authorization server and will validate the signature of the JWT locally.

In this example, we use JWT access tokens. In previous sections we have already configured the authorization server (sample01) and the Order Processing microservice (sample02) to work with JWT. Now let's see how to set up the Inventory microservice. The code corresponding to the Inventory microservice is in the ch12/sample03 directory. The way it works is almost same as the Order Processing microservice in sample02. To enable JWT authentication, make sure the following property is uncommented in the sample03/src/main/resources/application.properties file.

```
security.oauth2.resource.jwt.keyUri: https://localhost:8443/oauth/token_key
```

Now we can start the Inventory microservice with the following Maven command, run from the sample03 directory. The service starts on HTTPS port 10443.

```
\> mvn spring-boot:run
```

To execute the end-to-end flow, we need to place an order at the Order Processing (sample02) microservice. It will talk only to the Inventory (sample03) microservice. Before we run our cURL client against the Order Processing microservice, let's look at its code, which talks to the Inventory microservice. We use OAuth2RestTemplate to talk to the Inventory microservice, which will automatically pass the access token (Order Processing microservice) it got from the client application. The corresponding code is available in the sample02/src/main/java/com/apress/ch12/sample02/client/InventoryClient.java file. The Order Processing microservice gets the complete order from the client application, then extracts the list of items from the request, and updates the inventory by talking to the Inventory microservice.

```java
@Component
public class InventoryClient {
  @Autowired
  OAuth2RestTemplate restTemplate;
  public void updateInventory(Item[] items) {
      URI uri = URI.create("https://localhost:10443/inventory");
      restTemplate.put(uri, items);
  }
}
```

Assuming the OAuth 2.0 authorization server (sample01) is running, let's run the following cURL command to get an access token. Be sure to replace the values of $CLIENTID, $CLIENTSECRET, $USERNAME, and $PASSWORD appropriately. Also note that we pass both foo and bar as scope values.

```
\> curl -v -X POST --basic -u $CLIENTID:$CLIENTSECRET -H "Content-Type:
application/x-www-form-urlencoded;charset=UTF-8" -k -d "grant_type=password
&username=$USERNAME&password=$PASSWORD&scope=foo bar"
https://localhost:8443/oauth/token
```

This will produce a JWT access token. Along with that token, let's place an order by talking to the Order Processing microservice (sample02) by running the following cURL command.

```
curl -v  -k -H "Authorization: Bearer $TOKEN" -H "Content-Type:
application/json" -d '{"customer_id":"101021","payment_method":{"card_type":
"VISA","expiration":"01/22","name":"John Doe","billing_address":"201, 1st
Street, San Jose, CA"},"items":[{"code":"101","qty":1},{"code":"103","
qty":5}],"shipping_address":"201, 1st Street, San Jose, CA"}' https://
localhost:9443/order
```

If all works fine, we should see the 201 HTTP status code at the cURL client and the order numbers printed on the terminal that runs the Inventory microservice.

Service-to-Service Communication Secured with TLS Mutual Authentication

In this section, we see how to enable TLS mutual authentication between the Order Processing microservice and the Inventory microservice. In most cases, TLS mutual authentication is used to enable server-to-server authentication, while JWT is used to pass the user context between microservices.

One primary requirement to enable mutual authentication is that each service should have its own key store (keystore.jks) and a trust store (trust-store.jks). Even though both are key stores, we use the term key store specifically to highlight the key store that stores the server's private/public key pair, while the trust store carries the public certificates of the trusted servers and clients. For example, when the Order Processing microservice talks to the Inventory microservice, which is secured with

TLS mutual authentication, the public certificate of the certificate authority that signs the `Order Processing` microservice's public key must be in the trust store (`sample03/ trust-store.jks`) of the `Inventory` microservice.

Since we use self-signed certificates here, we have no certificate authority, hence we include the public certificate itself. The `Order Processing` microservice, which acts as the TLS mutual authentication client, uses its keys from the key store (`sample02/ keystore.jks`) during the TLS handshake for authentication. It also has to store the public certificate of the certificate authority that signs the `Inventory` microservice's public key, in its trust store (`sample02/trust-store.jks`). Once again, since we do not have a certificate authority, we store the public certificate itself. Figure 12-3 illustrates what we discussed here.

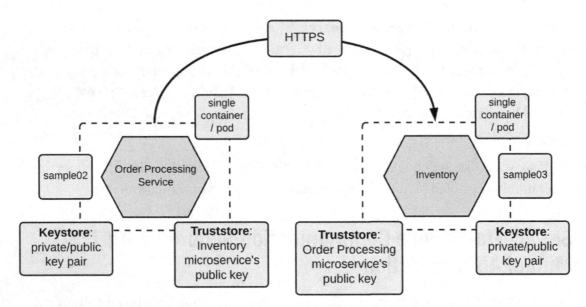

Figure 12-3. *Distribution of certificates to facilitate TLS mutual authentication*

Let's revisit the steps involved in setting up the key stores in the `Order Processing` microservice. First, make sure that we have the key store at `sample02/ keystore.jks` and the trust store at `sample02/trust-store.jks`. The following properties related to both the key stores are set appropriately in the `sample02/src/ main/java/com/apress/ch12/sample02/OrderProcessingApp.java` file. Also, we already added the public certificate of the `Inventory` microservice to the `sample02/ trust-store.jks` file.

```
System.setProperty("javax.net.ssl.trustStore", path + File.separator +
"trust-store.jks");
System.setProperty("javax.net.ssl.trustStorePassword", "springboot")
System.setProperty("javax.net.ssl.keyStore",  path + File.separator +
"keystore.jks");
System.setProperty("javax.net.ssl.keyStorePassword", "springboot");
```

Once we have the javax.net.ssl.keyStore and javax.net.ssl.keyStorePassword system properties set, the client automatically picks the corresponding key pair to respond to the server's challenge to request the client certificate, during the TLS handshake.

Now, let's look at the server-side configurations. The Inventory microservice should have its key store under /sample03/keystore.jks and trust store under sample03/trust-store.jks. The following properties related to trust store are set appropriately in the sample03/src/main/java/com/apress/ch12/sample03/InventoryApp.java file. Here we have only set the trust store properties. There is no need to set properties related to the key store unless it's acting as a TLS client.

```
System.setProperty("javax.net.ssl.trustStore", path + File.separator +
"trust-store.jks");
System.setProperty("javax.net.ssl.trustStorePassword", "springboot");
```

To enable TLS mutual authentication for the Inventory microservice, set the following property in the sample03/src/main/resources/application.properties file.

```
server.ssl.client-auth:need
```

Now we can test the end-to-end flow by invoking the Order Processing microservice with a valid access token. To cater to the request, the Order Processing microservice talks to the Inventory microservice, which is protected with TLS mutual authentication.

```
curl -v  -k -H "Authorization: Bearer $TOKEN" -H "Content-Type:
application/json" -d '{"customer_id":"101021","payment_method":{"card_type":
"VISA","expiration":"01/22","name":"John Doe","billing_address":"201,
1st Street, San Jose, CA"},"items":[{"code":"101","qty":1},{"code":"103",
"qty":5}],"shipping_address":"201, 1st Street, San Jose, CA"}'
https://localhost:9443/order
```

Securing Actuator Endpoints

Spring Boot provides out-of-the-box monitoring capabilities via the actuators. For any Spring Boot microservice, you can add the following dependency to activate the actuator endpoints.

```
<dependency>
  <groupId>org.springframework.boot</groupId>
  <artifactId>spring-boot-starter-actuator</artifactId>
</dependency>
```

A sample microservice project with this dependency is available at `ch12/sample04`. Let's spin up the `Order Processing` microservice from the `sample04` directory with the following command. The service will start on HTTPS port 8443.

```
\> mvn spring-boot:run
```

Since we have not engaged in any security at this point, if we run the following cURL command, it will successfully return a response.

```
\> curl -k https://localhost:8443/health
{"status":"UP"}>
```

To enable security, we need to add the following dependency to the `sample04/pom.xml` file.

```
<dependency>
  <groupId>org.springframework.boot</groupId>
  <artifactId>spring-boot-starter-security</artifactId>
</dependency>
```

Now, uncomment the `@Configuration` class-level annotation in the `sample04/src/main/java/com/apress/ch12/sample04/config/SecurityConfig.java` file. By default it was kept commented, so that Spring Boot won't pick the overridden configuration in that class and we can try the non-secured scenario. In the same class, the following code snippet introduces a user called `admin` to the system with the `ACTUATOR` role. When the actuator endpoints are secured, only the users in the `ACTUATOR` role will be able to invoke the endpoints.

```
@Override
public void configure(AuthenticationManagerBuilder auth) throws Exception {
  auth.inMemoryAuthentication().withUser("admin")
                               .password("admin").roles("ACTUATOR");
}
```

Now restart the service and try the same cURL command with admin/admin credentials.

```
\> curl -k --basic -u admin:admin  https://localhost:8443/health
{"status":"UP"}
```

Summary

In Chapter 11, we discussed the common patterns and fundamentals related to securing microservices. This chapter focused on building those patterns with microservices developed in Spring Boot. In the next chapter, we discuss the role of observability in a microservices deployment.

CHAPTER 13

Observability

Collecting data is cheap, but not having it when you need it can be expensive. In March 2016, Amazon was down for 20 minutes and the estimated revenue loss was $3.75 million. Also in January 2017, there was a system outage at Delta Airlines, which caused cancellation of more than 170 flights and resulted in an estimated loss of $8.5 million. In both cases if we had the right level of data collected, we could have predicted such behavior or could have recovered from it as soon as it has happened by identifying the root cause. The more information we have, the better decisions we can make.

Observability is the measure of how well internal states of a system can be inferred from knowledge of its external outputs[1]. It is one of the most important aspects, which needs to be baked into any microservices design. We need to track the throughput of each microservice, the number of success/failed requests, utilization of CPU, memory and other network resources, and some business-related metrics. In this chapter, we discuss the need for observability, the role logging, metrics, and tracing play in observability, how to build a distributed tracing system with Spring Cloud Sleuth, Zipkin, and Jaeger, and how visualization, monitoring, and alerting work with Prometheus and Grafana.

Three Pillars of Observability

Observability can be achieved in three ways: *logging, metrics,* and *tracing,* which are also known as the three pillars of observability. Logging is about recording events. It can be anything. Each transaction that goes through a microservice can be logged with other related metadata, including the timestamp, the status (success/failure), initiator, etc. Combining data from measuring events derives metrics. For example, the number of

---

[1]https://en.wikipedia.org/wiki/Observability

© Kasun Indrasiri and Prabath Siriwardena 2018
K. Indrasiri and P. Siriwardena, *Microservices for the Enterprise,* https://doi.org/10.1007/978-1-4842-3858-5_13

transactions processed in a unit time and the transaction success/failure rate are metrics about your microservice. Metrics are an indication of how well (or how poorly) your service is doing. Another example would be the latency. The logs capture the timestamp of every request that hits a microservice and the corresponding responses. The difference between those two timestamps is the latency of a given request. The average latency of a given service is derived by taken into consideration all such time differences over the time, which is a metric. Here, latency as a metric helps us decide whether our microservice is slow or fast. Also, when we want to set alerts, we always pick metrics. If we want to be alerted when the system starts to perform slower than the expectation, we probably could set up an alert on latency. When the average latency falls behind a preset threshold, the system will trigger an alert. In summary, metrics help us identify trends.

Tracing is also derived from logs. It's a different view on how a system behaves, which takes into consideration the ordering of each event and the impact of one on another. Say for example that tracing helps you find the root cause of why a request that comes to the Billing microservice fails, by tracing it back to the Order Processing microservice. It doesn't need to be across different systems all the time; it can be just within one system. For example, if it takes 90 milliseconds to place an order, the tracing should show us where exactly the delay is and how different components contribute to it.

Distributed Tracing with Spring Cloud Sleuth

Distributed tracing helps in tracking a given request, which spans across multiple microservices. Due to the nature of microservices, in most cases, to cater a single request from a client, more than one microservices are consumed. Figure 13-1 shows all the interactions between microservices that could happen during a single request to place an order. Some requests are direct service-to-service invocations, while others are asynchronous based on a messaging system. Irrespective of how service-to-service communication takes place, distributed tracing provides a way to track a request, which spans across all the microservices required in building the response to the client.

Distributed tracing adds value not just for microservices, but also for any distributed system. Whenever a request passes through different components (say an API gateway, Enterprise Service Bus) in a network, you need to have the ability to track it across all the systems. That helps you to identify and isolate issues related to latency, message loses, throughput, and many more.

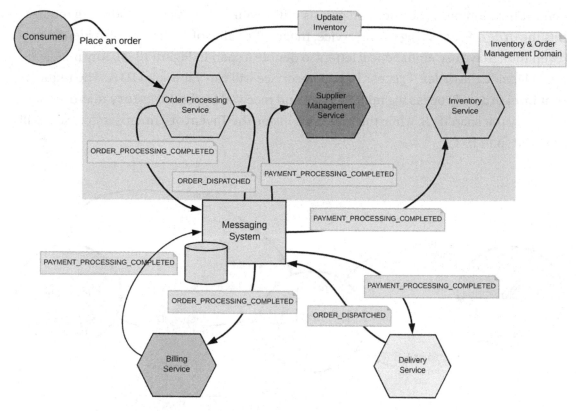

Figure 13-1. *Communication between microservices*

Spring Cloud Sleuth

Spring Cloud Sleuth implements a distributed tracing solution for Spring microservices[2]. Sleuth borrows many concepts and terminology from Dapper[3], which is Google's production distributed systems tracing infrastructure. The basic unit of work in Sleuth is called a *span*. A span represents the work carried out between two points in a communication network. For example, the `Order Processing` microservice (see Figure 13-1) receives an order from a client and processes the order. Then it synchronously talks to the `Inventory` microservice and, once it receives the response, publishes the `ORDER_PROCESSING_COMPLETED` event to the messaging system. Figure 13-2 shows how spans are identified between different points in the complete

[2]https://cloud.spring.io/spring-cloud-sleuth/

[3]https://storage.googleapis.com/pub-tools-public-publication-data/pdf/36356.pdf

communication network. The span gets its initial value once the corresponding request hits the Order Processing microservice. In fact, the value of span is a 64-bit identifier (even though we use alphabetical letters to denote a span in Figure 13-2). Any message logged inside the Order Processing microservice will carry the span ID A. The request sent from Order Processing microservice and received by the Inventory microservice will carry the span ID B, while the request is inside the Inventory microservice, so it will hold the span ID C.

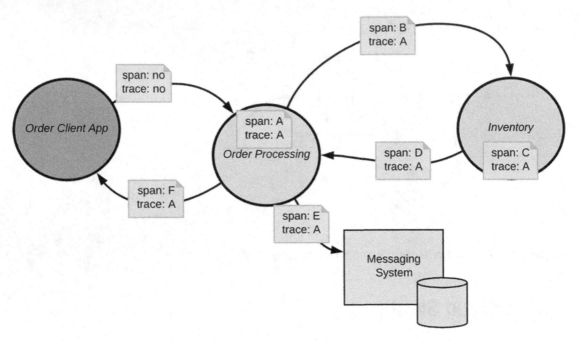

Figure 13-2. *Distributed tracing*

Each span has a parent span. For example, the parent span for span B is span A, while the parent span of span A is null. Similarly, span A is also a parent of span E. Figure 13-3 arranges spans by the parent-child relationship. A set of spans forming a tree-like structure is known as a *trace*. The value of the trace remains the same through out all the spans for a given request. As per Figure 13-2, the value of the trace is A, and it carries the same value across all the spans. The trace ID helps correlate messages between microservices. Once all the logs from different microservices are published into a centralized tracing system, given the trace ID, we can trace the message across different systems.

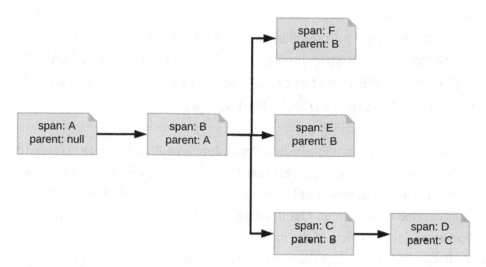

Figure 13-3. *A set of spans forming a tree-like structure*

Let's get our hands wet! Let's see how to use Spring Cloud Sleuth to do distributed tracing with a set of example Spring microservices.

Note   To run the examples in this chapter, you need Java 8 or latest, Maven 3.2 or latest, and a Git client. Once you have successfully installed those tools, you need to clone the Git repo: `https://github.com/microservices-for-enterprise/samples.git`. The chapter's examples are in the `ch13` directory.

`:\> git clone https://github.com/microservices-for-enterprise/samples.git`

Engaging Spring Cloud Sleuth with Spring Boot Microservices

Engaging Sleuth with Spring Boot is quite straightforward. Once you download all the examples from the Git repository, you can find the source code related to this example available in the ch13/sample01 directory.

> **Note**   A comprehensive introduction to Spring Cloud Sleuth is out of the scope of this book, and we recommend readers looking for details to refer to Sleuth documentation available at `https://cloud.spring.io/spring-cloud-sleuth/single/spring-cloud-sleuth.html`.

Let's look at some of the notable Maven dependencies added to the `ch13/sample01/pom.xml` file. The `spring-cloud-starter-sleuth` dependency brings in all the dependencies related to Sleuth. Once engaged to a Maven project, Sleuth spans and traces will be automatically added to all the logs. Sleuth intercepts all the HTTP requests coming to a given microservice and inspects all the messages to see whether any tracing information is already available. If so, will extract them out and make those available to the corresponding microservice. Also, Sleuth injects the tracing information to the Spring Mapped Diagnostic Context (MDC), so that logs created from a microservice will automatically include the tracing data. When an HTTP request goes out from a microservice, once again Sleuth injects the tracing information to the outbound request or to the response.

```
<dependency>
        <groupId>org.springframework.cloud</groupId>
        <artifactId>spring-cloud-starter-sleuth</artifactId>
        <version>2.0.0.RC1</version>
</dependency>
```

Let's look at the source code (`ch13/sample01/src/main/java/com/apress/ch13/sample01/service/OrderProcessing.java`), which logs data related to the order retrieval requests. The logging API used here to log messages has nothing related to Sleuth—it's simply the `slf4j`[4] API.

```
import org.slf4j.Logger;
import org.slf4j.LoggerFactory;

@RequestMapping(value = "/{id}", method = RequestMethod.GET)
public ResponseEntity<?> getOrder(@PathVariable("id") String orderId) {
 logger.info("retrieving order:" + orderId);
 Item book1 = new Item("101", 1);
 Item book2 = new Item("103", 5);
```

---

[4]`https://www.slf4j.org/`

```
PaymentMethod myvisa = new PaymentMethod("VISA", "01/22", "John Doe",
                                          "201, 1st Street, San Jose, CA");
Order order = new Order("101021", orderId, myvisa, new Item[] { book1,
                         book2 },"201, 1st Street, San Jose, CA");
return ResponseEntity.ok(order);
}
```

Before we run the code, there are couple of important properties to configure in the ch13/sample01/src/main/resources/application.properties file.

```
spring.application.name=sample01
spring.sleuth.sampler.percentage=0.1
```

The value of the property spring.application.name is added to the logs as the service name, along with the trace ID and span ID. Once Sleuth is engaged, the service name, trace ID, span ID, and a flag indicating whether the logs are published to Zipkin will be appended to the logs. In the following example, sample01 is the service name (picked from the property file), d25a633196c01c19 (first one) is the trace ID, d25a633196c01c19 (second one) is the span ID, and false indicates that this log is not published to Zipkin. We look into Zipkin later in the chapter, so for the time being, think about it as a server capturing all the tracing information in a microservices deployment.

```
INFO [sample01,d25a633196c01c19,d25a633196c01c19,false] 27437 --- [nio-
9000-exec-2] c.a.c.sample01.service.OrderProcessing: retrieving order:11
```

The spring.sleuth.sampler.percentage property in the application.properties file indicates what percentage of the requests must be traced. By default it is set to 0.1, which means that only 10% of all the requests will be published to Zipkin. By setting it to 1.0, all the requests will be published.

Now, let's see how to run the Order Processing microservice and invoke it with the following cURL command (run this from the ch13/sample01 directory).

```
\> mvn clean install
\> mvn spring-boot:run
\> curl http://localhost:9000/order/11
```

This cURL command will print the order details, and if you look at the command console that runs the Order Processing microservice, you will find the following log, which includes the trace ID and the span ID along with other metadata.

```
INFO [sample01,d25a633196c01c19,d25a633196c01c19,false] 27437 --- [nio-
9000-exec-2] c.a.c.sample01.service.OrderProcessing: retrieving order:11
```

Well, we are not surprised if you do not find the example by its own that helpful. It does nothing more than logging—no tracing at all. The next section will clear your doubts and probably will convince you of the value of tracing.

Tracing Messages Between Multiple Microservices with Spring Cloud Sleuth

Let's extend the example we discussed so far with multiple microservices and see how a given request is traced throughout the communication network. If you have already started the Order Processing microservice (sample01) as per the instructions in the previous section, keep it running. In addition to that you also need to start the Inventory microservice. Let's spin up the Inventory microservice by running the following command from the ch13/sample02 directory.

```
\> mvn clean install
\> mvn spring-boot:run
```

Now when we run our cURL client to place an order with the Order Processing microservice, it will talk to the Inventory microservice to update the inventory (see Figure 13-1).

```
\> curl -v  -k  -H "Content-Type: application/json" -d '{"customer_
id":"101021","payment_method":{"card_type":"VISA","expiration":"01/22","nam
e":"John Doe","billing_address":"201, 1st Street, San Jose, CA"},"items":[{
"code":"101","qty":1},{"code":"103","qty":5}],"shipping_address":"201, 1st
Street, San Jose, CA"}' http://localhost:9000/order
```

Let's look at the command console, which runs the Order Processing microservice. It should print the following log with the tracing information.

```
INFO [sample01,76f19c035e8e1ddb,76f19c035e8e1ddb,false] 29786 --- [nio-
9000-exec-1] c.a.c.sample01.service.OrderProcessing   : creating order
:10dcc849-3d8d-49fb-ac58-bc5da29db003
```

The command console, which runs the Inventory microservice, prints the following log.

```
INFO [sample04,76f19c035e8e1ddb,be46d1595ef606a0,false] 29802 --- [io-
10000-exec-1] c.a.ch13.sample02.service.Inventory     : item code 101
INFO [sample04,76f19c035e8e1ddb,be46d1595ef606a0,false] 29802 --- [io-
10000-exec-1] c.a.ch13.sample02.service.Inventory     : item code 103
```

In both logs printed from the two microservices, the trace ID (76f19c035e8e1ddb) is the same, while each has its own span ID (76f19c035e8e1ddb and be46d1595ef606a0). In the next section, we see how to publish these logs to Zipkin and visualize the complete path of a request across multiple microservices.

Data Visualization and Correlation with Zipkin

Zipkin[5] is a distributed tracing system that helps visualizing and correlating the communication paths between microservices. It also helps in diagnosing latency issues by gathering timing data. All the microservices can be instrumented to publish the logs along with tracing information to Zipkin (see Figure 13-4).

Note   A comprehensive introduction to Zipkin is out of the scope of this book, and we recommend readers looking for details to refer to the Zipkin documentation available at https://zipkin.io/.

Setting up Zipkin is quite straightforward with Docker. In Chapter 8, "Deploying and Running Microservices," we discussed Docker in detail, and assuming you have Docker up and running in your machine, you can spin up a Docker container with Zipkin, with the following command. In case you want to try Zipkin without Docker, refer to the installation guide available at https://zipkin.io/pages/quickstart.html.

```
\> docker run -d -p 9411:9411 openzipkin/zipkin
```

This command binds port 9411 of the host machine to port 9411 on the Docker container. Once the Zipkin node gets started, you can access its web-based console from the host machine, via http://localhost:9411/zipkin/, or simply with http://localhost:9411 (see Figure 13-5). The next step is to update the configuration

---

[5]https://zipkin.io/

of the Order Processing and Inventory microservices (from the previous section, sample01 and sample02) to publish logs to Zipkin. If you have both the microservices running, first stop them and update the application.properties file with the following. You need to do this for both microservices. The spring.zipkin.baseUrl property carries the server URL of the Zipkin server.

```
spring.zipkin.baseUrl=http://localhost:9411/
```

In addition to setting up this property in the application.properties file, we also must add the following dependency to the pom.xml file of both the microservices to complete the Zipkin integration. The spring-cloud-sleuth-zipkin dependency takes care of publishing logs to the Zipkin server, and those have to be in a format understood by Zipkin.

```
<dependency>
    <groupId>org.springframework.cloud</groupId>
    <artifactId>spring-cloud-sleuth-zipkin</artifactId>
    <version>2.0.0.RC1</version>
</dependency>
```

Start the Order Processing and Inventory microservices and use the following cURL command to place an order with the Order Processing microservice. Do it for few times, so we gather enough logs at the Zipkin. Also, keep in mind that not all the logs are sent to Zipkin—it depends on the value you set for the spring.sleuth.sampler. percentage property in the application.properties file. In a typical microservices deployment the data volume can be very high, hence the volume of traced data. Based on the volume of requests you get and the business criticality of the operations performed by the microservices, you can decide what percentage of requests needs be sampled or sent to Zipkin.

```
\> curl -v  -k  -H "Content-Type: application/json" -d '{"customer_
id":"101021","payment_method":{"card_type":"VISA","expiration":"01/22",
"name":"John Doe","billing_address":"201, 1st Street, San Jose, CA"},"items":
[{"code":"101","qty":1},{"code":"103","qty":5}],"shipping_address":"201,
1st Street, San Jose, CA"}' http://localhost:9000/order
```

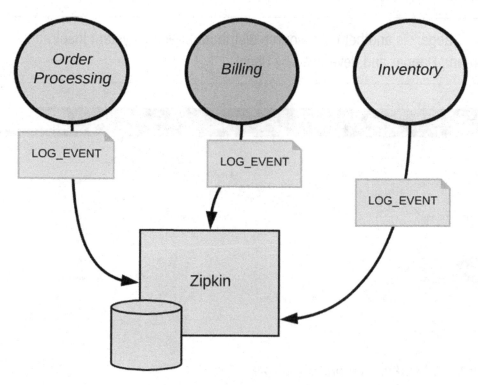

Figure 13-4. *Each microservice is instrumented to publish logs to Zipkin*

For the traced data, which is published from each microservice to Zipkin, you'll find the following logs printed on the command console, which runs each microservice. Notice that the fourth parameter of the tracing information added to each, which indicates whether the logs are published to Zipkin, and that is set to `true`.

```
INFO [sample01,bf581ac0009c6e48,bf581ac0009c6e48,true] 30166 --- [nio-9000-
exec-1] c.a.c.sample01.service.OrderProcessing : retrieving order:11
INFO [sample02,1a35024149ac7711,98239453fa5582ba,true] 30153 --- [io-10000-
exec-7] c.a.ch04.sample04.service.Inventory : item code 101
INFO [sample02,1a35024149ac7711,98239453fa5582ba,true] 30153 --- [io-10000-
exec-7] c.a.ch04.sample04.service.Inventory : item code 103
```

What happens underneath here is that Sleuth instruments your application to generate tracing information in a format understood by Zipkin. Zipkin is the data collector and once all the microservices publish traced data to Zipkin, it helps you to do the distributed tracing. To do distributed tracing, you need both the parts.

Note   Jaeger[6] is another open source distributed tracing system inspired by Zipkin and Dapper and developed by Uber.

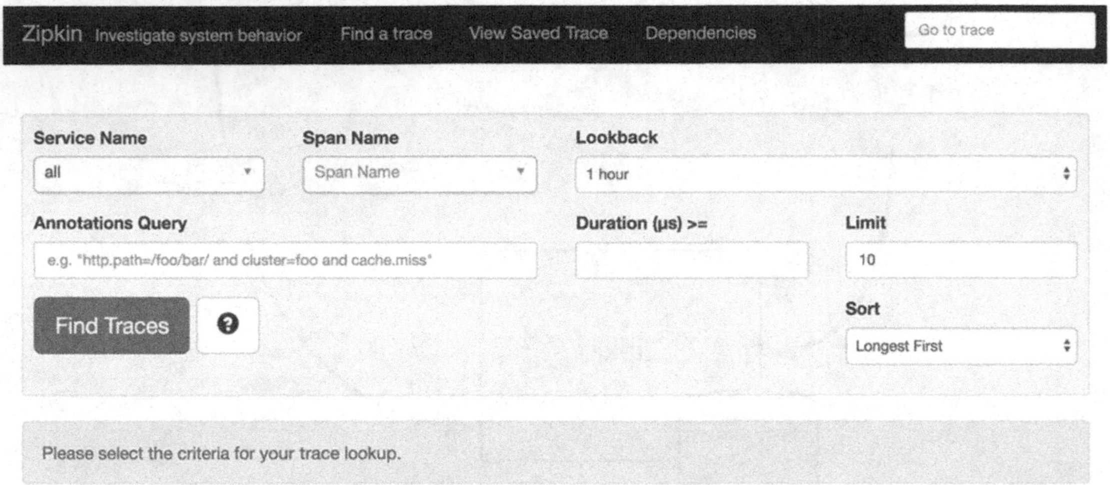

Figure 13-5. *Zipkin web-based console*

Now let's see how to find some useful information from the Zipkin server with the published tracing information. On the home page of the Zipkin web console, in the Service Name dropdown box, you will notice that we have two names: sample01 and sample02. Those are the service names associated with our two microservices and by picking one service name there, you can find all the tracing information related to that microservice. Figure 13-6 shows the tracing information related to sample01 or the Order Processing microservice.

Note   The Zipkin architecture is built with four main components: collector, storage, search, and web UI. The traced data published from applications (or microservices) first hits the collector. The collector validates, stores, and indexes the data for lookups. The storage of Zipkin is pluggable and it natively supports Cassandra, ElasticSearch, and MySQL. Once the data is indexed and stored, the search component of Zipkin provides a JSON API to interact with traces, which is mostly used by the web UI.

---

[6]https://www.jaegertracing.io/

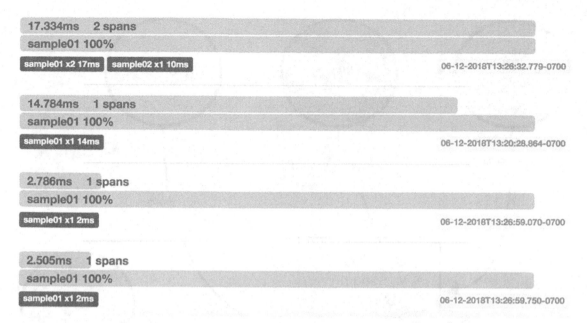

Figure 13-6. *Tracing information related to the Order Processing microservice*

Zipkin also has another nice feature, which builds a dependency graph for your microservice by analyzing inbound and outbound traffic patterns. This is quite useful when we have many microservices in our deployment. Anyway, in this particular example it's a very simple graph between the `Order Processing` (`sample01`) and `Inventory` (`sample02`) microservices, as shown in Figure 13-7.

Figure 13-7. *Dependency graph between the OrderProcessing and Inventory microservices*

Event-Driven Log Aggregation Architecture

Let's revisit Figure 13-4, which is the high-level design of what we are going to discuss in this section. The design here is bit different from what we proposed in Chapter 2, "Designing Microservices" (see Figure 2-17). Figure 13-8 depicts the redone design as per the recommendation for a log aggregator architecture in Chapter 2.

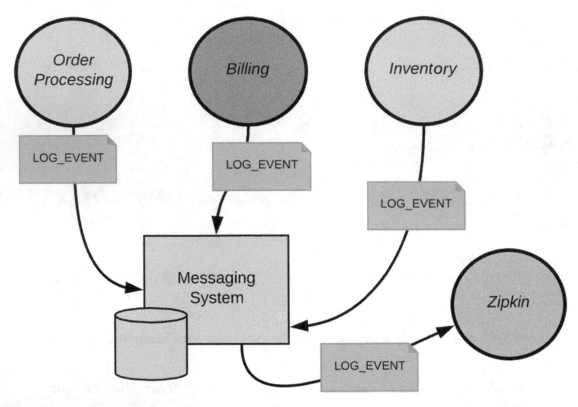

Figure 13-8. *Zipkin with event-driven log aggregation architecture*

Unlike in Figure 13-4, here there is no direct coupling between the Zipkin server and the microservices. Each microservice publishes the logs to a messaging system, which can be either RabbitMQ or Kafka, and Zipkin picks the logs from the messaging system. The advantage of this model is that even if the Zipkin server is down for some time, microservices can independently keep on publishing logs and Zipkin picks them all from the messaging system when it reboots.

Introduction to Open Tracing

Distributed tracing becomes quite tricky when different microservices in the same microservices deployment use different tracing modules. For example, the Order Processing microservice may use Sleuth to generate spans and traces, while the Inventory microservice uses another module. Both can publish the traced data to Zipkin, but unless both the modules share the same definition for spans and traces, and respect the traced data generated from the each other, this information will be useless. This forces developers to use the same tracing modules in all the microservices, which is sort of a violation of the polyglot architecture, which we proudly talk about with respect to microservices. *Open tracing*[7] is an initiative to address this concern by building an open standard. It precisely defines what's a span and what's a trace under the open tracing data model.

Open tracing has to work across multiple programming languages. At the time of this writing, it defines language-level APIs for nine programming languages: Go, Python, JavaScript, Java, C#, Objective-C, C++, Ruby, and PHP. There are several implementations of these APIs already. Jaeger, the open source distributed tracing system developed by Uber, has support for open tracing and includes open tracing client libraries for several programming languages: Java, Go, Python, Node.js, C++, and C#.

Distributed Tracing with Open Tracing Using Spring Boot Microservices and Zipkin

Zipkin has support for open tracing, but not the Sleuth. You can think about Sleuth as the tracing client, while Zipkin is the server that collects all the traced data. In the examples we discussed in previous sections, Sleuth was used as a tracing client for Zipkin, and it used a Zipkin specific format, which won't work with open tracing. In this section, we see how to publish traced data from a Spring Boot microservice, which is compatible with open tracing. The source code related to this example is available in the ch13/ sample03 directory.

Let's look at some of the notable Maven dependencies added to the ch13/sample03/ pom.xml file. The opentracing-spring-cloud-starter and opentracing-spring-zipkin-starter dependencies bring in all the dependencies required to publish open tracing compatible tracing information to Zipkin.

```
<dependency>
    <groupId>io.opentracing.contrib</groupId>
    <artifactId>opentracing-spring-cloud-starter</artifactId>
    <version>0.1.13</version>
</dependency>
```

---

[7]http://opentracing.io/

```
<dependency>
    <groupId>io.opentracing.contrib</groupId>
    <artifactId>opentracing-spring-zipkin-starter</artifactId>
    <version>0.1.1</version>
</dependency>
```

Assuming you are still running the Zipkin node from the previous section, add the `opentracing.zipkin.http-sender.baseUrl` property to the `application.properties` file , which carries the server URL of the Zipkin server.

```
opentracing.zipkin.http-sender.baseUrl=http://localhost:9411/
```

Now, let's run the `Order Processing` microservice and invoke it with the following cURL command (run from the `ch13/sample03` directory). Do it a few times and observe the data recorded at Zipkin via its web console running at `http://localhost:9411/zipkin/`.

```
\> mvn clean install
\> mvn spring-boot:run
\> curl http://localhost:9000/order/11
```

Distributed Tracing with Open Tracing Using Spring Boot Microservices and Jaeger

In the previous section we explained how to publish open tracing compatible traces to Zipkin. Since it's open tracing, not just Zipkin, any other product supporting open tracing should accept it. In this section, we see how to publish traced data from a Spring Boot microservice to Jaeger, which is compatible with open tracing (see Figure 13-9). Jaeger is another open source distributed tracing system inspired by Zipkin and Dapper and developed by Uber. The source code related to this example is available in the `ch13/sample04` directory. We can spin up a Jaeger Docker instance with the following command, which will start running on HTTP port 16686 and UDP port 5775. After it starts, we can access its web console via `http://localhost:16686/`.

```
\> docker run -d -p 5775:5775/udp -p 16686:16686 jaegertracing/all-in-one:latest
```

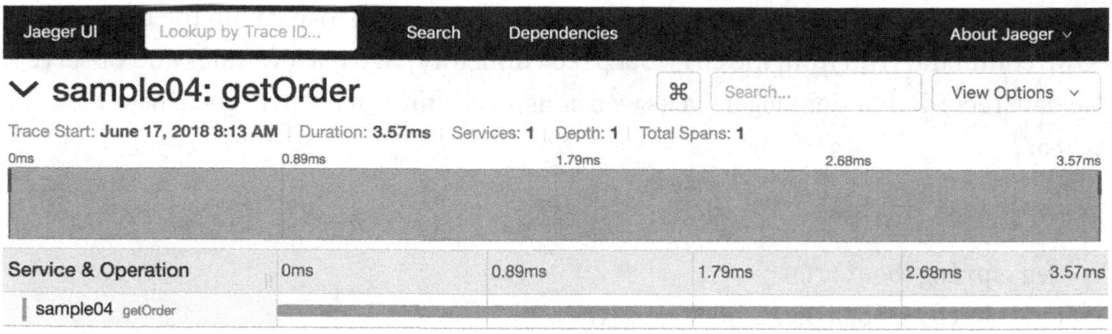

Figure 13-9. *Jaeger web console*

Note   A comprehensive Introduction to Jaeger is out of the scope of this book, and we recommend readers looking for details to refer to the Jaeger documentation available at `https://www.jaegertracing.io/docs/`.

Let's look at some of the notable Maven dependencies added to the ch13/sample04/ pom.xml file. The opentracing-spring-cloud-starter and opentracing-spring-cloud-starter-jaeger dependencies bring all the dependencies required to publish open tracing-compatible tracing information to Jaeger.

```
<dependency>
    <groupId>io.opentracing.contrib</groupId>
    <artifactId>opentracing-spring-cloud-starter</artifactId>
    <version>0.1.13</version>
</dependency>

<dependency>
    <groupId>io.opentracing.contrib</groupId>
    <artifactId>opentracing-spring-cloud-starter-jaeger</artifactId>
    <version>0.1.13</version>
</dependency>
```

From our Spring Boot microservice we use UDP port 5775 to connect to the Jaeger server to publish traces. We need to add the opentracing.jaeger.udp-sender.host and opentracing.jaeger.udp-sender.host properties to the application.properties file.

```
opentracing.jaeger.udp-sender.host=localhost
opentracing.jaeger.udp-sender.port=5775
```

389

Now, let's run the `Order Processing` microservice and invoke it with the following cURL command (run from the `ch13/sample04` directory). Do it a few times and observe the data recorded under Jaeger via its web console running at `http://localhost:16686/`.

```
\> mvn clean install
```

```
\> mvn spring-boot:run
\> curl http://localhost:9000/order/11
```

Metrics with Prometheus

Prometheus is an open source system for monitoring and alerting. In this section, we see how to use Prometheus to monitor a microservices deployment. The way it works is that all of your microservices will expose their own endpoints to expose their metrics outside and Prometheus will periodically poll those endpoints (see Figure 13-10).

Note   A comprehensive introduction to Prometheus is out of the scope of this book, and we recommend readers looking for details to refer to the Prometheus documentation available at `https://prometheus.io/`.

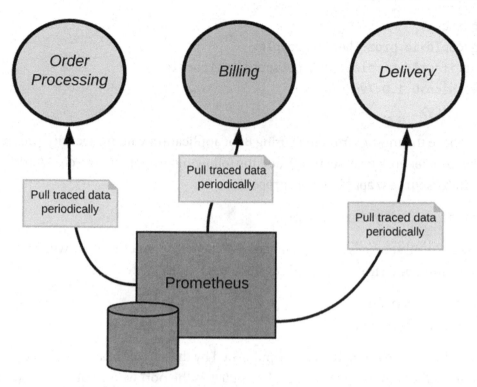

Figure 13-10. *Prometheus pulls traced data from the connected microservices*

Exposing Metrics from the Spring Boot Microservice

First, let's see how to instrument our Spring Boot microservice to expose metrics in a format understood by Prometheus. The source code related to this example is available in the ch13/sample05 directory. Let's look at some of the notable Maven dependencies added to the ch13/sample05/pom.xml file. The simpleclient_spring_boot and simpleclient_hotspot dependencies bring all the dependencies required to expose metrics to Prometheus. The simpleclient_spring_boot dependency introduces the two class-level annotations, @EnablePrometheusEndpoint and @EnableSpringBootMetricsCollector, which are added to the ch13/sample05/OrderProcessingApp.java class file.

```
<dependency>
    <groupId>io.prometheus</groupId>
    artifactId>simpleclient_spring_boot</artifactId>
    <version>0.1.0</version>
</dependency>
```

```
<dependency>
    <groupId>io.prometheus</groupId>
    <artifactId>simpleclient_hotspot</artifactId>
    <version>0.1.0</version>
</dependency>
```

To expose the metrics from the Spring Boot application with no security (we can probably use network level security), add the following property to the ch13/sample05/src/main/resources/application.properties file.

```
management.security.enabled=false
```

Now we're all set. Let's spin up our Order Processing microservice with the following command (from the sample05 directory).

```
\> mvn clean install
\> mvn spring-boot:run
```

Once the service is up, the metrics published by the service is accessible via http://localhost:9000/prometheus. Here, 9000 is the port where your microservice is running. The following text lists the truncated output from the previous endpoint.

```
# HELP httpsessions_max httpsessions_max
# TYPE httpsessions_max gauge
httpsessions_max -1.0
# HELP httpsessions_active httpsessions_active
# TYPE httpsessions_active gauge
httpsessions_active 0.0
# HELP mem mem
# TYPE mem gauge
mem 549365.0
# HELP mem_free mem_free
# TYPE mem_free gauge
mem_free 211808.0
# HELP processors processors
# TYPE processors gauge
processors 8.0
# HELP instance_uptime instance_uptime
```

```
# TYPE instance_uptime gauge
instance_uptime 313310.0
# HELP uptime uptime
# TYPE uptime gauge
uptime 317439.0
# HELP systemload_average systemload_average
# TYPE systemload_average gauge
systemload_average 2.13720703125
# HELP heap_committed heap_committed
# TYPE heap_committed gauge
heap_committed 481280.0
# HELP heap_init heap_init
# TYPE heap_init gauge
heap_init 262144.0
# HELP heap_used heap_used
# TYPE heap_used gauge
heap_used 269471.0
# HELP heap heap
# TYPE heap gauge
heap 3728384.0
# HELP nonheap_committed nonheap_committed
# TYPE nonheap_committed gauge
nonheap_committed 71696.0
```

Setting Up Prometheus

Setting up Prometheus is quite straightforward with Docker. First we need to create a prometheus.yml file, which includes all the services Prometheus will monitor. The following example shows a sample file, which includes our Order Processing microservice (sample05) and the Prometheus instance itself. A given prometheus.yml file can have multiple jobs. Here the prometheus job takes care of monitoring itself (which runs on port 9090), while the orderprocessing job is set up to poll 10.0.0.93:9000 endpoint every 10 seconds. Keep in mind that here we need to use the IP address of the node, which runs the Order Processing microservice, and it has to be accessible from the Docker instance, which runs Prometheus.

```
scrape_configs:
  - job_name: 'prometheus'
    scrape_interval: 10s
    static_configs:
      - targets: ['localhost:9090']
  - job_name: 'orderprocessing'
    scrape_interval: 10s
    metrics_path: '/prometheus'
    static_configs:
      - targets: ['10.0.0.93:9000']
```

Now let's spin up the Prometheus Docker instance, with the prometheus.yml file.

```
:\> docker run -p 9090:9090 -v /path/to/prometheus.yml:/etc/prometheus/
prometheus.yml prom/prometheus
```

Once the Prometheus node is up, go to the URL http://localhost:9090/targets, and it will show all the services, Prometheus monitors, and the status of individual endpoints (see Figure 13-11).

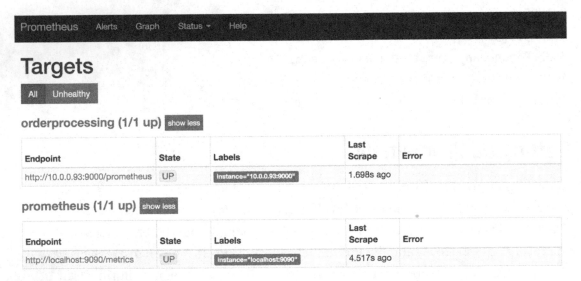

Figure 13-11. *Prometheus targets and the status of individual endpoints*

Building Graphs with Prometheus

Now we've have all the metrics from our Spring Boot microservice, published to Prometheus. Let's see how to build graphs to monitor those published stats.

First, go to `http://localhost:9090/graph` and pick the metric that you want to monitor. For example, we picked `heap_used`. Then when you click on the Graph tab, we should be able to see the used heap graph against time (see Figure 13-12). That way, you can add any number of graphs.

Note   Prometheus was born as an open source project released under Apache 2.0 license at SoundCloud in 2012. It's mostly written in Go and the community around Prometheus grew up in last few years. In 2016 it was the second project to get the membership of Cloud Native Computing Foundation (CNCF).

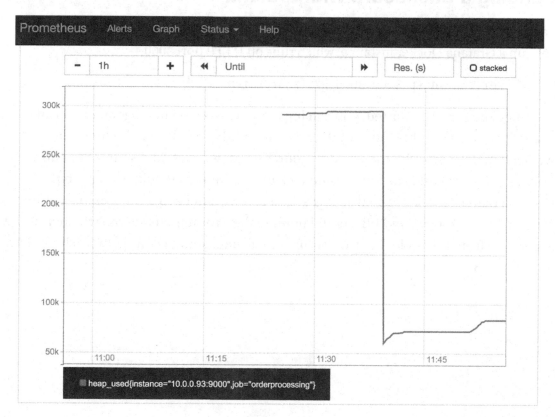

Figure 13-12.   *Using Prometheus to monitor the used heap of a Spring Boot microservice*

Analytics and Monitoring with Grafana

Grafana is an open source product for analytics and monitoring, and it is more powerful than Prometheus to build dashboards. In fact, it is recommended to use Grafana to build dashboards with Prometheus. Prometheus had its own dashboarding tool called Promdash, but with the advancements in Grafana, Prometheus developers let it go and started promoting Grafana.

Note   A comprehensive introduction to Grafana is out of the scope of this book, and we recommend readers looking for details to refer to the Grafana documentation available at `http://docs.grafana.org/`.

Building a Dashboard with Grafana

Setting up Grafana is quite straightforward with Docker. Use the following command to spin up a Grafana Docker instance, which runs on HTTP port 3000.

```
:\> docker run -d -p 3000:3000 grafana/grafana
```

Once the server is started, you can log in to the Grafana management console via `http://localhost:3000` with the credentials admin/admin. The first thing we need to do is introduce a new data source. Grafana uses data sources to build graphs. Click on Add Data Source and pick Prometheus as the data source type. Give it a name, let's say `prometheus_ds`. The rest we can keep as it is, except for the HTTP URL property. This URL should point to the Prometheus server, which must be accessible from the node that runs Grafana. The data source configuration looks like Figure 13-13.

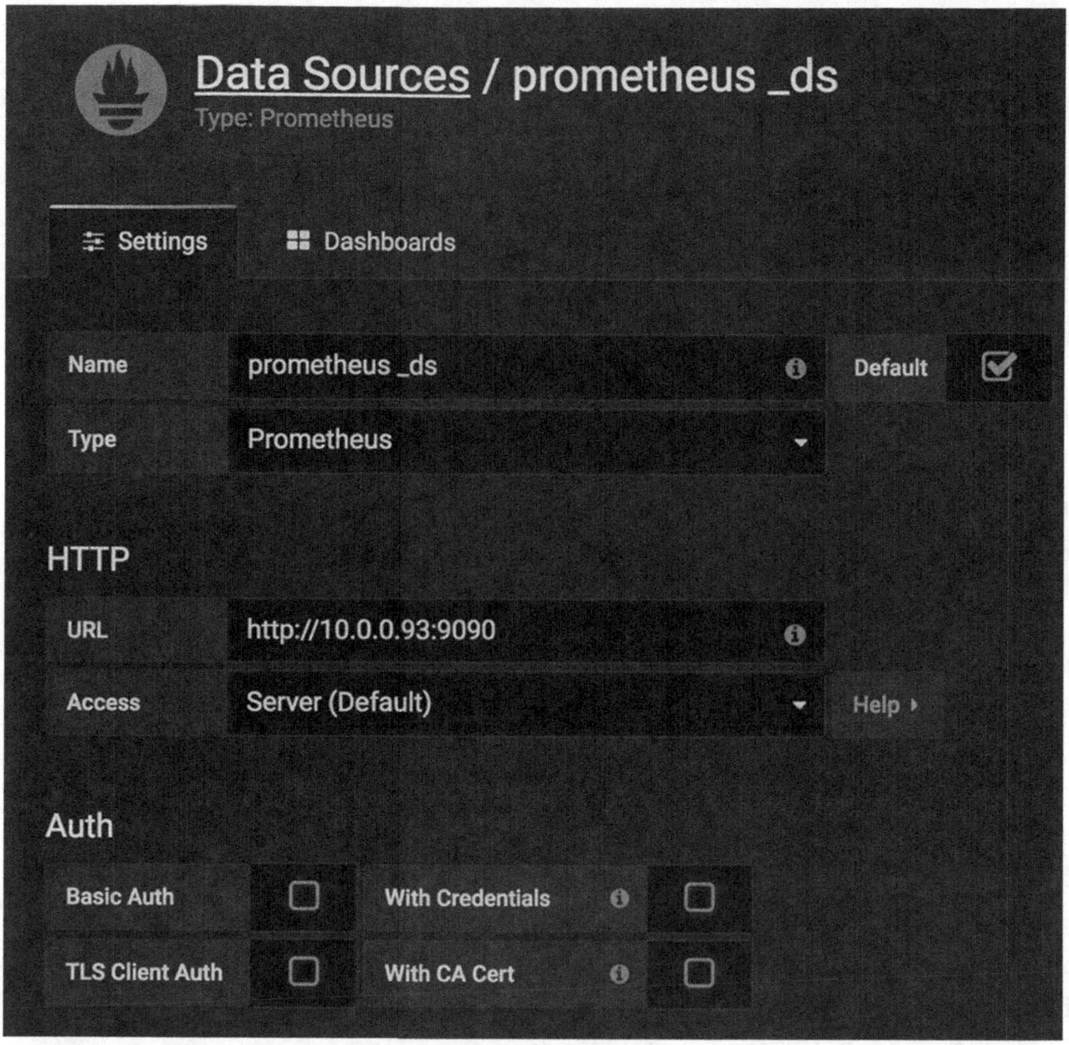

Figure 13-13. *Grafana data source properties*

Note   As per the configuration shown in Figure 13-13, we expect the Prometheus endpoint to be open or not protected. If it is protected, Grafana supports multiple security models, including basic authentication and TLS client authentication.

Now we can create a new dashboard via `http://localhost:3000/dashboard/new`. Choose the Graph, and then click on the Panel Title and click on Edit. Under Metrics, you choose any metrics made available via the selected data source. As shown in

Figure 13-14, we can define multiple queries. Here we have picked heap and heap_used. A query defines which information we need to pick from the metrics pulled from the Prometheus endpoint, and the graphs are rendered accordingly.

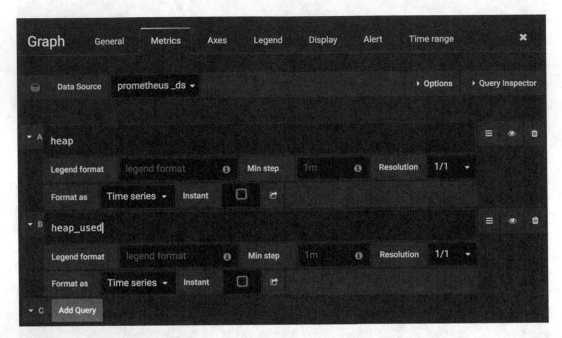

Figure 13-14. Setting up queries to build a dashboard with Grafana

Once we complete this process, we can find the dashboard that we just created, listed on Grafana home page under Recently viewed dashboards. You can click on it to view the dashboard, which will appear as shown in Figure 13-15.

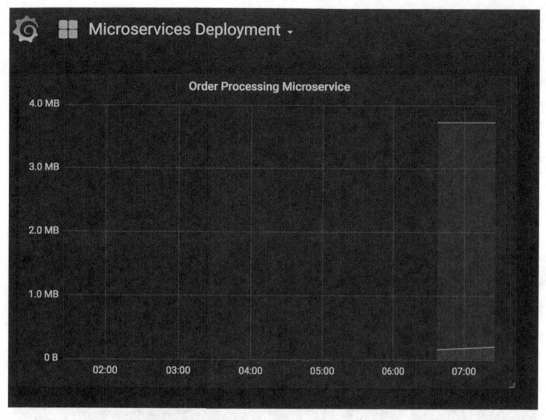

Figure 13-15. *Grafana dashboard to monitor the microservices deployment*

Creating Alerts with Grafana

Grafana lets you create alerts and associate them with a graph (or a dashboard panel). To create an alert corresponding to the dashboard we created in the previous section, first we need to edit the graph (see Figure 13-16) by clicking on its title and choosing Edit. Under Alerts, we can create a rule, which states under which conditions the system should raise an alert (see Figure 13-17). The only type of condition that Grafana supports at the moment is a query and for an alert rule, you can add multiple queries linked to each other (with an AND or an OR).

Note   Grafana alerting support is only limited to the data sources: Graphite, Prometheus, ElasticSearch, InfluxDB, OpenTSDB, MySQL, Postgres, and Cloudwatch.

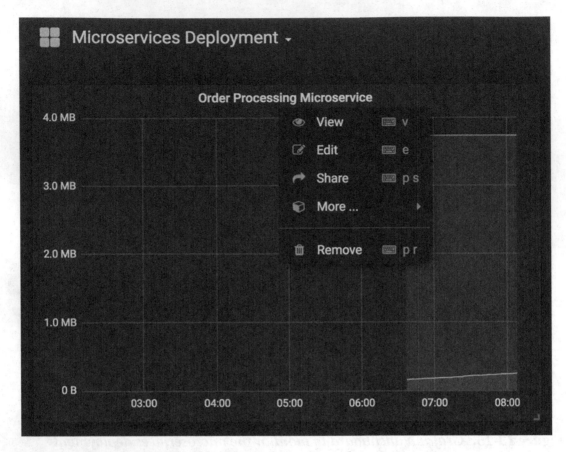

Figure 13-16. *The Grafana dashboard monitors the microservices deployment*

The following query indicates that when the maximum value of the metric A (see Figure 13-14, in our case heap) is above 3 for the next five minutes, raise an alert. This rule is evaluated every 60 seconds.

```
WHEN max() OF query(A, 5m, now) IS ABOVE 3
```

In addition to the `max()` function, Grafana also supports `avg()`, `min()`, `sum()`, `last()`, `count()`, `median()`, `diff()`, `percent_diff()`, and `count_non_null()`. See Figure 13-17.

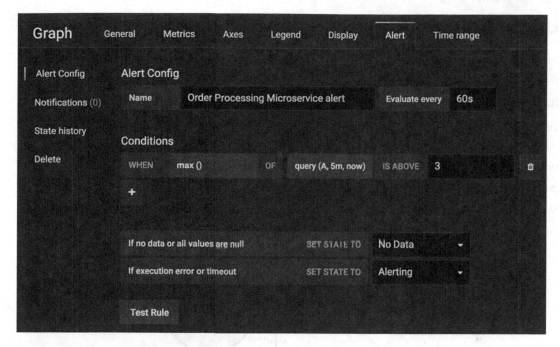

Figure 13-17. *Configuring alerts*

Once the alert rules are set, we can configure whom to send the notifications along with a message, under the Notifications menu, when an alert is raised (see Figure 13-18). Grafana supports multiple notification channels, including Email, PagerDuty, Telegram, Slack, and many more.

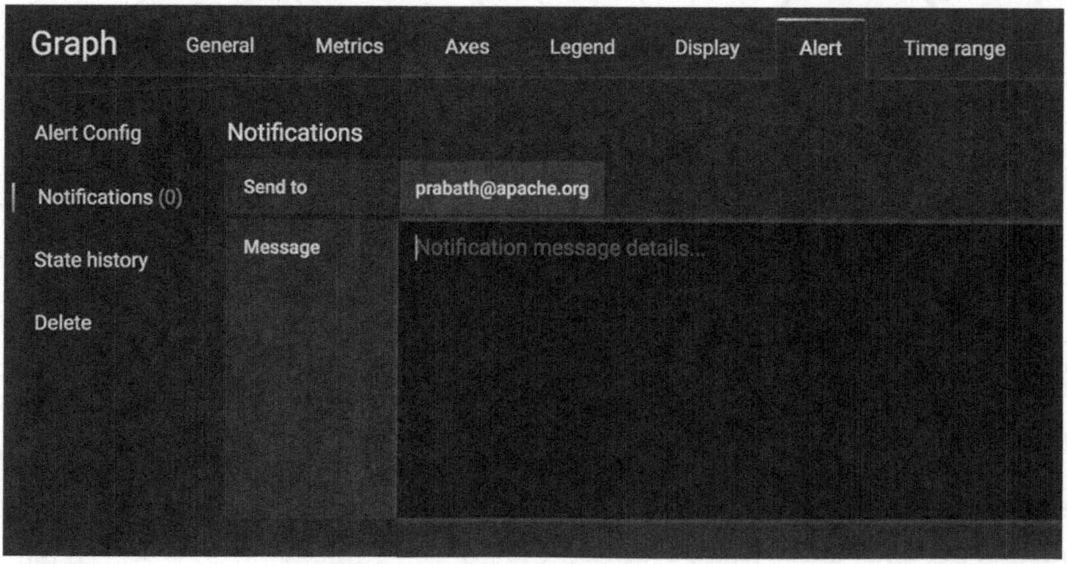

Figure 13-18. *Configuring notifications*

Using Fluentd Log Collector with Docker

Fluentd is an extensible data collection tool that runs as a daemon. Microservices can publish logs to Fluentd. It has a rich set of plugins, which can read logs in different formats from different sources and parse the data. Also, it can format, aggregate, and publish logs to third-party systems like Splunk, Prometheus, MongoDB, PostgreSQL, AWS S3, Kafka, and many more (see Figure 13-19). The beauty of Fluentd architecture is that it decouples data sources from target systems. With no changes to your microservice, Fluentd can change the target system of your logs or add new target systems. Also it can do content filtering on log messages and, based on certain criteria, decide which systems to publish the logs.

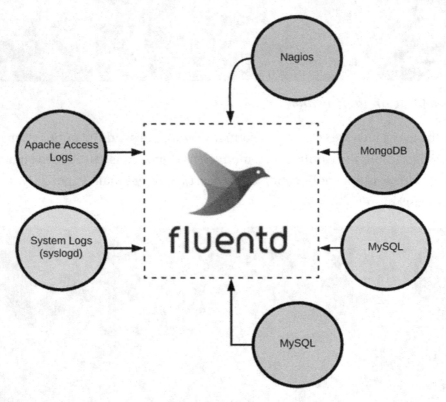

Figure 13-19. *Multiple input sources and target systems with Fluentd*

In the following sections, we see how to publish logs to Fluentd from a microservice running on a Docker container. First we'll set up Fluentd and then see how to spin up a microservice and publish logs to Fluentd.

Starting Fluentd as a Docker Container

The easiest and the most straightforward way to spin up Fluentd is using a Docker container. In practice, this is the most common approach too. In a production setup, where all your microservices are running in a Kubernetes environment (which we discussed in Chapter 8), the Fluentd node (which acts as a daemon) will run in the same pod, along with the corresponding microservice. In fact, you can treat the container running the Fluentd as a sidecar to the microservice (see Figure 13-20). The microservice, by default, will publish the logs to `localhost:24224`, which is the port Fluentd is listening to over TCP.

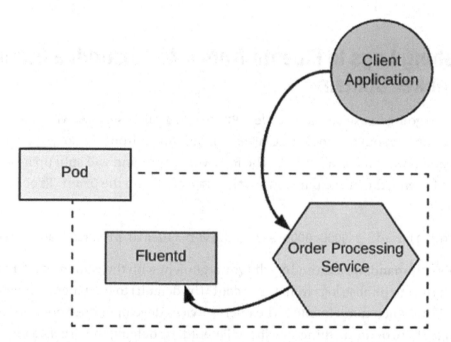

Figure 13-20. *Microservice and Fluentd containers are running in the same pod*

Let's use the following command to spin up the Fluentd Docker container. Before that, make sure you have a directory called data in the the home directory of the host filesystem—or you can have your own directory instead of ~/data.

```
:\> docker run -d  -p 24224:24224 -v ~/data:/fluentd/log  fluent/fluentd
```

As we learned in Chapter 8, containers are immutable. In other words, when a container goes down it will not save any of the changes we have done to its filesystem while running. By default all the logs published to Fluentd by the

`Order Processing` microservice will be stored in the `/fluent/log` directory in the container filesystem. To persist that data permanently, we need to use a Docker volume. Using the `-v` option in the previous command, we map the `~/data` directory in the host filesystem to the `/fluent/log` directory in the container filesystem. Even when the container goes down, we should be able to find the log files in the `~/data` directory. The `-p` option in the previous command maps the port `24224` from the Docker container (the port Fluentd listens by default) to port `24224` of the host machine. `fluent/fluentd` is the name of the container image, which will be pulled from the Docker Hub.

Once we get the Fluentd up and running, we can start a Docker container with the `Order Processing` microservice.

Publishing Logs to Fluentd from a Microservice Running in a Docker Container

Here we are going to use the same `Order Processing` microservice, which we discussed through out the book, but instead of building it from the source code, we are going to pull it from the Docker hub. The following command will spin up a Docker container (having the image name `prabath/sample01`) with the `Order Processing` microservice.

```
:\> docker run -d -p 9000:9000 --log-driver=fluentd prabath/sample01
```

In this command, we use the `log-driver` argument with the value `fluentd`[8]. Docker uses this driver to publish logs from the `stdout`[9] (by default) to the Fluentd daemon (or the container, which runs Fluentd). The microservices developer does not need to make any changes here or do anything specific to Fluentd. By default, the `fluentd` log driver connects to `localhost:24224` over TCP. If we run Fluentd on a different port, we need to pass the `fluentd-address` argument to the `docker run` command, with a value pointing to the Fluentd container (e.g., `fluentd-address=localhost:28444`).

If it all works fine, once the `Order Processing` service is started, we should see some logs available in the `~/data` directory in the host filesystem. This is the directory we used to create a Docker volume before.

---

[8]https://docs.docker.com/config/containers/logging/fluentd/
[9]Stdout (standard output) is the default file descriptor where a process can write output.

Note   A comprehensive introduction to Fluentd is out of the scope of this book. We recommend readers looking for details to refer to the Fluentd documentation available at `https://docs.fluentd.org/`.

How It Works

Fluentd uses a config file, which defines the input sources and the output targets. By default it is in the `/fluentd/etc` directory of the container filesystem where Fluentd is running. The file is called `fluent.conf`. Let's look at the default content of `fluent.conf`. The source tag defines where the data comes from. Under that we have `forward` and `port` elements, which make Fluentd accepts messages on port 24224 over TCP. The responsibility of the source tag is to accept messages and hand them over to the Fluentd routing engine as events. Each event has three elements: tag, time, and record. The sender (in our case the fluentd driver) defines the value of the tag.

Note   You can find all the configurations related to the fluentd Docker image from here: `https://hub.docker.com/r/fluent/fluentd/`. It also explains how to override the default Fluentd configuration file, which ships with the image.

```
<source>
  @type   forward
  @id     input1
  @label  @mainstream
  port   24224
</source>

<filter **>
  @type stdout
</filter>
```

```
<label @mainstream>
  <match docker.**>
    @type file
    @id    output_docker1
    path            /fluentd/log/docker.*.log
    symlink_path /fluentd/log/docker.log
    append          true
    time_slice_format %Y%m%d
    time_slice_wait   1m
    time_format       %Y%m%dT%H%M%S%z
  </match>

<match **>
    @type file
    @id    output1
    path            /fluentd/log/data.*.log
    symlink_path /fluentd/log/data.log
    append          true
    time_slice_format %Y%m%d
    time_slice_wait   10m
    time_format       %Y%m%dT%H%M%S%z
  </match>
</label>
```

The match element will tell Fluentd what to do with the matching messages. It matches the value of the tag element in each event with the criteria defined in the match element. In our case, it checks whether the tag starts with the word docker. The most common use case of the match element is to define the output targets. In the previous configuration, the output is written to a file in the /fluentd/log directory (in the container). If we want to send the output to different other systems, we can use any of the available Fluentd plugins[10]. Finally, the label element defined under the source element acts as a reference. For example, when the match element gets executed, if there is a label defined under the source, then only the match element under the corresponding label will get executed. The objective of the label element is to reduce the configuration file complexity.

---

[10]https://www.fluentd.org/plugins/all#input-output

> **Note**   Logstash[11], which is part of the well-known ELK (ElasticSearch, Logstash, Kibana) stack, provides similar functionality to Fluentd. Before you pick a logging solution for your enterprise, we recommend evaluating the pros and cons of both Fluentd and Logstash.

Using Fluentd in a Microservices Deployment

In this section, we see how to extend this Fluentd example architecturally to fit into a production microservices deployment. As we discussed (and as shown in Figure 13-21), each Kubernetes pod (which we discussed in Chapter 8) will have an instance of Fluentd running in a container. This container can be treated as a sidecar. Each microservice in our deployment will have a similar setup. Each Fluentd node can filter out the logs they need and publish them to another Fluentd node, which can do the log aggregation. This Fluentd node also can decide what other target systems it has to publish logs.

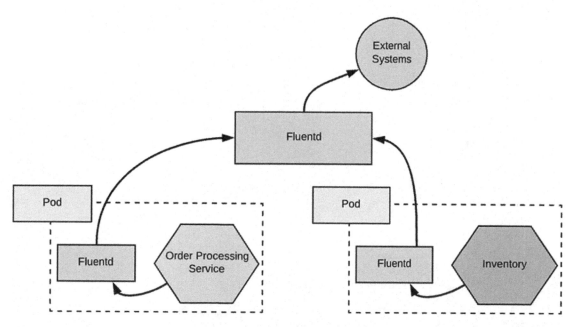

Figure 13-21.   *Fluentd in a production deployment*

---

[11]https://www.elastic.co/guide/en/logstash/

Summary

In this chapter, we discussed one of the key aspects of the microservices architecture—the observability—and the three pillars behind observability—logging, metrics, and tracing. We also discussed distributed tracing, which is in fact the most important enabler of observability. Distributed tracing helps tracing a request, which spans across multiple systems. We used Spring Cloud Sleuth, Zipkin, and Jaeger to build a distributed tracing system and used Prometheus and Grafana for visualization, monitoring, and alerting. Finally, we discussed how to use Fluentd, an extensible log-collection tool, in a containerized deployment.

Index

A

B

M

T, U

V

Printed in the United States
By Bookmasters